T5-AFS-409

THE CHINESE CLASSICAL WORK

COMMONLY CALLED

THE FOUR BOOKS

THE

CHINESE CLASSICAL WORK

COMMONLY CALLED

THE

FOUR BOOKS

(1828)

TRANSLATED,

AND ILLUSTRATED WITH NOTES,

BY THE LATE REV. DAVID COLLIE

A FACSIMILE REPRODUCTION

WITH AN INTRODUCTION

BY

WILLIAM BYSSHE STEIN

GAINESVILLE, FLORIDA

SCHOLARS' FACSIMILES & REPRINTS

1970

SCHOLARS' FACSIMILES & REPRINTS

1605 N.W. 14TH AVENUE

GAINESVILLE, FLORIDA, 32601, U.S.A.

HARRY R. WARFEL, GENERAL EDITOR

ISBN 8201-1079-5
L. C. CATALOG CARD NUMBER: 75-122487

Manufactured in the U.S.A.

CONTENTS

INTRODUCTION

For Thoreau, Confucius was not simply a Chinese philosopher: he was an archetypal Wise Old Man. Like his traditional counterparts in other civilizations, he was both the exemplar of moral perfection and the teacher of the disciplines of moral perfection. Like a Solomon, a Saadi, a Cato, or a Kapila (all alluded to in *Walden*), he was the heir, custodian, and interpreter of the meaning of the cultural experience of his people. While the reformative knowledge he taught was devised to remedy specific historical conditions of decay and corruption, it still derived from a much older perennial philosophy of man's nature and destiny—a view of the universe shared by an intellectual elite whose origins have been lost in immemorial time. Regardless of its religious investiture (especially the abracadabra of doctrine), this form of wisdom was pragmatic in orientation. It stressed the acquisition of those virtues which would enable the individual to bear all the burdens of existence, to weather all the crises and ordeals, moral and physical, that marked the passage from birth to death. Thus every Wise Old Man expounded a practical and practicable version of truth. He addressed himself to the problems that were common to mankind—the essential meaning of universal—and whatever the path of virtue that he chose to describe, it always led to the summit of the mountain where the vision of the horizon of truth was the same for all men. Here historical identity had no meaning; here the conveners were one—the Old Wise Man incarnate.

So Thoreau conceived of Buddha, Manu, Confucius, and Pilpay whose ethical writings he excerpted for publication in the *Dial,* the organ of the Concord Transcendental Club. Not, however, Emerson the sponsor of the project. He found these so-called bibles of mankind useless unless they were the direct agencies of inspiration. Most of his followers shared this belief in intuitive experience. Unlike Thoreau, they did not see the fallacies of the simplistic reductionism. Or perhaps they did not want to. The invisible wings of inspiration insured ascendance into the realms of glory without the need of any kind of self-discipline. On the lecture platform, in conversation, and in the privacy of his journals, Emerson always found the rhetoric to justify his formula of transcendence. Even when confronted by the matter-of-factness of the Confucian writings, Emerson did not lose his sangfroid. Despite the reluctance of the Chinese sage and his disciples to discuss the supernatural, he experienced no difficulty in translating their speculations into spiritual terms, as take for example his commentary on a dialogue from page 249 of the *Four Books*:

> "I fully understand language," he said, "and nourish well my vast-flowing vigor."—"I beg to ask what you call vast-flowing vigor." said his companion. "The explanation," replied Mencius, "is difficult. The vigor is supremely great, and in the highest degree unbending. Nourish it correctly and do it no injury, and it will fill up the vacancy between heaven and earth. This vigor accords with and assists justice and reason, and leaves no hunger. . . ." We give to this generalization the name of Being. . . . Suffice it for the joy of the universe that we have not arrived at a wall, but at interminable oceans. Our life seems not present so much as prospective; not for the affairs on which it is wasted, but as a hint of this vast-flowing vigor (*The Complete Works*, Centenary Edition, III, 72-73).

Emerson's inference derives from his conception of spiritual metaphors, unique figurations of God that are the cohesive force of various religions, like love in Christianity or fire in Zoroastrianism. Of course, this emblematic logic is based on his analysis of language in *Nature* where he equates words and natural facts with symbols of divine reality. Unfortunately, the context in Mencius does not permit such an interpretation, for immediately following the excerpt in the passage above comes this statement: "It [vast-flowing vigor] is produced by an accumulation of righteous deeds and not by a few accidental acts. If our actions do not give pleasure to our hearts, they leave an aching void" (pp. 249-250). In fine, what he attempts to describe is how disciplined recitude generates moral energy, not how some ubiquitous spirit extends the boundaries of moral freedom. But a distinction like this was only a form of quibbling for Emerson, who refused to impose limits upon the mystical resources of intrinsic being. Thus his pronouncements were not meant to accord with any criterion of reason or logic. Like scriptural truth, they had to be accepted upon the grounds of faith.

Quite the opposite view of morality in the *Four Books* attracted Thoreau. It was a tradition of virtuous conduct that had been handed down from sage to sage for countless generations, long before Confucius appeared on the historical scene. Though he universalized this inherited ethic by insisting upon moral cultivation for all men, he still invoked the authority of the past (the recurrent citations from the *Book of Odes*) to validate his teachings. Century after century his disciples maintained the pupillary system of knowledge, preserving the core of the ancient wisdom as the foundation of truth in all the situations of life. Of course, what Thoreau deplored about his own culture was the lack of any such unifying tradition. According to his writings, the members of his society shared no common belief in a vital purpose for existence. They exhausted their energies in the pursuit of a sterile, egotistic individualism, devoid of any reverence for nature or human nature. Thoreau conceived of individualism as a product of cultivated individuation—of a self-identity completely realized in freedom and responsibility. This is the lesson that neither the Hippies or Yippies have learned from their alleged prophet of rebellion. If viewed from the standpoint of his unwavering glorification of the teachings of the Wise Old Man of all ages and cultures, Thoreau was an incorrigible conservative, an iconoclast only in his insistence that his contemporaries were ignorant of the meaning of ignorance.

Confucius is no less concerned with unenlightened mentality. The *Analects* (*Memoirs* in the translation below) record the conversations of the sage with his disciples and other interlocutors on what only can be called the nature of virtue in action. Confucius betrays little or no interest in metaphysical definitions of morality. He is concerned primarily with empirical reality—with the effects of human conduct in the alleviation of misery and the promotion of happiness. For him knowledge per se is meaningless unless it vitalizes social and political existence. This attitude is evidenced in the way he talks to his students. He never tries to choose their vocations; instead he directs their attention to the responsibilities of the positions for which they aspire, insisting that they carry out their prescribed duties faithful to themselves and to the established order of things. What this counsel embraces is the doctrine of *tao,* a form of brotherly love based on the belief that sincerity is the foundation of all human truth. For if every individual carries out his duties in this spirit, then every member of society shares in the fruits of probity. This ethic shaped the resiliency of the Chinese character over the generations, giving life a purpose and a direction wholly independent of historical development. In exalting the cultivation of the self above all else, it established a place in the sun for all men, irrespective of rank or class, who did not allow the affairs of the world to corrupt their individual integrity.

Thoreau's first *Dial* selection of the Confucianist sayings came from the *Analects* (the translation of Joshua Marshman), but he chose to illustrate the doctrine of *tao* in a purely subjective fashion. Instead of emphasizing its essentially practical orientation, he focused almost entirely on its disengaged outlooks:

> Chee says, if in the morning I hear about the right way, and in the evening I die, I can be happy.
>
> A wise and good man was Hooi. A piece of bamboo was his dish, a cocoa-nut his cup, his dwelling a miser-

> able shed. Men could not sustain the sight of his wretchedness; but Hooi did not change the serenity of his mind. A wise and good man was Hooi (*Dial,* III [October, 1843] 493).

The choice of these and other excerpts have baffled the commentators on Thoreau's Confucianist interests, though wholly without reason. Even as in *Walden* and *A Week on the Concord and Merrimack Rivers,* the attainment of unshakable serenity marks the ultimate fruition of wisdom. It indicates that the mind has acquired absolute control over the erratic impulses of the body, over the tyrannical demands of pain and pleasure. In this perspective the attitudes of Chee and Hooi transcend the doctrines of a specific philosophy: they simply illustrate the efficacy of ascetic renunciation. Thoreau's immediate fascination with this subject can be traced to the extracts from the *Laws of Menu* which he published in the previous issue of the *Dial,* III (January, 1843), 331-40. In the light of his emphasis on the Hindu sage's injunctions to practice self-denial, we can only conclude that Thoreau searched the *Analects* for the expression of similar ideas—incidentally, an undertaking that required a meticulous examination of the text. In any event, this bias confirms his preoccupation with the perennial philosophy, but in a manner quite different from that of the other Concord Transcendentalists. Thoreau could not separate the understanding of any principle of truth from its practical application.

When Thoreau for the second time published a series of quotations from the Confucianist writings in the *Dial,* he drew on the *Analects, The Doctrine of the Mean,* and the *Memoirs of Mencius.* For some unknown reason he ignored the *Great Learning,* probably the most urbane of the *Four Books.* But, needless to say, he went about this task subjectively, converting Confucius into a figure compatible with his image of the Wise Old Man. Thus, apart from displaying him in his role as a teacher, he concentrated on the principles of his philosophy, particularly those associated with the pursuit of *tao*. At the outset he excerpted the writings of Mencius for the traits which display the active meaning of righteous conduct:

> The superior man's nature consists in this, that benevolence, justice, propriety, and wisdom, have their root in his heart, and are exhibited in his countenance. They shine forth in his face and go through to his back. They are manifested in his four members (p. 274).

Here Thoreau isolates the moral formula which many modern scholars consider to be the chief contribution of Mencius to the Confucian movement. The crucial nexus between inward beliefs and outward actions is not especially important in the reminiscences of the pupils who studied directly under the Master. Consistent with the pragmatic outlook of Confucius, they tend to emphasize the social consequences of virtue—the way it vitalizes filial, fraternal, and political relations. In fine, they center on the manner in which *jen* (love of others) helps to promote the cultivation of *tao* on all levels of human intercourse. Mencius, of course, has this same end in mind, but, teaching more than a hundred years after the death of Confucius, he apparently desires to spiritualize the conception of ethics. The passage in question exalts the individual who upholds in his conduct what he upholds in his heart. In other words, the superior man is never conscious of any conflict between what he feels and what he does. He has transcended the illusion of a divided moral self. In accord with this ideal, Thoreau again quotes Mencius to show how the practice of virtue affects the beholder:

> To be full of sincerity, is called beauty. To be so full of sincerity that it shines forth in the external conduct, is called greatness. When this greatness renovates others, it is called sageness. Holiness or sageness which is above comprehension, is called divine (p. 390).

Read out of context, certain words in this passage can be misleading. "Holiness" and "divine" are not meant to suggest the influence of a supernatural force, as no doubt Emerson would assume. For to judge by Thoreau's sensitive reading of Mencius, it is not unlikely that he recognized the function of such rhetoric. Very conscious of tradition, both Confucius and Mencius endow the inherited wisdom of the past with sacred qualities simply because they look upon enduring truth as independent of temporality. As a manifestation of *tao,* it is the bond that unites man to man, man to nature, man to his ancestors, and man to posterity. In this perspective historical circumstances are inconsequential. The true purpose and direction of life never changes.

Thoreau is very conscious of this belief when he turns his attention to the *Doctrine of the Mean* (*Chung Yung*). According to most scholars, this book was written by Tzu-ssu, the grandson of Confucius. As indicated by the title, it is a systematic exposition of the state of equilibrium subsumed in the union of *Chung* ("not to incline to either side," hence middle or mean) and *Yung* ("not to change," hence fixed law). To attain this goal is to attain mental and emotional harmony. Then all extremes of thought and feeling are avoided, and imperturbable sagacity alone determines conduct. And as Thoreau perceives in the passages that he quotes in the *Dial,* the sustaining virtue of the mean in action is sincerity (*cheng*):

> Sincerity is the *Taou* or way of heaven. To aim at it is the way of man (p. 49).

> From inherent sincerity to have perfect intelligence, is to be a sage by nature; to attain sincerity by means of intelligence, is to be such by study. Where there is sincerity, there must be intelligence. Where intelligence is, it must lead to sincerity (p. 50).

This concept of sincerity has little in common with its English meaning. It embraces the idea of essential natural goodness—a human-heartedness that is achieved without effort and without thought and that asserts itself spontaneously. As another of Thoreau's excerpts seeks to show, it is in man and can be cultivated by man: "the superior man employs man (that is, what is in man) to reform man" (p. 39). Of course, regardless of the terminology used by the various compilers of the *Four Books* to define the path of virtue, *tao* is ultimately the principle that is under discussion. As the word of the Master, it is cherished and nurtured as a revelation of absolute truth, as the matrix of divine wisdom. If we are to understand its impact upon Thoreau and perhaps Emerson, then its intimations about the nature of man are of key importance. All of Thoreau's quotations in the *Dial* tend to support the belief that man is innately good and has the capacity to perfect himself by his own efforts. This notion of the development of the self is most clearly elaborated in *Walden* and in the essays on walking, significantly without reflecting the influence of Emerson's outlook on the matter. The latter's conception of the process is essentially romantic. Intuition is the vehicle of self-realization, and, as a consequence, there is no need for physical or mental exertion, that is, barring leisurely contemplation from which springs the mystical awareness of the unlimited possibilities of being. Conversely, Thoreau always conceives of the growth of such insight in terms of a formalized discipline of sensory consciousness. How much the *Four Books* contributed to this conviction is of no real import. What matters is that we recognize Thoreau for what he is—an advocate of a perennial philosophy that actually tests the integrity of mind and body. Of course, the supreme trial is self-renunciation: detachment from pleasure, possession, and ambition.

Though Thoreau fails to quote the *Great Learning* in his *Dial* selections, the book merits a brief examination because of the way ethics are blended with politics and the curse of craving is overcome. The main thesis of the author is that the knowledge of *tao* "consists in clearly illustrating brilliant virtue, renovating the people, and resting only in the summit of virtue" (Introduction). As this belief is argued, it gradually evolves into a panacea for all social diseases, embracing the happiness of the individual, the family, and the state. Step by step, we witness the operation of the principle of moral extension. According to the *Odes* (the inherited wisdom of the past and the authority for conduct in the present), the ancient sages illustrated their virtue by ruling justly. But before they undertook the responsibilities of government, they learned to keep order in their families. However, before they could accomplish the latter, they had to cultivate personal virtue. What this involved was the rectification of the heart through the practice of sincerity. Thus the moral formula of the *Great Learning* insured the development of a well-balanced individual, a well-ordered family, a well-governed state, and a happy, stable world. To be sure, the attainment of this goal was not easy. It involved, as a summary of the creed indicates, the strenuous fostering of divine nobility on the plane of human existence:

> Benevolence, justice, fidelity, and truth, and to delight in virtue without weariness, constitute divine nobility. To be a prince, a prime minister, or a great officer of state constitute human nobility. The ancients adorned divine nobility, and human nobility followed it.
>
> The men of the present day cultivate divine nobility in order that they may obtain human nobility; and when they once get human nobility, they throw away divine nobility. This is the height of delusion, and must end in the loss of both (p. 361).

Appropriately, Thoreau includes this passage in his *Dial* offerings, and perhaps we have here the explanation for his neglect of the *Great Learning*. He may have thought that all the teachings of this short work are more clearly presented in the other writings of the *Four Books*. This is true in the sense that the voice of Confucius is seldom heard.

Filtered through surrogates, the sayings he was later to popularize somehow or another lose their dramatic cogency. Thus, without direct recourse to the *Great Learning,* Thoreau preserves the scope of the Chinese philosophy in his selections.

There is reason to believe that Thoreau never quite trusted Collie's translation of the *Four Books.* For as Lyman V. Cady has proved, eight out of the nine quotations on Confucianism found in *Walden* are Thoreau's translation from the French of G. Pauthier, a noted Oriental scholar. Unquestionably, what led Thoreau to suspect Collie were the innumerable footnotes in his edition which challenged the validity of all moral systems outside the Christian tradition, as for example the following remark:

> It is to be feared that the standard of perfect virtue, formed by the Chinese philosophers [in the *Great Learning*] is very low, hence the ruinous notion that man may, unaided by divine influence, make himself perfectly virtuous, but it ought never be forgotten, that the question is not whether man in his fallen state may not of himself practice virtues, and upon the whole be a useful member of Society, but whether he may without divine renovation, render the homage to his Creator which both scripture and reason require (Footnote, p. 19).

Thoreau answers this complaint several times in both *Walden* and *A Week on the Concord and Merrimack Rivers,* but this fact hardly compares with the importance of his obvious desire to become acquainted with the most accurate translations of the *Four Books,* a predilection also carried over in his approach to the Hindu scriptures. The early translators, most of whom were either missionaries or devout Christians, corrupted the originals by the introduction of vapid theological doctrines. Hence, Thoreau scoured the Latin, German, and French translations of scholarly Orientalists for more precise renderings of the ethnical bibles. In the case of the *Four Books* Pauthier apparently satisfied Thoreau's desire for intellectual (and spiritual) self-integrity in such matters.

This brief introduction does not pretend to exhaust Thoreau's particular understanding of Confucianism. It represents my personal viewpoint, one arrived at through countless readings of his major and minor works. However, my claim that he was fascinated by the archetype of the Wise Old Man has been fully substantiated in a number of published articles. Still others soon to appear will further elaborate the complex nature of this interest. Without advocating my approach to the *Four Books,* I sincerely believe that a patient and conscientious reading of these works will further illuminate the analogical texture of *Walden* and *A Week,* for example, his adaption of the polarity of *Yin* and *Yang* which receives careful examination in Collie's footnotes. Nor is the handling of natural imagery in the *Four Books* unrelated to Thoreau's own view of the universe. In short, the texts below can be used to explore stylistic effects, not simply echoes of Confucian philosophy. Thoreau's art is a poetics of perception. It is a way of seeing into knowledge.

WILLIAM BYSSHE STEIN

State University of New York
Binghamton
January, 1969

THE

CHINESE CLASSICAL WORK

COMMONLY CALLED

THE

FOUR BOOKS;

TRANSLATED,

AND ILLUSTRATED WITH NOTES,

BY THE LATE REV. DAVID COLLIE,

Principal of the Anglo-Chinese College,

MALACCA.

PRINTED AT THE MISSION PRESS.

1828.

PREFACE.

The following Version of the Four Books was undertaken, in the first instance, for the purpose of acquiring some knowledge of the Chinese Language. After the whole had been written, it occurred to the Translator, that if carefully revised and illustrated by quotations from the most approved Comments, and by occasional remarks on the fundamental errors in religion and morals, which, in too many instances, the work discovers, it might perhaps be of some use to the Chinese who study English in the College, not only by assisting them in acquiring the English Language, but especially in leading them to reflect seriously on some of the fatal errors propagated by their most celebrated sages. This circumstance forms the only apology which the Translator can offer for the frequent repetition of what must, to the European reader, appear common place remarks, but which it is hoped, may, by the divine blessing, prove useful to some of the deluded heathen who read the translation. At the time when the version was rewritten, along with the Notes and Remarks, there was little intention of publication: for although the

Translator by a kind of enthusiastic, and what to some may appear an unreasonable fondness for the Chinese Language, did not feel the Four Books to be by any means so dull and common place as there is reason to fear most readers of the translation will deem them, still he was not by any means so blinded by enthusiasm for his favorite study, as to lead him to suppose, that the work could possibly be made interesting to the generality of readers, and had he not been encouraged by friends whose judgment he highly values, in all probability the present version had remained in manuscript, for the sole use of those for whom it was originally intended. It is not meant by these remarks, however, to convey the idea, that the Four Books are wholly void of interest to a certain class of readers. To those who are but commencing their Chinese studies, and who may not have the assistance of a Teacher, the present version, imperfect as it confessedly is, will be, it is hoped of considerable service. Nor will it fail to interest those who take pleasure in tracing the operations of the human mind under all the varied aspects in which it is presented to our view For, the Four Books may be considered a fair specimen of what men in the age and circumstances in which their authors were placed could attain in the Science of Religion and Morals. What their attainments were, we shall leave the reader of the following pages to judge for himself, merely remarking, that the Christian who peruses them will see abundant reason to be grateful that he has been taught a "More excellent way," while the Infidel will find little in support of his favorite theory, viz. that a special Revelation of the Divine Will is unnecessary.

The Four Books, as the title denotes, consist of four separate pieces, which are arranged by the Chinese in the following order.

I. The Ta Heŏ which was compiled by Tsăng Tsze, a disciple of Confucius, from materials chiefly composed of the sayings of the Sage, and of quotations from the standard works of the Ancients. The scope of the work is to point out the truly philosophical mode of attaining perfect, personal and social virtue, and to trace the connection which indissolubly exists between individual worth and the proper regulation of the family, the good government of small Provinces and the virtue, prosperity and happiness of great Empires. It exhibits some beautiful theories, but generally founded on false principles. *

II. The Chung Yung, or "Golden Medium." This Tract was compiled by Kung Kĕih, who was a grandson and disciple of Confucius. Its object, as its title denotes, is to direct men how to find and maintain the due medium in all things. It is more abstruse and mystical than any other of the Four Books, and frequently puzzles the reader with a number of high sounding terms to which he cannot attach any definite idea. †

* We have seen two English Translations of the Ta Heo,—One by Dr. Morrison, and another published at Serampore in 1814, and ascribed to Mr. John Marshman, Son of the Rev. Dr. Marshman, who has executed a Chinese Version of the Bible, an English translation of the Shang Lun, a Grammar of the Chinese Language, &c.

† M. Abel-Remusat, de l'Académie royale des Inscriptions et Belles-Lettres,

III. The Lun Yu (Dialogues) This work consists of conversations between Confucius and his disciples, which were collected and committed to writing by the latter. It is divided into two volumes, called the Shang Lun and Hea Lun. The subjects of which it treats are of a miscellaneous nature, relating, principally, to the duties of Prince and Minister, Father and Son, Master and Scholar. The Lun Yu abounds with what some would call truisms, and repetitions in almost the same words are rather frequent. These Dialogues, however, discover considerable skill in the management of human nature, and often exhibit no small degree of adroitness on the part of the Sage, in adapting his instructions to the peculiar dispositions and talents of his disciples. *

IV. The Shang Mung and Hea Mung. This work is the production of Mung Tsze (Mencius), who flourished about 100 years after Confucius, and seems to occupy the next place to him in the estimation of his countrymen. In this treatise we have the substance of his political and ethical doctrines. His style excels the above-mentioned pieces in point of imagination, vigour and ornament. A considerable part of his book consists of conversations held on various occasions with the petty Princes of the day, with whose system of Government the Sage was far from being satisfied. He made it his constant practice to point out what he considered false in principle, or wrong in practice with the utmost

Professour de Langue et de Littératnre chinoises et tartares au College royal de France has translated this work into French and Latin

* An English translation of the Shang Lun, i. e. first Volume of the Lun Yu, was published at Serampore in 1809, by Dr. Marshman and dedicated to Lord Minto.

freedom, and reproved crowned heads without the least ceremony whenever he judged them culpable. Like Confucius, when he confines himself to political maxims and moral precepts, he speaks like a man of a sound and vigorous mind, but when he launches into the depths of metaphysical jargon, he frequently loses himself in mystical speculations, which seem to answer no other end than that of affording an additional proof, that no human intellect is of itself capable of discovering the truth on the momentous subject of Religion.*

Before concluding this Preface, we beg to say a few words respecting the execution of the version now presented to our readers. But on this subject we had better, perhaps, say little, for nothing we can urge will afford any sufficient apology for the faults and defects with which we are well aware the work abounds. Some will say, that in many instances the rendering is too literal and in others too free, and in many cases the spirit and force of the original have been lost. Others may observe so many Chinesisms and Scotticisms in the style that they will be apt to say it does not deserve the name of an *English* version. To such charges we are ready to plead guilty; but trust that the frequent obscurity and uniform conciseness of the original, will, in some degree, be admitted as our apology. At least if such considerations as those do not tend to soften the severity of criticism, we have no other to offer, for the translation was written with due deliberation and with

* Stanislaus Julien published a Latin translation of part of the first volume of Mencius in 1821.

good native assistance, and with the same assistance every page of it has been again carefully compared with the original; nor has the Translator failed to avail himself of the aid to be derived from the English and Latin Versions of part of the Four Books to which he had access, and although he has often taken the liberty to differ from his highly respectable Predecessors and been guided principally by native Commentators, still he has frequently received considerable assistance from the former. So that either the difficulty of the task, or the ignorance of the Translator, or both, can form the only apology for the faults of the version. For the Translator cannot accuse himself of negligence, nor can he complain of the want of all needful aid. In fact, when he considers the comparatively little value of the work, and the important engagements which form his proper employment, he feels that he ought rather to apologize for having bestowed so much time upon it, than for not having succeeded in giving a good and faithful version.

N. B. The Notes at the foot of the page are not a literal translation of any one Commentator, but rather the substance of various Comments. A small line separates these Notes from the remarks of the Translator.

Anglo-Chinese College,

March 1828.

MEMOIRS

OF

CONFUCIUS.

The Ancestors of the Sage were originally natives of Sung, but had for six generations, held official situations in Loo. When Confucius was born, there was a hollow on the crown of his head, on which account he was named 丘 *Kew* (a hollow on the top of a hill). His literary name was 仲 尼 *Chung Ne*, and his family name 孔 *Kung*. When a child, he was fond of enquiring into the nature and reasons of things, and was in the habit of making imitations of the sacred vessels used in the Temples, and of imitating the various ceremonies used in the worship of the gods and of ancestors. Being nine cubits, six inches high, people admired him and called him the *tall man*.

He was endued with an intuitive knowledge of all things, and was not under the necessity of pursuing a regular course of study, yet from his youth he paid the most serious attention to the doctrines of the former Sages and embodied them in his writings.

When young, he was poor and in low circumstances, and consequently obliged to have recourse to manual labour for his support. In consequence, however, of his great intelligence, and eminent virtue, when about twenty years of age, he was appointed by the Government of Loo, his native Country, to be superintendent of grain, cattle, &c.

He afterwards visited the Provinces of Tse and Wei, and returned again to his native Country. By the permission of his Sovereign, he subsequently went to Chow to avail himself of the instructions of 老子 *Laou Tsze*, a celebrated scholar of the day. Previous to this he had seventy disciples, but on his return the number of his pupils increased.

About the 35th year of his age, in consequence of the disorders which took place in Loo, he went to Tse and became Steward to a Mandarin of that Country, and was thus introduced to the Prince of Tse. Here he conversed on the principles of music with the master musician of the Court. It was there that, in consequence of hearing the Chaou or music of the famous Monarch Shun, during a period of three months he knew not the taste of flesh. *

He talked to the Prince of Tse of the reciprocal duties of Prince and Minister and of Father and Son, The Prince was pleased with his principles and was about to give him an appointment when one of his Counsellors dissuaded him by representing the Joo sect, or sect of the Learned, to which Confucius belonged,

* See Shang Lun Chap. vii. Sec. 12.

as a self-conceited haughty, unmanageable class of men, and this representation induced the Prince to dismiss the Sage. The latter being disappointed in his attempts to establish his principles in Tse, returned once more to his native Province. But in consequence of all the Government Officers of Loo having assumed improper authority, he declined being in office, and retired to revise the collection of odes called the 詩經 *She King*, the historical work called the 書經 *Shoo King*. and the treatise on ceremonies and forms of polite intercourse called the 禮記 *Le Ke*. He also improved or revised the art of music. His disciples now became very numerous and came from all quarters to receive his instructions. After he was upwards of 50 years of age, he was appointed by Prince Ting of Loo to be Governor of a district. While in this office he produced a thorough renovation of manners ni all around him: He was afterwards to be advanced to higher offices, and for a short time acted as Prime Minister of Loo. Whilst in this Office, the Government of Tse, a neighbouring state, observing the influence which the excellent politics of the Sage produced on the people of Loo, became alarmed lest the latter should speedily become an overmatch for Tse, and sent a band of female musicians to the Court of Loo, hoping thereby to lead the Prince and his Ministers into some gross irregularity which would induce the Sage to resign. The scheme succeeded completely; for the Prince and his principal Courtiers were so enchanted with the Songsters of Tse, that for three days they entirely neglected the business of the nation and forgot to send the sacrificial flesh to the high Officers of State. Consequently Confucius resigned and left the Court.

After this he went to the Wei Country, where he remained ten months and had some interviews with the Prince of Wei, and then left for the Province of China. On the way, his life was in danger from the people of Kwang, who mistook him for a person who had excited their rage by his tyranny. The Sage, however, confided in heaven and escaped. After this he offered his services to the Government of Wei, but that Prince not liking his benevolent politics, excused himself for not employing the Sage on the ground that he was too old to be guided by such a Minister; upon which Confucius departed with the intention of visiting Tsin, but in consequence of some unlucky omens which presented themselves, he returned to Wei. Some time after this, one of the principal Officers of Loo on his death bed commanded his son and successor to employ Confucius, declaring that his having so offended Confucius, on a former occasion, as to cause him to resign, had endangered the Country. The young Courtier, after the death of his Father, would have called Confucius to office, but was prevented by a friend, who stated that in consequence of not being able to retain the Sage in office on a former occasion, they had been laughed at by the neighbouring Princes, and that by calling him back to office they would only increase their disgrace, as it was not likely that they could so act as to keep him long in any Government office. It was after this that he formed the resolution of ceasing from his peregrinations and returning to his native Province, for the purpose of fully instructing his disciples, so that they might hand down his principles to future ages; * and of revising the ancient books called the 禮記 *Le Ke*, 詩經 *She King*, and 書經 *Shoo King*, and compiling the 春秋 *Chun Tsew*. The latter work which is of an historical nature, seems to have been among the last of his literary labors, and was intended to reprove the Princes and Ministers of the day. In all his writings, his grand object was to hand down to posterity the great principles of political economy practised by the renowned founders of the Hea, Shang and Chow dynasties, believing these principles to be derived from heaven, and admirably calculate . to promote the happiness of man.

Soon after the completion of the *Chun Tsew*, a period was put the labours of the Sage by death. His ancient disciples erected a booth at his grave, and there spent three years in mourning for their deeply lamented Master; after which they returned home. Tsze Kung, however, remained at the tomb three years longer. Such was the high esteem cherished for their leader, by the followers of this celebrated Moralist. That he was a man of considerable abilities, and of regular moral habits, seems to be a matter of fact we see no reason to dispute. We also admit, that among his numerous sayings, there are many excellent maxims; but we really have not been able to find any ground for the lofty epi-

* See Shang Lun, Chap. v. Sec 21.

thets applied to him by some celebrated opponents of divine truth.

In the whole compass of his writings, there does not appear to us to be a single idea above the reach of any plain man at all accustomed to reflection. As to the all important points, for the certain developement of which, Divine Revelation seems to us absolutely necessary, Confucius leaves them entirely untouched. On the nature and Government of the Supreme Being, he says little;—of a future state, almost nothing;—and on the method by which a guilty world may be restored to the image and favor of God, he has given us no information which is not as much at variance with sound philosophy, as it is with revealed truth. His information on most subjects connected with the character of God, and the duty of man to his Creator, seems to rank considerably below that of some of the Grecian Sages, especially Socrates; a circumstance, we think, which may be accounted for by the fact, that the latter lived nearer that favoured Country where the light of Revelation first shone. We have no reason, however, to suppose that Confucius was an Atheist; for, although he gives us no satisfactory view of the attributes and Government of one Supreme God, he often speaks with much apparent reverence of some high Ruler, which he calls 天 *Teen;* and his works afford sufficient proof that he believed in "Gods many and Lords many." It is supposed, however, that the generality of his pretended followers of the present day have sunk into absolute Atheism.

He seems to have lived in times of great degeneracy, especially among the higher ranks of Society; and it does not appear that his labours produced either a general or very permanent reformation notwithstanding the lofty things that are said by himself and his admirers, as to the all-renovating influence of his omnipotent virtue. * He himself frequently lamented that his doctrines were not embraced, and that his exertions had little influence on his depraved countrymen. In fact during his life, his fame does not seem to have been very great, and perhaps what has contributed, more than any thing else, to his having become an object of lasting admiration to his countrymen, is his having collected the scattered fragments of ancient legislators, moralists, and poets, and handed them down to posterity. It is on this very account that he is pronounced by some of their most respectable writers, to have been far superior to the great Monarchs Yaou and Shun, who are pronounced to be the patterns of all future princes.—These great Monarchs, say they, only benefited one age by their wise and benevolent Government, but Confucius, by transmitting their principles to ten thousand † ages possesses ten thousand times their merit. This circumstance has given his sayings published by his followers, and his compilations of ancient writers, a permanent hold on the veneration of the Chinese, and rendered them the standard classics in all their Seats of Learning.

* See the conclusion of the Chung Yung and many other passages of the Four Books.

† Ten Thousand is a general expression for all, or a great number.

TA HEO.

Superior learning* consists in clearly illustrating brilliant virtue, renovating the people, and resting only in the summit of excellence. The summit of virtue once ascertained, the mind determines to attain it—the determination once fixed, the mind becomes stable, being stable, it feels at ease—being at ease, it can fully investigate—having fully investigated, it attains its object. Things have an origin and a consummation, actions have

* "Superior learning," means the learning proper for men, in opposition to that of children "Brilliant virtue" is the pure, unclouded mind, which all men originally receive from heaven and which by the polluting, blinding influence of external objects, becomes obscure and disordered. The first object of genuine learning, is by a thorough scrutiny of the nature of things, to restore the mind to its original purity and brightness. This great object will infallibly be attained by that perfect knowledge which is the result of a complete investigation of all things. The mind being once restored to its pristine glory, universal happiness follows as the inseparable consequence. But, if any one suppose that he can promote the happiness of others, while he neglects to purify his own mind, and adorn his own person with virtue, he acts the part of him, who expects abundance of good fruit from the branches, while he neglects the proper culture of the root.

** The above passage looks beautiful in theory, and contains some important truths, but there is one grand fallacy at the foundation of the system, viz, that an extensive and accurate knowledge of things, will produce purity of heart, and rectitude of conduct. We are not left to theoretical conjecture on this all important point; for the history of man supplies us with numerous instances, in which men, the most eminent for their extensive knowledge of nature, have by no means been exemplary in their moral conduct. This shews that an extensive knowledge of things, however desirable, is still insufficient for effecting the great work of moral renovation, and strongly confirms the truth of divine revelation, which affirms that it is only the right knowledge of the Creator, and Saviour of the world and a spiritual renovation by the power of the Divine Spirit, that can produce that purity of heart, singleness of intention and moral rectitude of conduct, which are at once the preparation for, and antepast of never ending and unmingled felicity.

first principles and ultimate consequences. He who understands the regular order of things, has approximated to perfection.

The ancient (Princes) who felt desirous that the brilliancy of resplendent virtue might shine through the whole Empire, first promoted good order in their own provinces;—wishing to establish order in their own provinces, they first regulated their own families;—in order to effect the regulation of their own families, they first adorned their persons with virtue, in order that they might adorn their persons with virtue, they first rectified their own hearts; wishing to rectify their hearts, they first purified their motives; in order to purify their motives, they first extended their knowledge to the utmost. When knowledge is perfect, it rectifies the motives;—single motives regulate the inclinations;—virtuous inclinations lead to exemplary personal conduct;—such conduct (in the head of the family) leads to domestic order;—when the family of the Prince exhibits an example of domestic order, good order will prevail through the whole province;—when good order prevails in individual provinces, the whole Empire will enjoy peace and plenty. For all, from the son of heaven (the Emperor) to the meanest subject, there is but one rule, which is to make personal virtue the root. That the root should be disor d and the branches in good condition cannot be: for no man, if he treat lightly what is of most importance, will attend pronerlv to what is secondary.

The above section contains the words of Confucius, recorded by Tăang Tsze. He delivered ten sections which contain his own ideas, and were recorded by his disciples. In the ancient copies there were some errors;—the present, as corrected by Ching Tsze, and the text as examined by us, stands regulated as below.

SEC. I.

The Kang Kaou says, that Wăa Wang was able to illustrate brilliant virtue. The Tae Keă (speaking of Tang) says, he constantly kept his eye on the resplendent gift of heaven, (original virtue) and the Te Teĕn speaking of Yaou, says, he was capable of clearly exhibiting illustrious virtue * All these brightened their own original virtue. This first section shews what is meant by " Clearly illustrating brilliant virtue."

SEC. II.

The motto engraven on the bathing tub of Tang, said, " Sincerly renovate all day, daily renovate, constantly renovate." The Kang Kaou says, " Renovate the people." The ode says, Chow although an old country, has obtained a new decree.† Hence it is evident that the superior man, in all respects, carries every

* The Kang Kaou, Tae Kea, and Te Teen, are ancient Poems. The former praises the virtue of Wan Wang the father of the brave and virtuous Woo Wang, who conquered the tyrant Chow, (last Emperor of the Shang Dynasty,) and became the first Emperor of the Chow Dynasty, which commenced about 1130 years before the Christian æra. The Tae Kea was written by the celebrated E Yin, Prime minister of Tae Kea, grand-son and successor of the famous Tang who founded the Shang Dynasty. Tae Kea in the commencement of his reign did not bid fair as a ruler. hence E Yin wrote the Tae Kea ode to remind him of the virtues of his grand-father. With the intention of rousing him effectually to the imitation of so eminent an example, he advised him to spend three years at the tomb of his deceased ancestor. The young sovereign complied with the advice of his minister, and on returning from his solitary habitation, shewed the beneficial effects of such a course by performing the duties of his exalted station to the satisfaction of the whole Empire. The Te Teen extolls the exalted virtue of the ancient Monarch Yaou, who flourished about 2300 years before Christ. These sayings of the poets are quoted with the view of shewing, that those ancient worthies restored the original virtue conferred upon all men by heaven, to its pristine brightness, and of proving that this great work is in every man's own power. * *

† That is heaven made the rulers of Chow, Emperors, because through the influence of the virtue of Wan and Woo Wang, the people were renovated.

---

* * It is to be feared that the standard of perfect virtue, formed by the Chinese Philosophers is very low, hence the ruinous notion that man may, unaided by divine influence, make himself perfectly virtuous, but, it ought never to be forgotten, that the question is not whether man in his fallen state, may not of himself practise many virtues, and upon the whole be an useful member of Society, but whether he may, without divine renovation, render that homage to his Creator which both scripture and reason require.

duty to the utmost extent. This second section explains what is meant by renovating the people.

SEC. III.

The ode says, for one thousand miles around the Imperial residence, is the place where the people dwell. The poet says, the notes of the yellow bird, rest in the groves of the mountains, upon which Confucius observes, it knows its place, and shall not man equal the birds! The ode says, how profound the virtue of King Wăn! with what glory and dignity did he occupy his proper station! As a Prince, he rested in benevolence—as a minister, in respect—as a son, in filial piety—as a father, in paternal tenderness,—and as a member of society, in fidelity.

The ode says, behold on yonder banks of the Ke, how luxuriant is the green bamboo! Thus elegantly adorned with virtue i the superior man! (Alluding to King Wăn.) As we carve and smooth the ivory—as we cut and file the precious gem, so did he model his conduct. How majestic! how commanding! how illustrious, was the learned Prince! To the latest ages he will not be forgotten! As we carve and smooth the ivory, so did he cultivate his mind by the study of divine principles:—as we cut and polish the precious gem, so did he adorn his person with virtue. "How majestic," expresses the awe which he inspired "How commanding!" expresses, the respect which his dignity produced. "The learned Prince can never be forgotten," means that the people can never forget his abundant virtue, and consummate excellence. *

---

* According to Chinese history, these Princes, who are to this day renowned by the inhabitants of the celestial Empire, lived in a time of such tyranny, that man of moderate virtue, holding an official situation, must have been viewed with no common degree of respect, by the cruelly oppressed people who longed to be relieved from the yoke of tyranny: hence it is not improbable, that these chieftains were as much indebted for that permanent fame which they have acquired to the circumstances in which they were placed, as to the virtues which they possessed.

The ode says the former Kings (Wăn and Woo) are not yet forgotten! Good Princes still esteem those virtuous whom they esteemed virtuous, and still feel attached to such as they did. The people rejoice in the joy, and profit by the advantages of which they were the authors. To the latest ages they will not be forgotten! This third section illustrates the phrase, "Make the summit of virtue the point of rest."

SEC. IV.

1. Confucius said, in deciding law suits, I can do as well as others; but it is necessary to put an end to litigations:—to prevent the unprincipled from telling their stories, by filling the people with awe. This is what we call knowing the root. This fourth section illustrates what is said of the "Root and branches." *

SEC. V.

The fifth section, which illustrated the proposition, "The perfection of knowledge lies in a thorough investigation of the nature of things," is now lost. I, after having deliberately considered the subject, adopt the ideas of Ching Tsze to supply the deficiency. When it is said that the perfecting of knowledge, consists in scrutinizing the nature of things, the meaning is, that if we wish to perfect our knowledge, we ought to examine to the utmost the laws of existing things: for the human mind is certainly capable of acquiring knowledge, and among all things under

* The grand scope of the fourth section, is to shew that the sages by their profound and accurate knowledge of things, and by their consumate virtue, make bad men ashamed of their wicked deeds, and produce an universal renovation in human nature. * *

* * This theory receives little support from the history of the human species.

heaven, there is nothing without fixed laws. But if these laws be not thoroughly investigated by man, his knowledge must be incomplete. Hence the Ta Heŏ commences by sending the student to examine all things under heaven, that by reasoning from what he already knows, he may extend his knowledge to the utmost limit. When the mind has thus for a long time exerted its energies, at last, it becomes expanded and attains a perfect comprehension of all things, so that there is nothing either in the exterior, or interior,—in the more subtile, or more obvious principles of things, to which its knowledge will not extend:—thus the whole powers of the mind will be completely illuminated. This explains what is meant by the. " Perfection of knowledge, consisting in a thorough acquaintance with all things. " *

SEC. VI.

That which is called rectifying the motives, is this; do not deceive yourself; hate vice as you do an offensive smell; love virtue as you love beauty. This is called self-enjoyment. Hence the superior man will carefully watch over his secret moments.

The worthless man, when in secret, practises vice; nay, there is no length of wickedness to which he does not proceed, but when he observes the superior man, he attempts to conceal his vices, and puts on the appearance of virtue. Men who observe him, as it were see his very heart and reins; what then does he

* It is not very obvious what is meant by the expressions " All things under heaven" and " Scrutinizing the laws of all things." On the one hand, it is perfectly evident that the Chinese sages of antiquity, confined their inquiries, principally, to the nature and duties of man, and payed little attention to the laws and properties of matter; but on the other hand, it must be evident, to all who have attended to their speculations respecting the Yin and Yang principles, that they consider a knowledge of these imaginary powers, essential, not only to complete human knowledge, but even to fit man for the proper discharge of his incumbent duties. As they consider that every thing in nature belongs, either to one, or other of these principles, and as the superiority, or inferiority of every thing is ascertained by its belonging, either to the superior or inferior principle, so the knowledge of them becomes necessary in the most trival concerns; even a common meal cannot be placed on the table, in a proper manner, without a careful attention to the Yin and Yang, for as every inferior object belongs to the Yin, so in placing the different articles of food on the table, all that belong to the Yin principle must be set on the least honorable place and vice versa.

profit himself. This is what is meant by the adage, "What is really within, shews itself without." hence the superior man, must be careful over his conduct, when no human eye sees him.

Tsăng Tsze says, that which ten eyes gaze upon, and ten fingers point to, requires rigorous watchfulness. As riches adorn a mansion, so when the mind is expanded, the body is at ease: hence the superior man will rectify his motives. This sixth section explains the phrase "Rectify the motives." *

SEC. VII.

What is meant by saying that "Adorning the person with virtue, depends upon rectifying the heart," is this, if the mind be under the influence of rage, it cannot obtain this rectitude—if it be distracted by fear, it cannot attain a proper medium—if it be lifted up with excessive joy, it cannot obtain the proper medium,—and if it be depressed with grief, it cannot obtain the due equilibrium. If the mind be absent, we may look, without seeing, listen without hearing, and eat without relish. This shews what is understood by saying, that the cultivation of personal virtue, depends upon rectifying the heart. This seventh section illustrates the meaning of "Correcting the heart, and adorning the person with virtue"

SEC. VIII.

That which is meant by saying, that "The proper regulation of the family depends upon the cultivation of personal virtue," is

---

* There are two grand fundamental principles wanting in this system of moral renovation. In the first place, it recognizes no supreme being, to whom the constant and highest homage of all intelligent beings is due, and in the second, as a natural consequence of the first, excludes divine influence from occupying any share in forming the mind to virtue, and divine omniscience from taking notice of human thoughts and actions. Thus man is made a sort of deity, whose original virtue is capable of carrying him to the summit of rectitude and felicity, and who is responsible to no supreme ruler for his actions. This system is exceedingly gratifying to human pride, but how it will prepare a man for standing before an infinitely holy God, is another and most momentous question.

this; some men in loving their relatives, are partial—in hating the worthless, illiberal—in revering superiors, servile—in compassionating the distressed, too indulgent—in their treatment of inferiors, proud and haughty. Wherefore to love a man, and yet be sensible of his faults, and to hate a man and at the same time acknowledge his excellencies, are rare things under heaven. Hence the common adage, "A father knows not the faults of his children, and the husband-man knows not the growth of his corn." This shews that if a man does not cultivate personal virtue, he cannot properly regulate his family. This eighth section shews the connection between adorning the person with virtue and domestic order. *

SEC. IX.

That which is said respecting the necessity of regulating the family previous to being able to govern a country, may be thus explained: a man who is incapable of instructing his own family, cannot possibly instruct a nation. Wherefore, the superior man goes not beyond his own family, in order to finish a system of instruction, sufficient for a nation: for filial piety is that by which a Prince should be served—fraternal affection, is that by which superiors should be served, and paternal tenderness, is that by which all the people should be treated.

* To rectify the mind, is to bring it back to that state of pure, spiritual, unclouded intelligence, and perfect freedom from the least degree of impartiality, in which it is originally received from heaven. If mental purity and rectitude be not attained, there cannot be truly virtuous conduct. * *

---

* * Here, as to the result, the sages and the sacred writers agree, but the former send us to depraved human nature, as the source whence purity of heart and rectitude of conduct may, by personal exertion, be derived; while the latter direct us to the fountain of infinite purity, as the only source of virtuous sentiments and conduct. Let calm, unprejudiced reason decide who are the safest guides.

The Kang Kaou says, "*Nourish the people* as a mother does her tender offspring." If a mother really seeks to know the wants of her child, although she may not hit exactly upon them, she will not be far mistaken. There are none who first learn to nourish children, and then enter into the ma rimonial state.

If one family (that of the Prince) be virtuous, then the whole nation will flourish in virtue. If one family be polite and condescending, the whole nation will delight in politeness and condescension. If one man (the Prince) be avaricious, confusion will prevail through the whole kingdom. Of such importance is the prime mover; which confirms the adage, that "One word will ruin an affair, and one word will establish a nation. *"

Yaou, and Shun led the Empire by virtue, and the people imitated them. Keë and Chow † led the Empire by violence and the people imitated them, when what they commanded was contrary to what they themselves loved, the people did not

* Every family is in itself a nation in miniature, and every nation is but one great family: both should be governed by precisely the same rules and bound by the same ties. As a man who does not exhibit in his own conduct a pattern of virtue, is utterly unable to instruct and rule his own family, so a Prince whose own person is not ornamented with virtue, is totally incapable of instructing and governing a nation; but on the other hand, the truly virtuous father will find some difficulty in establishing domestic order in his family, nor will the good Prince find it a hard task to govern his people; for it is a fixed principle in nature, that inferiors are always influenced and led by superiors, and that whatever virtue or vice is found in the former is always exemplified in the latter. * *

---

† Keë was the last Emperor of the Hea Dynasty, which closed about 1756 before the Christain era; and Chow was the last of the Shang or Yin Dynasty, which terminated about 1112 B. C. These two tyrants seem to have been the Neros of China. History scarcely records any thing which surpasses their cruelty and brutality. The famous Tang cut off the former, and Woo Wang dethroned the latter.

* * Although there is a great deal of truth in these remarks, yet some will be apt to think that a subject placed under the same control and authority as that of a child, would not enjoy a sufficient degree of freedom, while on the other hand few Princes will consider themselves bound to exercise all that tender solicitude for their subjects that a father ought to feel for his own offspring. Nor will it be granted by those who possess a tolerable acquaintance with mankind, that a good example in superiors is quite so powerful in its influence on inferiors as the Chinese writers generally maintain. On both these points they seem to push good principles rather too far.

obey; therefore the Ruler must first have virtue in himself, and then he may call for it in others; he must first be free from vice himself, then he may reprove it in others. If we ourselves cherish and practise what we do not wish in others, we cannot possibly enlighten them. Hence, the good Government of a kingdom depends upon the proper regulation of the family.

The poet says "The peach tree how beautiful! Its foliage how luxuriant! Such is the bride when she enters the house of her husband, and duly regulates the family." Let a man first regulate his family, then he may instruct a nation. The Sho King says, "Perform aright the incumbent duties of elder and younger brothers, then you may instruct a nation. "The ode says, "He who shews a perfect example will rectify the manners of these four nations,"(or of all the nations within the four quarters of the Globe). His conduct as a father, a son, an elder and younger brother being worthy of imitation, the people will follow his example. This says that the good government of a kingdom, depends on the due regulation of the family.

Sec. X.

That which is meant by the proposition, "The good government of provinces will establish peace and happiness through the whole empire," may be thus explained: when the Sovereign venerates his aged, the people will take delight in filial piety; when he honors his seniors, the people will delight in showing due respect to their seniors; when superiors compassionate the destitute, the people will not rebel. Hence, the superior man (or the Prince) possesses the means of measuring and squaring (the hearts of others.).

That which you hate in superiors, do not practise in your conduct towards inferiors; that which you dislike in inferiors do not practise towards superiors; that which you hate in those before you, do not exhibit to those who are behind you; that which you hate in those behind you, do not manifest to those before you; that which you hate in those on your right, do not manifest to those on your left, and that which you hate in those on your left, do not manifest to those on your right. This is the doctrine of measuring *others by ourselves.* The ode says, " How delightful is it when a Prince is the father and mother of his people! " He who loves what the people love, and hates what the people hate, is the father and mother of his people.

The Poet exclaims, " Look at yonder south mountain, how lofty and terrific " such is the minister YIN ! all the people view him with terror! The ruler of a nation ought cautiously to guard against a deviation from the right path. If he do not, the loss of the empire will be the consequence. The She says: " Before the Princes of the Yin Dynasty lost the hearts of the people, they could stand before the most High." You ought to look at Yin as a mirror! It shews you that he who gains the hearts of the people, gains the throne, and that he who loses the people, loses the throne.* Hence, the good Prince first pays serious attention to virtue. Having virtue he obtains men; having men he obtains

* The appointment of Princes depends on heaven, and the mind of heaven exists in the people. ** If the Prince obtain the affections of the people the Most High †† will look upon him with affectionate regard, and he will secure the throne, but if he lose the hearts of the people, the Most high will frown upon him in wrath, and he will lose the throne.

** Thus it appears " vox populi vox Dei " is not a doctrine of yesterday, but was held by the ancient politicians of that country the government of which has been considered a master piece of despotism. A principle constantly inculcated by Mencius, and others is that whenever the reigning Prince lost the affections of the great body of the people, by acting contrary to what they deemed for the general good, he was rejected by heaven, and ought to be dethroned by some one who had by a good and benevolent discharge of the duties of his station, won the hearts of the nation. On these principles Tang is by these writers, justified in dethroning the monster Këe, and Woo Wang in driving the brutal Chow from the Imperial Seat.

†† The term 上帝 Shang Te, literally high, or Supreme Ruler, is seldom used in the four books, but from the circumstance of the same acts being in this place ascribed to 天 Tëen, Heaven, that are ascribed to 上帝 Shang Te, namely the setting up and putting down of earthly Princes, it would appear that by Shang Te and Heaven they meant one and the same supreme Deity.

territory; having territory he obtains revenue; having revenue he has sufficient supplies for all useful purposes. Virtue is the root; revenue the branches. If you lightly esteem the root, and attend principally to the branches, you excite disorder and rapine among the people. Hence it is that by accumulating wealth, you scatter the people, and by liberally diffusing wealth you unite the people. Therefore, as unreasonable language, is met by unreasonable answers, so wealth gained by unjust means, will be lost in the same way.

The Kang Kaou says," The decree of heaven * is not fixed in one man " (or one reigning family): this says, that virtue gains and vice losses it (the throne). The Tsoo book says, " The Tsoo nation does not esteem gems valuable; it esteems nothing precious but virtue." Kew Fan said," Exiles esteem nothing important except filial piety." †

The Tsin book says, " Had I a minister of unbending fidelity, although he might appear to possess no other talent, yet were his mind enlarged and generous, when he saw a man of eminent talents, he would view his talents as if they were his own The man of vast intelligence and virtue, he whould not merely praise with his lips, but really love him in his heart, and embrace him in his regards. Such a man could preserve my children, and my people. Would not such a man be of great advantage!

* " The decree of heaven—" He who so acts as to gain the hearts of the people, obtains the decree of heaven, that is the Imperial sceptre, but he who loses the hearts of the people loses the right which heaven gives to govern. Thus the divine will is known by the gaining or losing of the people's affections.

† Formerly, Wan Kung, son of the Prince of Tsin was by a wicked faction driven from his native province, while in exile his father died; upon which Muh Kung instantly sent a messenger to Wan Kong advising him to return, and seize the present and only opportunity he had of ascending the throne of his father. Wan Kung, instructed by his uncle Fan. Answered the messenger, by saying, that to him, an exile, the obtaining of a throne, was of no importance, compared with the proper discharge of the funeral and sacrificial rites of his deceased father (who had sought his life) and that were he during the time of mourning for his father, to raise an army and thus obtain the throne, it would be of no value in his estimation.

But if a minister is jealous of men of talents, opposes and keeps from notice those who possess eminent ability and virtue; not being able to bear them, such a man is incapable of protecting my children and people; nay how dangerous may he prove! It is only the virtuous man, who will banish such a character, and drive him out of the middle country (China) to live among barbarians. This shews that it is only the virtuous man, that can either love or hate a man. To see a man of eminent virtue and talents, and not to promote him; to promote him and not raise him to a high station, shews disrespect; to see a base man and not to dismiss him, to dismiss him, and not to send him to a great distance, is an error. The (Prince) who loves those who are the objects of general detestation, and hates those who are generally beloved, does an outrage to human nature. The divine judgments will certainly fall on such a man. Hence, the Prince, possessed of the great principles of government must hold them fast by fidelity and truth: by pride and extravagance he must lose them.

There is one great principle by which revenue may be produced; let those who raise it be many, and those who spend it few: let the producers have every facility * and the consumers practise economy; thus, there will be constantly a sufficiency of revenue. The virtuous man (or Prince) by his wealth, raises

* There is one great principle by which government may by just measures, always obtain sufficient supplies. Let there be no idle people, then there will be many who raise revenue; let there be no sinecures, then the number of those who consume revenue will be small. Never employ the people in government service, during seed time and harvest, then they will have an opportunity of raising sufficient supplies, regulate the expenditure by the income: this is a proper economy. * *

---

* * The present tyrannical mode of forcing the people to do government work at all seasons is a gross violation of the principles inculcated by Confucius, Mencius, and all the ancient sages. These politicians laid down certain rules, which ought to regulate the sovereign in calling for the services of his people. Seed time and harvest they viewed as peculiarly the people's own time, given them by heaven for the purpose of providing the necessaries of life for themselves and families, and that on this account the Prince had no right to call them during these seasons to do government work. Nor did they scruple to affirm, that none but tyrants would do so.

his character, but the vicious man degrades his character in accumulating wealth.

It has never happened that when the Prince loved benevolence, the people did not love justice; nor have the people, when they loved justice ever neglected the public service; and in such circumstances it has never been seen, that there was not a sufficient supply in the public treasury.

Mung Keen Tsze says, those who keep horses and chariots ought not to inquire about fowls and pigs. Those who use ice in their sacrifices, ought not to feed oxen and sheep. A family of one hundred chariots, ought not to keep a rapacious minister. A minister who is a robber is preferable to one who is rapacious. This shews that it is by equity, not by riches that a nation is profited.

When the Sovereign bends his whole mind to the accumulation of wealth, he must be led by a worthless minister, although the Prince may esteem him virtuous. The administration of such a worthless minister will at once call down upon the government divine judgements, and the vengeance of the people. When affairs arrive at this height, although a minister of talent and virtue be employed what can he do? This shews that the prosperity of a nation depends upon equity; not on riches.*

The tenth section illustrates how the good government of individual provinces, produces equity and peace through the whole empire.

In all there are ten sections; the first four contain the outline and general scope of the whole; the last six clearly elucidate its various branches; the fifth points out clearly the importance of virtue; the sixth shews where lies the source of personal perfection,

* If the Prince love his people, and do not oppress them by levying heavy taxes, in order to support extravagant wastefulness, the people will love their Prince and do their utmost to serve him. Rather than have a rapacious minister who whould extort enormous sums from the people, it is better that the Prince should employ a minister who would rob his master and treat the people with lenity. * *

---

* * Not a very palatable doctrine for kings.

CHUNG YUNG.

INTRODUCTION.

Ching Tsze says, that not to incline to either side, is called *Chung* (middle); and not to change, is called *Yung*. *Chung* is the path of universal rectitude. *Yung* is the fixed law of the universe. This treatise was handed down memoriter by the followers of Confucius. *Tsze Sze*, fearing lest through lapse of time it might be corrupted, committed it to writing, and delivered it to Mung Tsze. The Essay commences with one principle, —towards the middle it is extended to all things and at the close is again wound up in one. If you extend it, it will reach to every part of the universe; fold it up and it retires into deep obscurity. The relish is inexhaustible. It is genuine learning. Good reader! muse on it with delight, and having made it your own, practise it to the end of life:—You cannot exhaust it.

SEC. I.

What heaven has fixed, is called nature. To accord with nature, is called *Taou*. To cultivate *Taou*, is called learning. *

* Heaven by the *Yin* and *Yang* and the five elements of water, fire, wood, metal, and earth, formed all things. By 氣 *Ke* they are moulded into regular forms; then heaven confers upon them 理 *Le*. This principle, before it is conferred by heaven, is called 理 *Le*. after it is conferred, it is denominated 性 *Sing*, (nature.) To act agreeably to Sing, is called

道

Taou may not be departed from for a single moment. That which may be departed from, is not *Taou*. Hence, the man of superior virtue, is cautious of what he sees not, and fearful of what he hears not. There is nothing more open than what is concealed, and nothing more manifest than what is minute. Hence, the truly virtuous man is careful how he acts when alone. When the passions of joy, anger, grief and delight, are not manifested, they are said to be *Chung* (in the due medium). When they are manifested, and all in proper order, they are said to be *Ho*, (Harmony) *Chung*, or Middle, is the great foundation of all things, and Harmony is the all pervading principle of the universe. Extend *Chung* and *Ho*, (Middle and Harmony) to the utmost and heaven and earth will be at rest and all things will be produced, and nourished according to their nature. *

* Heaven, earth and all things are substantially the same with me. If my heart be correct, the heart of heaven and earth will be correct, and if my *Ke* (spirits) act regularly and according to nature, so will the *Ke* of heaven and earth. **

道 *Taou* (path of duty). The superior man walks in it,—the worthless man leaves it. But, although departed from, a man may by his own efforts return to it again, and thus gain the primitive perfection of his nature.†

The five elements, are water, fire, wood, metal and earth. The Yin and Yang are the male and female principles, which according to Chinese philosophy pervade all nature. Thus, heaven it seems employed these two principles and the elements of water, fire, wood, metal and earth, to form all things, i. e. Heaven is the primary cause in creation; the Yin and Yang are the instrumental cause, and the five elements are the materials employed. It is farther said that by 氣 Ke these are moulded into regular forms and finally inspired with Le 理. But a question arises, what do they mean by heaven? and what are Yin and Yang? How were the five elements originally produced? what are Ke and Le? 天 Teen (Heaven) is sometimes said to be an immaterial principle and the same as 理 Le. They sometimes speak of the Yin and Yang as if they were a kind of spiritual beings. 氣 Ke seems to be a sort of ethereal substance. Perhaps the animi mundi of the west. 理 Le seems to be some spiritual principle, which pervades all beings. But how the five elements were first produced, is wrapt in midnight darkness.

**It is worthy of remark that the word which we have here translated heart, is that by which the Chinese generally, express. the intelligent principle in man which makes him a moral agent. Now, if we take the word in that sense here, it will follow, that the heavens and the earth, and all other material substances are as much intelligent beings as man is. And this idea

In the 1st. sections Tsze Sze has delivered the sense of what he had learned, in order, First, to establish the doctrine that Taou originated in heaven, and is unchangeable, that it exists in ourselves, and may not be departed from. Secondly, to shew the importance of preserving, nourishing and narrowly examining it, and lastly to show the extent of the renovating virtue of the holy sages. For, he who wishes to learn this Taou must turn round and seek it in himself, and having obtained it, he must put away all the selfishness of external temptation and fill up the measure of virtue which he originally and naturally possesses. This shews why Yang She deemed this Book vastly important. The ten following sections are the words of Confucius, quoted by Tsze Sze for the purpose of completing the sense of this section.

SEC. II.

Confucius says, the superior man keeps the due medium, the mean man opposes it. The superior man in keeping the due medium, accords with time and circumstances. The mean man in losing the due medium, acts the part of a low man who is void of caution.

SEC. III.

Confucius says, the golden medium how great! Alas for a long time but few of the people have heen able to maintain it!

however absurd, is not only apparent in the above quotation, but agrees perfectly with their speculations about Heaven, Earth, and Man being three great Powers, or Deities capable of producing, nourishing and preserving things —See *San Tsze King*.

Kung sun Kung when he was called upon by Woo Te, one of the Emperors of the *Han Dynasty*, to give his opinion as to the best mode of governing a nation, among other things, delivered the following sentiments; viz, that when the conduct of rulers harmonizes with virtue, then the people harmonize with their rulers; hence the hearts of all will harmonize. When hearts harmonize *Ke* 氣 or temper harmonizes, tempers harmonizing, then forms harmonize, when forms harmonize, heaven and earth harmonize, hence the *Yin* and *Yang* harmonize, consequently the wind and rain come in season, all kinds of grain grow, the cattle are numerous, the hills produce abundance of grass and the rivers are never dry (or there is always a supply of water) this is the summit of harmony.—History of the Han Dynasty.

SEC. IV.

Confucius says, I know the reason why the right path is not walked in. The well informed pass over it, and the ignorant come not up to it. I likewise know why this path is not made plain and clear:—It is because men of talents and virtue pass over it, and the mean and worthless do not reach it. All man eat, but few know the true flavour of things! *

SEC. V.

Alas! that the right path is not trodden.

SEC VI.

Confucius said, great was the knowledge of Shun! Shun loved inquiry, and delighted in the investigation of truths, deemed common and simple. He concealed what was bad and proclaimed what was good. He took hold of things by the two extremes,

Taou (or the right and middle path of virtue), is what divine reason renders fit to be done in the nature of things. It is the due medium and no more. As to the intelligent and the dull, the virtuous and the vicious, the one class passes over Taou and the other does not reach it.

By the intelligent, we mean those who know or seek to know things beyond the due medium, because they do not consider this middle path worth while walking in. By the ignorant, we mean those whose knowledge does not extend to the due medium, and who know not how to maintain it. By the virtuous, we mean those who do more than the due medium requires, because they esteem it not worth practising. By the worthless, we mean those who do not in their actions attain the due medium, and who do not ask by what means they may attain the knowledge of it. These are the causes why Taou is not illustrated. *

**The idea of the sage seems to be, that those who possess some intelligence and virtue, esteem common place, self evident and practical truths unworthy of their attention, and employ their talents in abstruse and useless speculations, and in like manner despise those every day virtues, which any person may easily practise, and aspire after some extraordinary feats of what they esteem superior excellence. On the other hand, the ignorant and depraved, sink down into a state of apathy, esteeming the straight path of virtue utterly above their reach, on which account they make no effort to get at it.

and in his treatment of the people maintained the golden medium. This was what made him Shun. *

SEC. VII.

Confucius said, every one says I know; and then rushes into the net, falls into the pit, and is taken in the trap, but knows not how to make his escape. All men say we know it, and when they choose the due medium, cannot maintain it for one month.

SEC. VIII.

Confucius said, Hwuy was the man who could choose the golden medium. When once he obtained it, in any one virtue, he held it fast. With profound reverence he fixed it in his breast, and never lost it.

SEC. IX.

Confucius says, there are those who can divide the government of an empire with another,—refuse a lucrative salary, and tread on the mouth of a sword, who still are unable to reach the due medium. †

---

* Shun was one of the most celebrated monarchs of antiquity, and flourished about 2100 years B. C. He was sucessively a husbandman, a fisher, and a potter. The great Yaou, having heard of his extraordinary talents and virtue, gave him his two daughters in marriage, and resigned the throne to him. His filial piety and other virtues, both as a man and a sovereign, are extolled by the Chinese in the most exalted terms that language can supply. One of the peculiar features of his character was to obtain all the knowledge he possibly could acquire from all descriptions of people, and it is said of him that whenever he heard a good sentiment uttered, he rejoiced and immediately put it in practice. It was a sentiment constantly urged by Confucius, Mencius, and the other sages of that School, that every good Prince, must be formed on the model of *Yaou*, and *Shun*. These two are said to be sages by nature. The greater part of the other sages arrive at a state of absolute perfection, by a long course of laborious study, but these patterns of all excellence never lost the bright intelligence and immaculate purity of man's original nature, hence, found no necessity for study to chase away the obscurity contracted by most other minds, through the influence of external objects. Some statements respecting them seem to contradict this opinion.

† These three are works of knowledge, virtue and valor and the most difficult things under heaven. But they all lean to the one side or the other. They gratify human ambition; hence, one may force himself to practise them. But as to the due medium, unless a man have the knowledge of Shun, and the virtue of Hwuy; and be perfectly matured in justice, purity and benevolence without one particle of the selfishness of human lust, he cannot reach it. The three things above mentioned are difficult, yet easy.—The golden medium is easy, yet difficult.

SEC. X.

Tsze Loo asked *Confucius* what was true valour! Confucius replied, do you ask respecting the valor of the south, or of the north, or about your own valor? To teach men with a patient, mild spirit, and not to revenge unreasonable conduct, constitutes the valor of the south, and is the constant habit of the man of superior virtue. To lie under arms, and fearlessly meet death, is the valor of the north, and the element of the valiant man. *

Hence, the superior man, in according with others, does not descend to any thing low, or improper. How unbending his valor! He stands in the middle, and leans not to either side. How firm the valor of the superior man! When a nation treads in the right path he changes not what he held fast previous to his promotion to office. How undaunted his valor! When a nation departs from the right path, he changes not his course, even till death. †

SEC. XI.

Confucius said, to dive into mysteries, and practise wonders,

* The Chinese have an idea, that climate has a powerful influence on on the mind and temper of men.

According to the idea of the sage, in the above passage, the mild climate of the south, produces a mild, generous disposition, while the cold northern climate induces a bold, rash, martial spirit.

Although the Chinese seem to carry their speculations on this point too far, it cannot be denied, that climate has a very considerable effect on the mental as well the bodily constitution of man.

† If we may give full credit to the ancient records of China, on this point, no country under heaven can boast of more independent, upright and magnanimous statesmen, than China has produced at various periods of her history.

The translator has now in his possession, a document laid before Taou Kwang, the present Emperor, in 1822, by two Officers of Government, complaining of certain abuses, which manifests a spirit of fearless independence, and a firm determination to do their duty without regard to consequences. At the close, they boldly inform his majesty, that if he should subject them to the axe or the boiling caldron they are not afraid. The Emperor, however, declared, that they had shewed themselves great and faithful ministers, and imbued with the spirit of the celebrated statesmen of antiquity.

in order that future ages may record them, is what I will not do.*

The superior man follows right principles in his conduct. To proceed half way and then fail, is what I cannot do. †

The man of superior virtue accords with the golden medium, and feels no dissatisfaction at being unobserved by the world. It is only the Holy Ones that can act thus.

SEC. XII.

The principles of the superior man are extensive, yet minute. The most ignorant of common men and women, may know them (in some measure) but as to their utmost extent, although a man be a sage, he cannot fully comprehend them. The most degenerate of common men and women may in some degree practise them, but when extended to the utmost, there is something in them that even the sage cannot practise. Nay, even great heaven and earth, men find cause to murmur at them When the superior man speaks of the extensiveness of his principles, then the universe cannot contain them; when he speaks of their minuteness, no being in the universe can split them. The ode says "The Yuen bird mounts to heaven and the fishes sport in the deep"—This says, that the principles of great men illuminate the whole universe above, and below. The principles of the superior man commence with the *duties* of

* By searching into mysteries and working wonders, the sage means, deeply investigating obscure, low, or vile principles, and practising strange feats in order to impose upon the world and steal a name. Such things, the sage was incapable of. It does not appear that Confucius wished to publish false, unfounded principles, or to impose upon mankind either by abstruse speculations, or by pretensions to miraculous powers, but, that he has, through gross ignorance of that truth of all others the most important to man, deceived millions of immortal beings, must be evident to every impartial mind, which has studied his system.

† One Commentator says, that there is a class of " Keun Tszes (i. e. men of superior virtue) who pay high respect to right principles, and commence a career of virtue, but have not sufficient strength to proceed to perfection, hence stop half way. According to this comment, the passage should be rendered thus, " There are some good men who honor good principles for a time but fail of reaching perfection (or give over the practice of virtue) but this I cannot do. "

common men and women, but in their highest extent they illuminate the universe *

This twelfth section is the words of Tsze Sze employed to amplify and illustrate the doctrine of the first section, viz. that Taou is not to be departed from. In the following eight sections he intermingles with his own the words of Confucius in order to illustrate the sense

SEC. XIII.

Confucius says, *Taou* is not far removed from man. If men suppose that it lies in something remote, then what they think of, is not Taou † "The ode says cut hatchet—handles." This means

* Although a common man and woman may comprehend the most simple parts of *Taou* (or divine reason) yet even the sage, although he has arrived at the height of perfection, cannot comprehend its highest branches. Although, the degnerkte husband and wife may practise the easier parts of *Taou*, yet the sage possesses not sufficient strength to perform all its duties. There are impediments in the way which prevent him from seeing clearly the most remote bearings of this *Taou*. Not only is the sage incapable of fully comprehending, and completely practising divine reason, but even heaven and earth err. Heaven errs in producing and overshadowing things. Earth errs in perfecting and containing (or sustaining them). Hence, calamities are sent by heaven, when they ought not to be sent, and on this account, men have cause to murmur at heaven and earth for not always according with divine *Taou*. This Taou is so vast, that the universe cannot contain it and nothing is beyond it. At the same time it is so minute that nothing however small can enter or split it. It embraces all things within its mighty compass, and yet in its incipient principles, it is so minute as to be absolutely invisible, and indivisible. It fills and illuminates the universe, yet dwells with the simple husband and wife. It contains all things, and yet is contained in all things.

† *Taou* is merely to follow nature, hence all men may both know and practise it. It is constantly near men, but if any should despise what is common, and easy to practise, and consider it not worth while, but bend their attention to something lofty, remote and difficult, then that which they pursue is not Taou.

---

‡ This *Taou* of which such lofty, and incomprehensible things are uttered, is sometimes said to be eternal, uncreated, omnipresent and the original cause of all changes in the universe. In fact, the Chinese *Taou*, as it is sometimes defined, seems to come nearer to the scripture character of the supreme being, than any thing that we have met with in their writings respecting their deities. It is true, they often speak of heaven, as the supreme ruler and frequently talk as if heaven, earth, and man, or the sages, were three Powers placed above all things and possessed of the same, or nearly equal power. But, it is observable, that in the passage now under consideration, they speak of Taou not only as being above and beyond heaven, and earth, and the sages, but as being sometimes violated by these three powers, or as containing principles above their comprehension. Their speculations are, however, so mysterious, and to us, contradictory, that it is extremely difficult, if not impossible to obtain any distinct idea of their sentiments on these abstruse subjects. How happy they who possess the light of divine revelation!

of doing it is not remote. You have only to take hold of one handle, and use it to cut another. Yet if you look aslant at it, it will appear distant. Hence, the superior man employs man (i. e. what is in man) to reform man. * He reforms him and then desists. He who is faithful and benevolent, is not far from *Taou.* What he himself likes not, he does not do to others.

Confucius said, there are four things in the superior man, neither of which I am able to practise.—That which I require in a son, I cannot do in serving my father.—That which I require in a minister I cannot practisein serving my Prince.—That which I require in a younger brother, I cannot perform in serving my elder brother, and that which I require in a friend, I cannot fulfil to my friends. The superior man in the practice of every-day virtues, and in guarding his words, if in the former there be any deficiency, he dares not not exert himself to make it up; if in the latter he has said too much, he will not dare to practise them to the utmost. (Perhaps the true sense, is that if he has formerly spoken rashly, he will in future not say quite so much as might be said.) Thus, in speaking, he pays serious regard to his actions and in actions, he pays serious regard to his words. Why should not the superior man be sincere and faithful!

* The superior man when he wishes to reform, or renovate men, does not employ any thing that is distant, or remote from man, but uses what is in man to reform man; as we employ the handle of one hatchet in cutting another.* *

** This notion seems to be founded on the Chinese doctrine, that considers man even in his fallen state, still possessed of those divine principles, which by a long course of study, and self Government, will raise him to the highest elevation of intelligence and virtue. But all who are in the least acquainted with the histories of the most eminent heathen philosophers of antiquity, know, that this is but a vain dream, equally at variance with divine Revelation and fact. Did not many of the ancient sages of Greece, seek with the most unwearied perseverance for the truth? They sought it in themselves,—they sought it in others, and they sought it in every object of nature, but neither they themselves, nor those who have studied their works were satisfied in their own minds that they had found it. Now, if men whose whole life was devoted to the search of truth, could not reach it, how can we conclude with the sages of China, that it is near, nay even within every man? Does not this fact rather lead to the conclusion, that truth is not in man by nature, but that it comes from above?

SEC. XIV.

The superior man looks at his situation, and acts accordingly. He concerns not himself with what is beyond his station. If he possess riches, he acts as a rich man ought to do. If poor, he acts as a poor man ought to act. To a stranger, he acts the part of a stranger. If a sufferer, he acts as a sufferer ought to do. The superior man enters into no situation, where he is not himself. * If he hold a superior situation, he does not treat with contempt those who are below him. If he occupy an inferior station, he does not court the favor of his superiors. He corrects himself and blames not others. He feels no dissatisfaction. Above, he grumbles not with heaven—below, he feels no resentment towards man. Hence the superior man dwells at ease, calmly waiting the will of heaven. But the mean man, walks in dangerous paths, and covets what he has no right to obtain. Confucius said, the man of superior virtue, may be compared to the archer, who when he fails to hit the mark, turns round and blames himself.

SEC. XV.

The Taou of the superior man, may be compared to going a long journey, where you most commence at the nearest point,

* The situations of men in this world are very different, but there is no situation which has not its proper duties, which ought to be performed to the utmost degree of human ability, The superior man is always content with his station whatever it be, and without grasping at what does not belong to that station, he bends his whole strength to the performance of its peculiar and incumbent duties. If he fail in any part of his duty, he neither lays the blame on heaven nor man, but on himself only.**

**These excellent remarks, afford a pleasing contrast to the jumble of incomprehensible notions, which some of the preceding and following sections present. Thus, the Confucian system is compounded of a number of self-evident, sound, practical truths, intermingled with many abstruse, high sounding, false, and highly dangerous theories. The student ought carefully to examine, reject the false, and follow what is good.

and to the climbing of an eminence, where you must begin at the lowest step. *

The Ode says, "When a man lives in peace with his wife and children, it resembles the perfect harmony of musical Instruments. When peace and harmony reign among brothers, then there is pleasure and joy, nay abundant delight. Regulate your family, rejoice with your wife, children and grand-children." †

Confucius says, they who act thus, please and delight their parents.

SEC. XVI.

Confucius exclaimed, how vast the influence of the Kwei Shin! (i. e. Spirits, Genii or Gods). If you look for them you cannot see them. If you listen, you cannot hear them: they embody all things and are what things cannot be separated from, (or be without). When they cause mankind to fast, purify and dress themselves, in order to sacrifice to them, every thing appears full of them. They seem to be at once above, on the right and on the left (of the worshipers). The ode says, " The descent of the Gods, cannot be comprehended; with what reverence should we conduct ourselves! Indeed that which is

* Although, the Taou of the superior man be omnipresent yet he who would advance in this path, must do so in regular order. If you would arrive at the consummate perfection of your nature, you must begin with the five human relations. and practise the common, every-day virtues. Just as when you wish to go to a great distance, you must start from the nearest point. If you do not, then you have no possible means of arriving at the most distant. So it is in this case: if the common and easy virtues are neglected, there is no possibility of attaining the consummate perfection of our nature. * *

† Confucius quotes these words of the ode, to illustrate the meaning of commencing a long journey at the nearest point, and of ascending an eminence from the lowest step.

* * The doctrine of the above passage is good, as far it goes, but it takes for granted, that man by his own exertion, commences and perfects the work of moral renovation in himself. Does not the doctrine of divine revelation which ascribes this mighty transformation to the omnipotent grace of God, accord better with the numerous facts supplied by the history of man in all ages, and in all countries of the world?

most minute is Clearly displayed. They cannot be concealed?"*

* Ching Tsze says, that the Kwei Shin are the kung yung (literally meritorious work) of heaven and earth and the traces of creating and renovating, or rather of production and destruction. Choo Foo Tsze says, for my part I think if we speak of the two i. e. the Yin and Yang principles separately, then the Kwei is the soul (or ethereal part) of the Yin; and the Shin is the soul of the Yang. But if we speak of these two principles unitedly as one; then, if they are extended, they are Shin; if they are reverted, they are Kwei. These gods are immaterial, and without voice. That which occasions the beginning, and end of things, is nothing but the uniting and separating of the Yin and Yang. Thus they constitute the substratum of things, and what things cannot exist without.

All the operations of the universe are produced by the ethereal parts of the Yin and Yang, and the place where these ethereal parts reside is called kwei Shin (i. e. gods.)

The Kwei Shin, are merely the 氣 ke i. e. subtile, ethereal part of the Yin and Yang. They are called Kwei Shin, merely on account of their pure, subtile, excellent, flowing, and moving qualities.

Choo Foo Tsze says, that there is not one thing in the universe without Kwei and Shin: for the coming of the vital principle (i. e. production and growth of things) belong to the Yang, and death or the destruction of things belong to the Yin principle. Before noon is Shin, after noon is Kwei, From the first three days of the moon to the 16th. is Shin;—from that to the close is Kwei. The springing and growth of trees is Shin. The falling of the leaves, the decay and down fall of trees is Kwei. Man from his childhood to his manhood, is Shin;—from the time he begins to decay till old age is he Kwei. All moving, operating properties belong to Yang (i. e. Shin,) all inert properties belong to Yin, (i. e. Kwei) The ability of obtaining knowledge, belongs to Shin; and that of recollecting things to Kwei. Things did not first exist and then, Kwei Shin, but Kwei Shin first existed and then things. When once things existed, then they could not be without Kwei Shin. So that Kwei and Shin are like the bones of things. The union of the Yin and Yang, is the beginning of things, the separating of Yin and Yang, is the close, or end of things. They separate and again unite, hence we have the end of things and again the commencement. This is production after production, going on by a self-moving power without end. **

** From the above extracts, it will be seen, that the Chinese doctrine respecting these spiritual, invisible beings, is not much more comprehensible than their notions about Taou. Indeed I hav sometimes been inclined to think, that their Taou and their Kwei Shin, are but different names for the same thing. If they mean any thing by what they say on this subject, it seems to be, that the Kwei Shin is some extremely fine, subtile spirit, employed by heaven and earth the great creators, as the substratum of all things, and the secondary cause of all the phenmomena of nature: perhaps gravitation, or the electric fluid. It will be observed that according to the above quotations, they do not include heaven and earth among what they call all things, for they expressly state, that, the Kwei and Shin existed before all material things, and at the same time say, that Kwei and Shin are the souls of the Yin and Yang principles, by the union and disunion of which heaven and earth create and distroy all things, Indeed I have never met with any thing in any of their writings, which intimates, that they have any notion of heaven and earth ever having been created, while they themselves are uniformly represented as the creators of all things.

Plato talked of the supreme being, having from that substance which is invisible, and always the same, and from that which is corporeal and divisible, compounded a third kind of substance, participating of the nature of both. This substance which is not eternal, but produced, and which derives the superior part of its nature from God and the inferior from matter, Plato supposed to be the animating principle of the universe pervading and adorning all things. In the Platonic system this third principle in nature, is inferior to the deity, being derived from, that divine nature which according to that school, is the seat of the ideal world. Does not this all animating principle of Plato in some respects strongly resemble the Kwei Shin of the Chinese sages? They are both a kind of intermediate principle between the supreme being end the material creation which pervades and animates all nature, and both seem essential to material existences, while neither is properly material. It is true, that in some respects, these imaginary principles seem to differ, but thus is no more than is to be expected of every erroneous system. Truth is one and harmonizes in all its branches, but error

SEC. XVII.

How great, said Confucius, was the filial piety of Shun! * In virtue a sage, in honor, the son of heaven, as to riches, possessed of all within the four seas. He sacrificed to his ancestors in the ancestorial Temple and his posterity maintained the throne. Such eminent virtue could not but obtain the throne, riches, and longevity. Therefore, heaven in producing and nourishing things, regards them according to their true nature; hence, what is upright, it nourishes, what is bent and inclined to fall, it overthrows. The joy giving man of great worth, his virtue how brilliant! He acts as he ought, both to the common people, and to official men—receives his revenue from heaven, and by it is protected, and highly esteemed. Hence, great virtue must obtain the decree (Empire.)

* Shun had a vicious father, and brother, by whom he was treated with great cruelty, and who even attempted his life, but such was his unparalleled filial piety, and brotherly affection, that after a long and unwearied course of obedience, and kind services he at last gained their affections. It is said of him, that he considered the throne to which his virtues and talents had raised him, nothing in comparison to the gaining of his fathers affection, and confidence; hence, suceeding ages have extolled his unrivalled filial piety.

---

cannot be made accord to with itself. It is however worthy of notice, that two of the most celebrated sages of antiquity, who lived nearly at the same period, but far distant from each other, when groping after the truth, should have formed theories of the universe so nearly resembling each other.

It seems rather strange, that these gods (or genii) which from their own account appear to be nothing else but a certain modification of the Yin and Yang, neither of which is said to possess intelligence, should be the objects of such profound reverence, as the sages declare them to be. By the Shin or Gods they seem, sometimes to denote the spirits of the dead. Thus, they say that the God of the furnace which is worshipped to the present day, is the ancient King Yen, who first invented the mode of obtaining fire from wood.

Much of what they say about the Yin and Yang, bears a strong resemblance to the doctrine of two principles in nature held by many of the western philosophers of ancient times, and by the Hindoos, of the present day. The Manicheans a sect of ancient heretics followers of Manicheaus by birth a Persian, and educated among the Maji, held that there were two opposite principles in the universe, one good and the other evil! The first a most fine and subtile matter, which they called Light, did nothing but good; and the second, a gross and corrupt substance, which they called darkness, did nothing but evil. Now, the Yang principle of the Chinese so far answers to the Light of Mancheaus, that it is said to be clear and splendid, and the cause of the production and nourishing of all things; while the Yin, like his darkness, is said to be dark and sombre, and the cause of the decay, and destruction of all things. Moreover the Shin of the Chinese, which they consider they soul of the Yang principle, is the term by which they denominate good spirits or Angels; while the Kwei, the soul of the Yin principle is the designation which they give to bad spirits, or Demons.

Sec. XVIII

Confucius said, the man who was free from grief, was Wăn Wang. His father Wang Ke—his son Woo Wang. His father commenced the career of virtue, and his son continued it. Woo Wang continued the virtuous course of Tao, Wang Wang Ke and Wăn Wang. He only once buckled on his armour, and he gained the Empire. His personal conduct was such, that he never lost his illustrious name in the Empire. As to honor, he was Emperor, and in riches, he possessed all within the four seas. He sacrificed to his ancestors in the ancestorial Temple, and his posterity preserved the empire (or rather he preserved the empire to his posterity).

Woo Wang, was in the decline of life when he received the appointment of heaven. (i. e. the Empire) Chow Kung perfected the meritorious deeds (or wishes) of Woo Wang. Paid royal honors to Tae Wang, and Wang Ke, and sacrificed to their ancestors, according to the rites due to the Emperor. He extended these sacrifical rites to the Princes, great officers of state, literati and common people. If the father held a high office, and the son was one of the literati, then he was buried according to the rites of great officers, and the subsequent sacrifices were those of the literati. If the father was one of the literati, and the son a great officer, then his funeral rites were such as belong to the literati, and his sacrificial rites such as belonged to a great officer. *

* Wan Wang was a petty prince who lived near the close of the Dynasty Shang, about 1112 years before Christ. His virtue and abilites as a ruler, were such, that two thirds of the Empire felt desirous of having him put upon the Imperial throne. His father was Wang Ke a man of superior virtue, and the famous Woo Wang, who near the end of his life rebelled, against the Tyrant Chow, was one of his sons. Woo Wang having expelled Chow, the last Emperor of the Shang Dynasty, was by universal consent raised to the Emperial throne, and they became the founder of the Dynasty Chow. Thus he carred on, or rather completed, the virtuous intentions of his illustrious ancestors, and his family held the throne upwards of eight hundred years. Wan Wang the father, aud Woo Wang the son, are two of the most celebrated characters in Chinese history. Their virtue is said to have produced such lasting effects, upon the minds of their subjects, that it required a long sucession of bad Princes, to completely vitiate the nation. Hence notwithstanding the many vicious Princes that disgraced that Dynasty, it lasted to a period of exraordinary length. This seems to explain what is meant by WooWang preserving his posterity.

SEC. XIX.

Confucius exclaimed, the filial piety of Woo Wang, and Chow Kung is universally talked of. Now, filial piety consists in rightly accomplishibg the intentions of men, and in properly completing men's actions. In the spring and autumn they put in order the ancestorial Temples, arranged in proper order the vessels of sacrifice, put the clothes of their ancestors on a person to represent them, and offered the sacifices of the season. By the rites in the Temple of ancestors, are separated the different generations, according to their regular succession. By the order of rank are distinguished the nobles from the commons: By the order of office, are distinguished those possessed of virtue and talents. In the general feast, the inferior classes serve the superior; hence, this feast extends to the lower ranks, and here the aged according to their order, are distinguished by the colour of the hair. They filled the situation, practised the ceremonies, and used the music of their ancestors. They respected what they honored and loved those whom they made their associates. They served the dead as they did when they were alive, and those who are buried as when they were with them. They served the great supreme by the sacrifices offered to heaven and earth, and offered the sacrifices of the ancestorial hall to their ancestors. They clearly understood the manner of sacrificing to heaven and earth, and the nature of the Te (a great sacifice offered every five years)Hence, to them the Government of a kingdom was as plain as the plam of the hand. *

SEC. XX.

Gae Kung asked about the mode of governing a nation. Confucius replied, the laws of Wăn Wang were written on boards

* The Emperor had seven ancestorial halls. The tributary Princes five. Great officres of state, three. The superior rank of literati two, and the inferior class one. The sacrifical vessels were valuable vessels, which were kept by ancestors "Robes," mean garments left by ancestors, which at certain sacrifices were put on a person to represent some one of the dead and to whom for the time, the same worship was offered as was due to the rank of the deceased. In high antiquity these robes were put on a living person,' but now they are put on the effigy of the deceased.

and slips of bamboo. While men of his mind reigned, these laws flourished, but when the men were gone, the laws ceased to operate. * The true principles of man naturally produce good government, just as the earth nuturally produces trees. Good government is like the Poo Loo tree.(i. e. easy and speedy in its growth). Good government depends on obtaining proper men. The highest exercise of benevolence is tender affection for relatives. Justice is what is right in the nature of things. Its highest exercise is to honor men of virtue and talents. To love relatives, according to the degree of their nearness, or remoteness, and to honor the virtuous according to the degree of their worth, are what propriety leads to. Hence the good Prince ought most undoubtedly to cultivate personal virtue. Wishing to cultivate personal virtue, he must serve his parents. Wishing to serve his parents, he must not neglect to know men. Wishing to know men, he must know heaven. The path of duty for all men embraces five branches. The means of walking in it are three. The respective duties of Prince and minister, father and son, husband and wife, elder and younger brother, and the treatment of friends. These five constitute the general rule of life for all men. Knowledge, benevolence and magnanimity are the three cardinal virtues all under heaven. The means of practising these is one. *

Some are born with the knowledge of these. Some by study attain the knowledge of them, and others by severe effort, obtain this knowledge; but when once the knowledge is obtained, it is one. Some practise them with perfect ease, some with considerable effort, and others with great exertion, but when

* As long as men of the stamp of Woo Wang lived and were employed in the administration of government, the laws of this famaous monarch prospered, but when these men were no more to be found, of what value was the dead letter of the law ? Good government depends upon men, not on dead laws.

It is one of the best maxims of the Chinese, and one which is often in their mouths, that the virtue and good government of a nation, depend upon the personal worth of the Prince. But they sometimes carry this doctrine too far. For the history of human nature will not bear them out, when they maintain as they often do that if the Prince shew an example of genuine virtue, virtue must flourish in every family in the Empire.—See the Ta Heo &c.

once they reach the practice of them in perfection, their merit is the same. * Confucius says he who loves study, is near knowledge. He who acts vigorously, is near benevolence. He who knows how to feel ashamed, is near magnanimity (or bravery). He who knows these three, knows by what means to cultivate personal virtue. He who knows how to cultivate personal virtue, knows how to rule men. He who knows how to rule men, knows how to govern the whole Empire. All who hold the reins of Government have nine standard rules, by which to act. These require them to cultivate personal virtue, honor the virtuous, love their relatives, respect great officers, consider the whole of their ministers as members of their own body, view the people as their children, encourage all the trades, treat foreigners (those who come from a distance) with kindness, and to manifest a tender care for tributary Princes.

If the Prince cultivate personal virtue, then good principles will be established. If he honor men of virtue and talent, he will banish scepticism:—If he treat his relatives with affection, uncles and brothers will not grumble with him:—If he respect his great officers, then there will be no interruption to the pro-

* Men's natures are originally and equally virtuous, but their natural abilities are not equal. The minds of some never lose their orignal purity, such was the case with Yaou and Shun, who were born sages. In others the original purity and perfect intelligence of the mind are in some measure sullied and obscured by the influence of external objects; hence, study is necessary in order to chase away the moral pollution and mental gloom and bring the mind back to its pristine glory. This was the case with Woo Wang and Tang. There are others again, whose minds are polluted to such a degree, that it requires a long vigilant course of painful study, to effect a complete renovation. But, as people who travel on different roads all arrive at the same city, so by whatever means men obtain perfect knowledge and complete holiness, they are all alike when they do obtain perfection; which all may do by personal exertion.**

According to the above dogmas, there are men who find themselves by nature possessed of perfect intelligence, and who have no more need for study, than has the Omniscient God. Such men, they tell us were the famous Chieftains Yaou and Shun, who lived in high antiquity; but with the exception of Jesus, who was God as well as man, in what other country under heaven, have such men ever been heard of? And since they have not made their appearance in any other nation, what adequate reasons can be assigned for their appearance in China? But, here, however, as in many other cases, the infallible sages of the celestial Empire, flatly contradict themselves, for Mung Tsze, when it suited his objects to praise Shun, for his humble, docile disposition, and for his love of learning, declares, that he rejoiced when any one gave him new information on subjects with which he was previously unacquainted.

per discharge of business:—If he consider all his ministers as members of his own body, the gratitude of the learned will be great:—If he treat th people as his children, they will comply with his admonitions.—If he encourage the trades, his resources will be sufficient:—If he treat foreigners well, then people of all quarters will come over to him:—If he cherish tributary Princes, all under heaven will reverence him.

To prepare the mind by fasting, wear the proper robes, and do nothing contrary to propriety, are the means by which to adorn the person. To banish flattery, send lust to a distance, despise riches and honor virtue, are the means by which to stimulate men of abilities and worth. To respect their office, give them good salaries, love what they love, and hate what they hate, is the way to stimulate relatives. To have abundance of men for the proper discharge of business, is the way to lead on the great officers of state. To treat them with fidelity and and confidence, and grant them large emoluments, is the way to encourage inferior officers. To call them out at proper seasons, and exact little tribute, is the best way to lead on the people. To examine daily and try monthly, and reward according to their merit, is the means by which to stimulate all descriptions of workmen. To accompany those who are departing, and meet those who are coming, to praise the virtuous and pity the weak are the means by which to shew kindness to strangers. To connect again the broken line of succession, raise up fallen states, regulate those which are in a state of disorder, save those which are in danger, call them to audience at the proper seasons, bestow liberally and receive sparingly, is the way to cherish tributary Princes.

There are nine standard rules, which ought to be attended to by all who govern an Empire, and the means of practising them is one (sincerity or truth). Let every affair be previously studied, and determined, then it will be established; if not, then it will fail. Let your words be previously fixed, then you will not stumble. Let your affairs be before determined, and they will not be fettered. Let your actions be previously fixed, and they will not be feeble. Let your path of virtue be fixed and it will be endless.

If those in inferior stations do not obtain the good opinion of their superiors, they will not be able to manage the people. There is a proper method of securing the good opinion of superiors: If one is not confided in by his friends, he cannot have the good opinion of his superiors. To obtain the confidence of friends, there is a proper method: If one be not obedient to parents he will not be confided in by his friends. There is a proper way of shewing obedience to parents: If on self-examination one find that he is insincere, then he is not truly obedient to his parents. There is a way of attaining personal sincerity: If one does not clearly understand the doctrines of virtue, he cannot have attained to sincerity. *

Sincerity is the Taou or way of heaven. To aim at it, is the way (or duty) of man. The sincere (or perfect) hit the due medium without effort, obtain it without thought, and practise it spontaneously. Such are sages. Those who aim at sincerity, are such as select what is good and steadfastly adhere to it. Such extensively learn it (i. e. sincerity), judge and inquire about it, sincerely reflect upon it, clearly discriminate and stead fastly practise it. If there are things which he (the superior man) has not studied, when he studies them, and does not at first

* Not to clearly understand the doctrines of virtue, shews want of ability to examine the foundation of the human heart, and of the decrees (or will) of heaven, so as to perceive clearly where sincerity rests. * *

---

* * 誠 " Sincerity " Is a term much used in the remaining part of this work. I am quite sensible that our word sincerity does not by any means express fully the sense of the original word, and yet I cannot find any term which seems to come so near it. The Commentators define the word to be reality without any thing untrue, or disorderly, and some may be apt, from the manner in which it is used in this work, to deem our word perfection a better rendering than the word sincerity. But still, there are objections to the word perfection, as a correct rendering of the original word, such as the sign of the superlative degree being attached to it. &c.

comprehend them, he still exerts himself. When he begins to think of what he had not thought of before, although he may not at first understand it still he continues to consider it There are things between which he has not previously discriminated, if in attempting to do so he do not at first succeed' he desists not from his efforts. As to those things which he has not before practised, if he do not at first succeed in practising them faithfully, he ceases not until this is accomplished. To what others have attained by one effort, he will employ an hundred. If others have succeded by ten efforts, he will use a thousand. He who acts thus, although naturally dull, will become intelligent; although naturally weak and timid, will become strong and valiant. *

Sec. XXI.

From inherent sincerity, to have perfect intelligence, is to be a Sage by nature, to attain sincerity by means of intelligence is to be such by study. Where there is sincerity, there must be intelligence; where intelligence is, it must lead to sincerity.

Sec. XXII.

On the right, is the twenty first section, in which Tsze Szo connects the sense of the above section in order to establish the doctrine of Confucius respecting the Taou (or path) of heaven

* To be all equally virtuous and void of moral evil is human nature in its original state, in which every man receives it from heaven. In this, all men are equal. Inequality as to dullness and intelligence, strength and weakness, is called inequality of talent. In this men differ. To aim at sincerity, is the means by which to return to what all men at first equally possessed. (i. e. perfect moral rectitude) and to change talents originally not good, into good talents, requires an hundred fold effort. Without this it cannot be effected,—with this it may, and the man of inferior talents, may by his own strenuous efforts, raise his natural abilities to an equality with the highest degree of native talent. **

** It is one of the most favorite doctrines of this haughty people, that all men are by nature equally virtuous; and that all are perfectly so. But nothing can be more opposite, to revelation and universal experience. These infallible guides teach us, that men are all naturally vicious, and that if in practice they differ, the cause of such difference is not to be found in themselves, but in something external, principally to the renovating and restraining grace of God That men's natural abilities are very unequal, is a fact subtanstiated by the universal experience of more than five thousand Years, but that they may, by human exertion, be brought to any thing like an equality, the same extent of experience proves to be impracticable Nor does it appear to be the will of the great Creator that they should ever be equal.

and of man. The twelve following sections contain the words of Tsze Sze in which he views the subject in various lights, in order to illustrate fully the sense of this section. It is only the man possessed of the highest sincerity, * that can perfect his own nature—he who can perfect his own nature, can perfect the nature of other men.—he who can perfect the nature of other men, can perfect the nature of things;—he who can perfect the nature of things, can assist heaven and earth in producing and nourishing things. When this is the case, then he is united with heaven and earth so as to from a trinity.

Sec. XXIII.

The next order of men (i. e. the next to the Sages above mentioned), bend their attention to the straightening of their deflections from the path of rectitude. Those who can do so have sincerity. Having sincerity, it gradually accumulates and makes its appearance: after this it begins to shine, and at last becomes brilliant. Having become brilliant, it then moves others to virtue;—this being the case, others begin to yield to its influence, so that at last it effects in them a complete renovation. It is only those of the highest sincerity under heaven, that can thus renovate.

* The highest sincerity, means the reality of the virtue of the sages. There is nothing under heaven that can increase it; hence, it is perfectly free from selfishness. In this case the will or decree of heaven exists in oneself. Examine it, try it. Its whole body, its minute parts finer and purer qualities as well as its grosser, are all there:—not a single hairs-breadth is deficient. The nature of men and things is also our nature, but the Hing Ke (literally form and animation) given them differ from ours. To perfect these, means to know them perfectly, and to use them exactly as they ought to be used. To be united with heaven and earth, means to stand equal with heaven and earth so as to form a triad. These are the actions of the man who is by nature perfect, and who needs not to acquire perfection by study. **

** So it appears the Chinese, as well as most other nations have their trinity. But certainly it is sufficently ridiculous, to form a trinity of three beings so different in their nature and capacities, as heaven, earth and man are. If by heaven and earth, they mean those material created bodies, which generally receive that appellation, then man has no reason to be fond of being put on an equality with them. But, if, as we have often suspected, they mean, that heaven, and earth are the self-existent Creators of the universe, man included, then to put the best of men on an equality with them is the confounding of all order, and is downright blasphemy.

SEC. XXIV.

The Taou (or reason) of the supremely sincere, enables them to fore-know things. If a nation is about to flourish, there will be happy omens, and when about to come to ruin there will be unhappy omens. These will appear in Sze (an herb by which they divine) and in the tortoise and in the airs and motions of the four members. When either happiness, or misery is about to come, the sages will fore-know both the good and the evil, so that the supremely sincere are equal to the gods. *

SEC. XXV.

Sincerity is to perfect one's-self. Taou or reason is what men ought to practise. Sincerity is the origin and consummation of things. Without sincerity there would be nothing: hence, the superior man considers sincerity of much importance. Sincerity does not merely perfect one's-self, but is the means of perfecting others. It is benevolence by which one's-self is perfected, and knowledge by which one perfects others. This is the virtue of nature; the way of uniting the internal and external. Hence, every thing is done according to its season and order. †

* It is only they who carry sincerity to the highest point, and in whom there remains not a single hairs-breadth of hypocrisy, that can fore-see the hidden springs of things. The gods (Shin Kwei) because they embody all things, and never leave any thing, can move the secret springs of things, and the sages having a perfect acquaintance with all things, can fore-see by their hidden motions when good or evil is about to come. * *

† All things under heaven are produced by a true principle, hence, this principle must first exist, and then we have things. When this principle ceases to exist, things of course come to, an end. Hence, if in the mind there be one thing not genuine or sincere, then, although the man act it is still as if he did not. Hence, the superior man deems sincerity valuable: for man's heart may be without any insincerity, and may perfect itself: This depends on ourselves; there is no good work which we may not perform.—Moreover, although sincerity is that by which we perfect ourselves, yet it does not rest here but spontaneously flows out to others.

---

* * Thus in one paragraph we are told, that the sages are both Prophets, Sorcerers, and gods, or equal to the gods ! ! !

SEC. XXVI.

Hence the utmost sincerity is interminable. Not stopping, it will endure long;—enduring long, it will become manifest;—becoming manifest, it will extend far;—extending far, it will become thick and substantial;—becoming substantial, it will rise high and shine forth. Its thickness is that by which it contains things.—Its height and brightness are what overspread things:—its extent and duration, are that by which it perfects things. By its thickness and substantiality it equals earth; and by its height and splendour it equals heaven. Its extent and duration are without limit. He who possesses this *sincerity*, without shewing himself, he will shine forth, without moving he will renovate others; without acting, he will perfect them. * The law of heaven and earth may be expressed in one word,(i. e. sincerity). They do not create things double: hence, their mode of producing things is incomprehensible.

The way of heaven and earth is substantial, thick, high, splendid, extensive, and permanent. Heaven, although it appear but a small bright spot, is infinite in extent. The sun, moon, stars, and constellations, are suspended in it, and it overshadows all things. The earth, although it appear but a small heap of dust, yet by its extent and thickness, it sustains the mountains Hwa Yŏh, and feels not their weight. It contains the rivers and suffers them not to flow away. It sustains all things. The mountains, although they appear like the size of a stone, yet they are so extensive, that trees and grass grow

* Ching Tsze says, that what is called the virtue of the highest sincerity, shines forth to the four winds of heaven, and is preserved in the centre. When it has continued long, then its evidences come forth, and it increases in extent without end. When it extends to a great distance, then it accumulates, becomes broad, deep and thick;—being substantial and thick, it issues forth, rises high, and shines forth in full splendour.

on them,—birds and beasts dwell on them, and pearls are concealed in them. The waters, although they appear like a spoonful, yet they are unfathomable, and the Yuen To, the Keaou Lung, and the Yu Pēĕ dwell in them, and vast treasures are produced by them. The ode says "How excellent are the ways of heaven!" This speaks of the reason why heaven acts like heaven. It likewise says, how brilliant are the purity and virtue of Wăn Wang! This also speaks of the reason why Wăn Wang was Wăn Wang. His purity was also endless. *

Sec. XXVII.

How great is the way of the sage!—It is vast and flowing as the ocean. It issues forth and nourishes all things! It is exalted even to heaven! How abundant! It contains three hundred outlines of ceremonies, and three thousand minute particulars thereof. It waits for its men, and then is walked in (or practised) Hence it is said, that without a man of the most exalted virtue, the supremely excellent doctrines cannot be concentrated. Therefore, the superior man honors virtue and studies in order to carry it to the utmost extent, and to exhaust its sub-

* Since, in the above sections the meritorious operations of the highest sincerity, had been declared equal to heaven and earth. (two of their supreme deities), ** we are now called to take a view of heaven and earth, in order that we may form some idea of consummate sincerity: for although heaven and earth are great, yet their governing principle may be expressed in one word; that is, the true, undeviating, single, pure and permenant principle by which all the movements of the Yin and Yang are regulated. †† Again, as the principles by which heaven and earth act, are perfectly void of the least selfishness, and are unceasing in their operations, so Wan Wang being by his supreme virtue as it were absorbed into heaven and earth, his virtue was likewise without the least mixture of human passions, and interminable in its renovating power.

** Had the above paragraph carried the matter no farther, than to maintain, that it is the duty of men to imitate the holiness of the Supreme Being; and that genuine holiness is the same in nature, though not in degree, in good men as it is in God, then both reason and revelation would corroborate the sentiment. But to place created man on a perfect level with the supreme creator, which appears to us to be the intention of this, and several other passages of this extraordinary treatise, is a sentiment which none but those who are grossly ignorant both of God and man can possibly entertain.

†† Are there not faint traces of the divine character to be observed in these expressions? There is at least a reference to some principle superior to, and constantly regulating the operations of the great Yin and Yang.

tile and minute parts. He rises to the highest elevation and splendor, yet walks in the due medium. He makes himself perfectly acquainted with the old, and at the same time studies the new, and pays great respect to the decencies and proprieties of life. Hence, if placed in a high situation, he is not haughty. If he occupy an inferior station, he does not oppose authority. When a country is under, the Government of reason, his words are sufficient to raise him to an official situation (perhaps to the throne). When a country is not governed by reason, his silence protects him. The Ode says, "Thus intelligence and prudence protect his person." This passage agrees with what is here said.*

Sec. XXVIII.

Confucius says. Upon the man who is ignorant, and yet pushes himself into office, who holding a low situation, assumes authority, who, although living in the present age, returns to the ways of the ancients, the divine judgments will surely come It is only the Emperor who has a right to fix the ceremonies, regulate the laws, and adjust the language. But, although, one sit on the throne, if he be without virtue, he dares not (or ought not) to institute ceremonies, and music; and although he possess the requisite virtue, yet if he sit not on the throne, he has no right to institute ceremonies.†

---

* One Commentator says, that what is said in this Section is not intended to extol the sage, but his Taou. As we have already observed, it seems impossible to comprehend what this Taou is. Here, as in many other parts of their writings, it is said to be omnipresent and to fill and influence all things. Now the very same is repeatedly said of the virtue of superior men and of the sage.

† Did the power, which according to this section the Emperor possesses, extend merely to the civil laws of the Empire, and to the ceremonies of polite intercourse among men, we se- little reason to object to it, although we are of opinion, that all human laws should be founded on those which are stamped with divine authority: But, when we take into consideration, that those cerimonies over which the Emperor possesses a sovereign power, embrace all the forms of homage and worship due to the gods, as well as the forms of politeness due to our fellow creatures, we feel ourselves warranted, both by reason and revelation, to declare, that no created being, whether man or Angel, has the smallest degree of right to prescribe to his fellow creatures, the mode in which they ought to pay their homage and adoration to their Almighty Creator, Preserver, and Benefactor.

Confucius said, I can speak about the rites of the Hea Dynasty, but the Kingdom Ke has not left sufficient records of them. I have studied the rites of the Yin Dynasty, but it is only the Kingdom of Sung, that has preserved them. I have also studied the ceremonies of the Chow Dynasty: they are practised at present; I follow Chow.

Sec. XXIX.

There are three important things for those who govern the Empire, and where they exist the errors of men will be few. Although, the ancient kings understood these well, yet there now exists no sufficient documents to prove them. Without proof, there is no credit, not being credited the people do not follow them. The present sages, although, they understand these things, yet they hold not high situations.—Not holding high situations, they are not believed;—Not believed, the people will not follow them. The virtuous Prince possesses the root of high principles in himself, and manifests them to the people. He examines the laws of the three kings, and errs not. He stands as one with heaven and earth, and rebels not. He confronts the gods without any misgiving. He waits a hundred ages till a sage come, and does not doubt. He who confronts the gods, without any misgiving, knows heaven; He who waits a hundred ages till a sage comes, without doubting, knows men. Hence, the virtuous Prince, moves and for ages shews the Empire the way. He acts and for

* These three important things are the regulating of the ceremonies,—fixing the laws, and adjusting the language. It is only the Emperor (the Son of heaven) who possesses authority to regulate these important things. Where they are properly regulated the Government of kingdoms will not differ, the customs of families will be the same, and the errors of men will be few. But, although the ancient kings of the Hea and Shang Dynasty, such as Tang and Woo Wang, understood these things, yet there are no authentic documents left, sufficient to prove to the people what their laws and ceremonies were and, although sages of the present day, such as Confucius understand these important matters well, yet as they do not occupy high official situations they are not credited by the people. Hence it is only the sage, forming as he does one of a triad with heaven and earth, and the all renovating power of whose virtue extends to every part of the universe, who ought to sit on the throne, because it is only such a man who unites in himself that virtue and authority, which are necessary in order to effect the complete renovation of men.

ages gives laws to the Empire. He speaks and for ages gives a model to the Empire. Those who are at a distance look to him with respect; those who are near are never wearied with him. The ode says, "There, not hated, here, not rejected." Perhaps the fame of such a one will continue night and day forever! the virtuous must be such a man (consequently will soon obtain fame in the Empire.)

SEC. XXX.

Confucius took his principles from Yaou and Shun and elegantly exhibited Wăn Wang. Above, he imitated the seasons of heaven; below, the laws of water and earth. He may be compared to heaven and earth, in their supporting, containing and overshadowing all things;—to the regular revolutions of the seasons, and to the successive shining of the sun and moon. All things are nourished together, without any mutual injury. The laws of nature move together without any mutual opposition. The feeble energies of nature resemble the flowing of of rivers, and the more powerful, the abundant production and changes of things. These are the reasons why heaven and earth are great. *

* As the conclusion of this section shows why heaven and earth are great, it is likewise here stated that Confucius was the same as heaven and earth. For he united in his own person, all the virtue of heaven and earth, as well as the whole body of the sages. The utmost fulness of divine virtue was manifested in Yaou and Shun. Confucius, therefore viewed them as his ancestors and received and handed down their doctrines. There were no laws, more complete than those of Wan and Woo Wang, hence, Confucius exhibited them in their beauty. The revolution of the seasons are fixed and move on with self-existent power, hence the sage made them his pattern. There exists nothing whatever which is not supported, overshadowed, and nourished by heaven and earth, in the same manner, the astonishing, all-moving virtue of the sage, pervaded the universe. Thus it is evident that, Confucius united in his own mind all the virtue of the holy gods, and in his conduct, all the laws of the ancient, and sacred kings. * *

---

* * From such statements as this, one is almost led to conclude that the admirers of Confucius, consider his virtue more extensive than that of the gods? that being the case, it is not to be wondered at, that the Chinese to this day pay divine honors to this frail, fallible, sinful mortal. Had they but one such view of the divine glory and majesty, as the Prophet Isaiah was favored with, * * they would shudder at the idea of offering religious homage to the most eminently virtuous among mortals who, when compared with the Most High, are but feeble and polluted worms of the dust.

* * Isaiah Chap. VI.

SEC. XXXI.

It is only the most holy man under heaven who is possessed of that clear discrimination, and profound intelligence, which qualify him for filling a high situation,—who possesses that enlarged liberality, and mild benignity, which fit him for bearing with others.—who manifests that firmness and magnanimity, that enable him to hold fast good principles—who is actuated by that benevolence, justice, propriety and knowlege, which command reverence—and who is so deeply versed in polite learning and good principles, as to qualify him rightly to discriminate. Vast and extensive are the effects of his virtue! it is like the deep and living stream, which flows unceasingly.—It is substantial and extensive as heaven, and profound as the great abyss! When manifested, not one of the people but reverences it. His words not one of the people disbelieve. In his actions, not one of the people but take delight. Hence, his fame fills and passes over the boundaries of China and reaches to the barbarians. Wherever ships sail, or chariots run, wherever human strength extends, wherever the heavens overshadow and the earth sustains, wherever the sun and moon shine, or frosts and dews fall, among all who have blood and breath, there is not one which does not honor and love him. Hence it is said that he equals heaven. *

---

* This Section speaks of the intelligence of which some are possessed when born. It does not appear however but what they consider such perfect omniscience attainable by those who have not the good fortune to be born with it. Their most extravagant assertions in reference to the effects of such virtue and knowledge. as the most eminent sages are said to have possessed, are not only destitute of the least shadow of evidence, but are made in direct contradiction to the most satisfactory evidence. They are without evidence; for, according to their own historical records, the virtue of Confucius (by far their greatest sage) was so far from filling the middle country (China) and passing over the boundaries of the celestial Empire, to the barbarians, so as to excite their admiration and renovate their morals, that it had extremely little effect on the far greater part of those by whom he was immediately surrounded. They are contradicted by the most satisfactory evidence; for, when he who was as superior to the most eminent sages of antiquity, as the heavens are higher than the earth, tabernacled among men, he was so far from being generally admired and imitated, that he was the object of derision and hatred to a rebellious and obstinate race.

Sec. XXXII.

It is only he who possesses the highest sincerity under heaven, who is capable of discriminating and fixing what are the proper duties belonging to each of the human relations, who can establish the great foundation of the Empire, and who comprehends the manner in which heaven and earth produce and nourish. Who should such a man rely upon! How ardent his benevolence! How profound his virtue! How vast his heaven! Unless a man possess the knowledge of the bright discerning sage, he cannot know such a man. *

Sec. XXXIII.

The Ode says, " Put on an upper garment above ornamented Robes; detest display of ornament." Hence, although the path of the superior man, appear secret, yet it daily becomes more splendid, while the path of the mean man, although, he strive to exhibit it, daily vanishes from sight.—Although, the principles of the superior man seem tasteless, yet they do not produce dislike. Although, apparently plain, they are still elegant. Although, his conduct may appear confused, it is nevertheless according to reason. He knows the near beginnings of distant results,—the source of manners, and the bright manifestations of what is minute: such a man can enter the path of virtue.

The superior man studies for his own good, and is careless whether men consider him a scholar or not, hence, he bends his whole attention to fundamental principles. Once established in these, his virtue naturally shines forth and cannot be concealed. The low man, on the contrary, studies with a view to catch the admiration of men, hence, he bends his attention to external ornament, and neglects the root, the consequence of which, is, that his shewy virtue soon decays and comes to nothing.

---

* It is presumed that few will feel disposed to call in question the concluding sentence of this section, namely, that none but a man of the brightest intelligence can understand what sort of man the Chinese sage is. Poor man, he seems to be lamentably ignorant himself on this important point. He seems to have forgotten that he is a finite creature, and from the blindness of his mind and haughtiness of his heart, imagines himself the omnipotent and omniscient God. Thus, esteeming himself infinitely wise, he labors under the destructive influence of the most gross and dangerous ignorance, viz. Ignorance of his Creator and ignorance of himself.

The Ode says. " Although what is deep, be concealed, yet it shines out at some aperture." But, when the superior man examines himself, he finds no cause for shame or self-reproach. It is the conduct of the superior man, when unseen by human eye, that cannot be equalled.

The Ode says, " Look into your own chamber, whether you have cause for shame in the presence of your household gods." Hence, the superior man is respectful, even when he moves not, and sincere when he speaks not. Again, the Ode says, " Advance in silence to worship the gods, renovation takes place without noise or strife. " Hence, the man of superior virtue, without exhorting the people, causes them to receive instruction, and without being angry, makes them more afraid than the instruments of punishment can do. The Ode farther says " He makes no display of his virtue, yet all his officers imitate it. " Thus the superior man (i. e. virtuous prince) by his simple, solid gravity gives peace to the Empire. The ode says " I cherish that illustrious virtue which is without great noise and without colour." Confucius says, sound and colour are things of the least moment in the renovation of a people. The Ode says " Virtue is light as a hair, " But a hair has comparisons. The highest comparison we can make (of the sage's virtue) is the containing power of heaven above, which is without sound or scent.*

CONCLUSION.

On the right is the 33rd. Section. Tsze Sze having in the former sections carried the discussion to the highest point, in this turns back and examines the source. He begins again at the commencement of moral science, which consists in paying the most serious attention to our secret thoughts and actions, and pushes the reasoning till it reach that simple, solid gravity

* Had they contented themseleves simply with saying that virtue is not composed of any material substance, all men would have understood their meaning but when they compare that quality in moral agents, which men call virtue, to the containing and overshadowing power of the material heavens, they are evidently talking about what neither they themselves, nor any other person can form an idea of.

which produces abundance of peace and tranquility through the whole Empire; and praises its admirable beauty, until he speak of it being without sound or scent, and then stops. For he takes up the most important ideas in the treatise and draws them to one point. His intention in thus repeating again and again for the instruction of men is most deep and important Will not the student do his utmost to understand the doctrine? *

* In this treatise which contains the leading doctrines of the Confucian Phoilosophy, there are two grand and fundamental defects. In the first place, it presents us with no accurate account of one self-existent, Almighty, Omnipresent, and Infinitely Gracious and Holy Being as the Creator and Father of the universe. From this as a natural consequence another sad defect arises viz. the perfect absence of a single direction how guilty depraved man may regain the favor and image of his Creator.

Although reverence to the gods, be inculcated, there is nothing said of these beings in the least degree calculated to inspire the mind with that reverence and love which man should always feel towards the supreme Being. He who was honored with the distinguished appellation "The wisest of men" declared that the fear of the Lord is the beginning of wisdom, but here is a whole fabric of wisdom built without that which the wise monarch of Israel considered the foundation stone.

SHANG LUN.

CHAP. 1.

1. Confucius says, to learn and constantly digest, is it not delightful! *

Is it not also pleasant to have a friend come from a distance! †

Is not he a superior man, who does not feel indignant when men are blind to his merits! ‡

2. Yew Tsze says, it is seldom that he who practices filial piety, and manifests fraternal affection, takes pleasure in disobeying superiors:—not to feel pleasure in disobeying superiors, and yet to be guilty of rebellion, is a thing which never happens.

The man of superior virtue bends his undivided attention to fundamental principles. Once established in these, virtuous practice naturally follows. Do not filial piety and fraternal respect constitute the stem of virtuous practice? ¶

3. Confucius says, that fine speech and a fair exterior are seldom associated with virtue.

4. Tsăng Tsze said, I daily examine myself in three things; viz. whether I have been unfaithful in transacting business for men, whether in my intercourse with friends I have been insincere, and whether I have neglected to reduce to practice the instructions of my Teacher.

5. Confucius says, he who rules a country of a thousand chariots, should pay serious attention to business;—obtain the

* When the knowledge we acquire by study, is by long and repeated meditation perfectly matured, and wrought into the mind, it becomes a source of pure delight.

† By a friend is meant one of the same class, or disposition with yourself. When your knowledge and virtue attract those who live at a distance, then those who are near will know you; and when you can extend your virtue to others it becomes a source of joy.

‡ Whether I possess knowledge or not, depends on me, but to know whether I have knowledge or not, depends on others: hence should they not know me, what cause have I to be angry.

¶ Filial piety is the stem of benevolence, but virtue is the source of benevolence. ‡

---

‡ This doctrine is defective, because it views obedience to parents, as the highest and first branch of benevolence, or virtue, and thus excludes our duty to the Supreme Being altogether. But if we ought to love, revere and serve our parents, more than we love, and serve other men, because our obligations to parents, are greater than to other men, then upon the same principle, our first and chief love, reverence, and obedience are due to our Father in heaven, to whom our obligations are unspeakably greater, than they can possibly be to the best of earthly parents.

confidence of the people;—be economical in his expenditure, and employ his people at the proper seasons.*

6. Confucius says, let a son, when at home, practice filial piety, and when abroad, perform the duties of a younger brother; be diligent and sincere, shew universal benevolence, and make friends of the virtuous, and if he have leisure, let him spend it in study.

7. Tsze Hea said, he who esteems the virtue of others, and turns his mind from the love of lust; who, with his whole might serves his parents,—devotes his person to the service of his Prince, and is sincere in his intercourse with friends, although he may be deemed unlearned, I must esteem him truly learned.

8. Confucius says, if the superior man be not grave in his conduct, he will not be respected, nor will his learning be solid. Be ruled by fidelity and sincerity. Have not a friend inferior to yourself. If you err, fear not to reform.

9. Tsăng Tszo said, be careful to perform aright the funeral rites of parents (or deceased relatives,) and offer sacrifice to distant ancestors, then the people will return to substantial virtue.

10. Tsze Kin asked Tsze Chung, saying, when our master comes to the province, he must hear what are its politics: will he himself ask the Prince, or will it be told him? Tsze Chung replied, our master is benign, upright, respectful, polite, and condecending; by these he obtains information. His mode of enquiring differs from that of other men.†

11. Confucius says, while his father lives, observe the bent of his mind; when his father dies, look at his conduct. If for three years (after his father's death), he change not from the principles of his father, he may be called a filial son.‡

* The Prince should not call upon the peo le to do government work either in the spring, when they ought to plow and sow the fields, or in the harvest when they are employed in reaping; but in winter, when they have spare time; this is what is intended by employing the people seasonably.

† Such was the eminence of the sage's wisdom and virtue, that when he arrived in any country, the Prince informed him how he conducted the affairs of government and asked his opinion.

‡ If a man before three years, after the death of his father, deviate from his principles, although his conduct may be virtuous, he cannot be considered a dutiful son.

12. Tsze Yew says, in the practice of politeness a mild deportment is of the greatest moment. This adorned the conduct of the former kings. But there is a mild pliability which ought not to be indulged. When one knows only how to be pliable, and does not regulate his pliability by propriety, this is what ought not to be done.

13. Yew Tsze says, he who makes just agreements can fulfil his promises. He who behaves with reverence and propriety, puts shame and disgrace to a distance. He who loses not those whom he ought to treat with kindness and respect, may be a master.

14. Confucius says, that the superior man seeks not to pamper his appetite, nor to live at ease: he is diligent in the practice of his duty, cautious in his words, and comes to men of right principles that he may be corrected. Such a man may be said to be a lover of learning.*

15. Tsze Loo asked what may be said of him who is poor, yet free from servile adulation; rich yet void of haughtiness. Confucius replied, he may pass, but is not equal to him who though poor, yet joyful; rich yet a lover of propriety.†

Tsze Kung replied, the ode says, cut then smooth, carve then polish. Confucius answered Ssze (Tsze Kung) begins to be capable of quoting the poets. Tell him the past, and he knows the future, (or give him a hint and he knows the conclusion.)‡

16. Confucius says, be not sorry that men do not know you, but be sorry that you are ignorant of men.

* The superior man's mind is not much concerned about high living and elegant mansions, but is bent upon the duties of his station, always anxious to reform his former errors and make up his former deficiencies; hence his readiness to apply to men of virtue and knowledge that he may learn of them to correct his mistakes.

† Tsze Loo a disciple of Confucius, had formerly been poor, but afterwards become rich. In both situations he had endeavoured to preserve himself from falling into the two evils to which ordinary men in these situations are liable, namely servile flattery, and haughty extravagance; hence he put this question to the sage, and the latter answered him, so as to praise him for the attainments he had made, and at the same time to stimulate him to aim at greater eminence than he had yet reached.

‡ Tsze Kung having heard what the sage said of being able to rejoice in the midst of poverty, and to delight in propriety even when rich, inferred that he meant more than he had expressed; wherefore the sage complimented him on being able to quote the poets in illustration of his master's ideas.

CHAP. 11.

1. Confucius says, he who governs by virtue, resembles the north polar star, which remains in its place, while all the other stars revolve round it, and incline towards it.*

2. Confucius says, the sense of the three hundred odes may be expressed in this one sentence,† "Let not your thoughts be impure"

3. Confucius says, if you lead the people by the laws and regulate them by penal infliction, they will escape punishment, but be void of shame; but lead them by virtue, and regulate them by propriety; then they will feel ashamed of vice and advance in virtue.‡

4. Confucius said, at fifteen I was bent on study;¶—at thirty my mind was firmly established;—at forty I had no doubts;—at fifty I understood the ways of heaven, and at seventy the wishes of my heart passed not the proper limits.

5. Mung E Tsze asked what is filial piety. Confucius replied, not to oppose (propriety). FAN-CHE driving his carriage, Confucius told him, that Mung E had asked him what filial piety was, and that he had told him it was not to oppose. FAN-CHE said, what did you mean? Confucius replied, when living,

* The north polar star, means the north pole. The south pole is within the earth thirty degrees, the north pole extends outside the earth thirty degrees. From this circumstance the south pole is invisible; consequently the north pole is employed to illustrate this point. The north pole is the axle of the heavens, it remains in its place and all the heavenly bodies revolve round it, and tend towards it. In the same manner the Prince of genuine virtue, without any effort on his part, occupies his royal seat, and such is the all pervading influence of his virtuous example, that all his subjects are attracted and renovated by it.

† "May be expressed in one word," this does not say that if you have this one word you may cast away all the odes, but that the whole sense of these odes resolves itself into this one sentiment.

‡ "Lead the people by the laws". Laws and punishments are but the means of putting in force those political principles of which virtue and propriety ought to be the foundation, but if the Prince vainly depend on laws and punishments, while he neglects to inculcate the radical principles of virtue and proper behaviour, the people will merely endeavour to avoid punishment, but will still retain their evil dispositions and wax worse and worse. On the other hand, he who leads them by virtue and regulates them by propriety, will not only make them ashamed of their vices, but will excite them to self-examination, and reformation.

¶ "I was bent on study." The sage was born with perfect knowledge and needed not to advance step by step; but he laid down this as a rule for students in general.

serve them (i. e. parents) according to propriety, when dead, bury them according to propriety, and afterwards sacrifice to them according to propriety.*

6. Mung Woo Pih asked about filial piety, Confucius replied, a Father and Mother alone are grieved for their children's sickness.†

7. Tsze Yew asked what is filial piety? Confucius replied that in the present day, merely to nourish parents, is considered filial piety, but we feed our dogs and horses; hence if we do not honor our parents, what preference do we give them.

8. Tsze Hea asked respecting filial piety. Confucius said. it is in the manner, (or countenance) that the difficulty lies.‡

9. Confucius said, I converse with Hwuy the whole day, and he never calls in question my doctrines. He appears dull, but when he retires, he investigates in secret, so that he can illustrate my doctrines. Hwuy is not dull.

10. Confucius says, observe what a man does. Look at his motives. Examine where his mind rests. How can men conceal themselves! How can men conceal themselves!

Confucius says, make yourself completely master of what you know and constantly learn new ideas, then you may be a teacher of others.

11. Confucius says, the superior man is not a mere machine, which is fit for one thing only.

* Fan Che was a disciple of the sage and was driving his carriage on the occasion. Confucius fearing that Mung E might misunderstand his answer, and suppose that he meant to say that not to oppose the will of parents was filial piety, hence he entered into conversation with Fan Che in order to explain the point, which was, that not to act contrary to the fitness of things, is filial piety. At that time the families of three of the great officers of Loo had assumed the performance of ceremonics above their station. Confucius wished by this answer to arouse them to a sense of the impropriety of their conduct.

† An ancient book says, that the filial son gives no cause of grief to parents, by doing any thing wrong; hence the only thing they are concerned, or grieved for, is his sickness. Some Commentators say, the meaning is, that parents feel constantly and deeply concerned for the sickness of their children, even at the time when they are well, and that the filial child embodies this spirit in himself, and constantly feels the most tender concern for his Parents.

‡ Tsze Hea was too grave and formal in serving his parents and elder brothers. Thus being deficient in suiting his external deportment to the act he was performing, he failed in according with the feelings of his parents.

Ching Tsze says, that the instruction given to E Tsze, was suitable to all men. That given to Woo Pih, was imparted on account of his being a man which caused much grief to people. Tsze Yew nourished his parents, but was deficient in shewing respect. Tsze Hea was correct and just, but somewhat wanting in mildness and pliability. Each was taught according to the superiority, or inferiority of his talents, and according to his short comings. This commendable mode of communicating instruction was generally adopted by the sage.

12. Tsze Kung asked who is a superior man? Confucius replied he who first practices his words and then speaks accordingly.

13. Confucius says, the superior man possesses general benevolence without selfish partiality. The mean man is selfish, partial and void of general benevolence.

14. Confucius says, if you read and do not reflect, you will lose what you learn :— if you think and do not study, you are uneasy and in danger.

15. Confucius says, oppose false principles, for they are injurious.

16. Confucius said, Yew, permit me to tell you what is knowledge. What you are acquainted with, consider that you know it, what you do not understand, consider that you do not know it; this is knowledge.

17. Tsze Chang studied with the view of obtaining a government appointment.

Confucius says, hear much, that you may diminish your doubts. Be careful what you say, then you will seldom err. See much in order to lessen dangerous uneasiness. Pay much attention to your actions and you will seldom repent. He who in words rarely mistakes, and who seldom finds cause to repent of his actions, already possesses an official emolument.

18. Gae Kung asked how he might secure the submission of the people. Confucius replied, promote the upright and put down the vicious and the people will obey. Promote the vicious and put down the upright and the people will not obey.

19. Ke Kang asked by what means the people might be made respectful and faithful, and stimulated to the practice of virtue. Confucius replied, rule with firmness and dignity, and they will behave respectfully. Exemplify filial piety and tenderness, and the people will be faithful. Promote the virtuous and instruct the ignorant, and they will be stimulated.

20. Some one asked Confucius why he was not in an official situation; to which he replied, the Shoo-King when speaking

of filial piety says, in good government nothing is manifested, but filial piety and fraternal affection; he who practices these governs; why consider him only who holds a government situation to be acting the part of a ruler?

21. Confucius said, I know not how a man who is destitue of truth can proceed. How can a large carriage go without a bow, or a small one without a yoke?

22. Tsze Chung asked whether the affairs of ten generations might be foreknown. Confucius replied, it may be known from the Yin Dynasty, what it took from, or added to the rites of the Hea Dynasty; and from the Chow Dynasty it may be known what it took from, or added to the rites of the Yin Dynasty. Suppose any other succeeds the Chow Dynasty, then the affairs of the Empire may be known for a hundred ages to come.*

23. Confucius says, it is adulation to sacrifice to a god, to whom we ought not to sacrifice, and to know that a thing is right and not to do it, is weakness.†

CHAP. 111.

1. Confucius said, Ke She uses eight bands of musicians at his family feasts; if he can bear to do this, what may he not do?

2. The three families used the Yung Che (a kind of music played at the removal of the Imperial sacrifices) Confucius said, this Ode says, "It is only the Princes who assist; the Emperor looks mild and benignant." How can this apply to the Hall of the three Mandarines!‡

* The sage knew the future only by reflecting on the past, and not by any low arts as people of after ages pretended to do. Thus Confucius renounces all claim to the being inspired with the knowledge of future events.

† Every man has gods, whom those in his station are bound to worship. For instance the Emperor sacrifices to Heaven and Earth.—The Prince to the local deities.—The high Officers to the houshold gods, and the common people to their ancestors. If any person sacrifice in the public Temples to any god which does not belo g to his class, it is with the view of flattering the deity in order to obtain happiness.

‡ Ke She was one of the superior officers of the Loo country. The Emperor employed eight bands, or ranks of musicians at his feasts; the Princes six, and the great Officers of state four. Ke She used the music and ceremonies of the Emperor; on which account Confucius remarked that since he was capable of doing such a thing as this, there was nothing so bad that he would not do it.

When the Emperor sacrificed in the ancestorial Temple they sang the Ode called Yung, while the sacrifices were removing. This Ode says, that the Emperor looks benignant, and it is only tributary Princes who assist him. The three Mandarines had at that time taken upon them to sing this Ode at their sacrifices. But as its language could not apply to their sacrifices, Confucius ridicules their ignorance and irregularity in singing it.

3. Confucius says, how can a man devoid of virtue practice propriety! How can a man destitute of virtue play music!

4. Ling Fang asked what is the source of propriety? Confucius exclaimed, an important question indeed! In the performance of ceremonies, narrow economy is better than extravagance; and in mourning, deep sorrow is preferable to external ceremony.*

5. Confucius said, the western and northern barbarians have rulers and are not like us the multitudes of Hea (China), who have lost them.†

6. Ke She sacrificed to Tae Shan (a mountain). Confucius said to Yen Yew, cannot you prevent him. He replied I am unable. Upon which Confucius exclaimed, alas what you say of Tae Shan, shews that are you inferior to Ling Fang! ‡

7. Confucius says, that the superior man wrangles not. If he do, it is at shooting matches. But he yields the place to his unsuccesful antagonist, and ascends the hall, then descends and drinks with him. This is the wrangling of the superior man.

8. Tsze Hea said (the ode says) "Smiling with a well formed mouth and a fine rolling eye; first the fair ground, then paint." What ideas does this convey? Confucius replied, first make the fair ground, then adorn with colours. Tsze Hea said, you mean politeness comes last. Confucius exclaimed you have caught my idea Shang! Now you can converse with me on the poets.¶

* In all our concerns we ought neither to be parsimonious, nor extravagant; but the former is preferable to the latter. In mourning and rites, inward grief, and external order ought to be regulated by due decorum, but it is better that grief exceed due bounds and external order be a little overlooked, than that there should be too much external shew and a deficiency of inward sorrow.

† Yin She says, Confucius was grieved at the disorders of the age, and thus lamented them. They had not completely lost their rulers, but those they had, could not do their duty; and the distinctions of society were nearly lost.

‡ Ko Sho the Prime Minister of Loo, presumed to sacrifice to the god of Tae Shan; a god who should be worshipped only by the sovereign of a country. Yen a disciple of the sage was Ke She's head servant, hence Confucius considered it to be his duty to reprove his master for this fault, or rather to advise him not to do such a thing, but on finding that he rather accorded with his master in this matter; he mentioned Ling Fang who had just asked what was the source of propriety, and hinted that Yen was inferior to him; this he did from a wish to arouse Yen to a sense of his duty.

¶ As the painter cannot make a good drawing without a fair white ground, so unless the radical principles of virtue be seated in the heart, there is no foundation for a truly polite carriage. This is the scope of the metaphorical language of the Poet.

9. Confucius said, I can speak of the laws and ceremonies of the Hea Dynasty, but Ke is incapable of substantiating what I say. I can likewise teach the rules and ceremonies of the Yin Dynasty; but here too, Sung is not capable of verifying my words.*

10. Confucius said, in the great royal sacrifice, after the libation is poured out to invoke the descent of the gods, I wish not to be a spectator any longer.†

11. Some one asked what was the intention of the great Royal sacrifices. Confucius replied, I do not know: to him who knows this, every thing under heaven, is as plain as this; at the same time putting his finger into the palm of his hand.

12. Sacrifice to ancestors as though they were here. Worship the gods as if they were present. Confucius said, I do not worship as if I were not worshipping.

13. Wang Sun Kea, asked what was meant by saying that it is better to flatter the god of the corner, than the god of the furnace? Confucius replied, not so, he who offends heaven has none to whom he can pray.‡

14. Confucius said, the founders of the Chow Dynasty inspected the polity of the two preceeding Dynasties, and how richly did they adorn it! I follow Chow.¶

* The country Ke was given to the descendants of the reigning family of the Hea Dynasty, the country Sung was given to the descendants of the Yin, or Shang Dynasty; but both these countries were deficient in men of merit and in authenticated records, and hence insufficient to confirm the words of the sage, in reference to the polity of the Hea and Yin Dynasties.

† In the great royal sacrifice, called Te, the Chief Ministers of Loo, in the commencement of the ceremonies, appeared to manifest some sincerity, and might be witnessed, but after the libation was poured on the ground for the purpose of invoking the descent of the gods they fell into a lazy careless manner, which the sage could not endure to behold.

There was nothing in which the former kings manifested their grateful remembrance of ancestors more deeply, than in the sacrifice called Te. Unless a man's benevolence, filial piety,—sincerity, and reverence, were of the highest order, he could not perform this sacrifice aright; hence the remark of the sage, that he who was capable of offering this sacrifice properly, could easily govern the Empire.

‡ The god of the corner, was considered more honorable, than the god of the furnace. Wang Sun Kea was a Ta Foo of Loo, and wished to assume the place of his Prince; hence comparing the Prince to the god of the corner, and himself to the god of the furnace, he in a jeering manner insinuated to the sage, that it would be more advantageous, to pay court to him, than to the Prince. But Confucius silenced him by telling him that, when a man violates the will of heaven (as he had done) there is no atoning for this fault by praying to any other god whatever.

¶ The Hea and Shang Dynasties did not arrive at perfection in their laws and ceremonies, but the Princes Wan and Woo and the Prime Minister Chow Kung, examined the system of these two Dynasties, lopping off what was superfluous, and adding what was deficient, and thus formed a most elegant and complete political and religious system

15. When Confucius entered the great Temple, he minutely enquired about every thing. Some one said, who will say that the man of Tsow's Son knows propriety? When he enters the great Temple, he asks about every thing! Confucius having heard this, said, even this accords with propriety.

16. Confucius said, in shooting at the target, not to send the arrow through the leather, because men's strength is not equal, was the custom of the ancients.

17. Tsze Kung wished to abolish the sacrificial lamb, offered on the first of the (12th.) moon. Confucius said, Sze, you are concerned about the lamb, I about the custom.

18. Confucius said, if a man (at present) serve his Prince with the utmost propriety, people say that he is a flatterer.

19. Ting, Prince (of Loo) asked how a Prince should employ his Ministers, and how Ministers should serve their Prince. Confucius replied, a Prince should employ his Ministers with propriety, and Ministers should serve their Prince with fidelity.

20. Confucius said, the joyful strains of the Kwan Tseu (ode) do not excite licentious desires, nor do its mournful notes wound the feelings.*

21. Gae, Prince (of Loo), asked Tsae Go, about the altars, of the gods of the land and grain. Tsae Go replied, the people of Hea planted them round with the pine tree, the people of Yin with the cypress, and those of Chow with the chesnut, in order to make the people stand in awe. Confucius having heard this, said what is finished speak not of it; what cannot be done well give no advice about it; what is past blame not. †

* The Kwan Tseu ode refers to Wan Wang having fallen in love with a Lady of extraordinary virtue. When he first paid his addresses to her and was unsuccessful, his grief was so pungent that he could not sleep, but having ultimately been successful in his suit, all the instruments of music were employed to express his joy: yet in the grief expressed by the ode, there was nothing to wound the feelings, nor was there any thing in the expressions of joy calculated to excite licentious passions; hence the sage recommends this piece as a model of its kind.

† At that time the Prince of Loo was a weak man, and his Ministers were violent and tyrannical. Confucius, knowing that his disciple Tsae Go had not, in his answers to the Prince of Loo, given the true idea of the altars erected to the local deities, and being aware that what he had said about keeping the people in awe might induce the Prince to use harsh measures with the people, instead of suppressing the tyranny of the Mandarines, he uttered these words with the intention of reproving Tsae Go's careless and erroneous answer. His meaning was, that the words which escaped Tsae Go's mouth, could not be recalled, and now it was of no use, as to the effect they were calculated to produce. By this he wished to make his disciple more attentive to his words in future.

22. Confucius said, Kwan Chung was a man of small capacity. Some one said, was Kwan Chung niggardly then? Confucius replied, he had three Kwei (a sort of gallary) and did not employ one man for more than one office, how could he be called niggardly (or economical). Then did Kwan Chung know propriety? Confucius replied, the Princes of a Province had their doors enclosed by a screen; so had Kwan She. When two neighbouring Princes met, after having drunk together, they inverted their cups, so did Kwan She. If Kwan She knew propriety, who does not know it!

23. Confucius, conversing with the music master of Loo, said, you ought to be acquainted with the principles of music. In commencing an air, there must be the union of all the notes, and tones, when the tune swells, there must be perfect harmony, clearness, and regularity in order to complete the music.*

24. The Resident of E begged to be introduced to Confucius, saying, when men of virtue and talent come here, I have never been prevented from seeing them. The followers of the sage introduced him, and when he went out he addressed them thus, "why do you lament that your master has lost his situation? The Empire has long been in a state of anarchy, but Heaven will make him a great reformer."

25. Confucius said, the music of the Chaou is supremely excellent and perfectly mild in its spirit;—that of the Woo is also very fine, but the spirit is not perfectly mild.†

* At that time the knowledge and practice of music had decayed. Confucius wishing to revive this science, conversed with the Chief Musician of Loo on the subject, and gave him to understand, that if there was a single note wanting, or if the harmony of all the different parts was not complete, it was not worth the name of music.**

† Chaou was the designation of the music of the great Shun, and Woo was the name given to that of the famous king Woo. Shun was a man of a remarkably mild temper and gained the Empire by his humble benign disposition, hence his music breathed a sweet, mild spirit. Woo Wang was a valiant warrior, and by his bravery conquered the tyrant Chow, consequently his music partook of the severe and stern.

** It would appear from this paragraph, as well as from many other parts of their ancient writings, that the Chinese, at a very early period, studied music; which science like all their other systems, was founded upon the Yin and Yang Principles. Certain notes were considered as belonging to the Male, and certain to the Female principle, and if these were not properly blended the music was not worth the name, because it did not accord with the nature of things.

26. Confucius says, when men of high rank are void of liberality;—when in mourning there is no real grief, and ceremonies are not observed with respect, how can I look at such things!

CHAP. IV.

1. Confucius says, the virtue of villagers is beautiful: he who in selecting a residence refuses to dwell among the virtuous, how can he be considered intelligent?

2. Confucius says, those who are destitute of virtue, cannot long conduct themselves aright either in poverty or affliction, nor can they long manage themselves in the midst of prosperity, (or pleasure), but the virtuous find repose in virtue, and the intelligent earnestly covet virtue. *

3. Confucius says, it is only the virtuous that are capable of either loving, or hating a man.

4. Confucius says, if the mind be sincerely inclined to virtue, the man will not do any thing that is vicious.

5. Confucius says, riches and honor are what all men wish for, but if they cannot be obtained by just means, seek not to enjoy them. Poverty and low station are what all men hate, but if they cannot be avoided by proper means, seek not to get rid of them. If a superior man abandon virtue, how can he complete his reputation. The superior man does not for a single moment act contrary to virtue. When in great haste and confusion he still accords with virtue.

* Man's heart is originally perfectly virtuous; he who preserves his original rectitude, is unmoved by external circumstances, but he who loses it, if in poor and distressing circumstances, will give way to low and irregular feelings. If on the other hand, he lives in ease and affluence, he will indulge in every sort of extravagance and vicious pleasure.

The truly virtuous man is perfectly free from selfishiness and partiality, hence his love and hatred are constantly guided by reason. ††

†† That a man destitute of sterling principle, will not conduct himself aright, either in poverty or affluence, must be granted by all who know any thing of human nature; but, that man is naturally possessed of perfect rectitude, the sad experience of all ages and countries, proves to be utterly void of truth. The same experience proves that the heart of man is naturally "deceitful, above all things and desperately wicked," and that genuine virtue is not a plant which springs naturally in the soil of human nature, but is a tree of our heavenly Father's planting."

6. Confucius said, I have not seen any one who perfectly loves virtue, nor have I seen one who thoroughly detests vice. He who perfectly loves virtue, prefers nothing else to it; and he who has a thorough detestation of vice, will not permit it to approach his person. Were there any one, who would for one day apply his whole strength to the practice of virtue, then I have not seen a person whose strength is not sufficient for it. If there be any such people, I have not yet seen them.

7. Confucius says, men's faults correspond with the class to which they belong: observe their faults; and you will know whether they are men of virtue. *

8. Confucius says, if in the morning you hear divine truth, in the evening you may die. †

9. Confucius says, the scholar whose inclination is towards truth, and virtue, but who is ashamed of mean apparel and coarse fare, is not worth reasoning with.

10. Confucius says, that the superior man in every thing is void of prejudice, and obstinacy; whatever justice requires, that he follows.

11. Confucius says, the superior man fixes his mind on virtue, the worthless man thinks on a comfortable living;—the former regards the sanctions of the law, the latter regards gain.

* Confucius said, that the people of that age only knew that he who was free from fault was virtuous, but they were not aware that a man may from his very faults be known to be a virtuous man. Men are divided into two classes, the honorable and the mean. The honorable man's faults lean to the side of too much generosity, the faults of the mean man are the direct reverse: look then at a man's faults, and you will see to which of those classes he belongs.

† Divine principles are of the utmost importance to every man; if in the morning a man hear, understand, and firmly believe them, then in the evening he may die without regret. ‡ ‡

---

‡ ‡ It is the glory of the everlasting gospel, that the moment a man sincerely believes its sacred principles, and with his whole heart relies on that Almighty Saviour which it reveals, that moment he is pardoned and justified in the sight of God the Judge of all the earth.† But as the meritorious cause of his justification, is neither his knowledge, nor belief of the gospel, but the merits of the Divine Saviour, to whom this gospel directs his mind, it does not appear how the mere hearing and believing of the doctrines of the Chinese sages, which reveals no Saviour, could prepare a man for that awful change which he undergoes at death.

Bigotted prejudice proves the ruin of numberless millions of immortal beings. Nothing can be more foolish or injurious, than for a man to believe principles merely because his forefathers have adopted them. Every wise man examines impartially whatever he reads or hears, embraces true and rejects false principles, by whomsoever they may have been held. Had Confucius heard the gospel of Jesus, is it not likely that he would have joyfully embraced it!

† Acts XVI. 31.

12. Confucius says, he who pursues self-advantage, will be much hated.

13. Confucius says, that if a man is able by polite complaisance to govern a kingdom, where is the difficulty (of governing), but if he is not able to govern by polite complaisance, what shall we say of his politeness!

14. Confucius said, be not vexed that you have not a government appointment, but be anxious to possess the requisite qualifications: be not grieved that you are not known, but seek to be worthy of being known.

15. Confucius (addressing Tsăng Tsze) said, San, "My principles all unite in one harmonious whole." Tsang Tsze replied, right. When Confucius went out, his disciples asked the meaning fo what he had said? Tsang Tsze replied, our master's principles are nothing but consummate faithfulness, and benevolence. *

16. Confucius says, the superior man is influenced by the love of rectitude, the mean man by the love of gain.

17. Confucius says, when you see a man of virtue and wisdom, think whether you equal him; when you see a bad man, retire within, and examine yourself

18 Confucius says, in serving parents, reprove with mildness; if you perceive that they are not disposed to comply, still reverence them, and do not oppose their will; should they treat you severely, murmur not.†

19. Confucius says, while parents are alive, wander not to a distance: if you do, you must fix the place.

20. Confucius says, the age of father and mother we ought not to forget: it is at once a source of joy and fear.

21. Confucius says, the ancients said not what they could do, because they felt ashamed that their actions should not completely accord with their words.

* To perform our duty to the utmost, is faithfulness:—to do to others as we wish them to do to us, is benevolence. All the various branches of the Sage's doctrine resolved themselves into this one principle of fidelity and benevolence.

† A child ought to take supreme delight in rendering his parents happy. If at any time they act improperly, he ought with a mild countenance and low, gentle voice, to point out their mistakes, and admonish them to reform, but should they not feel disposed to comply with these gentle and respectful admonitions, they must still be treated with the highest respect. If the reproofs of a son should excite the wrath of parents, so as to lead them to treat him with extreme severity, he must not complain, nor diminish his endeavours to please them.

22. Confucius says, the cautious seldom err.

23. Confucius says, the superior man, wishes to be slow in speech, but prompt in action.

24. Confucius says, the virtuous will not be left alone, they will certainly have neighbours.

25. Tsze Yew says, he who serves a Prince, if he often reprove him, will get disgraced, and he who often reproves a friend, will be be treated with indifference.

CHAP. V.

1. Confucius said, Kung Che Chang may be married; although he be imprisoned, it is not his blame.—He gave him his daughter in marriage.

Confucius said, if the country be governed by reason, Nan Yung will not be dismissed; if the country be not governed by reason, he will escape punishment, and death. He gave him his brother's daughter in marriage. *

2. Confucius exclaimed, Tsze Tseen is a man of superior virtue. If the Loo country has no superior men, where did this man get such virtue?†

3. Tsze Kung said, what sort of a character is Sze (Tsze Kung), Confucius replied, you are a vessel. What kind of vessel? Confucius answered, a Hoo-leen (a highly ornamented vessel used in the ancestorial Temples.) ‡

* The conduct of Confucius, in these two instances, shews that the sage in choosing matches looked at the virtues, not at the happiness, or misery of the individual. Some one said that Nan Yung was more virtuous than Kung Che Chang, and that the sage on that account gave him his daughter; thus honoring his Brother.

† Tsze Tseen was a disciple of the sage, and a native of Loo. He selected virtuous associates, in order to perfect his own virtue, hence the sage intimates by the praise which he conferred on that gentlemen, that the Loo country possessed men of superior virtue, and talents.

‡ Tsze Kung hearing his master eulogize Tsze Tseen, felt desirous of knowing the sage's opinion concerning himself, upon which Confucius told him, that he was a vessel.—Tsze Kung knowing that there were valuable vessels, and likewise those of little worth, asked farther what kind of vessel, on which the sage told him, that he might be compared to the Hooleen, intimating that he possessed virtue and abilities capable of serving his country, and that his talents and virtues were adorned by the graces of an elegant education.

4. Some one said, Yung is a good man, but destitute of a clever address. Confucius said, why use a clever (or artful) address! Disputing with men, often procures their hatred. I do not know whether he (Yung) be a virtuous man, but why attach importance to artful address?

5. Confucius was about to appoint Tseih Teaou Kae to an official situation; he replied I am still unable completely to comprehend your doctrine. Confucius was delighted. *

6. Confucius exclaimed, alas good principles do not prevail; were I to ascend a raft and set out to sea, he who would have courage to go along with me, is Yew (Tsze Loo). Tsze Loo hearing this, rejoiced; upon which Confucius said, Yew, you are more valiant than I; but you cannot discriminate.

7. Mung Woo Pih, asked whether Tsze Loo was a virtuous (or benevolent) man, Confucius replied, I do not know. Having again asked, Confucius said, he is capable of commanding the military forces of a country of one thousand chariots, but I do not know as to his virtue. What may be said of Kew? He is capable of being Chief Magistrate in a city of one thousand houses; or governor of a family of one hundred chariots, but I am not certain as to his virtue. What is your opinion of Chĭh? Confucius replied, Chĭh girded with his official sash, is capable of waiting at court, and receiving guests, but in regard to his virtue I am uncertain. †

8. Confucius said to Tsze Kung, whether do you, or Hwuy excel? Tsze Kung replied, how can I presume to compare myself to Hwuy! if Hwuy hear one thing, he knows ten; ‡ if I hear one thing, I know two. Confucius replied you are not equal to him, I grant you are not.

* Tseih Teaou Kae considered that until he completely comprehended right principles, so as to have the entire management of himself, he was incapable of ruling others, hence Confucius sensible of his talents and virtue, rejoiced at his sincerity, and firm resolution to make himself master of the doctrines of rectitude.

† As to these three disciples, although they possessed considerable talents, they had not arrived at that entire freedom from all selfishness, and that consummate excellence, which merits the name of virtue, and Confucius would not lightly grant that a man was truly virtuous.

‡ The words one and ten, mean the commencement and close, including all the intermediate steps, denoting that Hway only wanted to hear the first principle of any truth in order to obtain an instant and complete knowledge of the whole subject." "One and two," mean this, and that, intimating that when Tsze Kung heard any idea, he instantly knew its opposite.

9. Tsae Yu having slept in bed during the day; Confucius said, rotten wood cannot be carved, a wall of dirty earth cannot be whitened: of what use is it that I should reprove Yu. Confucius said, formerly in my intercourse with men, when I heard them speak, I believed that they would act, but from this time, when I hear a man speak, I must also see him act. Tsae Yu has occasioned this change. *

10. Confucius said, alas I have not seen a truly inflexible man! Some one replied, is not Shin Chang an inflexible character? Confucius rejoined, Shin Chang is under the influence of lust, how can he be inflexible. †

11. Tsze Kung said, what I do not wish men to do to me, I do not wish to do to them. Confucius replied, Sze (Tsze Kung) you have not yet attained this.

12. Tsze Kung said, the virtue and elegant manners of our master, we may obtain the knowledge of; but his lectures on the nature of man, and divine reason, we cannot comprehend. ‡

13. When Tsze Loo heard any thing that he had not yet ful-

* Both these sentences were spoken by the sage with the intention of strongly reproving Tsae Yu. For he dreaded any approach to sloth, or laziness, in his students. The doctrine of the ancient sages was, that the scholar during his whole life, should, with close and unwearied application pursue his studies, and cease only at death. Hence the sharp reproof of the sage, even for one day's sloth. Tsae Yu, or Tsae Go, as he is called in the Hea Lun, was an eloquent speaker, but often failed in following up his words by action: hence the sage, with the view of rousing him, told him that from his conduct, he had learned to put no confidence in men who spoke well, until he also saw them act well.

† Confucius lamented that he could not find an inflexible man who might hand down his doctrines. Those whom the sage considered truly unbending characters were such as had obtained the straight Ke, (soul or breath) of heaven and earth, and who possessed reason and integrity sufficient to cultivate this divine gift, until they arrived at that state of firm inflexibility, which cannot, by the separate, or united influence of all external things be made to swerve one hair's-breadth from the line of rectitude. ††

‡ The nature of man, means the divine principles, which man originally receives from heaven. Divine reason, means the radical essence of celestial, self existent principles. The virtue, and elegant manners of the sage were daily exhibited to the eye of the disciples, so that they could all know them; but human nature and divine reason, were subjects rarely discussed by the sage, and some of his students were not prepared to study them. For in the schools of the sages, studies are pursued in regular order; there is no leaping over any intermediate step. Tsze Kung at that time had just begun to hear the sage treat on these high branches of knowledge, and thus extolled their excellence.

---

†† It is to be feared that few, if any have completely reached this standard; but we may venture to say, that such men as the Apostle Paul, and John Knox came pretty near it.

ly practised, he was afraid of hearing any thing else. *

14. Tsze Kung asked why Kung Wan Tsze obtained the epithet "Learned"? Confucius replied, he was clever, loved study, and was not ashamed to ask his inferiors, therefore he was termed learned.

15. Confucius said, Tsze Chan possessed four characteristics of the superior man: in his personal conduct he was grave;—in serving superiors respectful;—in providing for the support of the people, benevolent; and in employing them, equitable.

16. Confucius said, Gan Ping Chung, knew well how to maintain friendly intercourse with men: for a long period he kept up due respect. †

17. Confucius said, Chwang Wan Chung built a house for a great Tortoise; on the tops of the pillars he painted the pictures of mountains, and on the beams he drew the representation of water herbs: of what sort was his intelligence? ‡

18. Tsze Chang enquiring, said, the Ling Yin, Tsze Wan, three times obtained the office of Ling Yin, yet manifested no appearance of joy, and three times lost the office, without any appearance of displeasure. He informed the new Ling Yin, in what manner he had conducted the business of the office. What may be said of such a man? Confucius said, he was faithful. But was he perfectly virtuous? I do not know; why consider him perfectly virtuous.

Tsuy Tsze having assasinated the Prince of Tse; Chin Wan Tse, who possessed forty carriage horses, gave them all up, left Tse and went to another Province. On his arrival there he exclaimed, here also they have such Ministers as our Tsuy Tsze!

* Tsze Loo was of an ardent, bold disposition, hence when he heard any precept, he instantly put it in practice, and was afraid lest he should hear another before the first had been fully practised.

† When people have long lived on terms of close intimacy, they are apt to become careless and negligent in their intercourse with each other. Hence arises want of mutual respect. When therefore we see people after a long continued intimacy, still preserve due respect, we may judge that they understand the true principles of mutual intercourse.

‡ Chwang Wan Chung was one of the great Officers of Loo; he supposed that by preparing a house for a great Tortoise which they had in Loo, and ornamenting it with mountain scenery, he might have the power of happiness, or misery in his own hand by this his want of knowledge is clearly displayed.

He left and went to another country, but there also, he declared that their Ministers resembled Tsuy Tsze of his native Province. What (said Tsze Chang) shall we say of this man? Confucius replied, he was uncorrupted. But was he perfectly virtuous? I do not know; why should you esteem him perfectly virtuous. *

19. Wan Tsze always considered a thing three times, before he acted, Confucius hearing of it, said, twice may do.

20. Confucius said, Ning Woo Tsze, when the country was under the government of right principles acted wisely; but when the government lost right principles, he acted foolishly. His wisdom may be equalled, but his folly (or feigned ignorance) cannot.

21. When Confucius was in the Chin country, he exclaimed, "I will return! I will return"! My students at home, possess ardour, ability and learning, but they know not how to regulate themselves aright. †

22. Confucius said, that Pih E and Shuh Tse, did not think of men's former vices, hence men did not feel deeply offended with them. ‡

* From the sentiments of the sage respecting Tsze Wan, and Chin Wang Tsze, we may see that a man may be faithful and uncorrupt, and yet not perfectly virtuous. Faithfulness and uncorruptedness, are but two branches of 仁 jin (perfect virtue,) so that although a perfectly virtuous man must be faithful, and pure, yet it does not follow that because he possesses one, or both of these good qualities, that he is therefore completely virtuous. **

† When Confucius was in Chin, he saw that his principles were not embraced; hence he lamented the waywardness of man, and said at first I really wished to disseminate my principles, but now I see that during my own life, they will not be generally embraced. I will return home, for although my doctrines may not be received by this age, my disciples at home, are bold, intelligent, and aim at great things. Their learning is likewise considerable, but as they are not yet well acquainted with the golden medium and the proper manner of self government, they want farther instruction on these points, which having obtained I may commit my doctrines to them with the hope that they will transmit them to posterity: I will therefore return for this purpose.

‡ Pih E and Shuh Tse two brothers and sons of the Prince of Koo Chuh, could not bear to come in contact with bad men, but if men reformed and abandoned their former vices they received them into their society and thought no more of their former improper conduct: bad people knowing that this was their disposition did not feel a deep antipathy towards them.

** The word which we have, in this place, translated, "perfect virtue," is by some Translators rendered "benevolence," but it will appear to those who attend to the definitions of the word which often occur in Chinese writers, that unless we consider benevolence, and perfect moral excellence, synonymous terms, benevolence is an inadequate rendering of the original word. 仁

23. Confucius said, who can say that We Sang Kaou was an upright man? Some one having begged a little mustard of him, he (not having any) went and begged of his neighbours, and gave it to him.

24. Confucius said, Tso Kew Ming was ashamed to use fine speeches, put on a fair countenance, and shew excessive respect, and Mow (Confucius) is likewise ashamed of such things. Tso Kew Ming was ashamed to conceal enmity under the mask of friendship, and of such conduct, Mow is also ashamed.

25. When Yen Yuen and Ke Loo were standing by his side, Confucius said, why does not each of you express his wish? Tsze Loo said, I wish to have carriages and horses, and fine skin robes, that I may use them in common with my friends. If they should spoil them, I would not be offended. Yen Yuen said, I wish, not to brag of my virtue, nor to publish my merits. Tsze Loo said, I wish to hear the desire of our master. Confucius replied, I wish to give ease to the old, to be faithful to friends, and to cherish the young. *

26 Confucius sighing, exclaimed, alas! I have not seen those who are conscious of their errors, and inwardly accuse themselves.

27. Confucius said, in a village of ten houses, there may be those who equal Mow in fidelity and sincerity, but not in his love of learning. †

* Ching Tsze says, that Confucius rested in perfect virtue, Yen Yuen did not act contrary to it, and Tsze Loo sought after it: and that the great wish of all the three manifested a public spirit, but they differed as to the degrees of their virtue. Tsze Loo's valour exceeded his justice; Yen Yuen had no selfishness, hence he boasted not of his virtue, he knew that he was the same as other men, and he did not publish his merits. His aim may be called great, but he could not, however, avoid reflecting before he acted. But Confucius was equal to the renovating power of heaven and earth and moved on in his course without the necessity of thought, or reflection, and was steady and infallible as the laws of nature. This is the sage. **

† "Fidelity and sincerity equal to the sage," means an excellent natural disposition and good talents. Confucius was born with perfect knowledge, yet he never ceased to love study, and made this remark to stimulate others. His meaning is, that it is easy to find people of an excellent natural disposition, but that the highest knowledge and virtue, are difficult attainments. Those who reach them are sages; those who do not, are mere rustics; ought not men to exert themselves!

** If to be a sort of machine, moved on in its course by some extrinsic force, without the excercise of thought, or will, is to be a sage, we presume few who lay any claim to common sense, will covet the distinction.

CHAP. VI.

1. Confucius said, Yung may be employed as a ruler. *

Chung Kung (i. e. Yung) asked respecting Tsang Pih Tsze. Confucius replied, he may do (as a ruler); he is liberal. Chung Kung said, to maintain proper respect and yet manifest mild liberality in the administration of affairs, is not this proper? But if one be careless, or negligent in his own conduct, and mild and easy in the discharge of his official duties, is not this an excess of mildness? Confucius replied, your words are true Yung.

2. Gae Kung asked (the sage) which of his disciples excelled in the love of learning? Confucius replied, there was one, called Yen Hwuy, who really loved learning. He did not remove his anger (from the proper object), he did not twice commit the same mistake: but he was unfortunate; his life was short; I have lost him, and have not heard of another who truly loves learning? †

3. Tsze Hwa being sent into Tse; Yen Tsze asked rice for his (Tsze Hwa's) mother. Confucius said, give her one Foo; (Yen) asked more. Confucius said give her one Yu; Yen gave her five Ping of rice. Confucius (hearing of it) said, when Chih Tsze Hwa went to Tse, he rode fat horses, and wore fine clothes, now I have heard, that the superior man, assists the needy, but does not increase the wealth of the rich.

Yuen Sze being made a governor by Confucius, he gave him nine hundred measures of grain, which he refused. Confucius

* "A Ruler," Literally, may be placed with his face to the south, that being the position o Prince when on the throne, or bench.

† Yen Hwuy, the special favorite of his master, died at the age of thirty two. Confucius said, when he happened to be provoked he could not avoid being angry, but regulated his anger and did not remove it to an unoffending object. In the course of his life, he could not avoid erring from ignorance, but when once he knew his error, he never committed it again.

said, do not refuse it, give it to your hamlets, villages and towns.*

4. Confucius speaking of Chung Kung said, the yellow coloured, horned calf of a mixed coloured cow, although men may not use it (in sacrifice), will the river and mountain gods reject it!†

5. Confucius said, for three months Hwuy did not deviate from perfect virtue. The others, perhaps, may not do so only for a day, or a month.

6. Ke Kang asked whether Chung Yew was qualified to hold an Official situation? Confucius replied, Yew is certainly qualified to be an Officer of Government; what difficulty would he have? Is Sze fit for the Mandarinship? Why should he not? Sze has intelligence well suited to the situation of a high Officer of state. Is Kew capable of filling a government situation? Why not? Kew's elegant education renders him well qualified to be a superior Mandarin.

7. Ke She sent a messenger to Min Tsze Këën, asking him to accept the Office of Governor of Pe. Min Tsze Këën said to the messenger, I beg you will make a polite excuse for me, and should your master again call for me, by that time I shall be on the banks of the river Wan.‡

* Ching Tsze says, that Confucius should send Tsze Hwa and that Tsze Hwa should act as the Messenger of Confucius, was proper; and when Yen Tsze asked grain for the mother of Tsze Hwa, Confucius, (not wishing to oppose men directly) offered him a little to shew him, that it was not proper to give any! When he asked more: the sage offered him a little more to teach him, that it was improper to give more. When he did not succeed in obtaining his request, and gave much of his own accord, this was wrong, and the sage blames it. For if Chih had really been in want, Confucius would not have waited till he was requested, but would have assisted him of his own accord. As to Yuen Sze; he was Governor, and had a right to a fixed salary. When he objected to it, as being too much, the sage said that it was what the government had fixed and that it was not at his option to refuse it; adding that if he found it more than he had use for, he ought divide it among the poor in the hamlets, villages, and towns of which he had the oversight. Chang Tsze, says that from these two cases, we may see how the sage employed property.

† Chung Kung's father was a worthless character, but he himself being a good man, the sage used this comparison to shew that, although his father was a bad man, yet he ought to be employed in government service. Yellow was the colour most esteemed by the people of the Chow Dynasty: a yellow calf of a party coloured cow would be an acceptable sacrifice to the gods; although its speckled mother would not.

‡ Ke She, Prime minister of Loo, was a man of revolutionary principles; Min Tsze Keen, was bred in the school, and had imbibed the principles of Confucius, consequently abhorred the idea of serving under such a man: wherefore he not only requested the messenger, to make an excuse to Ke She, but also shewed his decided unwillingness to serve him, by intimating that if he should call him a second time, he would have left the country before another message could reach him.

8. Pih New being sick, Confucius went to see him. From the window the sage took hold of his hand and exclaimed I shall lose him! That this man should have this sickness, is the decree of heaven! *

9. Confucius exclaimed, how virtuous is Hwuy! He has one bamboo of rice, one cup of water, and a mean narrow lane for his habitation: other men could not endure such distress; but it disturbs not the joy of Hwuy; how virtuous is Hwuy!

10. Yen Kew said, it is not that I do not delight in the doctrines of my Master, but my strength is insufficient. Confucius replied, those whose strength is not sufficient go half way and then fail, but you are feigning.

11. Confucius conversing with Tsze Hea said, let yours be the learning of the superior man, not that of the man of low character.

12. When Tsze Yew was governor of the city of Woo; Confucius asked him whether he had any men of worth. He replied I have one Tan Tae Mëë Ming, who in travelling takes not a near cut, nor does he ever come to Yen's house but on public business.

13. Confucius said, Mung Che Fan did not boast of his merits. When the army fled he was in the rear, but as they approached the gate he beat his horse and said it is not that I dared to be in the rear but my horse would not advance. †

* Le (Etiquette) required, that the sick should be placed under the north window of the house, and that when the Prince came to call and ask for the sick person, he should be removed to the south window in order that the Prince might look on him with his face towards the south, The family of Pih New observed this ceremony when Confucius called to ask for him, in order to honor the sage, but he would not presume to accept of such an honor, hence he did not enter the house, but reached his hand in at the window and took hold of the hand of his dying disciple; for he took an eternal farewell of him! Pih New, in point of virtue, was next to Yen and Min, hence the sage was the more sorry at seeing him near death.

† When an army is put to flight, to be in the rear is considered meritorious. Ming Che Fan, when the army of Loo was defeated by the troops of Tse, although he remained in the rear, endeavouring to repel the enemy, yet when the flying troops approached the city, so that all eyes could see him he beat his horse, calling out, that it was not his courage that kept him in the rear, but the laziness, or feebleness of his horse. In this he showed his modesty, and exhibited a pattern of humility which ought to be imitated. ††

---

†† The student ought to reflect that this soldier violated truth in order to manifest his humility. He told a direct falsehood, which is accounted a heavy crime in the sight of the God of truth. His humility ought to be imitated, but his disregard to truth, ought to be abhored,

14. Confucius said, if a man do not possess the insinuating address of Chŭh To, and the beauty of Sung Chaou, he will find it hard to pass in the present age.

15. Confucius said, who can go out but by the door? why will not men walk in the right path!

16. Confucius says, when a man's natural, honest, plainness, exceeds his ornamental accomplishments, he is a mere rustic; on the other hand, when his ornamental accomplishments exceed his natural, honest, plainness, he is a mere scribe (or fop): but when substantial plainness, and polite accomplishments, are properly blended, they form the superior man.

17. Man is born upright, if he swerve from uprightness, and yet avoid death it is mere good fortune. *

18. Confucius said, he who knows right principles, is not equal to him who loves them, nor is he who loves them, equal to him who delights in them. †

19. Confucius said, the higher branches of learning, may be taught to those whose abilities are above mediocrity, but not to those whose talents are below mediocrity.

20. Fan Che asked what constitutes knowledge? Confucius replied, to perform fully the duties due to men, to reverence the Gods,

and Confucius in recommending the one as an example to his disciples, ought to have warned them against imitating the other: but it is but too evident, that the sage himself, had little idea how abominable the sin of lying is in the eyes of the God of truth.

* Man is born with a principle of perfect rectitude, he ought to act agreeably to this divine principle; if he go astray, this principle is lost; and if after this, his life be preserved it is mere chance.

† Chang King Foo says, the thing may be thus illustrated, to know the five kinds of grain, is to know that they may be eaten, to love them, is to eat and relish them; to delight in them, is to eat and be satisfied. To know, and not to love good principles, shews that knowledge is not complete, to love and not delight in them, shews that love is not perfect. ††

---

†† These remarks are perfectly correct, and apply admirably to the doctrines of divine revelation. There is a superficial, speculative knowledge of these principles, which is not productive of love to them, and there is a sort of love, or partial approving of them, which is unaccompained by geninne delight in the truth: but when divine truth is clearly and spiritually understood, it must be loved, and when loved, it must prove a source of the purest and most sublime delight.

and keep at a due distance from them, may be called knowledge. * He then asked what is perfect virtue? Confucius answered, that which is at first difficult, but in course of time is attained, may be called perfect virtue.

21. Confucius says, the intelligent man resembles water, the virtuous man is like a mountain. The man of knowledge moves, the man of virtue is at rest. The man of knowledge rejoices, the man of virtue endures long. †

22. Confucius said, by one revolution Tse might equal Loo, and by one revolution Loo might attain to the government of reason. ‡

23. Confucius said, when a cornered cup loses its corners, shall it still be esteemed a cornered cup? Shall it still be called a cornered cup. ¶

24. Tsae Go asked, saying, if a man of perfect virtue, be told that a person has fallen into a well, must he descend and save him? Confucius replied, why should he! A superior man will do his utmost, but will not throw away his life. He may be imposed upon by what has the appearance of reason, but not by what is plainly unreasonable.

25. Confucius says, be extensively acquainted with literature and maintain what is important with propriety, then you will not oppose reason.

26. Confucius visited Nan Tsze (the Queen of Wei). Tsze Loo was displeased with him. On which the sage called on

* He who acts towards others as he ought, and who does not call in question what cannot be known respecting the Gods, nor treat them with irreverent familiarity, may be said to possess knowledge.

† True knowledge pervades all nature, as water flows wherever it has a tract. Perfect virtue is calm and solid like the mountains. The former produces joy, the latter leads to old age.

‡ Tse and Loo, under the government of Tae Kung and Chow Kung, at the commencement of the Chow Dynasty, were throughly brought under the sway of the principles of the two Kings Wan and Woo, but by the deposition of Wan Kung, Tse lost these principles. Loo still possessed them in some measure ; hence Tse was considered one step farther from the great principles of the ancients than Loo.

¶ These words were uttered, because at that time Princes and Ministers, had merely the name of Office, without any thing of the virtue and talent which the right discharge of Official duties requires. The conclusion is, that as a vessel which loses its corners, is no longer a cornered vessel, so Rulers without talents and virtue are not worthy to be considered Rulers.

heaven, saying, "if I have done wrong may heaven reject me! may heaven cut me off!"*

27. Confucius said, the due medium is virtue. This is the highest attainment; for a long time few of the people have reached it.

Tsze Kung said, suppose a man were to manifest general benevolence to the people, and promote the happiness of all men, what would you say of him? Might he be called perfectly virtuous? Confucius replied, why only virtuous? He must be a sage: even Yaou snd Shun seemed to come short of this. †

The virtuous man wishes to be established himself, and to establish others—he wishes to possess perfect intelligence himself, and lead others to perfect knowledge. To be capable of measuring the hearts of others by our own, mav be called the mould of virtue.

CHAP. VII.

1. Confucius said, I compile, and transmit to posterity, but write not any thing new. I believe and love the ancients, taking Laou Pang for my pattern. ‡

2. Confucius said, to meditate on what one has learned—to learn without satiety, and teach without being wearied; how can I attain to these!

* Nan Tsze was the wife of Ling Kung, Prince of Wei; and a woman of infamous character. Confucius having gone to Wei she desired an interview. At first he refused, but could not avoid visiting her. His disciple Tsze Loo, considered that his master had disgraced himself, by visiting a woman of such bad repute. The sage, in order to convince him, that he had done nothing improper, called on heaven to abandon him, if he had acted unworthy of his character, And indeed what could there be improper in the sage, whose virtue was absolutely perfect, seeing a person of bad character.

† This does not mean that these famous Monarchs, had not a disposition to treat all their people with the utmost kindness, and to make all men feel the happy effects of their benevolence; it only shews the difficulty of manifesting such favor, which arose from their paucity of means, and the narrow limits of their empire.

‡ Confucius said, those who compose original works, are sages. I only revise and transmit to future ages the doctrines of the former Kings, and do not write any original compositions. For the ancients have discussed all the principles of heaven and earth. In them there is an inexhaustible mine of admirable truths, I firmly believe them, without the least doubt, and because I sincerely delight in them, I never feel any satiety in the study of them; nor is this my opinion alone, for Laou Pang of the Shang Dynasty, likewise believed, loved and handed down the doctrines of the ancients.

3 Confucius said, I am grieved that virtue is not cultivated, that learning is not investigated, that when the principles of rectitude are heard, men do not advance in the practice of them, and that the vicious do not repent.

4. When the sage sat at leisure, his manner was easy, thus, and his countenance benign, thus.

5. Confucius sighed and said, how much I am decayed! For a long time I have had no dreams of Chow Kung.

6. Confucius said, let the inclination be fixed on the path of duty, hold fast goodness, accord with perfect virtue, delight in the arts, (or rather when you have leisure amuse yourself with the arts.) *

7. Confucius said, when a person comes and offers the usual presents, as an introduction, I always endeavour to instruct him. †

8. Confucius said, he who does not exert his mind, I do not explain matters to him; he who does not exert his mouth, I do not assist him to express himself. When I help a man round one corner, if he does not get round the other three, I do not again assist him.

9. When Confucius sat near one who was mourning, he could not eat a sufficient quantity. On the day in which he condoled with any one, he did not sing.

10. Confucius conversing with Yen Yuen, said, it is only you and I who, when the government wish to employ us, go into office, and when they dismiss us, retire into obscurity. ‡ Tsze Loo said, if you go out with a large army whom will you take

Confucius abridged and revised the She and Shoo King, fixed the rites and music, perfected the Yih King, and compiled the Chun Tsew. In all these works he only transmitted the doctrines of the former Kings, and did not publish any thing new. But although, his work was only that of a compiler, his merit was double that of the original authors.

* These are ceremonies, music, Archery, Horsemanship, Writing and Arithmetic.

† The presents here mentioned, are a few pieces of dried flesh. The sage meant that those who themselves come and in the proper manner ask for instruction, although their presents be of little value, yet they shew their sincerity, and that he would do his utmost to instruct such, but that he would not go and offer his instruction to those who did not come to him.

‡ The sage neither coveted an official situation, nor had he any predilection for the life of a recluse. If he could act on his own principles, he went into Office, when called to it; when he found that he could not act on these principles, he retired. Yen Yuen had imbibed the spirit of his Master, hence the high encomium of the sage.

along with you. Confucius replied, a man who without cause, would rashly engage a tiger, or wade a river and endanger his life without remorse, is one with whom I would not go out. I want one who is cautious in the management of affairs—who plans well, and then carries his schemes into effect.

11. Confucius said, if it were proper to seek riches, although I should become a groom to obtain them, I would do it; but as it is improper to seek them, I will rest in that which I love.

12. Confucius was very careful in worshipping the gods, in reference to war, and to sickness.

13. Confucius being in Tse, heard the music of Shun, and for the space of three months, knew not the taste of flesh. He said, I had no idea that music, at its best, had arrived at this pitch.

14. Yen Yew said, will our master assist the Prince of Wei? Tsze Kung replied, I will ask him; on which he entered and said, what sort of men were Pih E, and Shŭh Tse. (Confucius) replied, they were virtuous men of old. Were they dissatisfied? Ans. they sought virtue and obtained it, why should they have been dissatisfied? When he came out, he said, our Master will not assist the Prince (or he does not approve of his conduct.)*

15. Confucius says, coarse rice for food, water for drink, and one's bended arm for a pillow, even in the midst of these,

* Ling Kung, Prince of Wei, banished his eldest son, Kwae Kwei. When the Prince died, the people placed Che, son of Kwae Kwei, on the throne. The people of Tsin received Kwae Kwei but his son Che opposed him. When Confucius was residing in Wei, the people considered that Kwae Kwei had disobeyed his father, and that it was proper that Che his son should ascend the throne: hence Yen Yew doubted whether Confucius would approve of such a measure, and asked the opinion of Tsze Kung: the latter did not ask directly about the Prince of Wei's conduct, but about Pih E, and Shuh Tse. These two young men were the sons of the Prince of Koo Chih. When their father was near death he left an order that Shuh Tse (the youngest) should inherit the throne. But on the death of his father, Shuh Tse yielded the throne to Pih E: Pih E said, My Father has commanded that My Brother should reign: and forthwith absconded, Shuh Tse also refused the throne, and left the country. When Woo Wang went to conquer Chow, these two brothers reproved him, and when Woo Wang destroyed the Shang Dynasty, they felt ashamed to receive salary from the house of Chow; and hence concealed themselves in the Yang mountain, where they died of hunger. Pih E honored his father's commands, and Shuh Tse the divine institution: both acted according to divine reason, and therefore had no occasion to repent. When Tsze Kung had heard the sage's opinion of their conduct, he knew that he did not approve of the conduct of Che towards his father.

there is happiness: but riches and honors, gained by injustice are to me light as the fleeting cloud. *

16. Confucius said, were my age increased fifty years, till death I would study the Yih King, and would thus avoid great errors. †

17. The subjects on which Confucius daily spoke, were the She and Shoo King and the Le Ke. These he constantly spoke of.

18. Yih Kung asked, respecting the conduct of Confucius at Tsze Loo. Tsze Loo made no reply. Confucius said, why did you not say, that he is a man who in his zeal to obtain knowledge, forgets to eat, and in his joy on having obtained it, forgets the anxiety it cost him, and that he is insensible of the approach of old age: you might have answered him thus.

19. Confucius said, I was not born with knowledge. I love the ancients and study them with diligence that I may obtain knowledge.

20. Confucius did not speak of extraordinary feats of strength nor of rebellion, nor of the gods. ‡

21. Confucius said, if there are three of us walking on the way, the two besides me, would be my teachers. I would select the

* Ching Tsze says it is not that the good man rejoices in such things as coarse food, and water for drink, but such things cannot alter his joy. * *

† Some are of opinion that the sense has been altered and that it, ought to be read " were my life lengthened for some time I would till death study the Yih King." The sage at the time he uttered these words was seventy years old, and his mind was most completely under the influence of the admirable doctrines of the Yih King; but this remark was made to convince men of the vast importance of studying that work, and to stimulate them to the utmost exertion.

* * Mere heathen philosophy has in all ages, and in all countries taught men, that happiness is found not in riches and honors, but in virtue. But the hopes and prospects, as well as the principles and practice of the genuine christian, being far more pure and elevated, than that of the most eminent heathen sages, his happiness in the midst of poverty and affliction must of necessity be far more solid and satisfactory. The one can look forward with humble confidence to a glorious immortality, while to the other the future is enveloped in a gloomy uncertaintity.

‡ Thus it appears by the confession of the sage's own disciples, that his doctrines were confined to the concerns of this transitory life, and left man to grope in midnight darkness, as to the awfully momentous concerns of eternity. If there be a Supreme Ruler, it is of the utmost importance, that we the subjects of his government, be acquainted with his character and laws. Without this knowledge how shall we know, how to honor and serve him, or by what method shall we discover how we may regain his favour, which by disobedience to his will, we have lost. A knowledge of these infinitely important points, must be essentially necessary to the happiness of man, but in vain do we search the writings of Confucius, or of any other Chinese sage for the slightest hint on the subject. Let us then turn from these to that book where we find " life and immortality brought clearly to light."

good, and imitate him, I would look at the bad and avoid his ways.

22. Confucius said, heaven produced virtue in me, what can Kwan Tuy do to me!

23. Confucius said, you my disciples suppose that, I have some myterious doctrines, which I conceal from you. I have no secrets; whatever I do, all is laid open to your view: this is the manner of Mow.

24. Confucius taught four things, literature, virtuous practice, faithfulness, and sincerity.

25. Confucius said, a sage I cannot see, but could I see a man of eminent virtue it would satisfy me. I cannot see a man of genuine virtue, but could I see a single hearted, stedfast man it would be a consolation. *

Without it, and yet pretending to have it—empty, and yet pretending to be full—possessing little, yet boasting of great things; how difficult to find constancy among such people!

26. Confucius angled, but used not a net—shot birds, but not when perched. †

27. A Confucius said, to act without knowing on what principle, is what I never do. I hear much, select what is good, and practice it—see much and remember what is seen: this is the next step to knowledge.

28. It was difficult to talk to the people of Hoo Heang (i. e. it was difficult to instruct them). A boy from thence havingwaited on Confucius, the disciples doubted the propriety of admit-

* "Sage" is the epithet given to a holy man, who possess divine and unfathomable knowledge. "Keun Taze" is the name given to those whose talents and virtues are of a superior cast "Virtuous" is the denomination of those whose minds are wholly bent towards virtue and not at all to vice. The "Stedfast" are those who are not double minded. Chang King Foo says a sage and superior man receive their designation from their learning, while the virtuous and stedfast are so named from their unadorned sincerity. I (says Choo Foo Tsze) consider, that there is a great difference between the height of the sage and the lowness of the stedfast, yet the latter may arrive at the perfection of the former.

† Confucius when young was poor, and was often obliged to fish, and hunt in order, to obtain a livelihood, but he did not intentionally kill all, but gave both fish and birds an opportunity of escaping for their life. From this may be seen the real disposition of the virtuous man's heart. Since be treated animals thus, we may see how he would treat men. Since in small matters he acted thus, we may judge how he acted in matters of great importance.

ting him. On which the sage said, when a man purifies himself in order to enter (the school) I commend his having purified himself, and forget his past conduct,—praise his having thus come forward, and do not commend (or guarantee) his future conduct; why are you so extremely strict?

29. Confucius exclaimed, is virtue far off! I only wish for virtue, and virtue comes.*

30. The Judge of Chin asked whether Chaou King (Prince of Loo) understood propriety? Confucius replied, that he did know propriety. The sage having gone out (the Judge) introduced Woo Ma Ke and said, I have heard that the superior man did not connive at men's faults; but I see the superior man does connive: for the Prince married a lady of the Woo Family, who are of the same family name with himself, and has changed her name to Woo Mung Tsze; if then the Prince knows propriety, who does not? Woo Ma Ke informed Confucius of these remarks; upon which the sage replied, Mow is a fortunate man, when he errs, men are sure to know it.†

31. When Confucius met with any one who sung well, he caused him to sing the same piece a second time, and then joined with him.

32. Confucius said, in learning I am equal to others; but I cannot by any means exhibit the man of superior virtue in my conduct.

33. Confucius said, how dare I presume to consider myself equal to a sage, or to a man of perfect virtue! All that can be said of me, is that I practice their doctrines without satiety, and teach them to others without weariness. Kung Se Kwa replied, even this we students cannot learn.

* Chin Tsze says the practice of virtne originates in one's self: only wish for it, and it comes, why consider it to be far off!

† Chaou Kung was well acquainted with the rules of propriety, hence, although contrary to propriety, he married a lady of the same family name, Confucius looking at his general conduct might justly say that he knew what was proper, when the affair of his irregular marriage was distinctly mentioned to him, his humility induced him to confess that he had erred. This unwillingness to point out the faults of his Prince and readiness to confess his own, exhibits a pattern to all future ages.

34. Confucius being very sick, Tsze Loo begged him to pray. Confucius said, is it right that I should? Tsze Loo replied, it is; the Lay says "Pray to the celestial and terrestrial gods." Confucius rejoined, Mow has prayed long!*

35. Confucius says, extravagance leads to disobedience, and parsimony to meanness. Meanness is better than disobedience.

36. Confucius says, the superior man is composed and easy, the mean man always appears anxious and restless.

37. Confucius was mild, yet firm—majestic, but not harsh, grave, yet pleasant.

CHAP. VIII.

---

1. Confucius said, the virtue of Tae Pih, may be said to be, of the highest order. He resolutely refused the Empire, and yet the people saw nothing for which to applaud him. †

2. Confucius says, to be respectful without knowing etiquette, is irksome—seriousness without a knowledge of propriety, degenerates into excessive timidity—courage without propriety, leads to insubordination, and uprightness where propriety is wanting, induces confused haste.

If superiors treat their Parents and elder relatives properly, then the people will advance in virtue. If they do not forget their old friends and servants, they people will not act rudely.

* The gods to whom Tsze Loo exhorted the sage to pray, were heaven and earth. When a man offends these deities, he ought to repent of his sin, pray for pardon, and amend his conduct: but the sage had no sins to repent of: his conduct perfectly accorded with the mind of the gods; why then should he pray to them! **

† Tae Pih was the eldest son of Tae Wang, the grand-father of the famous Wan Wang. Tae Wang seeing that the royal family of the Shang Dynasty, had degenerated, wished to dethrone the reigning prince, by which means his son Tae Pih might have been raised to the Imperial throne. The latter, however, resolutely refused to assist his father in such a project, deeming it improper to rebel against one's lawful sovereign; hence in order to avoid all concern in this affair, he absconded, and took up his residence among barbarians, on which account the people had not an opportunity of seeing the exhibition of his exalted virtue.

** This language betrays the grossest ignorance of the divine character, and of the human heart. The natural consequence of such ignorance, is that ineffable pride which such assertions as this exhibits. He who knew what is in man says, "There is none righteous, no not one" "Shall man be pure before his maker." Reader look into your own bosom, and say whether it does not contain the most conclusive evidence, that these are the words of truth and soberness.

3. Tsang Tsze being sick (near death), called his disciples, and addressed them thus: "Uncover my feet, uncover my hands." The Poet says "Be cautious, and tremble as if on the brink of an abyss, or as if treading upon the ice." Now and ever after, I know that I shall escape. Little children (think on this). *

4. Tsang Tsze being sick, Mung King went to see him. Tsang Tsze said, when a bird is near death, its notes are mournful; when a man is about to die, his words are virtuous. There are three things to which the superior man pays great attention. He takes care that his demeanour be far removed from harshness and negligence: his countenance is a true index of his heart; (rather "his countenance is properly regulated,") this is near to sincerity: his words are duly tempered; this is far from lowness, or opposition. The vessels of sacrifice have their keepers. †

5. Tsang Tsze said, to possess ability, and yet to ask of those who do not; to know much, and yet to inquire of them that know little; to possess, and yet appear not to possess; to be full, and yet appear empty; I once had a friend who acted thus. ‡

6. Tsang Tsze says, may the man to whom you can commit a young orphan (heir to the throne), and the government of a country of an hundred Le, and who in times of great emergency maintains inviolable fidelity, be called a man of superior virtue? He is truly a man of superior virtue.

* The idea of Tsang Tsze in wishing his disciples to look at his hands and feet, was to shew them, that from a principle of filial piety he had most carefully preserved his body whole and entire, as he received it from his parents. The quotation from the Poet shews what constant care and caution are necessary in order to the right performance of this all important duty. *

† To adorn the person with virtue is the foundation of good government; as to vessels of sacrifice and such like things, they must be attended to, but the superior man does not consider them of much importance.

‡ Woo She was of opinion, that this friend whom Tsang Tsze eulogizes, was the famous Yen Yuen, the favorite disciple of Confucius.

---

* * The Chinese consider every inattention to one's person and conduct a breach of filial piety, on the principle, that our bodies are bequeathed us by our parents, so that a want of proper care to our person, and actions, shews contempt of the donors. Thus every virtue is resolved into filial piety, of which every vice is considered a breach. This is good as far as it goes, but reason requires, that the principle should be acted upon in reference to the great author of soul and body.

7. Tsang Tsze says, a scholar should be a man of an enlarged, liberal, and unbending mind, that he may sustain the weight of his office, and finish his distant course. To be perfectly virtuous, is his duty, and is not this a weighty concern? To stop only at death, is not this a long course?

8. Confucius says, be aroused to an early attention to the poets—be established by the study of the Le (manners and customs, or the rules of propriety) finish the whole by the study of music. *

9. Confucius said, you may cause the people to practice what is proper, but you cannot make them understand the grounds of their duty. †

10. Confucius says, that a man fond of valour, when vehemently pressed by poverty, will rise in rebellion: and if you shew an immoderate degree of hatred towards a bad man, you will drive him to rebellion.

11. Confucius says, suppose a man possess the elegant talents of Chow Kung; yet if he be proud and parsimonious, his other qualities are not worth looking at.

12. Confucius says, it is not easy to find one who will study three years, without having his mind inclined towards the emoluments of office.

13. Confucius says, he who believes firmly, delights in study and holds fast even till death; finishes his duty well.

* The frequent recitation of the poets, excites the minds of youth to the love of virtue, and the abhorrence of vice; hence an early attention should be paid to this branch of study:—the study of the Le Ke (a work on the rules of politeness, and propriety among the ancients) will establish the young mind in the principles of virtue and decorum; and an acquaintance with music, excites all the finer feelings of the soul, and gives the last polish to a man of education: Hence the man who makes himself perfectly acquainted with these branches of learning, is an accomplished scholar. * *

† Although the people may be led on to the practice of the incumbent duties of life, yet the reasons and natural fitness of these duties, lying deep in the will of heaven, and nature of man, can be discovered only by long and severe study: for which reason the common people cannot be brought to comprehend them. † †

---

* * To this opinion, men of science and literature in the present day, will not subscribe. No man can justly be termed an accomplished scholar, who has not made himself well acquainted, with the works and revealed will of the Great Creator, and Supreme Governor of the Universe:—of the former the most eminent Chinese sages knew little, and of the latter nothing at all, to purpose.

† † Divine revelation, has made it an easy task, even for the uneducated, common people, to know their duty and likewise to comprehend the reasons on which it is grounded.

A country on the brink of danger, enter not—a country thrown into disorder, dwell not in it. When the Empire is under the government of reason, go into office, when it loses reason, retire. If a Province be governed by reason, poverty and meanness are a disgrace—if it is not, riches and honor are disgraceful.

14. Confucius says, if you hold not an official situation, interfere not with politics.

15. Confucius exclaimed, how charmingly did Cho commence his performance of the Kwan Tseu! *

16. Confucius says, forward and not upright, stupid and not attentive, empty and not faithful, I acknowledge not such men.

17. Confucius says, study as if you could never reach it, as if you felt afraid that you should lose it.

18. Confucius exclaimed, how great and majestic the government of Shun and Yu! yet to themselves it appeared as nothing.

19. How great, exclaimed Confucius, was the regal conduct of Yaou! Vast and extensive,—equalled only by heaven! †

It was only the virtue of Yaou that was thus vast, and thus high, the people could find no name for it. How vast his merits! How brilliant the laws and rites which he established!

* Che was at that time master of music in the Loo country. The Kwan Tseu, is a national air. Confucius had returned foom Wei to Loo, with the intention of regulating the music of his native Province. Che had just been appointed to the Office of Master Muscian, and the sage on first hearing his performance of the Kwan Tseu, was highly delighted with his abilities, and praised him in this manner.**

---

† That the Chieftain Yaou loved his country, and established laws and Institutions which he sincerely wished might promote the happiness of its inhabitants, there is little reason to doubt; but what foundation does, even Chinese History, lay for such extravagant, unmeaning, nay blasphemous, eulogiums as this! If by heaven, the sage means the supreme ruler of the universe, in what respect could the man Yaou equal heaven! The dominion of heaven (i. e. of the Supreme Being) extends to innumerable worlds; the government of Yaou, reached only to a very small spot of this solitary Globe—the beings rendered everlastingly, and perfectly happy by the laws and despensations of Heaven, neither man nor Angel can number—those who reaped a partial and temporary benefit, from the institutions of Yaou, were at most but a few millions. But why spend time in contrasting the merits of a creature of the dust, with the infinite Glory of the Great Eternal! Alas for the ignorance of God and man which dictated such empty eulogiums, as that under consideration! Alas for the blindness that continues to extol them, while it never thinks of inquiring into their absurdity O! that man would learn to know God and himself, then would such assertions as this fill him with horror.

20. Shun had five ministers, and the Empire was well governed.

King Woo said, I have ten ministers, who are able statesmen. Confucius said, is it not true, that it is difficult to obtain men of real worth? In the space between the time of Yaou and Shun till the time of Woo Wang, the most hat could be obtained (at one time) were nine men, and one woman *

Two thirds of the Empire, came over to him (King Wăn); with these he served the Shang family: the virtue of Chow (Wan Wang) may be said to have been of the highest order. †

21. Confucius said, I see no flaw (crevice) in the character of Yu. His food was coarse, but his sacrifices in the hall of ancestors, full and rich—his common apparel was mean, but his sacrificial robes, and cap were finely adorned—he lived in a mean palace, but exhausted his strength, in making ditches and water courses (for the good of the people). I see no defect in Yu. ‡

* The scope of this passage is to shew how difficult it is to procure men of sterling talent and virtue. It was an ancient saying, that "Talents are difficult to find." Confucius says, that the Emperor Shun obtained only five men of worth, and ability, and the most that Woo Wang could obtain, were nine. The Hea and Shang Dynasty intervened between these two princes, and although those two families held the throne for the space of nearly 1100 years, yet they never, at any period of their reign, obtained ten or even nine men of real virtue, and talents; does not this prove the ancient saying true, viz. that "Talents are difficult to find."

† Wan Wang governed a small Province during the latter end of the Shang Dynasty. Such was his virtue and merit, when contrasted with the vice and outrageous tyranny of the infamous Chow, then Emperor, that two thirds of the Empire wished to rebel, and place Wan Wang on the throne; he however continued faithful to the House of Shang; not deeming it right to dethrone the Emperor, unless the whole body of the people had been unanimous in such a measure.

‡ Yu, the successor of Shun, is said to have been employed by that Emperor to drain the Empire after the deluge, so as to carry off the overplus of water. Such was his zeal in this highly meritorious work, that during the eight years in which he attended to it, although he passed his own door three times, he did not enter. ‡‡

---

‡‡ Some are of opinion—that the flood here referred to, which took place according to Chinese Chronology about 2200 years before Christ, is the same as that recorded by Moses, and that Noah and Yu are one and the same person. The student who is acquainted with Chinese and old Testament History, will find some points of resemblance between the Chinese flood, and that recorded in the sacred volume, and likewise between Noah and Yu; but whether there be sufficient grounds to identify those persons and events, we shall not take upon us to decide.

CHAP. IX.

---

1. Confucius seldom talked of gain, fate, or perfect virtue. *

2. A person belonging to the village of Tă Hang exclaimed, how vast and extensive the learning of Confucius! Alas that he has not done any thing to complete his fame! Confucius hearing of this, said to his disciples, what shall I bend my attention to, shall I become a charioteer, or an archer? I will become a charioteer.

3. Confucius said, to wear a cap made of fine linen, accords with etiquette; at present, one made of silk is worn; because more economical: in this I will follow the multitude. Etiquette requires that obeisance should be done to the Prince below stairs; at present people ascend the hall and then bow: this is pride, I will follow the custom of bowing below, although I should differ from all. †

4. Confucius was perfectly void of four things; he had no selfishness—no prejudice—no bigotry—no egotism.

5. Confucius being alarmed when in Kwang, said, that

* Although the sage explained every subject, yet he seldom conversed much on these three things, wishing his pupils to follow justice, and not scheme about gain, to adorn themselves with virtue, and not vex themselves about fate, and to practice the virtues of which they were capable, and not think of leaping at once to the summit of excellence.

† Confucius said, that in reference to the materials of a cap, or such things, although they may not be made of the same cloth as ancient custom requires, yet there is nothing in this contrary to justice. I will therefore imitate the many in such cases; but as to bowing above stairs, instead of doing it below, according to ancient usage, since it springs from pride and disrespect, which ought to be crushed, I will in such cases dare to be singular in following the ancient and proper mode. ††

---

†† This was acting the part of an upright man. Our first object ought to be to discover what reason and religion point out as the path of duty; and having once found this celestial path, we ought not for a moment to hesitate about walking in it, although we may walk alone, and by our singularity provoke the foolish jeers of a deluded world. This is the only way to find present peace of mind, and to secure everlasting felicity.

since Wăn Wang is now no more, does not the regulation of the laws and ceremonies depend on me? If heaven had wished to put an end to this order of things, then the successor of the dead, would not have been disposed to hand down this regulation of manners and laws, and since heaven does not wish to put an end to this regulation, what can the men of Kwang do to me! *

6. A great Officer of state once asked Tsze Kung saying, is not your Master a sage? Has he not numerous accomplishments? Tsze Kung replied, certainly heaven has granted him unbounded talents and virtue and may make him a sage; he likewise possesses many accomplishments. Confucius hearing of this, said, does this Mandarin know me? When I was young, I was in low circumstances, hence learned many of the arts, but these things are of little value. Do many such accomplishments make a superior man? No; Laou said, Confucius was wont to say, "I was not employed by government, hence attended to the arts." †

7. Confucius said, do I really possess knowledge! I have no knowledge; but if an ignorant person make inquiries, although he appear perfectly empty, I shew him all the bearings and fully explain the sense of his questions.

* Yang Hoo having acted a tyrannical part in Kwang, and the appearance of the sage bearing a strong resemblance to his; the people, through mistake, surrounded him, as if about to do violence to him, but although the sage was a little startled at such a procedure, he said to his followers, that heaven had put it into his heart to revise, and hand down to posterity, the excellent laws and rites of Wan Wang, and that since this famous Prince had been long dead (about 430 years) and heaven had raised him up to adorn and transmit his laws, the men of Kwang were not able to oppose heaven and injure him. **

† This Mandarin deemed the numerous accomplishments of Confucius a proof of his sageship. Tsze Kung considered that the virtue and abilities which heaven had granted him without measure, were what constituted him a sage, and that his knowledge of the arts were to be viewed, rather as appendages than essential elements of his sage-ship. But although he believed him to be in reality a sage, he did not decidedly affirm so, but modestly insinuated, that he was on the point of becoming one. Confucius as modestly denied that any importance ought to be attached to the arts of angling, archery, horseman-ship, and such like things, which he learned in youth, only because he was not employed by the public, remarking that a knowledge of a number of such things, is not essential to the character of a superior man.

** It appears from these remarks of Confucius, that he thought himself the only person capable of transmitting to posterity a knowledge of what he considered the principles which are essential to the happiness of man. Mung Tsze, who lived more than 100 years after Confucius, and who ranks next to him in the estimation of his countrymen, expresses a similar opinion respecting himself.

8. Confucius exclaimed the Fung bird comes not, the rivers send not forth the Too, it is all over with me! *

9. When Confucius saw one in a mourning habit, or wearing the cap and robes of office, or blind, although younger than himself (when sitting), he rose; if he passed the person (sitting) he walked fast.

10. Yen Yuen in admiration (of the sage's way, "Taou") exclaimed, when I look up to it, how high! When I attempt to penetrate it how firm! When I view it as before me, suddenly it appears behind me. My master led me gradually on, expanded my mind by learning and bound me by the knowledge of propriety. When I wish to stop I cannot: when I have exhausted my abilities it (the doctrine of the sage) as it were stands fixed, although I wish to reach it I have no means of doing so.

11. Confucius being very sick, Tsze Loo sent a disciple as his minister. When the sickness abated a little, Confucius exclaimed, how long will you continue to err Yew! Not to have a minister and yet be attended by one, whom do I insult by this? I insult heaven! Rather than have died in the hands of this minister, I would have preferred dying in the hands of my disciples: although I should not have obtained a great funeral; should I have died on the high way! †

12. Tsze Kung said, suppose I had a handsome jewel, ought I to keep it concealed in a case, or should I ask a good price for it and sell it? Confucius replied, sell it, sell it; but I would wait till I got its value. ‡

* In the time of Shun, the Fung Lin bird made its appearance, and in the time of Wan Wang its notes were heard on the Ke mountain, and in the days of Fuh He (the inventor of the characters) an animal appeared in the river having the body of a horse and the head of a dragon, with a map on its back: these were felicitous omens and the precursors of good Princes and a benevolent government. Their non-appearance in the days of the sage, led him to despair of being the renovator of his degenerate country.

† Confucius was at that time out of office, and had no right to such an official servant. A great burial means such as a Prince or Minister of state should have.

‡ Tsze Kung, by this comparison, referred to his master, who although possessed of talents and virtue, was not in Office. Confucius signified by his reply, that he really desired to serve his country, but that he would not ask for an Official situation.

13. Confucius expressed a wish to reside in Kew E (among the eastern barbarians). Some one said, what a wretched situation! Confucius replied, where the superior man dwells how can there be wretchedness. *

14. Confucius said, when I returned from Wei to Loo, I corrected the music, so that each of the notes and tones obtained its proper place. †

15. Confucius says, when you go out, serve your Prince and his Ministers, when at home, serve your father and elder brother. In funeral and sacrificial rites, do not dare not to do your utmost. In drinking do not indulge so far as to confuse your mind; how can I lay claim to such conduct!

16. Confucius being on a river, exclaimed, this rolls on, night and day, it stops not! ‡

17. Confucius said, I have not seen any one who loves virtue as we love beauty.

18. Confucius said, if in raising a mound, I stop when it wants one basket more to finish it, my stopping depends on myself, and if there be but the contents of one basket laid on the level ground, yet if I advance, this going forward likewise depends on myself.

19. Confucius said, he who never flags, under my instructions, is Hwuy.

20. Confucius speaking of Hwuy; said alas! I saw him advance, bnt never did I see him stop.

21. Confucius says, the blade my spring, and yet produce no blossom, the blossom may appear, and may never give the ripe grain.

* This wish of the sage arose from a conviction that to the end of his life, his principles would not be embraced, and is of the same kind with his desire to cross the sea on a raft. By this reply he meant, that wherever the superior man lives, he renovates the manners of those among whom he resides.

† In the winter of the 11th. year of Gae Kung, Confucius returned from Wei to Loo (his native Province). At that time, the rites of Chow were observed in Loo, but poetry and music were in rather a mangled state, having lost their due regulation. Confucius had been travelling to all parts of the Empire making inquiries on the subject, and collecting what information he could obtain, and seeing that his principles were not likely to be embraced during his life, he returned to his own Province to correct its music.

‡ The moral which the sage wished to be derived from this, was that as the revolutions of nature are unceasing, so should the student be in his application to learning.

22. Confucius says, a young student may be worthy of veneration. Who knows but his knowledge may yet equal mine? But if a man arrive at forty, or fifty, without having acquired knowledge, he can never be worthy of veneration.

23. Confucius says, straight forward language, (or reproof) will not men assent to it? But it is reformation which is valuable Insinuating words, will not men be pleased with them? But to investigate the source of the evil is the grand point? What can I do with those who are pleased and do not probe the root of the evil—who assent and do not reform? *

24. Confucius says, the general of a large army, may be seized, but the will of a common man cannot be forced.

25. Confucius says, Yew is the man who in mean apparel, and tattered garments, can sit with those who wear furred robes, without feeling ashamed. Neither hurtful, nor covetous, how can he practice vice.

Tsze Loo (i. e. Yew) constantly recited these words, on which Confucius observed, how is this sufficient to be considered virtue. †

26. Confucius says, when the cold season arrives, then you will know the Sung and Pih trees (perhaps the Pine and cypress) by their durable foliage.

27. Confucius says, the truly intelligent have no doubts—the truly virtuous, no sorrow—and the truly brave, no fear.

28. Confucius says, a man may apply to learning, and yet not hit on right principles, he may hit on right principles, and yet not become established in them, he may be established in them, and yet not be capable of weighing things aright.

* Straight forward, faithful language, is what men fear, hence they must assent to it. Insinuating words, do not take occasion of men's faults, hence they must give pleasure. But the consent which is not followed by reformation, is merely a temporary and external thing, and the pleasure that does not send one to examine his conduct to the bottom, shews that the person is incapable of perceiving where the hidden idea lies.

† Tsze Loo by constantly repeating the terms in which the sage had praised him, shewed that he was delighted with himself, and made no farther effort to advance in the path of virtue. Therefore the sage again referred to this in order to arouse him.

29. "The Tang Te flower waves from side to side, and do not I think on you, but your abode is distant." Confucius says, men do not think of it (virtue). How is it distant! *

CHAP. X.

1. Confucius in his native village was sincere and respectful, and appeared as if unable to speak. †

In the Temple of Ancestors, and in the Court, he conversed minutely about every thing, but with respectful caution. ‡

2. In the Court, he talked to the inferior Officers with straight forward fidelity, and to the superior Officers he talked with pleasing frankness. When the sovereign was present, he shewed a respectful and dignified demeanour.

3. When sent by his Prince to receive a guest, his countenance suddenly changed, thus, and he walked with a short and quick step, thus; in bowing to them (i. e. surrounding officers), he moved his hands left and right, but his robes hung straight, both before and behind. ¶ He entered again with quick step, and his hands stretched like the two wings of a bird. When the guest retired he reported to the Prince, saying "the guest is out of sight,"

* This is a quotation from an ancient ode; the former two clauses have no meaning and are quoted, merely, to introduce the latter two.

† Yang She says, Confucius daily practised the principles which he taught, and never departed from them. Consequently his disciples minutely observed and recollected his every motion, and most trifling action. His native village, was the residence of his parents, elder brothers and kindred, hence his humble retiring deportment while there.

‡ The Ancestorial Temple, is the depository of the rules respecting rites and ceremonies. The Court is the place from which the national laws issue, hence what belongs to these ought to be minutely inquired into,

¶ When bowing to those on his left, he moved his hands to the left, when bowing to those on his right, he moved his hands to the right, but stood so as to keep his robes straight.

4. When he entered the Palace door, he crouched down in this manner, as if the door could not admit him. He stood not in the middle of the door, nor did he walk on the threshold. * In passing the (empty) seat of the Prince, his colour changed, thus: he walked, with short and hasty step thus; and in speaking he appeared unable to express himself. Holding up his robes he ascended the hall, bending his body, thus, and repressing his breath as if he did not breathe. When he went out and descended one step, he relaxed his countenance a little, assuming a mild and pleasing deportment; when he reached the foot of the stair, he expanded his arms like a bird's wings, thus. On returning to his seat, he put on a serious, grave countenance, thus.

5. When receiving the seal of office he bent his body as if unable to bear it; holding it as high as the hands are raised in making a bow, and as low as if delivering any thing—his countenance wearing the appearance of fear and lifting his feet with short and cautious step, as if intangled. In presenting the public presents his countenance was mild and placid—in presenting private presents, still more pleasant.

6. The superior man (Confucius) did not wear clothes with a deep green, or crimson collar. He did not wear clothes of a reddish, or brownish colour, as his common apparel. In hot weather he wore a robe of fine, or coarse linen as an upper garment. Black clothes he lined with the skin of a (black) lamb; white robes with the skin of the deer—yellow with that of the fox.

Common clothes he wore long with the right sleeve short. His night gown was one length and a half of his body. At home he wore thick warm clothes made of the hair of Hoo Hŏ (a kind of fox). When he put off his mourning robes he failed not to wear all the customary ornaments. Unless a we Shang (an under garment) he had his lower garments plaited. With lamb-skin robes and sombre coloured cap he did not go to condole. On the first of the month, he always put on his court robes and waited on the Prince.

* The middle of the door ("or rather the middle door") was that by which the Prince went out and came in.

7. When he fasted he dressed himself in clean clothes,—changed his food and his sitting place.

8. He did not dislike delicate food, nor had he any objection to meat cut very small. Rice too hot, or with a bad flavor—stinking fish and spoiled meat, or changed in flavor, discoloured flesh, or what had a bad flavour he did not eat. Food over done, or out of season, he did not eat. Whatever was not properly cut he did not eat, nor did he eat any thing without its proper sauce. Although there were abundance of flesh, he did not take an undue proportion of it: although he had no fixed standard as to the quantity of wine he drunk, he never took so much as to injure his mind. Wine bought in the market he did not drink—dried meat which was bought he did not eat. He never omitted taking ginger to his food. He never eat too much. When assisting at the public sacrifices, he kept not the flesh, which he received, through the night. The flesh used in his family sacrifices, he gave not away after being kept three days: if given away after three days it would not be eatable. When eating he did not give his opinion, when reposing he proposed not any subject of conversation. Although it were coarse food, vegetables or soup, he first poured out a little as a libation: this he did with solemn reverence.

9. If the mat was not laid straight, he sat not down.

10. When the men of the village who used staves left a convivial party, he also left. When the villagers brought the No * he put on his court robes, and stood out side his door to receive it.

11. When he sent a messenger to inquire for a friend in another Province, he bowed twice and accompanied him a short way. Kang Tsze having sent some medicine to him, he bowed and received it, but said Mow is not acquainted with it, and dares not eat it. His stable being burnt down; when he returned from Court, he asked whether the people were injured, but did not enquire about the horses.

* A sort of exhibition by which they expelled dæmons, or diseases occasioned by dæmons.

12. When the Prince sent him food he first had it placed properly on the table, and then tasted it. When the Prince presented him with raw flesh, he had it dressed and then offered it to his deceased ancestors. If the Prince gave him a living animal, he fed it. When with his Prince at table, on the Prince pouring out a libation, he first tasted it. When sick, if the Prince went to visit him, he laid his head to the east, threw his court robes over him, and put on his great sash. When the Prince called him, he waited not for his carriage, but walked on foot. When he entered the great temple he asked about every thing. When a friend died, who had no relative, he said "let the care of burying him devolve on me." When a friend presented him with a gift, if it were a carriage and horses, unless there was flesh, that he could offer in sacrifice, he did not bow. He did not sleep as if dead, nor did he appear stiff and formal in his own house. When he met one in a mourning habit, although his familiar acquaintance, he shewed him respect. When he saw one wearing the robes of office, or a blind person, although in the habit of seeing him daily, he did him honor. When he met a person in mourning, he bowed even to the front cross beam of his carriage, he did the same to the person bearing the census of the people. When he saw his host spread a full table for him, he changed his countenance, and rose to shew his respect. In time of loud thunder, or violent winds he manifested awe.

13. When he mounted a carriage, he stood upright and took hold of the cords—when in a carriage he did not gaze about, talk fast, nor point at people.

14. At the countenance (of a man) a bird rises, flies about (till he pass) and then returns. It is said that the Tsze bird was enjoying itself near a mountain bridge, when it saw Tsze Loo it gave three shrieks and rose. *

* This is a fragment seemingly unconnected with what goes before.

CHAP. XI.

1. Confucius said, in former times, those who excelled in the knowledge of propriety and music are (by men of the present age) esteemed mere rustics—but in the present day, those who are versed in the knowledge of propriety and music, are esteemed accomplished Scholars. In practice, I follow those of former ages. *

2. Coufucius said, of those who followed me in Chin and Tsae, none now call at my door. Those who excelled in the practice of virtue, were Yen Yuen, Min Tsze Keen, Yen Pih New, and Chung Kung. The most eloquent were Tsae Go and Tsze Kung. Those who were best versed in politics, were Yen Yuen and Ke Loo. The most eminent in literature, were Tsze Yew and Tsze Hea.

3. Confucius said, Hwuy does not asist me. I say not any thing in which he does not delight. †

4. Confucius said, how eminent was the filial piety of Min Tsze Keen! There was no man who did not credit the testimony of his parents and brothers (concerning his filial piety.)

5. Nan Yung, daily repeated the Pih Kwei, three times: Confucius gave him his brother's daughter in marriage.

6. Ke Kang asked which of the disciples loved study most, Confucius replied, there was one Hwuy, who delighted in study, but unfortunately his life was short. He is dead, and now I have no such man.

* In former times, men possessed a due proportion of plain, honest sincerity, duly blended with ornamental accomplishments; at present, the learned have more polish than substantial virtue

† Hwuy had such a clear perception of every doctrine which the sage delivered, that he never came to have his doubts resolved. Hence his delighted master said, I receive no assistance from Hwuy, as it respects the advantages resulting to the teacher from the frequent discussion of difficult points: for Hwuy has no difficulties to solve. This was not said because the sage needed the assistance of his disciples, but proceeded from humility and a wish to extol Hwuy.

7. When Yen Yuen died, Yen Loo begged Confucius to sell his carriage and buy an outside coffin for him, to which request Confucius replied, talents or not talents, every man says he is my son. When Le died, he had an inner, but no outer coffin. I cannot walk on foot in order that he may have an outer coffin. Since I hold the office of a Ta Foo I ought not to walk on foot. *

8. When Yen Yuen died, Confucius deeply lamented him exclaiming, heaven has ruined me! heaven has ruined me!

9. When Yen Yuen died, Confucius wept bitterly. His followers said, does not our Master lament too bitterly! Should I not do so! If I do not lament such a man, whom shall I lament! †

10. When Yen Yuen died, the other disciples wished to give him a splendid funeral, Confucius said, it is improper: but they buried him in a splendid manner (on which account) the sage said, "Hwuy looked on me as his father, that I could not treat him as a son, is not my blame, but that of my disciples. ‡

11. Ke Loo asked how the gods ought to be served. The sage replied, you cannot yet serve men, how can you serve the gods? I presume to ask concerning death. You do not yet know life; how can you know death. ¶

12. Min Tsze stood by with steady mildness in his looks, Tsze Loo appeared firm and bold. Yen Yew and Tsze Kung manifested a soft pliability. Confucius was pleased, but said, Yew will not die a proper death.

* Yen Loo was the father of Yen Yuen, and Le was the son of Confucius. As the sage buried his own son without an outer coffin, he justly considered, that although Le's talents were not equal to Yen Yuen's yet, as he was his own son, it would be improper to treat another with more respect.

† He lamented that he did not succeed in burying Hwuy in a proper manner, as he interred his own son Le, and this he did in order to reprove his disciples.

‡ In funerals it should be considered whether the family possesses means or not. It is not agreeable to reason that poor people should have expensive funerals, on this ground the sage gave his veto to the request of his disciples.

¶ The gods and men ought to be served on the same principles and so should the living and the dead. Consequently he who knows how to serve men, must know how to serve the gods, and he who is acquainted with the principles of life, knows the principles of death. ¶ ¶

¶ ¶ As to serving the dead, in the manner of the Chinese, it is evidently gross idolatry, and consequently condemned by the law of the only living and true God: but must it not appear to every unprejudiced mind, at the first glance, that there ought in many respects to be a vast difference between the services which we render to God, and that which we render to our fellow creatures! And is it not a palpable fact, that many are in a great measure acquainted with their duty to man, who are at the same time totally ignorant of the very first principles of their duty to God, Thus confounding things which are so vastly different, is one of the fatal effects of being unacquainted with the revealed will of God.

13. The store keeper of Loo wished to erect a new granary Min Tsze Keen said, why not repair the old one? What necessity for altering it? Confucius said, this man is not a man o words, but if he speak, it is always to the point.

14. Confucius said, how does Yew's harp suit my Porch (school)! *

For this reason the other disciples shewed less respect for Tsze Loo, on which Confucius said, Yew has ascended the great hall, but has not yet entered the inner chambers of science.

15. Tsze Kung asked whether Sze, or Shang was the more learned and virtuous. Confucius replied, Sze goes too far, and Shang goes not far enough. Then Sze excels? Confucius replied, to go too far, is as bad, as not to go far enough.

16. Ke She was richer than Chow Kung: Kew collected the taxes for him, and (by extortion) increased his riches. Confucius said, he is not my disciple. Little children drum him away.

17. Tsae is deficient in knowledge. San is dull. Sze, with a fine exterior, is wanting in sincerity. Yew is vulgar. †

18. Confucius said, Hwuy is near perfect virtue: he is often in great poverty.

Sze did not submit to the will of heaven, he coveted gain, planned well, and often succeeded.

19. Tsze Chang asked respecting the principles and practice of the Shen Jin (virtuous man). Confucius replied, he does not tread in the footsteps of the sages, nor enter the chambers of the learned. ‡

* Tsze Loo's harp had a harsh, warlike sound, which was ill suited to the mild doctrines taught in the school of the sage.

† Some think that the two words "Confucius said." Should be placed at the head of these four sentences: according to this, they express the opinion of the sage respecting these four disciples, and consequently the present tense ought to be employed.

‡ The Shen Jin (or virtuous man) is one who possesses an excellent natural disposition, and who does nothing vicious, but who has no inclination to learn, hence is unacquainted with the doctrines of the sages, and consequently does not follow their footsteps. ‡ ‡

‡ ‡ The sages of China, sometimes express themselves, as if they considered it imposible for a man to be virtuous, who is not a scholar; but from this sentence it appears, that a man destitute of learning may possess a considerable portion of virtue. The Protestant Missionaries to China, and we believe the Romish Missionaries also, have often used the words "Shen Jin," as the designation of a true Christian. The Chinese reader ought not however to suppose that the words, when thus applied, are to be taken in the sense given to them in this passage. In the mouth of a true servant of Jesus, Shen Jin, does not mean an unlearned person, of an excellent natural disposition, but a person, whether learned, or unlearned, whose depraved nature has been renovated by the Almighty power of the Holy Spirit.

20. Confucius said, can you know from a man's having reasoned well, whether he be a man of superior virtue, or a painted impostor?

21. Tsze Loo asked whether upon hearing a duty (recommended) he ought immediately to put it in practice? Confucius replied, your father and elder brother are alive, why should you act immediately on hearing a thing! * Yew likewise asked if he ought to act as soon as he heard a precept? Confucius said, act immediately. Kung Se Hwa said, when Yew asked whether he ought on hearing, to act immediately, you Sir, answered that his father and elder brother were alive: Kew asked the same question, and you replied, act immediately. I am in doubt as to your meaning, and presume to ask. Confucius replied, Kew is of a slow disposition, and I wish to spur him on—Yew is rash, and I wish to check him.

22. Confucius was alarmed (or in danger) in Kwang: Yen Yuen having fallen behind, when he came up, Confucius said, I thought you had been dead; to which he replied, how could I dare to die while my master is alive! †

23. Ke Tsze Yen asked whether Chung Yew, and Yen Kew might be called great statesmen. Confucius replied, I thought Sir, you were about to ask concerning something marvellous, and lo you merely ask about Yew and Kew! Those who deserve to be denominated great ministers serve their Prince according to what is right and just, and when they cannot so act, resign. At present, Yew and Kew may be considered as making up the number of the ministers. Then they will follow their master? Confucius answered, in assassinating a father, or a Prince, they would not follow him. ‡

* That is, he ought always to ask the advice of his father and elder brother before undertaking any thing.

† How ought I carelessly to expose myself to death, while my master lives, whom I ought always to protect. This sentence shews the strong mutual love and regard, which subsisted between the sage and his favorite disciple.

‡ Ke She had usurped great power and wished to kill, or dethrone his Prince. Those two gentlemen held offices under him, but could neither restrain him, nor would they resign; still they were too well acquainted with their duty to the reigning Prince to admit of their assisting Ke She in his treasonable designs.

24. Tsze Loo appointed Tsze Kaou to be governor of Pe; Confucius said, you have injured a man's son. Tsze Loo replied, there are the people to govern and the Temples to oversee, why should he read books before he be learned in these? Confucius answered, I hate loquacity. *

25. When Tsze Loo, Tsăng Seih, Yen Yew, and Kung Se Hwa were sitting by him, Confucius said, although I be a day older than you, let not that deter you from declaring your opinions. You say we dwell here and are not known, but suppose you were known, what would you do? Tsze Loo, with an air of levity, replied abruptly, send me to rule a country of one thousand Chariots, hemmed in between two powerful states, pressed by large armies, and at the same time distressed by famine, and in the space of about three years, I will make the people brave, and turn their minds to justice: Confucius smiled.

Confucius said, and what would you do Kew? Kew replied, were I employed in governing a country of about sixty, or seventy, or about fifty, or sixty Le, in the space of three years, I would cause the people to possess sufficient resources, but as to teaching them propriety and music, I should be obliged to leave that to a superior man. And what would you do Chĭh? Chĭh replied, I am not master of such things, but I wish to study them. When there is business in the Temple of Ancestors, or at the assemblies of the Princes, I would put on the proper robes, and cap, and act as a sub-assistant. Tĕĕn what is your wish? Tĕĕn drew his air to a close, laid aside his harp, rose and said, I differ from these three gentlemen. On which Confucius observed, what harm is there in that! Let each speak his mind? Tĕĕn answered, I should like, now in the close of spring, to put on my spring robes, and in company with five

* Tsze Kaou was a youth of an excellent disposition, but had not studied, on which account the sage considered that Tsze Loo in appointing him to the government of Pe had done him a serious injury, or robbed him, as the expression denotes. Tsze Loo wishing to have the last word, although he was conscious that he had acted wrong, insinuated that the duties of a governor did not require that a man should be deeply read, but that on the contrary he might by practice learn how to act.

or six capped companions, and six or seven youths, go and bathe in the E, take the air among the local temples, and return singing. Confucius exclaimed, I agree with Tĕĕn. *

These three disciples having gone out, Tsăng Seih stayed behind. Tsăng Sĕih asked what the words of the three disciples meant, Confucius replied, each merely expressed his opinion. Why did you smile at Yew? Confucius answered, a country must be governed by propriety; his language was not modest and yielding, therefore I smiled at him. But did not Kew also express a wish to govern a country? Ans. when was it seen that an extent of 60 or 70 Le, or 50 or 60 Le, was not considered a country. Does not Chĭh also wish to govern a Province? Who but rulers of Princes attend on the Emperor in the Royal Temples, and are present at levees? If Chih were a sub-assistant pray who would be great (or chief?)

CHAP. XII.

1. Yen Yuen asked in what perfect virtue (or benevolence) consists? Confucius replied, virtue consists in conquering self, and returning to propriety. When a man has conquered self, and returned to propriety, on that day all men will allow that he is virtuous. Does perfect virtue then originate in one's self or in others? Yen Yuen asked what are the several branches of perfect virtue? Confucius replied, what is contrary to propriety, look not at it—listen not to it—speak not of it—touch (or move) it not. Yen Yuen rejoined, although Hwuy is not clever, he wishes to act thus.

2. Chung Kung asked what is perfect virtue? Confucius said, when you go out, do it as if you were receiving a guest of high rank; command the people as if you were attending a great sacrificial festival. What you do not wish others to do to you, do not to them; then in the country none will be displeased with you: nor will any in the family feel disatisfied. Chung Kung replied, although I am not quick I wish to act thus.

* He aimed not at any thing beyond his station and abilities, but felt at ease in his situation, hence the commendation of the sage.

3. Sze Ma New asked what constitutes perfect virtue. Confucius replied, it is to find it difficult to speak. To find it difficult to speak! Is that perfect virtue? Confucius rejoined, what is difficult to practice, must it not be difficult to speak? *

4. Sze Ma New asked respecting the man of superior virtue. Confucius replied, he has neither sorrow nor fear. To have neither sorrow nor fear, does that constitute a man of superior virtue! Confucius rejoined, when a man examines within, and finds nothing wrong, why should he have either sorrow or fear.

5. Sze Ma New in grief, exclaimed all men have brothers, I alone have none! Tsze Hea said, I have heard, that life and death are decreed and that riches and honor depend on heaven. The man of superior virtue, is serious and respectful, and constantly so. To others he always manifests respect and politeness: hence all within the four seas are his brethren. How can the superior man be grieved, as if without brethren?

6. Tsze Chang asked what might be called superior intelligence. Confucius said, when a man can stop a slowly soaking slander, and a flesh cutting accusation, he may be called intelligent. The man, that can defeat the ends of a soaking slander, and a flesh cutting accusation, may be said to possess a high degree of intelligence. †

7. Tsze Chung asked respecting government. Confucius replied, let there be sufficient supplies, and plenty of troops, and gain the confidence of the people. Tsze Chung said, if one of these three must be dispensed with, which should be first given up. Ans. The military. Tsze Chung asked again saying if forced to give up one of the remaining two, which ought to be given up first? Ans. The supplies: from ancient days to the present

* Sze Ma New was a loquacious man, on which account the sage taught him in this manner in order to make him more cautious in his language. Had he merely spoken of perfect virtue in general terms little or no effect would have been produced on his rash and thoughtless pupil.

† He that can detect and prevent the object of that secret and slow attempt to ruin his character which resembles the gradual entrance of water into any substance, or frustrate the ends of that malice which would lead one to cut out a piece of his own flesh to present as evidence of having been wounded by another, may be said to possess superior sagacity.

time, all have died, but if the people have no confidence (in their rulers) they cannot be established.

8. Keih Tsze Ching said, the superior man is substantially virtuous and no more, what necessity for ornamental accomplishments! Tsze Kung said, alas for what you have said, Sir, of the superior man! Four horses cannot overtake the tongue. Ornament is as substance and substance as ornament. The skins of the Tiger, and leopard, when tanned, appear the same as the skins of the dog, or sheep when tanned. *

9. Gae Kung asked Yew Jŏ, saying, this year there is scarcity, and I have not sufficient supplies, what ought to be done? Yew Jŏ replied, why not take only one tenth in taxes. † To which the Prince replied, when two tenths are not sufficient, why take only one? Ans. If the people have plenty, how can the Prince want? If the people have not enough, how can the Prince have plenty?

10. Tsze Chang asked how virtue may be exalted, and doubts dissolved. Confucius replied, be governed by fidelity and sincerity, and constantly advance in rectitude, thus virtue will be exalted. If when you love a man you wish him to live, but when you are displeased with him you wish for his death, since you both wish him to live, and to die, this is to doubt. ‡

11. Prince King of Tse, asked about government at Confucius, Confucius answered, let the Prince act the Prince, the Minister the Minister, the father the father, and the son the son. ¶ To which the Prince replied, you have spoken excellently; for in truth, if the Prince neglect the duty of a Prince, the Minister that of a Minister, the father that of a father, and the son that of a son, although there may be abundance of provisions how could we enjoy them!

* That is, it is only learning and politeness that distinguish the superior man from the rustic, just as it is only by the hair, that we distinguish the Leopard's skin from that of the dog or sheep, which when tanned appear the same.

† In the Chow Dynasty, one husbandman received one hundred Mow of land, and paid one tenth in taxes. But in the Loo country, from the time of Prince Seun, the Government exacted two tenths in taxes. Hence Yew Jo begged Prince Gae to return to the old custom of exacting one tenth. His intention was to persuade the Prince to be economical and to treat his people liberally.

‡ Life and death are determined by heaven, hence to wish for the one or the other, is to doubt the divine decrees.

¶ The minister of Kung, Prince of Tse, had been allowed to assume too much power. The Prince did not make his eldest son heir to the throne; thus neither Prince, Minister, father nor son, did, or could do his duty, hence the reply of the sage.

12. Confucius said, he who can with half a sentence put an end to litigations is Yew: For Tsze Loo acted with decision and promptitude. *

13. Confucius said, in hearing law suits I act like other men, but it is necessary to put an end to litigations. †

14. Tsze Chang asked respecting government. Confucius replied, let your mind dwell upon it without wearying and practice it with faithfulness.

15. Confucius says, the superior man, perfects men's virtues, but does not finish men's vices; the mean man acts the reverse of this.

16. Ke Kang Tsze asked Confucius respecting government, Confucius replied, government is rectitude. If you, Sir, lead by rectitude, who will dare to act contrary to rectitude!

17. Ke Kang was harassed by robbers, and consulted Confucius on the subject. Confucius said, if you, Sir, were not covetous, the people would not rob, even though you should hire them to do it.

18. Ke Kang asked of Confucius respecting government, saying, how would it answer to put to death the vicious, in order to bring forward the virtuous. Confucius replied, Sir, if you wish to govern well, why put men to death. If you only wish for virtue, the people will be virtuous. The virtue of the superior man (or of superiors) resembles the wind, that of inferiors resembles the grass. When the wind blows on the grass it must yield. ‡

* Tsze Loo was a man of sincerity, fidelity, and prompt decision; hence as soon as he uttered his words, men gave him credit, and yielded to him, nay they did not even wait till he had done speaking.

† Yang She said, Tsze Loo could with half a sentence decide a law suit, but he knew not how to rule a country by propriety, and humility; consequently, he could not prevent litigations among the people. On which account these words of the sage are recorded, to shew that he did not consider it difficult to decide law suits, but that what he deemed important, was to put an end to litigations altogether.

‡ The doctrines of Confucius were directly opposed to tyranny, or harsh government. His scheme was to lead men by reason and good example; and he constantly maintained, that if superiors were virtuous, inferiors would certainly be so too. ‡‡

---

‡‡ We have already observed that this principle, although good in itself, is carried a little too far by the sage and his followers.

19. Tsze Chang asked what the scholar must be who deserves fame. Confucius replied, what do you call fame? Tsze Chang answered, to be heard of through the province, and at home. Confucius said, that is only to be heard of, but not to have true fame. Now true fame consists in plain, straight forward sincerity—in the love of justice—in examining men's words—in reading their countenances—and in giving place to others; such a man must be famous through the country and at home.

He who aims at being heard of, assumes the appearance of virtue, but in his actions opposes it: yet he rests satisfied with himself, and doubts not of being right. Such a man will be heard of, both at home and abroad. *

20. While Fan Che, was walking along with Confucius, Woo Ke said, I presume to ask how virtue may be honored, secret vice suppressed, and doubts resolved. Confucius exclaimed, an excellent question indeed! Does not that which at first requires great labor, and is afterwards attained, honor virtue? To attack our own vices, and not to attack the vices of others, is not that to suppress secret vice? In one morning's rage, to forget its conquences to one's self and relatives, does not this shew doubt. †

21. Fan Che asked what benevolence (or perfect virtue) is Confucius replied,—to love men. What is knowledge? The sage answered, to know men.

* Ching Tsze says, that the student ought to bend his undivided attention to reality, and not to permit the love of fame to come near him. He who covets fame, has lost the fundamental principles of genuine learning. He who studies for a name, is a hypocrite. The students of the present day, for the most part, study in order to gain fame and through fame to get gain,

Yin She says, that the fault of Tsze Chang's learning, lay in his not bending his whole attention to realities. Wherefore Confucius answered him in this manner: wishing him in all things to be sincere and substantial. This internal fulness would be manifested externally. If the disciples who themselves received the instructions of the sage, erred in this manner, how much more must those of after ages!

† The man who in a fit of anger brings on himself and relatives great misery, shews the highest degree of indiscrimination between what is light and heavy; hence, in reference to just principles, he may be said to be undecided, or in doubt. Although the sage does not in so many words point out the method of resolving doubts, an inference may be drawn from his words, viz. that the best method is to examine fully the first, or incipient motives to action.

Fan Che did not comprehend this. Confucius said, elevate the upright, and dismiss the perverse, thus you will make the depraved upright. *

Fan Che departed and waited on Tsze Hea, to whom he said, just now I had an interview with Coufucius, and when I asked what knowledge is, he replied, elevate the upright, and dismiss the depraved, thus you may make the depraved upright. What does he mean? Tsze Hea replied, rich are his words! When Shun was Emperor, he selected and elevated Kaou Yaou from among the multitude, and the vicious (or rather vice) went to a distance. When Tang was Emperor, he chose and exalted E Yin from the mass of the people, and vice fled to a great distance.

22. Tsze Kung asked how we ought to conduct ourselves in our intercourse with friends. Confucius replied, teach (or reprove) them with fidelity, lead them skilfully: if they will not follow, desist; do not disgrace yourself.

23. Tsang Tsze said. the superior man employs his learning to collect friends, and his friends to assist (or increase) his virtue.

CHAP. XIII.

1. Tsze Loo asked concerning government. Confucius replied, lead the people (by your example), and encourage them. I beg to ask what more is requisite? Be not weary in acting thus.

2. Chung Kung, when first minister to Ke She, asked respecting government. Confucius said, in the first place, have suitable Officers under you. Pardon small offences, and promote men of virtue and talents. But how shall I ascertain who

* Fan Che supposed that a knowledge of men would be injurious to the love of them; from the circumstance, that an acquaintance with the vices of men, would lead us to hate, rather than love them. But the sage wished to teach him, that a correct knowledge of men, would enable those in power to honor and promote the virtuous, and to disgrace and dismiss the vicious, so that in the end, the vicious would by this treatment be reclaimed, and hence would deserve to be loved. Thus the good man may with propriety love men in general.

possess virtue and talents, that I may promote them? If you promote those whom you know, will men conceal those whom you know not?

3. Tsze Loo said to Confucius, suppose, Sir, the Prince of Wei were to give you an official a appointment, what would you teach him to do first? Confucius replied, to establish his character. On which Tsze Loo exclaimed, indeed! You have shot far beyond the mark, Sir! Why should the establishing of his character be of the first importance!

Confucius replied, you are a simple rustic Yew. The superior man is not rash and heedless in those things which he understands not, as you are. If one's character is not correct, his words will be inconsistent, if his words are inconsistent, things will not be properly done.* If things are not properly done, propriety and music will not flourish. When propriety and music do not flourish, punishments are not equitable. When punishments are not equitable, the people will not know how to move hand or foot. Therefore the character of a superior man must be such as can be spoken of. What is said of it, must be such as may be practised.† A superior man is never rash and irregular in his words.

4. Fan Che begged to be instructed in husbandry. Confucius said, I am not a farmer. He next asked to be taught the art of gardening. Confucius said, I am not a gardener. When Fan Che went out, Confucius said, this Fan Che acts the inferior man.‡ When superiors love propriety, the people will not dare to be disrespectful. When superiors love justice, the people will not dare to disobey. When superiors love truth, the

* Whatever virtue you wish the people to practice, first practice it yourself, and they will certainly imitate you. Assist them in every case of necessity, and they will serve you with the utmost diligence and fidelity.

† At that time Ling, Prince of Wei, had expelled his eldest son. When Ling died the people of Wei crowned his grandson, who, when his father wished to return to his country, opposed him, hence the sage considered that it was of the first importance, for such a man, to redeem his character.

‡ There is nothing degrading in being a husbandman, or gardener, but Fan Che having entered the school of the sage, these employments were unsuitable to his situation.

people will not dare to be unfaithful. When matters are thus, the people will come from all quarters to serve you, carrying their young children in little bags on their backs. In such circumstances, what use is there for studying husbandry.

5. Confucius says, although a man may be able to recite the three hundred Odes; if, when he receives an appointment, he know not how to act, or when sent abroad as an Ambassador he is unable of himself to reply to the questions put to him; although he has read much, of what use is it to him?

6. Confucius says, that if your own conduct be correct, although you do not command, men will do their duty. But if your own conduct be incorrect, although you command, the people will not obey.

7. Confucius said, the political systems of Loo and Wei are brothers.

8. Confucius said, Kung Tsze King; managed his own family well. At first, having little, he said it will do. Afterwards having a little more, he said it is complete. When he became rich he said it is excellent!

9. Confucius having gone to Wei, Yen Yuen acted as his coachman. Confucius said, how numerous the people! Yen Yuen said, since the population is so great, what can be done for the farther good of the community? Enrich them. When they are made rich, what more can be done for them? Instruct them.

10. Confucius said, if any government would employ me; in the course of one year, I would do something, and in three years I would make a complete reformation.

11. Confucius said, it is an ancient saying, that, if a succession of virtuous men were to govern a Province for a period of one hundred years, an end would be put to tyranny, and capital punishments.* What think you of these words!

* Yin She says, that the overcoming of tyranny, and abolishing of capital punishments, merely put down the practice of vice. Since the merit of a virtuous man would reach to this, a sage would not require one hundred years, nor would the renovation which he would effect stop in this.

12. Confucius said, if we had a King, in one age (about thirty years) the people would be virtuous. *

13. Confucius said, if a man can rectify his own conduct, what difficulty will he find in governing others! If he cannot rectify himself, how can he rectify others!

14. Yen Tsze having returned from an audience, (with Ke She) Confucius said, why have you come so late? To which he replied, I have been at court, on public business. Confucius rejoined it must have been private business; had it been government business, although I am not now in office, I must have heard of it. †

15. Ting, Prince of Loo asked whether there was any one sentence, sufficient to lead to the prosperity of a country? Confucius replied, one word cannot contain so much as this. Men say that to be a King is difficult, and to be a minister is not easy. If you know that it is difficult to be a King, is not this one word which contains the germ of the prosperity of a Province? Is there any one word, which would lead to the ruin of a kingdom? Confucius replied, how can so much be expressed by one word. Yet men say I could have no pleasure in being a Prince, unless there were none who would oppose my words. Now if the Prince's commands are good, and none oppose them, is not this excellent? But if they are bad, and none oppose them, then does not the one word "none oppose" contain that which will lead to the ruin of a nation?

16. The governor of Yih, asked respecting government. Confucius replied, make glad those who are near, and those who are at a distance will come.

* If any one should say, that three years and one age (30 years) are very different, as to rapidity and slowness in the work of renovation: and ask why the sage says at one time, that this work may be done in three years, and at another time, that it would require thirty years, Chin Tsze, answers by remarking, that when Confucius spoke of three years, he meant that in that period a sage could put the laws and regulations in a state of order, and thus set in motion the elements of complete renovation, but, that it would require a period of thirty years, to gradually advance the people in virtue, and rub them into righteousness; so that virtuous principles shall have been thoroughly wrought iuto their very nature.

† Propriety required, that when the court had any public question to discuss, those who had formerly been in office, should be informed of it. But at that time, Ke She had usurped the power in Loo, and did not meet with his peers in the court house, to transact the affairs of the nation; but held private consultations with his own servants. Hence Confucius by this remark had a deep intention of repressing Ke She and of teaching his pupil Yen Tsze.

17. Tsze Hea when governor of Keu Foo, asked respecting government. Confucius said, be not rash, and regard not a trifling advantage. If you are in haste, you will not succeed. If you regard a small advantage, you will not be able to accomplish great things.

18. The Governor of Yih conversing with Confucius said, in my village there is a truly upright man. His father stole a sheep and he proved the theft. Confucius said, the upright in my village, differ from this. The father conceals the faults of the son, and the son those of the father: uprightness lies in this! *

19. Fan Che asked, what perfect virtue is, Confucius said, in retirement, be serious, in the discharge of the duties of your office, be respectful,—in your intercourse with men, be faithful. Although you go among barbarians, you must not cease to act thus.

20. Tsze Chung asked, what description of man may be styled an eminent scholar. Confucius replied, he who has a sense of shame, and who if sent abroad on an Embassy would not disgrace the authority of his Prince. I presume to ask who may be considered next in order? Those whom they of the same family style filial, and whom the people of the same village call fraternal. I beg leave to ask who are next to these? He who is sincere in his words, and determined in his actions, although dull, and of mean capacity, may be considered next in order! † What may the present ministers of state be called? They are mere measures, how are they worth speaking about.

21. Confucius said, since I cannot obtain men perfectly correct to whom I may deliver my doctrines, I must look for emulous and cautious men. The emulous will press forward

* That the father and son should conceal each others faults is in the highest degree accordant with divine reason, and the nature of man. * *

† Such a man does not inquire whether what he says, accord with reason or not, but keeps his word faithfully. In acting, he does not study whether what he does ought to be done or not but goes through with it.

* * This principle is good, to a certain extent, but if carried so far as to defeat the ends of public justice, it is pernicious, and must be abandoned by every truly upright man,

to the highest point. The cautious will do nothing wrong. *

22. Confucius said, the south country people have a proverb which says, that without stability a man can neither be a magician, nor a Doctor. Very good! (The Yih says) he who does not steadfastly persevere in the path of virtue, will be disgraced. Confucius says, this is only because he has not made himself a acquainted with the Yih. †

23. Confucius says, the superior man lives in harmony with men, without caballing. The mean man cabals, without living in harmony.

24. Tsze Kung asked, what may be said of a man, who is loved by all the people in the village? Confucius replied, you must not believe, that he is truly virtuous. What if all in the village hate him? Confucius answered, even then you must not believe that he is vicious. This is not equal to being loved by all the virtuous in the place; and hated by all the vicious.

25. Confucius says, the superior man is easily served, but difficult to please. If you wish to please him by what is contrary to right principles, he will not be pleased. He employs men according to their talents. The mean man is difficult to serve, but easily pleased. If you wish to please him by that which is opposite to just principles, he will be pleased. In employing men he requires them to be qualified for every thing. ‡

* It was the sincere and ardent wish of the sage, to obtain men who steadily and exactly kept the due medium, in all their actions, to whom he might commit his doctrines, in order that they might be handed down to future ages: but as he could not succeed in accomplishing this wish, he sought for men of ardent minds and great learning, and virtue, and who after proper cultivation would accomplish great things. He at the same time sought for cautious, steady men, who though deficient in knowledge, might be so moulded by a proper education, that they would steadfastly adhere to the path of virtue, and do much for the dissemination of the sage's principles. **

† One Commentator says, that the sense of this sentence is not clear. Another explains it by saying, that the Yih King clearly sets forth the disgrace of not perserving in the path of virtue, consequently, if a man fail here, it is because he has not made himself well acquainted with the Yih King.

‡ The superior and mean man, here spoken of, refer to the ministers of state, and great officers of that time. Nothing contrary to rectitude can delight the mind of the superior man. But in employing men, if they possess but one ta'ent, or know but one art, they will find employment in his service. Such is his liberal and candid disposition. The mean man is, in every thing, the direct reverse of this.

** Why could not the omnipotent virtue of the sage, which is said to be capable of renevating all nature, form his own disciples to perfect virtue, so that they should be in every respect what he could wish them to be?

26 Confucius says, the superior man is dignified, without pride: the mean man is proud, and destitute of ease and liberality.

27. Confucius says, the man who is firm, and magnanimous; plain in his manners, and slow in speech, is near perfect virtue. *

28 Tsze Loo asked, what is requisite, to render a man worthy of being called learned. Confucius replied, he must be sincere and open in his admonitions (or reproofs) and mild and pleasant in his temper. He must admonish his friends with frankness and sincerity, and live in harmony with his brothers. †

29. Confucius said, were a good man to teach the people for seven years, they might then be employed in war ‡

30. Confucius says, to lead out untaught people to war, is to throw them away.

CHAP. XIV.

1. Heen asked what things a man ought to be ashamed of? Confucius said, when a country is governed by reason to have a salary, (a sinecure) and when a country is not governed by right principles, to have a salary, are both shameful things. ¶

* These natural by good qualities only want to be adorned by literature in order to finish the man's virtue. * *

† Tsze Loo was deficient in these virtues, on which account the sage taught him in this manner.

‡ If you instruct the people in the knowledge of filial piety, fraternal affection, fidelity, sincerity, husbandry and war, then they will love their superiors, and die for them. When you have by education brought them to this, they are prepared for the field of battle.

¶ "To have a salary," here means to be concerned only about government emoluments, without discharging the duties of your office. Heen was backward in the performance of his duty. He knew that to have a salary in a country not governed by right principles, without acting, was disgraceful, but was not conscious that the same was the case, in a country governed by good principles, hence the sage spoke of both unitedly, in order to rouse him to a sense of his duty.

* * This is a fatal error. For although it must me allowed, that learning gives a polish to human virtue, and sometimes proves a means of leading to genuine sanctity of character; yet the world affords numerous and melancholy proofs, that mere human learning is totally inadequate to the genuine renovation of depraved human nature. Have not many of the most learned, been the most vicious, while many of the least learned have been the most virtuous of our species!

2. Heen said, may a man be esteemed perfectly virtuous, who represses the love of victory, boasting, anger and avarice? Confucius replied, this may be considered difficult, but I do not know that it is perfect virtue. *

3. Confucius says, the man whose mind cherishes the love of ease, and personal convenience, is not worthy of being esteemed a scholar.

4. Confucius says, when a state is governed by just principles, a man's words and actions may be high and independent. When a Province is not governed by right principles, his actions ought still to be independent, but his words may be a little pliable. †

5. Confucius says, he who possesses virtue, will be able to speak, but it does not follow that all who possess eloquence are virtuous. He who is virtuous will be brave, but it does not hence follow, that all who are bold, are likewise virtuous. ‡

6. Nan Kung Kwă asked Confucius saying, did not E the famous archer and Aou who pulled a boat over dry land, die in an improper manner? And were not Yu and Tseih, who were poor husbandmen, elevated to the Imperial throne? To this Confucius made no reply. Nan Kung Kwă having gone out, Confucius exclaimed, this is a superior man! This man exalts virtue. ¶

* The man of perfect virtue does not merely repress these evil passions, but they do not exist in his heart. * *

† The superior man ought at all times, and in all circumstances, to preserve one undeviating line of conduct; but in times of disorder, during the reign of unprincipled kings, and the administration of unjust ministers, he needs not endanger his personal safety by speaking out his mind.

‡ There is a mere blood and breath boldness (animal courage) and there is a just and reasonable boldness. He who possess the former, is not truly virtuous, he who has the latter, is the good and truly brave man. There is a mere ability to quibble and by artful and specious reasoning to make truth appear falsehood, and falsehood truth. Those who excel in such eloquence are not virtuous characters.

¶ Nan Kung Kwa wished to compare the men of power and authority of that time to the celebrated archer E, and the powerful Aou and to compare Confucius to the famous Yu and the renowned Tseih, the former of whom was elevated to the Imperial throne in his own person, and the latter in that of his posterity, which became the reigning family of the Chow Dynasty. He doubtless wished to encourage the sage, with the hope, that his virtue was such as would raise him to the throne, either in his own person, or in his posterity. Hence Confucius from modesty, made no reply, but on his retiring praised his knowledge and virtue.

* * This is true, but if we except the Saviour of the world, who was both God and man, in what age or country has any man been found totally free from these passions.

7. Confucius says, a superior man may do a bad thing, but there never was a mean man who at any time practised virtue. *

8. Confucius said, can you love them (children), and not train them rigorously? Can you be faithful, and not often instruct him (your Prince). †

9. Confucius said, the government of Chin employed Pe Shin to draw up the outlines of their official documents, She Shŭh examined and revised them. The messenger, Tsze Yu, adjusted them, and Tsze Chan of Tung Le ornamented them. ‡

10. Some one asked what kind of man Tsze Chan was? Confucius replied, he was a benevolent man. He than asked about Tsze Se. Confucius exclaimed, that man! That man! (speak not of him.) On which he enquired about Kwan Chung. Confucius replied, that man wrested from Pih She a town of three hundred houses, yet he (the latter) to the end of his life lived on coarse fare and uttered not a murmuring word. ¶

11. Confucius says, that it is more difficult to bear poverty, without murmuring, than to be be rich without pride.

12. Confucius said, Mung Kung Chŏ is more than competent for being Chief of the Ministers in the family of Chaou, or Wei, but he is not capable of being a Ta Foo (great officer) in Tăng or Sëĕ.

13. Tsze Loo asked what constitutes an accomplished man Confucius replied, if a man possess the knowledge of Tsang Woo Chung—the moderation of Kung Chŏ—the bravery of

* Perfect virtue is in complete accordance with divine reason. The superior man ought without a single moment's interruption to practise it, but there are some moments, in which from absence of mind, or when off his guard he may do something wrong; but the mean man, having completely lost his originally virtuous nature, never practises virtue.

† Soo She says, to love children and not to instruct, chastise, and cause them to exert themselves, is the mere blind affection of fowls and cows. To pretend faithfulness to a Prince, and not to admonish him frequently is the faithfulness of women and eunuchs.

‡ The intention of these remarks of the sage, was to shew that the government of Chin, knew well how to employ men properly. In preparing official documents, each minister had that part assigned to him, for which his talents qualified him.

¶ Hwan Prince of Tse took the city Peen from Pih She and gave it to Kwan Chung, but it was by the great talents of Kwan Chung, that the Prince accomplished this exploit: and so great were the merits of Kwan Chung, that they completely subdued the resentment of Pih She so that he patiently lived in poverty to the end of life.

Pëen Chwang Tsze, and the skill in the arts of Yen Kew, and were he to polish all these accomplishments by the knowledge of polite manners and music, he might be esteemed a perfect man. * But why is it necessary that perfect men of the present day should be thus. He who, when he sees an opportunity of getting gain, thinks on justice; who in times of danger is willing to give up his life, who forgets not his agreements, may likewise be esteemed a perfect man:

14. Confucius asked Kung Ming Kea, whether it was true that his master Kung Shŭh Wăn Tsze neither talked, nor laughed, nor took? Kung Ming Kea replied, you must have been wrongly informed, Sir. My master speaks when it is proper to do so; hence people are not tired of his conversation. On occasions of joy, my master laughs; hence men are not disgusted with his laughter, when it accords with justice, he takes; therefore people are not dissatisfied with what he takes. Confucius exclaimed indeed! Is this really the case!

15. Confucius said, when Chwang Woo Chung took possession of Fang, and asked the Prince of Loo to promote his son although it was said, he would not compel the Prince, I do not believe it. †

16. Confucius said, Prince Hwan of Tsin was crafty and not upright. Hwan Prince of Tsze was upright and not crafty. ‡

* This does not speak of the highest degree of perfection, it only treats of that degree of excellence which Tsze Loo was capable of attaining. If you speak of the highest excellence, then unless, like the sage, you completely perform all the duties of man, to the highest extent, it is not worth calling perfection. * *

† Chwang Woo Chung had offended against the laws of Loo, and fled to Choo. Afterwards he returned and took possession of Fang the place which he formerly ruled, and sent to ask the Prince of Loo to give his son a government appointment. This conduct in thus returning and taking possession of Fang said that if his request was not granted he would rebel and force the Prince.

‡ Both were men of great note, yet neither of them was truly virtuous. But they differed as o their straight forward or crafty manner of accomplishing their designs.

---

* * If by all the duties of man, they mean all the duties which a guilty human being, owes to God, as well as to himself, and fellow creatures, we should have no objection to this statement, but there is too much reason to fear, that their sages, although by those who knew no better, considered models of perfection, were radically defective in their duty to the supreme Being. This is a capital deficiency, and renders the Chinese worthies very inadequate models of perfect virtue.

Tsze Loo said, Kwan Kung killed Kung Tsze Kew, Chaou Hwŏ died with him, but Kwan Chung did not, is not this called want of virtue! *

Confucius replied, Prince Hwan through the merits of Kwan Chung, without the aid of the military, united and ruled all the Princes. Whose virtue is equal to his! Whose virtue is equal to his! †

17. Tsze Kung said, was not Kwan Chung void of virtue! Hwan the Prince, put Tsze Kew to death, and Kwan Chung could not die, but even became his minister. Confucius replied, Kwan Chung assisted Hwan the Prince (of Tse) to overawe all the Princes, and rectify the whole Empire. The people to this day reap the benefits of his administration. Had it not been for Kwan Chung my hair would have been dishevelled and my robes open on one side. ‡ Why should he act like a common man or woman, who commit suicide lie in a ditch and are never heard of!

18. The family minister of Kung Shŭh Wan Tsze, called Seen Yu, (afterwards) a high Officer of state, he advanced to the same rank with himself. Confucius hearing of this, said he (Shŭh Wan Tsze) deserved the epithet Wan (learned or accomplished.)

19. Confucius having said that Ling, Prince of Wei was a man of no principle, Kung Tsze replied, if it be so, how is it that he does not lose the throne!

Confucius rejoined Chung Shŭh Yu receives his guests, Shŭh To superintends the ceremonies in the Temples, and Wang Sun Kea manages the military; this being the case, why should he lose the throne!

* Kwan and Kew were the sons of Leang, Prince of Tse; Leang was a man of no principle and was killed by Woo Che Kwan previous to this event, in a time of commotion, he fled to Loo. After his father was killed, he succeeded in causing the people of Loo to send men and put Kew his brother to death. Kwang Chung and Chaou were at that time servants of Kew. The latter died with his master, but the other surrendered himself a prisoner to the people of Loo, and afterwards became the Minister of Kwan, the very man who put his old master to death. Hence Tsze Loo's doubts as to the virtue of Kwang Chung.

† Although Kwang Chung, was a man of eminent talents, he had not studied in the school of the sages, nor was his virtue equal to his abilities. He subdued men rather by force, than by reason. Yet such were his abilities, that he united the petty Princes of China, and checked the incursions of the barbarians, and thus preserved the chinese from the tyranny and rude customs of savage foreigners. On this account the sage praised him.

‡ That is I should have been a barbarian.

20. Confucius says, he who is not ashamed to speak great things, will find it difficult to act up to his professions.

21. Chin Ching Tsze assassinated Prince Këën (of Tse). Confucius bathed, went to Court, (the Court of Loo) and informed Prince Gae, saying, Chin Kwan has killed his Prince, I beg you to punish him.* The Prince replied, inform the three great Mandarines. Confucius said, since I held the office of Ta Foo, I dare not neglect to inform and lo the Prince says, announce it to the three Madarines! Having informed them, they deemed it improper to comply; Confucius said, since I held the office of Ta Foo, I dare not, neglect to announce (such an affair). †

22. Tsze Loo asked how a Prince should be served! Confucius answered, do not deceive him, and reprove him.

23. Confucius says, the superior man ascends higher in knowledge and virtue—the inferior man descends lower in ignorance and vice.

24. Confucius said, the ancients studied for their own good, the moderns that they may gain a name from others.

25. Kew Pih Yu sent a man to call on Confucius. Confucius made him sit down, and asked him what his master was doing. To which he replied, my master is attempting to lessen his errors, but cannot. When the messenger went out, Confucius exclaimed, (in approbation) a messenger a messenger indeed!

26. Tsăng Tsze says, the superior man's thoughts go not beyond his situation.

27. Confucius says, the superior man is ashamed to say much, but in his actions he exceeds (his words).

* When a minister assasinates his Prince, it throws the greatest confusion into the human relations, all men ought to punish such a man, how much more a neighbouring country!

† When Confucius went out, he said these things to himself. The three domineering families in Loo had assumed all the power in the state, and in reality did not wish for monarchical government. Hence in heart they accorded with Chin Ching in his rebellion. But, they pretended that as Tse was far superior in strength to Loo that it would be improper to interfere, especially as the murder of the Prince of Tse did not concern any other nation, but his own. These sentiments were directly opposed to the doctrines of the sage; who held that all men under heaven ought to avenge the murder of a Prince.

28. Confucius said, there are three things in the practice of the superior man, to which I cannot reach. He is intelligent and without doubt, virtuous and without sorrow, brave and without fear. Tsze Kung replied, my master depreciates himself.

29. Tsze Kung was fond comparing the merits and demerits of men. Confucius said, Sze, how virtuous! I have no leisure for such work. *

30. Confucius says, be not vexed that you are not known, but be concerned that you want abilities.

31. Confucius says, that he who does not before hand vex himself about being imposed upon, nor anxiously anticipate not being believed; and yet is sensible of these before hand, is a virtuous man. †

32. Wei Sang Mow, said to Confucius, how is it Mow, that you thus cleave to (or depend upon) others? Is it not because of your insinuating, artful address? Confucius replied, I dare not please men by artful language, but I hate bigotry. ‡

Confucius said, a fine horse is not praised for his strength, but for his docility and tractableness. ¶

33. Some one asked, what may be said of rewarding hatred by kindness.

34. Confucius said, in that case with what will you reward

* This was a severe reproof for Tsze Kung, intimating, that if a man pay proper attention to his own spirit and conduct, he will not have much leisure for criticising others.

† It is only the superior man who can so act in his intercourse with others, as to prevent them from either imposing on him, or not trusting him.

‡ Wei Sang Mow was a man of virtue and talents, but prided himself in retiring from public view, in times of confusion and bad government. The answer of the sage was a blow aimed at his bigotry.

¶ The great man is not praised for his talents but for his virtue. ¶ ¶

¶ ¶ An excellent maxim, but seldom attended to by men of the present day.

kindness? Reward bad treatment with justice, and kindness with kindness. *

Confucius said, alas no one knows me! Tsze Kung said, how is it that you are not known, Sir? Confucius replied, I repine not at heaven, I grumble not with men, I study the inferior branches of learning, and advance to a clear understanding of the superior. It is only heaven which knows me. †

35. Kung Pĭh Leaou calumniated Tsze Loo to Ke Sun, Tsze Fŭh King Pĭh informed Confucius of the circumstance, and said, that (Tsze Loo's master, Ke Sun) was prejudiced against him in consequence of what Kung Pĭh Leaou had said, saying if I had strength I would kill him and expose his corpse in the market. ‡

Confucius replied, that good principles should be practised, depends on the decree of heaven, and that they should be abandoned, likewise depends on the divine decree, how can Kung Pĭh Leaou affect the determinations of heaven!

36. Confucius said, men of eminent talents, and virtue (when the Empire is without the government of reason) retire from the world. The next class (when a Province is in a state of confusion) leave it. The next class when they see that the demeanour of the Prince towards them is not respectful, retire from his service, and the next class to them, when they cannot agree in opinion with the Prince, they retire from his service.

38. When Tsze Loo lodged in Shĭh Mun, the porter of the city gates said to him, whence come you? Tsze Loo said from

* Reward your enemies with strict justice, without the least degree of selfish feeling. Forget not favors bestowed, but reward them by other favors. * *

† Among the disciples of the sage, there was only Tsze Kung who was beginning to comprehend his most sublime and abstruse doctrines. But even he did not fully comprehend them.

‡ Tsze Loo was Ke Sun's steward, Kung Pih Leaou calumniated him to his master. The latter believed the calumny and in consequence felt averse to employ Tsze Loo. Tsze Fuh King Pih enraged at the villany of Kung Pih Leaou wished to put him to death, and expose his body to public view in order to make manifest his slander.

* * How different is this from the mild precept of the Prince of peace. "Love your enemies, do good to them who hate you, and pray for them who despitefully use you and persecute you!" Reader judge for yourself, whether the dictates of the Chinese sage, or the commandment of the Divine Saviour, appears most like the doctrine of the God of love.

Kung She, (Confucius) the porter replied, does he know that he cannot act and yet goes on thus.! *

39. One day when Confucius was playing on the King in Wei, a man carrying a grass basket exclaimed, the man who has a heart to save the Empire, is he who plays on the King. † Having said so, he exclaimed, simple rustic, what bigoted blindness. Not to know that you should give over at once. "When you ford a deep stream, do it with your robes down. When you cross shallow water hold up your under garments." Confucius said, truly to act thus, is no difficult matter.

40. Chang Tsze said, the Shoo King says, that Kaou Tsung mourned three years for his parents, without speaking (of government affairs); what do you say of this? Confucius replied, why say so of Kaou Tsung only; the ancients all did the same. When the Prince died, all the Officers met in the Office of the Prime Minister and received his commands.

41. Confucius says, when superiors love propriety, the people are easily managed.

42. Tsze Loo asked, respecting the character of the superior man. Confucius replied, he adorns his conduct with respectful behaviour. Tsze Loo said, is that all? Confucius rejoined, he thus acts that he may promote the peace and happiness of others. Tsze Loo again asked, saying is this all? Confucius replied, he cultivates personal virtue that he may give happiness to all the people. Now even Yaou and Shun in some measure fell short of this.

* This Porter was a man of eminent talents and virtue who had in consequence of the maladministration of government, retired into obscurity. He knew that he could do nothing for the salvation of his country, and hence very properly retired. But he did not understand, that there was nothing too much for the sage to do, in the way of individual, or general renovation, hence his censure of Confucius.

† The heart of the sage never forgot the good of the Empire, when this man heard the sound of his harp, he knew his feelings and sentiments.

43. Yuen Hwae sat down crossed legged waiting for Confucius. Confucius said, he who in youth is without filial piety, and fraternal affection, and who in mature age obtains no praise, if he live to be old, will be a thief, (having so said) he hit him on the ancle with his staff. *

44. (Confucius) employed a youth of the village Keuĕ to carry messages between the host and his visitors. Some one observed, this youth must have made great progress. Confucius replied, I have seen him sitting in the seat of a superior, and walking by the side of his teacher. He does not seek to advance in learning, but speedily to be a man. †

CHAP. XV.

1. Ling the Prince of Wei, asked Confucius about military tactics. Confucius replied, I have learned the business of the Tsoo Tow, ‡ but I have not studied the military art: next day he took his departure.

When in Chin, their provisions were cut off, so that his followers became sick, and were unable to rise. Tsze Loo manifested tokens of displeasure, and said, does the superior man also suffer want thus? Confucius replied, the superior man firmly maintains self-government in seasons of distress; but the mean man, when oppressed by want, gives way to all sorts of improper conduct.

* Yuen Hwae was an old acquaintance of Confucius. When his mother died, he sung, and on that occasion he sat waiting for the sage in a disrespectful posture. A thief here means an injurer of the name of man.

† Propriety requires that youths should sit in a corner and walk behind their teachers and seniors, Confucius said, I see that this youth does not thus act, hence I employ him to bear messages between host and guest that he may practically learn the distinction between superiors and inferiors and thus be accustomed to a polite humble demeanour.

‡ The tsoo tow is a sacrificial vessel. The sage meant to say that he understood, and could practise the ceremonies of worshipping the gods in the Temples, but neither understood nor cared for the art of war.

2. Confucius (addressing himself to Tsze Kung) said, Tsze do you suppose that I have learned many things and remember them? Tsze Kung answered yes: and instantly said no. Confucius said, no. I concentrate all in one princip le.

3. Confucius said, Yew! there are few who know virtue.

4. Confucius said, he who governed without any labour was Shun. What did he do? He merely sat on the throne in a respectful and dignified manner. *

5. Tsze Chang asked respecting a successful line of conduct. Confucius said, let your words be faithful and sincere, and let your actions be pure and respectful, then, although you be among the southern, or nothern barbarians, you will succeed. When you stand, let these things be before you. When riding in your carriage let them be on the front cross-beam, thus you will succeed. Tsze Chang wrote these words on his girdle.

6. Confucius exclaimed, upright was Sze Yu! When the province was well governed, he was straight as an arrow, when the province was without right principles, he was still straight as an arrow. (Confucius said) Keu Pih Yŭh was a man of superior virtue. When the Province was governed by right principles, he held an office: when it was not, he resigned and dwelt in secret.

7. Confucius says, if you speak not to a man who ought to be spoken to, you lose men. If you speak to a man who ought not to be spoken to, you lose words. The man of knowledge neither loses men nor words. †

8. Confucius says, the determined scholar and man of finished virtue, seeks not the preservation of life to the injury of virtue, but will give up life in order to finish his virtue.

* The predecessor of Shun, the great Yaou, had put the government in such a train of good order, and such were the abilities and virtue of the officers of government and the all renovating power of Shun's personal virtue, that the Empire governed itself and left nothing for him to do.

† According to one Commentator, the sage meant that when a man shews a disposition to listen and follow instruction, or advice, if you do not instruct him, it is losing or injuring him, but when a man is either too wicked to listen, or too stupid to understand you, by endeavouring to instruct him, you spend your words in vain.

9. Tszo Kung asked about the practise of virtue. Confucius replied, the mechanic who wishes to finish his work well, must first whet the edge of his tools. When dwelling in a province, then serve (or imitate) men of talents and virtue among the great officers, and form friendships among the virtuous of the literati.

10. Yen Yuen asked how a Province should be governed. Confucius said, follow the division of time made by the Hea Dynasty, ride in the carriages of Yin, wear the diadem of Chow, and use the music of Shun, restrain the music of Chin, * and put loquacious flatterers to a great distance:—for the music of Chin, is licentious, and loquacious flatterers are eminently dangerous.

11. Confucius says, to the man who does not concern himself about what is distant, sorrow must be near.

12. Confucius exclaimed, alas I have never seen one who loves virtue as we love beauty!

13. Confucius said, Chwang Wăn Chung was a secret robber of office. He knew that Lew Hea Hwuy was a man of eminent talents and virtue, and yet did not promote him to a place equal to his own.

14. Confucius says, be liberal in reproving yourself, and sparing in reproving others; thus you will put murmuring to a distance.

15. Confucius says, a man who does not say how can this be done, what will this lead to? I can do nothing for him. †

16. Confucius says, when a number of men club together and during the whole day converse not on the principles of justice, but delight in little, crafty schemes, it is difficult for such to become virtuous.

† That is the man who does not maturely reflect before he acts, cannot be saved from misery, even by a sage.

---

* Restrain the music of Chin &c. It appears that the ancient sages of China were not only extremely fond of what they esteemed good music, but that they believed it to have a powerful influence over the morals of the people. Confucius was so powerfully struck with the music of the great Shun, that for three months after he heard it, he knew not the taste of his food. The Chinese at the present day seem partial to music, and play on a great variety of instruments. But according to their own account, their music at present is far inferior to what it was in the golden ages of antiquity.

17. Confucius says, the superior man makes justice the foundation, builds according to propriety, adorns with humility and finishes by sincerity: such is a superior man.

18. Confucius says, the superior man is grieved at his own want of ability, not that men do not know him.

19. Confucius says, the superior man is grieved, if he die without a name. *

20. Confucius says, the superior man seeks it in himself, the mean man, seeks it in others.

21. Confucius says, the superior man acts with firmness, without wrangling—lives in harmony with others, without intriguing with them.

22. Confucius says, the superior man, does not employ men on account of their words, nor despise the words because of the man.

23. Tsze Kung asked, if there was any one word which expresses the conduct proper for one's whole life. Confucius replied, will not the word *Shoo* do it, i. e. do not to others what you do not wish them to do to you.

24. Confucius said, in my intercourse with men, whom do I slander? whom do I flatter? If I do flatter any one, I must have first tried him, For three Dynasties, this people have been treated with uprightness, why should I do otherwise. !

25. Confucius said, I have seen the day, that when the Imperial Historian was not certain as to the truth of any report, he left a blank in the record, and when he who had a horse, would lend him to another man; but now these days are gone. †

* These two remarks, though seemingly contradictory, are perfectly consistent with each other. For the only reason why the superior man is grieved that he has not attained a name, is because he knows that if he had really possessed genuine worth, he must have been praised. So that the want of a name, in his estimation, is a sure evidence of the want of worth.

† In this passage the sage laments the growing degeneracy of the age. Hoo She says, I am in doubt as to the sense of this sentence and dare not give a forced explanation.

26. Confucius says, sophistry confounds truth, and falsehood; he who cannot bear with little things, will ruin great undertakings.

27. Confucius says, although the multitude hate a person, still you should investigate, and although men in general love a man, it is nevertheless necessary to examine. *

28. Confucius says, man may enlarge the path of virtue, but it cannot enlarge him. †

29. Confucius says, he who errs and reforms not, errs indeed.

30. Confucius said, I have spent whole days without food, and whole nights without sleep, in abstract thinking, but this proved of no real utility. There is nothing equal to the study of the ancients.

31. Confucius says, the superior man, is concerned about right principles, not about food. Even the ploughman may be famished. But learning has its reward in itself. The superior man is grieved that right principles are not practised, but feels no concern about poverty.

32. Confucius says, although a man have knowledge sufficient to reach the point, yet if he have not virtue to hold fast what he has attained, he will lose it again. Although his knowledge be sufficient, and he has virtue to preserve it, if he do not conduct himself with dignity, the people will not reverence him. Although he have knowledge and virtue to hold it fast, and also conduct himself with dignity, if he do not treat the people according to the rules of propriety, he falls short of his duty.

Confucius says, the superior man cannot be known by small things, but he may by being entrusted with important concerns.

* It is only the truly virtuous, who are qualified either to hate or love others, hence if we either esteem or dis-esteem a man, merely because of the general opinion of the multitude and do not examine for ourselves, we are likely to be deceived.

† Beyond man there is no Taou (right path) and beyond Taou there is no man. But the human mind possesses an intelligent principle, while Taou cannot act of itself; hence man may diffuse Taou but Taou cannot enlarge man.

The inferior man cannot be known by being trusted with weighty matters, but may be known by little things. *

34. Confucius says, men are more dependant on virtue, than on water and fire. We see men in consequence of treading on fire, and water, die, but we never saw men die in consequence of treading in the footsteps of virtue.

35. Confucius says, maintain virtue and yield it not, even to your Teacher.

36. Confucius says, the superior man is upright and firm, but does not practise his words whether they be right or wrong. †

37. Confucius says, in serving your prince respect his work, and put salary in the back ground.

38. Confucius said, teach all without regard to what class they belong.

39. Confucius says, those whose principles differ, should not consult together (or they cannot do so).

40. Confucius says, it is sufficient that yonr language be perspicuous. ‡

41. Confucius in conducting Mëën, the blind musician, when he arrived at the stair, said this is the stair, when he came to the seats, he said these are the seats; when they had sat down,

* Those who employ men, ought carefully to examine and discover what their peculiar talents fit them for and employ them accordingly. A man of great abilities should never be employed in situations of minor importance, nor should men of inferior talents be intrusted with the duties of an important station. It is not certain but that a man of superior talents and worth may some times fail in the duties of an inferior office, while an inferior man may chance in some one instance to perform a great action.

† If at any time the superior man should through inadvertence, or from want of sufficient information, make a promise, the fulfilment of which would not accord with justice, he will not fulfil his promise at the expence of justice. Nor will he do any thing merely because it was done, or is now done, by men of virtue, and talents, but will always examine and act according to what is just and right. ††

‡ Confucius taught his disciples to employ such language as would convey their ideas perspicuously, and not concern themselves much about elegant diction.

---

†† This is one of the best definitions of the superior man we recollect to have met with in the Four Books. If the line of conduct here recommended were always adopted, the world would not, as it now does, present the monstrous spectacle of multitudes following numerous absurdities, both in theory and practice, merely because they were adopted by their ancestors.

Confucius said, such a one sits here, and such a person sits there. When the musician went out, Tsze Chang asked saying, is what you said to the musician agreeable to reason (or does it convey any instruction). Confucius replied, this is the way of assisting others.

CHAP. XVI.

1. Ke She wishing to reduce Chuen Yu, Yen Yew and Ke waited on Confucius and informed him, that Ke She would have an affair in Chuen Yu Confucius said, Kew, is not this your fault! The former kings appointed Chuen Yu Lord of Tung Mung. Moreover it lies within the precincts of the country, and is under the government, ministers of the crown, how ought he to attack it.*

Yen Yew said, our master wishes it, we two, his servants do not wish it? Confucius said, Kew, Chow Jin said, when you can employ your talents, hold an office, when you cannot, resign. If, when a man is in danger of falling, he be not supported, or if when he falls he be not helped up, of what use are his assistants! You speak erroneously. When the tiger and wild ox are permitted to leave their cages and the precious gem to spoil in the casket, who is to blame? Yen Yew replied, at present, Chuen Yu is strongly fortified, and it is in the vicinity of Pe, if we do not take it, it will be a source of vexation to posterity. Confucius said, I tell you Kew, that the superior man hates such a concealment of ones real wishes under false pretences*

* At that time Ke She (one of the high officers of the Loo country) had one half of the country under him, and Mung Sun, and Shuh Sun, each had one fourth. Ke She also wished to have the dependant country Chuen Yu which alone was under the control of the Loo government. As Kew assisted Ke She in peeling the people, Confucius reproved him only.

I have heard that rulers and masters of families, are not grieved because their people are few, but because every one obtains not his due. They do not grieve on account of poverty, but because of the want of harmony and peace. For when each obtains his due, there will be no poverty, when harmony prevails, there will be no want of people, and when peace is enjoyed, there will be no revolutions. Now if things are thus, and people at a distance after all do not serve you, then cultivate learning and virtue to entice them to come, when they come (or put themselves under your government) then make them happy. At present you two, Yew and Kew, assist your master, and people at a distance do not serve you, nor are you able to induce them to yield themselves up to your government. Your own province is rent to pieces, and in a state of disorder, and you are unable to manage it, and yet you are scheming about taking up arms to subdue a people not in your country. I am afraid that Ke She, will find, that the source of his grief lies not in Chuen Yu, but within the walls of his own town.

2. Confucius says, when the Empire is governed by right principles; rites, music, and decrees to put down the disorderly, proceed from the Emperor. When the Empire is not governed by right principles, rites, music, and edicts to subdue the disorderly, proceed from the tributary Princes. When these proceed from the Princes, it is seldom that they do not, in the space of ten ages, lose their power. When they proceed from the great Officers of state, it is a rare case, if they do not lose their power, in the course of five ages. When these proceed from the stewards of government Officers, (or Princes), it seldom happens, that they do not lose their influence in three ages. *

* When Taou (the principles of the former kings) flourishes in the Empire, it is well governed. The Emperor alone possesses the divine right of appointing the rites, regulating the music, and punishing the refractory. When this power is wrested out of his hands, it will descend from one rank to another till it arrive at the lowest and end in complete anarchy and the loss of the country.

When the Empire is governed by just principles, government does not depend on the great officers. When the Empire is well governed, the plebeians do not hold private consultations (on the measures of government).

3. Confucius said, for five ages, our Prince has been deprived of his revenue. For four ages, politics have been under the power of the great officers, so that the descendants of the three Kwans are become feeble. *

4. Confucius says, there are three classes of men who prove useful friends, and three who are injurious. The friendship of the upright, faithful, and intelligent is advantageous, that of the fop, the sycophant, and the loquacious, is injurious.

5. Confucius says, there are three things which it is advantageous to delight in, and three which it is injurious to rejoice in. To delight in discussing the principles and rules of propriety and music—in talking of (perhaps praising) the virtues of others—and in having many virtuous friends, is advantageous. To rejoice in the indulgence of pride, idleness and feasting, is injurious.

6. Confucius says, there are three errors to which he who stands in the presence of a virtuous Prince is liable, viz. speaking without being asked; which is rashness—not answering fully when asked, which is taciturnity (or concealing one's mind);—and speaking without observing the (Prince's) countenance, which is blindness.

7. Confucius says, there are three things which the superior man guards against. In youth, when his passions are fluctuating, he guards against lust. In manhood when his passions are vigorous, he guards against quarrelling and fighting. In old age when his passions have lost their vigour, he guards against covetousness.

* These three families had for four ages assumed the sole power in the state of Loo, so tha according to the principles of the sage, delivered above, their power was becoming feeble.

8. Confucius says, there are three things which the superior man venerates. He venerates the decrees of heaven—he venerates great men and he venerates the maxims of the sages. But the mean man knows not the will of heaven, insults great men, and despises the words of the sages. *

9. Confucius says, men of the first rate talents, are born with the knowledge of divine principles. Those who attain this knowledge by study, are next to them. Those who after long and severe labor, at last attain this knowledge, are next. Those who after long and painful toil, cannot attain the point, are the most inferior of men. †

10. Confucius says, the superior man has nine things that he thinks on. When he looks, he thinks of seeing clearly. When he hears, he thinks of hearing distinctly. In his countenance he thinks of manifesting benignity. In his words he thinks of truth. In his actions he thinks of respect. When in doubt, he thinks of inquiring. When in anger he thinks of suffering. When he sees an opportunity of getting gain, he thinks of justice.

11. Confucius said, look upon virtue as if unable to reach it, and upon vice as thrusting the hand into boiling water; I have seen the men who did so, and heard the maxim. I have heard of dwelling in secret in order to cultivate one's talents and virtue,

* The decree of heaven (which some render fate), means the original principles which heaven implants in all men.

† Heaven bestows upon all men the same nature, equally and perfectly virtuous, while it gives different degrees of ability to different individuals. But although the talents of him who knows divine principles without study, are far superior to the abilities of the man who must study hard to obtain this knowledge, yet the latter may, by long and severe effort arrive at the same eminence of perfect intelligence that the former occupies. ††

†† After such intellectual giants as Plato, Socrates, and Pythogoras, who had the best facilities which nature could afford, have spent their lives, and exerted their mental powers to the utmost in search of divine principles, and to the last proved unsucessful, it is rather too much to be told, that some men attain this high elevation without any mental effort. Had we not the works of the Chinese sages in our hands, from which we can estimate their knowledge and abilities, we should be apt to suppose, by such assertions, that the celestial Empire produced a certain class of divine personages clothed in the garb of human nature. But as the tree is best known by its fruit, and as we have tasted pretty freely of the fruit produced by these imaginary divine plants, we can say from experience that after all both root and branches smell strongly of the earth.

and then coming forth to a public station in order to employ their talents, but I have not seen any one who did so.

12. Prince King of Tse had one thousand four horse carriages, but when he died the people saw nothing for which they could praise him. Pih E and Shuh Tse died of hunger at the foot of the mountain Show Yang and the people praise them to this day.

13. Chin Kang asked Pih E, saying, Sir, have you heard any thing extraordinary (from your father)? I have not, replied the other. One day when he was standing alone, and I was passing thro' the hall, he asked me whether I had studied the She King; I replied in the negative. On which he remarked that unless I studied the She King, I could not have materials for conversation. I then retired and studied the She King. At another time, when he was alone and I was crossing the hall, he asked me whether I had studied the Le Ke, I said I had not. If, said he you do not study the Le Ke, you cannot be established in right principles, I have only heard these two things. Chin Kang retired highly pleased, saying, I asked one thing, and I have heard three. I have heard of the importance of the She King, and of the Le Ke and that the superior man keeps his son at a distance.*

14. The wife of a Prince of a Province is styled by the Prince himself Foo Jin.—She calls herself Seaou Tung.—The people of her own country call her Keun Foo Jin. To foreigners She is styled (or styles herself) Kwa Seaou Keun, but foreigners call her Keun Foo Jin.†

* Chin Kang suspected, that Confucius secretly taught his son some wonderful doctrines which he concealed from his disciples, and therefore asked Pih Yu in reference to this point.

† At home when the Prince is employed governing the people, his wife assists him by governing the household; hence her husband styles her. "Foo Jin" denoting that the is his equal. When she is in the preseuce of her husband, she styles herself "little girl" meaning that she is young and without knowledge, and presumes not to consider herself the equal of her husband. The people of the nation style her Keun Foo Jin, denoting that she assists the Prince in managing domestic concerns, and shares his honors. These are the terms by which she is designated in her own nation. In foreign countries her husband calls her "Kwa Seaou Keun" (i. e. deficient man's little Prince). This is the language of humility. The people of foreign coutries likewise style her Keun Foo Jin. Denoting that She is equal to the Queen of their own country.

CHAP. XVII.

1. Yang Ho wished to see Confucius.—Confucius did not go to call on him. On which he sent a Pig to induce a visit. Confucius chose a time, when Yang Ho was from home, to pay his respects, but happening to meet on the road, Yang Ho said to Confucius, come here I wish to speak with you. Can it be called benevolence to conceal one's gem, and leave his country in a state of moral stupefaction? Confucius replied, no. Can it be called intelligence to love business, and yet always lose the proper season for doing it? Confucius replied, it cannot.—Said the other, days and months are passing away, and time waits not for us. Confucius replied, right; I will go into office.*

2. Confucius says, by nature we are nearly equal, but by education very different. †

3. Confucius says, it is only those who possess the highest degree of intelligence, and the lowest degree of stupidity that cannot be altered.

4. When Confucius went to Woo Ching, he heard the sound of instrumental and vocal music, on which he smiled and said, when you kill a fowl, why use a knife employed to slay an ox. Tsze Yew replied, I have formerly heard you, Sir, say, that when the ruler studies right principles, he will love the people, and that when the people learn right principles, they are easily

* Yang Ho was steward to the usurper Ke She and wished a visit from Confucius, hoping to engage him as an auxiliary in their usurpation. Confucius, of course, would wish to avoid such a man; consequently he chose to pay his respects when he knew that he was from home.

† Chin Tsze says that it is the original talents of men, that are spoken of and not their original moral nature, (or as the words denote, the root of nature). For in the original nature of man, as to its moral qualities there is no difference. All having a nature perfectly virtuous.

ruled. Confucius said, my pupil Yen's (Tsze Yew's) words are just; I was only jesting.*

5. Kung Shan Fŭh having raised a rebellion in Pe sent for Confucius. Confucius wished to go. Tsze Loo was displeased and said you ought not to go. Why should you go at the call of Kung Shan She. Confucius said, do you think he has called me for no purpose. If he employ me I will establish the doctrines of Chow in the east.†

6. Tsze Chang asked Confucius in what virtue consisted? Confucius replied, he who possesses five things is virtuous, all over the world. (Tsze Chang) said I beg leave to ask what these are? Ans. They are gravity, liberality, fidelity, intelligence, and benevolence. Be grave and you will not be treated disrespectfully. Be liberal, and you will win the affections of all. Be faithful and you will be confided in. Be intelligent and you will be meritorious, benevolent and you will be able to manage men.

7. Pĭh Heĭh sent for Confucius, and the latter felt inclined to go. Tsze Loo said, I have formerly heard you Sir, say, that if a man's conduct was vicious, the superior man would not associate with him. Pĭh Heĭh has raised a rebellion in Chung Mow, why should you, Sir, go to him!

Confucius replied yes, I did say so; but I did not then speak of the hardness that cannot be diminished by rubbing, nor of the whiteness which cannot be stained by being put in the mud. Do you suppose that I am like a water-melon, which is to be hung up and not to be eaten!‡

* Tsze Yew was governor of Woo and, according to the instructions of his master Confucius, taught the people the rules of propriety and music, hence the sage was really highly pleased with him.

† Had Confucius received an official appointment in Pe, he would have brought the royal principles of Wan, Woo and Chow Kung into play in the east

‡ This means, that such was the firmness, and stability of the sage's virtue, that it could not be bent from the path of rectitude, by any temptation whatever; and such was its purity, that it could not be sullied by having intercourse with bad men. ‡‡

---

‡‡ Many will question the truth of this position, but few will deny, that the declaration would have come with a better grace, from some one else, than from the sage himself.

8. Confucius said, Yew, have you heard of these six words and of the six things which cloud them? Ans. No. Sit down and I will explain the matter.

A desire of being benevolent unaccompanied by the love of learning, is clouded by ignorance. A fondness for knowledge without the love of learning, is clouded by instability. A wish to be faithful unattended by the love of learning, is clouded by robbery. A love of uprightness without the love of study, is clouded by rashness. A love of bravery without the love of learning, is clouded by insubordination. A love of firmness without the love of study, is clouded by forwardness.

9. Confucius said, my pupils, why do you not study the She King? The She, will expand your ideas—teach you to discriminate—to live in harmony—to repress wrath—when at home how to serve your father, and when abroad how to serve your Prince—and to be extensively acquainted with the names of birds, beasts, herbs, and trees.

10. Confucius said, to (his son) Pih Yu, you ought to study the Chow Nan, and the Chaou Nan. If a man do not study the Chow Nan, and the Chaou Nan, he is like one standing with his face close to a wall. *

11. Confucius said, every one calls out Presents! Presents! but are mere gems and silks (without respect) presents? Every one calls out Music! Music! but is the mere ringing of bells and beating of drums (without harmony) music?

12. Confucius says, the man who puts on an external appearance of great firmness, but at heart is really weak and pusillanimous, resembles the mean fellow who bores through a wall to commit theft.

13. Confucius says, he who covets the praise of villagers, is the thief of virtue.

* The Chow Nan, and the Chaou Nan, treat of the cultivation of personal virtue, and the proper regulation of the family. The meaning of the phrase, ' 'standing with your face close to a wall,' ' is that if you do not study these two pieces, you cannot see any thing aright, nor advance a single step in the right path.

14. Confucius says, he who hears any thing on the road and prates about it on the road, throws away virtue.

15. Confucius said, how can a low man serve his Prince! Before he get into office, he is in distress how he may obtain it, and when he has obtained it, he is vexed about keeping it. In his unprincipled dread of loosing his place, he will go to all lengths.

16. Confucius said, the people in ancient times, had three failings which do not now exist. The ambitions of ancient times, aimed at great things, those of the present day break over all the bonds of propriety. The austere of ancient times, were moderate, those of modern times, give way to violent wrath. The dull of former days were upright, those of the present day are only deceitful.

17. Confucins said, I hate partial red, which assumes the place of the true vermillion. I hate the music of Chin, which confuses the music of the sages. I hate sharp mouths, which prove the overthrow of a state.

18. Confucius said, I feel inclined not to speak. Tsze Kung replied, if our Master speak not, what will his pupils have to transmit to posterity? Confucius replied, what does heaven say! yet the four seasons constantly revolve, and all things are produced, what does heaven say! *

19. Joo Pei wished to have an interview with the sage, the the latter refused to grant it, on the ground of being sick, but as soon as the bearer of this message went out, the sage took his harp and played that Joo might hear him. †

* That the four seasons constantly revolve and all things are produced, certainly manifests the constant operations of heaven. There is no need for words to make them obvious. Every movement of the sage was nothing else, but the manifestation of wonderful doctrines, and pure rectitude, why wait till he speak to illustrate them! This is truly heaven.

† Joo Pei, had been a student of the sage, but must have committed some misdemeanor, hence the sage deeply reproved him by this refusal. ††

†† Pray what moral renovation could this palpable falsehood effect on the beholders, or upon the reader of this barefaced lie! Does heaven thus deceive men! Truly such a man was a worthy compeer to the God of eternal and inviolable truth! It had been much better that the sage had not spoken at all, than that he should by his example encourage his admirers in a hateful practice, which if not deeply repented of, and pardoned through the atonement of Jesus, must be punished with everlasting woe. Is it in imitation of the sage that the Chinese of the present day distinguish themselves by telling falsehoods?

20. Tsae Go asked whether one year was not a long time to mourn for parents, observing, that if superior men, are three years without practising ceremonies, etiquette must be lost; and if they are three years without practicing music, music must come to ruin, and since the old grain is exhausted and the new springs up, and fire is taken from the different kinds of wood in one year, it is a sufficient period (for mourning). * Confucius replied, should you then feel easy in eating fine grain, and wearing ornamented clothes, (after your parents had been dead one year)? Yes (replied the other) I should feel easy. Confucius rejoined, if you can feel at ease, you may do so; but the superior man, when mourning for his parents, suppose you give him nice food, he does not relish it. Although he hear music, he does not enjoy it. If he dwell in a fine house, he feels not at ease. If you can enjoy such things you may do so.

Tsae Go having gone out, Confucius said, Yu is not virtuous, after a child is three years old, it may leave the arms of its parents. Hence three years mourning for parents, is proper for all under heaven, has Yu three years affection for his parents!

21. Confucius says, that the man who spends the day in eating, without employing his mind about any thing, is in a bad state indeed! The common chess-player is superior to him.

22. Tsze Loo asked, whether the superior man esteemed valor? Confucius replied, the superior man considers justice of the first importance. If a man in a superior situation, have valor without justice, he will act disorderly, if a man in an inferior situation, have valor without justice, he will be a robber.

23. Tsze Kung asked, saying, are there any whom (or whose conduct) the superior man hates? Confucius replied, there are: he hates those who publish the faults of others.—He also hates

* In the spring season they extract fire by boring, or rotatory friction, from the elm—in summer from the date tree—in autumn from the mulberry tree, and in winter from the Hwae Tan tree. So that in the course of one year, all things undergo a regular change. On which account Tsae Go thought one year a sufficient time to mourn for parents.

the man who slanders his superiors.—He hates those who are bold and know not propriety, and those who boast of great things which they are unable to perform.* Tsze Kung said, there are those whom I also hate. I hate those who secretly pry into the private affairs of others, in order that they themselves may be esteemed very knowing. I hate those who act a haughty part, in order that they may be thought brave. I hate those who spy out the vices of others, in order that they themselves may appear upright.

24. Confucius says, none are so difficult to bring up as women and men servants. If you treat them with familiarity, they become disrespectful, and if you treat them distantly, they grumble.

25. Confucius says, that if a man is hated for his vices, when forty years of age, there is an end to him (i. e. to his improvement. †

CHAP. XVIII.

1. Wei Tsze resigned;- -Ke Tsze became his (Chow's) slave, and Pe Kan, for reproving (Chow), was put to death. Confucius said, there were three men of sterling virtue in the court of Yin.‡

2. Leaou Hea Hwuy, had been chief Jailor and was three times discharged from office. Some person said to him, Sir, ought you not to leave your country. To which he replied,

* By the superior man Tsze Kung indirectly referred to Confucius. How She says, that sages and men of eminent talents and virtue hated such people as these. This explains what is meant by saying that it is only the virtuous, that can love or hate men aright.

† The ancients deemed forty years of age the period when human virtue is complete. After that time the spirits daily decay, and the man who has not forsaken his vices, and accustomed himself to the practice of virtue, before he is forty, will not do so to the end of life.

‡ When the tyrant Chow reigned, his uncle Ke Tsze, in consequence of having reproved him, had his hair cut like that of a slave, and was cast into prison. Another uncle called Pe Kan, was put to death, for the same offence. On which the brother of the tyrant, called Ke Tsze, thought it time to retire that he might preserve the ancestorial sacrifices (perhaps family name). These were the three men alluded to by the sage.

If I act uprightly in serving men, whither shall I go where I shall not be three times discharged from office. But if in serving men I act contrary to right principles, why should I leave the country of my parents! *

3. King, Prince of Tse, when consulting with his ministers respecting the mode of treating Confucius, said, I will not treat him with so much respect, as Ke She is treated; but will treat him on a medium between Ke and Mung; but added, I am now old, I cannot employ him at all, on which account, Confucius took his departure. †

4. The people of Tse sent a band of female musicians (to the court of Loo). Ke Hwan Tsze, received them and for three days held no court; wherefore Confucius marched off. ‡

5. The arrogant Tsëë Yu of Tsoo passing Confucius one day sang, King of the birds! King of the birds! how is thy virtue degenerated. What is past, cannot be altered by reproof, but as to the future, you may yet stop. Those who hold government offices at present, are in eminent danger. Confucius alighted and wished to converse with him, but he went off quickly, and avoided him, so that the sage could not speak with him. ¶

* Leaou meant, that if he followed the false principles and corrupt practices of the government of his native country Loo, he might hold his office in peace and quietness, but that such was the degenerate state of all the surrounding provinces that a man of upright principles and practice. would soon get expelled from office. On this account, he saw no reason to hope for better treatment in another country than he had experienced in his own.

† Of the three high officers of state in the court of Loo, Ke She was the chief, and Mung She was the lowest. Ke was a violent minister, and the Prince treated him with the highest degree of respect. Hence, when the Sovereign of Tse had some thoughts of giving the sage an official appointment, he thought that if he treated him on a medium between Ke and Mung, he would hit the mark. But no sooner had he declared his intentions on this point, than he intimated that he was now too old to employ such a man as Confucius. The latter being informed of this, instantly left the Tse country. Thus we see that when wishing to get into office, he did not refuse an appointment, because of the ceremonial treatment he was likely to meet with, but because he could not act upon his own principles.

‡ In the fourteenth year of Ting, Prince of Loo, Confucius held the office of criminal judge. The people of Tse, were afraid that by his principles and government, he might make the Loo country more than a match for Tse. Hence they employed this scheme with the hope, that they might offend the sage, and induce him to give up his office. In this design they completely succeeded.

¶ Tsee Yu was a man of talents and virtue who, in consequence of the mal-administration of the day, had retired into secret and was much offended at the sage because he would not give over his fruitless attempts to reform the country.

6. Chang Tsoo and Këë Neïh being at the plough together, Confucius on passing them one day, sent Tsze Loo to ask them where the ford was. Chang Tsoo said, who is that, who holds the reins? Tsze Loo replied, it is Kung Mow. Is it Kung Mow of Loo? Yes. O then he knows the ford. On which Tsze Loo inquired of Këë Neïh. Këë Neïh asked saying, who are you, Sir. To which Tsze Loo answered, I am Chung Yew. Are you a disciple of Kung Mow of Loo. He replied in the affirmative. On which Këë said, all under heaven are flowing down the stream of vice, and who can reform them? Why do you follow a master who only refuses office under certain men, and do not rather imitate us who retire from office entirely. Having said so they went on with their ploughing and stopped not. * Tsze Loo went on and informed Confucius. Confucius sighed and said, I cannot associate with birds and beasts! If I follow not men, whom shall I follow! If the world were in possession of right principles I should not seek to change it.

7. Tsze Loo having fallen behind the sage, chanced to meet with an old man carrying a basket on a staff. Whom he asked, saying, did you see my master, Sir? The old man replied, you are unaccustomed to labor, nor can you distinguish the five grains:—who is your master? He then stuck his staff into the ground and began to pull up the weeds. Tsze clasped his hands on his breast in a respectful manner and stood still. He kept Tsze Loo through the night, killed fowls and prepared food for him. He also brought out his two sons and presented them to Tsze Loo. Next day Tsze Loo walked on and told Confucius. Confucius said, he is a hidden one, and sent Tsze Loo back to have an interview with him. When Tsze Loo arrived, he had left.

* These were likewise two men of talents and virtue, who in consequence of the misrule which then prevailed among the different states, chose to lead a quiet country life, in preference to holding offices under Princes void of good principles. They likewise took this opportunity of shewing their displeasure at Confucius; because he had not like them abandoned the age to its fate.

Tsze Loo delivered the sentiments of the sage, saying, this man's not going into office is not right. The duties of juniors to their seniors, he dares not violate; how is it that he neglects the duties of a Minister to his Prince? Wishing to keep his own person pure, he confuses the greatest of human relations. The superior man goes into office, that he may put in practice his principles. I know that good principles are not now acted upon. *

8. Pih E, Shŭh Tse, Yu Chung, E Yih, Choo Chang, Lew Hea Hwuy, and Shaou Lëĕn, were all worthy and accomplished men without office.

Confucius said, the men who would neither crouch to another, nor taint their character, were Pih E and Shŭh Tse. It is said, that Lew Hea Hwuy, and Shaou Lëĕn, yielded and lowered their persons. But their words accorded with reason, and their actions were fair and altogether upright. It is said, that Yu Chung, and E Yih, dwelt in secret, and gave scope to their words, yet kept their persons pure and declined holding Offices. † Confucius said, I differ from these. I never predetermine whom I will, or will not serve.

9. Che, the chief musician of Loo went to Tse. Kan, master of the second meal band, went to Tsoo. Lew, master of the third meal band, went to Tsae. Keŭh, master of the fourth meal band, went to Tsin. Fang Shŭh, the Drummer, went and dwelt in Ho. Woo, who beat the Taou went to Han. The assistant master musician, Yang, with Seang master of the King, left and dwelt on an Island.

10. Chow Kung said to Loo Kung, the superior man, does not treat his relatives distantly, nor excite the murmurs of his

* The old man shewed by presenting his two sons to Tsze Loo, that he knew the proper gradations of human society. Of all the human relations, that which subsists between Prince and Minister, is the greatest. The man of superior accomplishments, wishes to go into office, that he may perform the important duties which that relation requires. Hence Confucius was displeased with eminent characters, who, without sufficient cause, retired into private life, and did not rather come forth to office, and use their utmost effects to reform a degenerate age.

† Mung Tsze says, that when it was proper to hold an office, Confucius accepted a government appointment, and when it was proper for him to resign, he did so. When it was right to remain long in office, he remained long, and when it was right for him quickly to leave it, he instantly resigned.

high Officers, nor forget his old friends, without good cause, nor does he look for every accomplishment in one individual.

11. In Chow there were eight eminent scholars named Pĭh Tă, Pĭh Kwă, Chung Tŭh, Chung Hwŭh, Shŭh Yay, Shuh Hea, Ke Suy, and Ke Wa. *

CHAP. XIX.

1. Tsze Chang says, the true scholar, when he sees his Prince, or parents in danger, will risk his life for their safety. When he sees an opportunity of getting gain, he thinks on justice. When offering sacrifices, he thinks of reverence. When mourning, he feels genuine grief; such a man merits the name of a scholar. †

2. Tsze Chang said, as to those who hold virtue, but not in a liberal manner, who embrace just principles, but not firmly; it is of little importance to the world, whether they exist or not.

3. The disciples of Tsze Hea, asked Tsze Chang, with whom they ought to associate as friends.—Tsze Chang said, what does your master say on the subject? He says, that we ought to associate with men of worth, and to keep at a distance the worthless. Tsze Chang replied, this differs indeed from what I have learned. I have heard that the man of superior virtue, honors men of talents and virtue, and bears with all; and that he praises the virtuous and pities the weak. In my intercourse with men, with whom will I not bear? But if I am not virtuous, men will first reject me, how can I reject them! ‡

* This is recorded to shew how abundant men of worth and ability were in the commencement of the Chow Dynasty, and likewise how much men had degenerated before the time of the sage. Some say that one mother bore all the eight at four births.

† These four are the great principles, by which one's character is established, if a man is wanting in any one of these, the others are not worth looking at.

‡ The doctrines of Tsze Hea, on the subject of holding friendly intercourse with men, were too narrow and rigid, and Tsze Chang very properly satirised him; but on the other hand, Tsze Chang's own principles on this point, were too lax. For although, in general, a man of eminent talents and virtue, bears with all; yet when there is just cause, he will cut off his intercourse with abandoned characters. It is true that a man who is himself destitute of virtue, ought not to reject others; but there are injurious friends who ought to be avoided.

4. Tsze Hea says, the inferior employments are still worthy of attention, but if those who follow them extend their thoughts to what is great and extensive, it is to be feared that they will not succeed: hence the learned do not attend to them.*

5. Tsze Hea says, he who daily learns what he did not before know, and monthly forgets not what he had previously learned, may be called a lover of learning.

6. Tsze Hea says, learn extensively, determine firmly, examine fully, and think homeward: for virtue lies in these.

7. Tsze Hea says, the mechanic dwells in his shop to finish his work, the superior man studies to complete his duty.

8. Tsze Hea says, the mean man puts a false gloss upon his faults.

9. Tsze Hea says, the superior man has three variations: look to him at a distance, and he appears stern; come near to him, and he is mild; listen to his words and they are severe.

10. Tsze Hea says, the superior man, gains the confidence of the people and then employs them. Did he not first gain their confidence, he might be considered severe. He is first faithful, and then reproves. Were he not faithful, he might be suspected of railing.

11. Tsze Hea says, in important things pass not over the proper limits; in lesser matters you may err without much injury.

12. Tsze Yew said, the disciples of Tsze Hea are mere children: they can sprinkle and sweep the floor, answer questions, enter and retire, but these are merely the branches, without the root, what are they worth?

Tsze Hea, hearing this sighed, and said, you are mistaken

* The inferior occupations are such as those of the husband-man, gardener, physician, diviner, &c.**

** It is presumed that a European M. D. would not think himself highly honored, by being classed with a husband-man, or gardener, and far less by being put on an equality with a fortune-teller.

Yew! Among the doctrines of the sages, which ought to be first taught, or which is to be considered last and not taught? For instance, among herbs and trees there are different classes. Why should we render void the doctrines of the superior man! It is only the sage that unites in one, commencement and close. *

13. Tsze Hea says, let men in the service of government employ their spare time in study, and let the scholar when he can spare time from study, go into office.

14. Tsze Yew says, in mourning for relatives if grief be carried to the utmost it is enough. (i. e. there is no need for external show).

15. Tsze Hea said, my friend Chang is for doing hard things (or impossibilities), but he does not attain to virtue.

16 Tsăng Tsze said, splendid is Chang's external appearance! but he neither will be assisted, nor assist in practising virtue.

17. Tsăng Tsze said, I have heard my master say, that a man cannot fully exhaust the abilities of his nature. If in any thing he can, it must be in mourning for parents.

18. Tsăng Tsze said, I have heard Confucius speak of the filial piety of Mung Chwang Tsze. In other things he may be imitated, but his not having changed his father's ministers, and mode of government is truly difficult.

19. When Mung She appointed Yang Foo to the office of criminal judge (the latter) asked Tsăng Tsze how he ought to act. Tsăng Tsze said, superiors have for a long time lost the

* According to the doctrines of the sages, you are not to consider the branches of greatest importance and attend to them first, nor to consider the root to be last and get wearied in teaching pupils to understand it. But there is among students a radical difference of talent, just as there exists a difference among trees and plants. If you do not inquire what their abilities are, but class them all together, this is only deceiving and insulting them. How could the superior man do such a thing!

right way, and the people have long been scattered; when you discover guilt, be grieved and pity them and rejoice not. *

20. Tsze Kung says, Chow was not so extremely vicious (as is reported); hence Princes should abhor dwelling in a low sink; for if they do not, all the vices under heaven will be imputed to them

21. Tsze Kung says, the errors of the superior man are like the eclipses of the sun and moon. His errors all man see, and his reformation all men look for.

22. Kung Sun Chaou of Wei, asked Tsze Kung, how Confucius learned. Tsze Chang replied, the doctrines of the Kings, Wan and Woo, have not yet fallen to the ground; they are still among men. Men of great abilities and virtue, remember their most profound and most important principles, and those of inferior abilities and worth, recollect their less profound and less important branches. Why should not Confucius study them? But why should he follow a fixed master? †

23. Shŭh Sun Woo Shŭh speaking of the great Officers of the court, said, Tsze Kung is a man superior in abilities and worth to Confucius. Tsze Fŭh King Pĭh informed Tsze Kung. Tsze Kung replied, we may be compared to the walls of a palace.

* The act of transgressing the laws, although the people's own, yet their not being instructed is to be imputed to their rulers; wherefore, when people under a government which makes no suitable provision for their education and instruction in right principles, are found guilty of violating the laws, their Judges ought in passing sentence upon them, to take into consideration, that they have been in a manner precipitated into crime, by the bad policy, or tyranny of unprincipled Rulers. By acting on this principle, they will be led to compassionate the people, and to administer fair and impartial justice. * *

† If men study right principles, they must, in general, have fixed and constant teachers. It was only Confucius who was an exception to this rule. The divine principles of the ancient Kings were still among men, and such were the super-eminent abilities of the sage, that he could learn them without the constant aid of a teacher. From superior men he learned their more important and from inferior men their less important branches.

---

* * The principles here inculated most approve themselves to every well regulated mind, as truly excellent. They are in perfect harmony both with reason and revelation. May not many Christian Rulers, learn a lesson on this point, from those who had only reason for their guide? Many Rulers who bear the Christian name, seem to think that implicit obedience, and revenue, are the only objects to which the Magistrate should look. But they would do well to consider, seriously, whether the gross ignorance, and consequent vices of their people, will not, on the awful day of retribution, be, in a great measure, charged upon them.

My wall is only shoulder high; if you only peep over the top, you may see all that is good in the house. But the wall of Confucius, is several jin high, if you don't get in at the door, you cannot see the beauty of the ancestorial Temple, and the riches of all the ministers. Few are those who get in at the door:—are not these words of your master reasonable! *

24. Shŭh San Woo Shŭh having reviled Confucius. Tsze Kung said, this is of no use. Confucius may not (or cannot) be reviled. Other men of talent and virtue, resemble the mounds and hills, which may be passed over, but Confucius resembles the sun and moon which cannot be passd over. A man may cut himself off from the sage, but how can he injure the sun and moon! He will only make it abundantly evident that he knows not his own measure. †

25. Ching Tsze Kin, conversing with Tsze Chung said, you Sir, are grave and respectful; how is Confucius more virtuous than you!

26. Tsze Kung said, the superior man for one word is deemed intelligent and for one word is deemed ignorant; ought we not therefore to be careful to our words. As the heavens can not be scaled, so Confucius cannot be equalled. Were Confucius to obtain the throne, he would establish the people, and they would be correct:—he would lead them, and they would follow:—he would console them, and they would come to him:—he would stimulate them, and they would live in harmony.—His life would be glorious and his death bitterly lamented; who can equal such a man!

* The expression, the beauty of the ancestorial Temple, is used in reference to the brilliancy of the sage's virtue and accomplishments, and the riches of all the ministers, refers to the abundant fulness of his virtue. As Shuh Sun Woo Shuh, had not ability sufficient to perceive the vast superiority of the sage. Tsze Kung gave an admirable turn to the subject, by not denying, but acknowledging the reasonableness of his remarks. For, as he had not been admitted into the Temple, how could he form any idea of its beauty and grandeur!

† Intimating that though a man may, by reviling the sage, and despising his doctrines, cut himself off from the benefit to be derived from learning these principles, and thus display his own ignorance, he cannot in the least degree injure the sun and moon (i. e. the sage) by refusing to behold their light.

CAAP. XX.

1. Yaou said, Ah! Shun, the decree of heaven now rests in you. Faithfully hold fast the due medium. If the people within the four seas suffer distress, heaven will cut you off forever. Shun gave the same charge to Yu. *

(Tang Wang) said, I Le a little child, presume to offer a black bull, and announce this case to the Great Supreme. His (Këë's) crimes I must not conceal. They are all known by the Supreme Being. If I offend, my sins are not occasioned by the people; but if the people offend, their crimes are chargeable on me. †

The Chow Dynasty bestowed liberal rewards, and made the virtuous rich. Books say, although Chow has many near relatives, they are not equal to (or a match for) the virtuous people (of Woo Wang.) If the people commit crimes they are chargeable on me. ‡

He (Woo Wang) paid great attention to the weights and measures—examinea the laws—restored to office those who had been put out of place; thus just government was practised in all parts of the empire. He re-established ruined Provinces—connected again the line of succession, where it had been broken —restored to place those who had retired into private life and the hearts of all under heaven submitted to him. ¶

What he deemed of most importance, was the support of the people, funeral rites, and sacrifices to ancestors. He was liberal, and hence obtained the hearts of the people;—faithful and the

* This refers to Yaou resigning the throne to Shun, and the latter giving it up in his turn to Yu.

† This is said in reference to Tang conquering the wicked Kee, last Emperor of the Hea Dynasty, and announcing the thing to the most high ruler, and to the different Princes of China. The announcement intimated that the crimes of Kee were too great to be forgiven, and that as Tang had received the divine decree to reign over the Empire, so, if he committed any crime, it was chargeable on himself alone, but if the people should act a vicious part, this was to be imputed to his misrule, and consequently charged on him.

‡ These were the expressions used by Woo Wang, in the form of an oath when he began to subdue the tyrant Chow. The meaning is, that although the relatives of Chow were numerous, yet their hearts were divided, and they had left the path of virtue, hence they were not equal to the numerous virtuous men who adhered to the house of Chow, and who were united in heart and in virtue.

¶ He gave the dignity of Princes to the descendants of Hwang Te, Yaou, Shun, and the royal families of the Hea and Shang Dynasties. He set Ke Tsze at liberty from prison, and restored to place those of the Shang Dynasty who had been displased.

people confided in him;—diligent (or quick), and therefore meritorious;—just, hence the people delighted in him. †

2. Tsze Chang asked Confucius how the affairs of government ought to be conducted? Confucius replied, honor five excellent and put away four evil things, then you may conduct aright the business of government. Tsze Chang asked what these five excellent things were? Confucius replied, be benevolent, without being wasteful;—employ the people, without causing them to murmur;—desire, and be not covetous;—be dignified, without pride;—and inspire awe, without being tyrannical.

Tsze Chang said, what do you mean by being bevevolent and not wasteful? Confucius repiied, to encourage the people to make gain by proper means; is not this benevolence without waste (or expense)? Select what work ought to be done, and employ the people at it, and who will murmur? To wish for virtue and to obtain it, is this covetousness? The superior man, whether the people be many or few; whether he attend to what is of great, or of small importance, never manifests disrespect, nor carelessness. Is not this being dignified without pride. He puts on his cap and clothes properly, and is grave and dignified in his looks and demeanour: hence the people look up to him with reverential respect. Is not this to inspire awe without being tyrannical?

Tsze Chang asked, what the four evil things were? Confucius replied, not to instruct the people and yet put them to death, is called cruelty. Not to give them previous warning, is called tyranny.—To delay your orders till the time when a thing should be done, is called robbery.—To hesitate in giving rewards through a niggardly disposition, is the action of an inferior officer (who has not power to do as he would) Confucius says, he who does not know the will of heaven, has no means of acting the superior man. He who does not know propriety, has not the means of being established. And he who does not know words, cannot know men.

* This is not recorded in the history of Woo Wang. We suspect that it is what some one has said, by way of a general remark on the government of the former kings.

MEMOIRS

OF

MENCIUS.

So little has been left on record concerning the celebrated subject of the following brief memoirs, that it is no easy task to give a correct outline of his character, much less is it practicable to enter into a minute detail of his public and private conduct: the following are some of the particulars of his life.

Mencius, whose name was 軻 *Ko* and literary title 子 *Tsze*, was a native of 鄒 *Tsoo*, now in the province of 山東 *Shan Tung*. He flourished about 350 years before the Christian era. His family were descended from 孟孫 *Mang Sun*, one of the 三家 *San Kea* whose usurpation of power, and consequent affectation of superior rank, Confucius severely reprehends in the four books. His father, it appears, died soon after Mencius was born: he was what the Chinese term a scholar, but was not distinguished for any peculiar virtues, and therefore is passed over in silence by Chinese writers. His mother, whose name was 伉氏 *Hang She*, is extolled as a prudent, clever woman, and recommended as an example to parents in bringing up their children. It is a maxim with

Chinese philosophers, that a good man will not dwell in a bad neighbourhood, lest, as they express it, all the pollution of the place should flow to him. It is recorded of Mencius's mother, that she changed her residence three times for the purpose of benefiting her son. In the first instance she lived near a butcher's shop ; but being apprehensive, from her son's apparent interest in the scenes of the slaughter house, and his desire of imitating them at home, that his feelings would become blunted and depraved, she determined on removing to a more eligible situation. Her next habitation was in the vicinity of a burial place, where Mencius soon began to imitate the practices of the mourners, who came to weep and offer sacrifices at the tombs of their deceased relatives: this was a new source of anxiety to his vigilant parent, who, fearing that he would habituate himself to mock the sacred rites of the people by imitating them in his boyish sports, deemed it advisable again to remove. Eventually she was more successful in the choice of a neighbourhood, having fixed upon a house opposite to a school. Mencius from observing here that the pupils were instructed in various branches of polite literature, commenced the practice of imitating them at home, which prodigiously delighted his mother, whose fond wishes respecting her son were now, she thought, about to be realized. He was accordingly sent to school, where he made great progress. Afterwards having heard of the fame of 子思 *Tsze Sze*, a worthy descendant of Confucius, Mencius became his disciple; and under him, we are informed, advanced rapidly in the knowledge of his master's doctrines. His mind having been thoroughly imbued with the principles of the philosophy of his sect, he set out to travel, and in the course of his wanderings arrived at the court of 宣王 *Seuen Wang* of 齊 *Tse*, and entered into the service of the king. But the king not being able to practise his doctrines, Mencius speedily withdrew, and went to 梁 *Leang*. 惠王 *Hwuy Wang* its king having been many times defeated in battle, humbled himself in his ceremonies, and sent many presents to the virtuous literati of the day, amongst whom was Mencius, inviting them to come to his assistance. They all obeyed his summons. 惠王 *Hwuy Wang* informed them that he was a man destitute of eloquence, his soldiers had been thrice defeated in battle, his eldest son was taken prisoner and his chief general killed. His enemies had depopulated his country, disgraced his ancestorial temples and the local deities, and he felt himself grievously insulted. You will not think a thousand *Le* too great a distance, said he to Mencius, if you can do me any good. Shame and misery have overtaken my country, what will profit it? Mencius replied, do not speak of profit. If the prince desires profit, then the officers of government will look for it. If the officers of government are anxious about it, the people will not be satisfied without it. Thus superiors and inferiors will wrangle about profit, and the nation's interests will be endangered. Those things about which a prince ought solely to be concerned, are benevolence and justice. 梁惠王 *Leang Hwuy Wang* laid a plain for attacking 趙 *Chaou*. Mencius said, 太王 *Tae Wang*, the father of 文王 *Wan Wang*, when his country was likely to be invaded, abandoned 邠 *Pin*, and retired to a hill rather than contend with his enemy. How could he unite with the prevailing irregular customs of the age? Can you take a square handle and insert it in the round socket of a chisel? 梁惠王 *Leang Hwuy Wang* did not apply what he said, but supposed it referred to something altogether remote from the present business. At that time the 秦 *Tsin* country employed 商君 *Shang Keun*, formerly of 魏, as it's prime minister; the nation was also rich in wealth and possessed of a powerful army The 楚 *Tsoo* and 魏 *Wei* countries employed 吳起 *Woo Ke* to wage war with 秦 *Tsin*. The rest of the Empire then united in a confederacy to attack and subdue it, and considered their conduct as virtuous. Mencius adhered firmly to his principles, and recommended the virtues of 堯 *Yaou* and 舜 *Shun*; but because the princes of the day did not unite with his views, he withdrew from office and gave himself up to the study of letters. He, with the assistance of some of his disciples, compiled the 詩經 *She King* and 書經 *Shoo King*; and handed down the doctrines of Confucius, with whose name his has now become associated in Chinese literature Like him he professed to seek the welfare of his fellow men, and advance the interests of his native country. By communicating a knowledge of the principles he had acquired, first to persons in official situations, and then to a number of private individuals who gathered around him for instruction, he endeavoured to diffuse his doctrines amongst the multitude at large, and effectually impress on the minds of his superiors, that the only stability of their times was the affections of the people. Thus inculcating the reciprocal duties of subjects and governors, he aimed at subjugating the whole Empire to the dominion of his principles. On the one hand he taught to the people the divine right of kings to reign, on the other he instructed kings that it was their duty to consult the wishes of the people, refrain from the exercise of tyranny, and in short become the father and mother of the nation. He was a man of independent principles; and unwilling to permit any oppression, in the governments with which he was connected, to pass without severe animadversion. His talents were of rather a superior order: he possessed a good knowledge of human nature, and displays in his writings considerable acuteness, in detecting the arbitrary measures of the reigning princes, and the insincere pretensions of inferior officers. In his doctrinal views he was proud to be considered an imitator of Confucius, and in his natural abilities seems to have excelled that renowned individual. Pride was evidently no stranger to his bosom; and though he unitormly assayed to conceal it, under the cloak of zeal for the public welfare and indignation at the oppressive conduct of bad rulers; it nevertheless not infrequently exhibits itself in characters too conspicuous to be mistaken. With all his pretensions to perfection in knowledge and practice, Mencius shows the same disposition to depart from the pure principles of morality and virtue, as the generality of men without the guidance of divine revelation. Whilst it is allowed that he excelled the majority of his country men in acuteness of intellect, and in research into such principles as were known and adopted by the sages of antiquity, and moreover deduced useful lessons of practice from experience and observation, it cannot be conceded that he is a fit instance to be adduced in favor of the non-essentiality of a divine revelation. He frequently inculcates principles at direct variance with common observation; and therefore of course also in opposition to truths established by infinite wisdom. His system is admirably adapted, as the event has shown, to captivate the minds of the people and procure their unlimited veneration for his character and writings. He lived to a great age, and communicated his principles to persons on whom he depended for their transmission to posterity. It is said he regretted the circumstance that himself and Confucius did not live at the same time, and on that account selected a worthy descendant of the sage's family for his preceptor. The tutor and pupil cultivated mutual esteem and respect, the one rejoicing to obtain a disciple in whose life and writings his doctrines should hereafter live, the other that he had been favored with so good a model of Confucius as 子思 *Tsze Sze*.

He died in the 94th. year of his age, and is buried by the side of his mother. Divine honours are paid to his memory, and sacrifices offered twice a year at his tomb.

SHANG MUNG.

CHAP. I.

1. Mencius having visited King Hwuy of Leang, his majesty said, my respected friend, since you did not deem one thousand miles far, you must have some scheme for the profit of my country. Mencius replied, O King why must you speak of profit! Benevolence and justice are sufficient. If your majesty ask how your kingdom may be profited, your Officers will ask how their families may be profited, and the people will ask how their persons may be profited. Superiors and inferiors will thus contend for profit, and the country will be endangered. The family of a country of one thousand chariots, will put to death the Sovereign of a country of ten thousand chariots, and the family of a country of one hundred chariots, will kill the Prince of a country of one thousand chariots.* That of ten thousand, one thousand should be taken and of one thousand, one hundred, is not little, but if you put profit first, and keep justice in the back ground, they will not be satisfied without seizing the whole.

It never has been that the virtuous neglected their parents, or that the just were slow in saving their Sovereign. Speak only of virtue and justice; why speak of profit!

* A Country of ten thousand chariots, refers to the territory immediately connected with the Imperial seat. It consisted of one thousand square Le and sent forth ten thousand war chariots. A family of one thousand chariots refers to the countries of the chieftains of small Provinces. Their territories consisted of one hundred square Le and sent out one thousand war chariots. A family of one hundred chariots was that of a great officer of one of of the petty Princes called Choo How.

2. Mencius having called upon Hwuy, king of Leang, found him standing on the side of a pond, looking at the geese and deer. On seeing him the king said, do men of virtue and talents delight in these things? Mencius replied, they are first virtuous, and then they enjoy such things. If they were not virtuous, although they possessed these, they could not enjoy them. The Ode says (of Wăn Wang) he planned an elegant pleasure house. Having formed the plan, the people in no time finished it. When they began, he told them not to be in haste; but the people flocked to it like children serving their parents. When the King in his elegant pleasure park saw the stag and its dam sporting at their ease, the stag and its dam were shining and fat. Resplendent were the feathers of the white bird (something like a stork). The King stood by the side of his beautiful fish ponds; how full were they of the playful fishes! Wăn Wang by the strength of his people made his pleasure house, and fish ponds, and the people rejoiced and exclaimed, his pleasure house how elegant! his fish ponds how beautiful! They were delighted to see his stags and his fishes. The ancients thus shared their joy with their people, and consequently enjoyed true delight.

The Tang she says "When will this sun expire? we will expire with him:" for the people thus ardently wished to die with him. Hence although he possesed pleasure houses and fish ponds, birds and beasts, how could he enjoy them! *

3. King Hwuy of Leang said, in ruling my kingdom I do the utmost in my power. When there was famine in Ho Nuy (within the

* The Tang she was an ode written in the time of the Shang Dynasty. These words refer to the tyrant Këe, last Sovereign of the Shang Dynasty, He compared himself to the sun and his possessing the throne to heaven having possession of the sun saying that when the sun was extinguished, so would he also. Hence the people in derision, and from detestation, excited by the tyranny of the monster, pointed to the sun and said, O sun! when wilt thou expire! we had rather expire with thee than suffer thus.* *

** If they uttered such complaints openly, they must have enjoyed more freedom of speech than many people of the present day who live under what are called liberal governments.

river) I removed the young and strong to Ho Tung (on the east of the river) and sent grain to Ho Nuy to support the old and infirm. When there was Famine in Ho Tung I acted on the same principle. I have examined the mode of government pursued in neighbouring states: their rulers do not exert themselves as I do: yet the population of the neighbouring provinces does not decrease, nor does the number of my people increase. What can be the cause of this?

Mencius replied, your Majesty is fond of war, allow me to use an illustration taken from the military profession:—At the sound of the drum the soldiers advance, but, if when the hostile ranks come to close quarters, some throw away their armour, trail their arms behind them and flee, some fifty paces, some an hundred; is it proper that those who flee fifty paces should laugh at those who flee one hundred? The king replied, it is not proper: For although they did not flee one hundred paces, still they did flee. Mencius rejoined, since your majesty understands this, you may (by this comparison) know not to hope for the increase of your people above the population of neighbouring states. *

Do not interfere with the time of the husbandman, and you will have more grain than you can consume.† Let not

* The design of the sage in employing this illustration, was to shew Leang Hwuy Wang that although he manifested some degree of regard for the good of his people, above what the neighbouring Princes did, yet he, as well as they, did not govern on the truly excellent principles of the celebrated monarchs of antiquity, and that on this account he had no more right to laugh at them, than the soldier who from cowardice flees fifty paces, had to mock him who from the same cause, flees an hundred; or had no more cause to expect, that the number of his people would increase, than the coward had to expect victory.

† The people should not be employed in government service during the spring, summer and harvest, which are the seasons of plowing, weeding and reaping, but in winter when they have leisure. In ancient times, they used no nets, the eye of which was not four inches. Fishes that had not arrived at ten inches long, were not sold in the markets, nor did people eat them. The marshes and forests belonged to the people in common, but there were prohibitions, that they should not enter the woods, to cut wood when the trees were covered with foliage but in the fall of the year, when the leaves were fallen. All these regulations were made before civil laws had arrived at perfection. In those days they followed the principles of nature. The ancient Princes considered the gaining of the people's hearts the fundamental principle of good government. † †

† † It is worth the serious consideration of modern rulers, whether they would not do well to imitate the ancients a little more in this particular.

narrow nets be employed in the muddy ponds, and you will have a superabundance of fish. Let the axe enter the forest at the proper season, and you will be overstocked with wood. Having more grain and fish than can be eaten, and more wood than can be used, the people will be able to nourish the living and sacrifice to the dead, and will be free from murmuring complaints. To nourish the living, and sacrifice to the dead, and to have no complaints, form the commencing point of royal (or good) government. In a five mow * dwelling place plant the mulberry tree, and persons of fifty years of age may wear silks. Let not the breeding of fowls, hogs, dogs and swine be neglected, and those of seventy years will have flesh to eat. Do not interfere with the time of those who possess one hundred mow and their families will not suffer hunger. Pay great attention to the education of the schools that you may give importance to the duties of filial piety, and fraternal affection, so that the grey headed may not be seen carrying burdens on the roads. When those of seventy years wear silks and eat flesh, and the young people suffer neither cold nor hunger, it never has been seen that good

* A Mow is much less than an English acre. In ancient times under what the sages denominate the Holy Kings, the lands were divided into portions of 900 Mow each. These were again subdivided into patches of one hundred mow. Eight of these patches were given to eight different families, and the centre hundred mow was considered public, or government property. Twenty mow of this public field were equally divided among these eight families, for the purpose of building houses upon, that is two and one half mow to each family. The remaining 80 mow were cultivated by the eight farmers conjointly--each farmer tilling 10 mow the produce of which was given to government, as a tax, or rent for their farms. In the spring season, the people went out and lived in the fields, and on the approach of winter, they returned to live in town. Hence they had two and a half mow in town for their dwelling place. The 5 mow in the text refer to the two and a half given to them from the public field, and to the two and a half which they were allowed in town, taken together. They were required to plant the mulberry tree for the nourishment of the silk worm, not in the fields lest they should injure the growth of the grain, but by the walls of their little gardens about their houses. It was the wish of the ancient kings that the young as well as the old should wear silks and eat flesh, but as the state of the country at the time would not admit of it, they took good care that the aged, who without silks could not be warm, and without flesh, could not be satisfied, should have sufficient supplies of these. To educate the young, and keep the old warm and comfortable, they deemed of the first importance, in the government of the people.

government did not prosper (or if you thus care for your people you will have no difficulty in governing them).

The dogs and swine eat the people's food, and you know not how to prevent them. The people are dying of hunger on the roads, and you do not issue supplies for their relief. When the people die, you say it is not my fault, but that of the season. What difference is there between this, and stabbing a man to death, and then saying, it was not I that killed him, it was the weapon. Let not your majesty blame the seasons, and all the people under heaven (or rather of the empire) will come over to you. *

4. King Hwuy of Leang said, I wish calmly to listen to your instructions. Mencius replied, what difference is there between killing a man with a stick, and doing the same with a sword? King, none. What is the difference between killing the people by the sword, and doing it by political measures? King, it is all one. There is plenty of fat meat in the kitchen, and abundance of fat steeds in the stable, but the people exhibit the picture of hunger, and the wastes are strewed with the bodies of those who have died of hunger. Thus the animals are led on to devour the people.

Animals that eat each other are hateful to men. If he who should be the father and mother of his people cannot keep clear of leading the brutes to eat them, how does he act the part of a father, and mother to his subjects! Confucius said, that he who invented the YUNG had no posterity, because he made the image of a man, and employed it; what then shall be said of him who starves his people to death! †

* In the time of Confucius the good principles disseminated by the founders of the Chow Dynasty, had still considerable influence on the minds of the rulers. But when Mencius rose to reform the age, their principles were nearly lost and in the contest maintained by the seven principal states, the people suffered so severely under their unprincipled and tyrannical masters, that had any of the Princes exhibited the practice of a kind, and benevolent government, the whole Empire would without doubt have reverted to him.

† In high antiquity they made bundles of grass or straw in the form of a human being, and interred them with the dead. In what is called middle antiquity, or about the time of Confucius, they made the YUNG which was a wooden image, made with springs so

5 Hwuy, the King of Leang replied by saying, that formerly there was no country under heaven more powerful than Tsin, is what you sir know very well. But since I have ascended the throne, we have been defeated by Tse on the east; my son has been slain; and on the west we have lost territory by Tsin. I am ashamed of such things, and wish in behalf of the dead to wipe off the stain. Under such circumstances what can be done? Mencius replied, with a province of one hundred Le you may become sovereign (of China *). Exhibit a kind, benevolent government; make the punishments lighter, diminish the taxes, let the people exert their whole strength in plowing and cleaning the fields. Let the young employ their leisure time in learning the principles of filial piety, fraternal affection, fidelity and truth.—Then when at home they will serve their fathers and elder brothers, and when abroad they will serve their superiors. Thus you may with sticks oppose the strong armour and sharp swords of Tse.

They (your enemies) rob the people of their time, so that

so as to move and appear as much like a human being as possible. This was buried along with the dead as their attendant. Confucius reprobated the inventor of the wooden image, because he made it so much more like a man than the ancient straw images were, and thus led men to practice what was inconsistent with true benevolence. For the sage could not bear to see any thing done, which had even the appearance of cruelty. † †

* At that time, the seven principal provinces of China were wrangling for Empire, the sage had formerly taught those Princes to whom he had access that would they but practice benevolent govrnment, such was the tyranny of the others that all the people would forsake them and flee for shelter to the Prince of kind and benevolent dispostion; thus without the use of arms (for which the sages had no partiality) he would become Emperor by the decree of heaven and by the choice of the people.

—

† † It is said to have been at one time a practice in some parts of China, when a person of any consequence died, that his servants and attendants together with his horses. &c &c were buried with him. The Scythians and some other barbarous nations observed the same custom. The Chinese to the present day when a relative dies fit out a complete household of paper servants, utensils &c and consume them by fire, with a view they say, to convey them to their departed relatives, in the unseen world. This superstitious pratice compared with the barbarous custom of sacrificing so many human lives, is certainly infinitely preferable, but seems to have originated in the same absurd notion, viz. that the dead can be benefited by the things of this world.

they have not time to plow and weed the fields for the nourishment of their parents. Their fathers and mothers are starved by cold and hunger. Their brothers, wives and children, are separated and scattered abroad. They have plunged their people into misery. Let your majesty go and rectify (or punish) them and who will oppose you? The ancients say, the truly benevolent have no enemies under heaven: do not question what I say.

6 Mencius having visited King Seang of Leang said, on coming out, when you see him from a distance, he has not the appearance of a King, and when you come near him, you see nothing to inspire veneration. * He asked abruptly how the empire was to be composed? To which I replied, it will be united in one. He asked who was capable of uniting it? I replied he who does not delight in killing men may unite it.† He then asked who would come over to him? I answered there are none under heaven who would not. Your Majesty understands the budding of the grain. During the droughts of the seventh and eighth months, the blade droops, but when the heavens blacken, the dense clouds are formed, and the copious showers fall, then the blade suddenly rises, and who can prevent it in such circumstances. At present, among all the Princes under heaven, there is not one who does not delight in killing men. If there were any one who did not delight in killing men, all the people under heaven would look up to him, and

* King Seang was the son of Hwuy, King of Leang. He had nothing dignified or majestic in his appearance and manner. The external manner and address answer to the measure of virtue which one possesses. Since therefore his outward demeanour was thus, what he cherished in his breast may be judged of.

†. At that time the petty sovereigns were a parcel of blood thirsty tyrants; hence the remark of the sage that were there a prince who did not delight in blood-shed he might conquer all the others by the power of his benevolence, unite all the discordant states in one as they had formerly been, during the Hea and Shang Dynasties, as well as for a long space of time under the Chow family, which at that time had so degenerated as to possess little or no power in the empire.

come over to him. Were it really thus, the people would flock to him, as water flows downward and who could prevent them !*

7 Seun, a Prince of Tse, asked Mencius, whether he could inform him of the affairs of Hwan of the Tse country, and Wan of Tsin? Mencius replied, the disciples of Confucius have not spoken of the transactions of Hwan, for which reason those of after times had no means of transmiting them to posterity; thus I have not heard of them, but if your majesty must have me to speak, then I will speak of the government of (good) kings. On which the king said, what virtues are necesary in order that one may rule well? Mencius replied, love and protect your people, and none will be able to oppose you. †

The King rejoined, may such a man as I be able to protect my people! You may. How do you know that I may sir? Your servant has heard Hoo Kih say that one day when your Majesty was sitting in the Hall, while some one led an ox past the Hall, your Majesty on seeing him asked where the person was leading the ox to. He replied I mean to consecrate a new bell with his blood. On which your Majesty said, set him at liberty; I cannot bear to see him trembling thus, since he is innocent and yet going to the ground of death. The person replied, then we must give up the consecration of the bell. ‡

* Soo she says, that the remarks of Mencius are not vague unfounded bombast, but if you do not deeply trace his meaning, and fully investigate the truth you will certainly consider them vague. I have observed from the time of Mencius to this day, that the founder of the Han Dynasty and Kwang Hoo as well as the founders of the Tang and Shang Dynasties, all of whom united the Empire in one, were Princes who had no delight in blood-shed, and that the other sovereigns who have reigned since that time, the more they have delighted in putting to death their people, the greater have been the anarchy and confusion of the empire. Were then the words of Mencius accidental, or spoken at random!

† Hwan of Tse and Wan of Tsin were a sort of tyrants or men who ruled by force, rather than by reason, and even the younger disciples of Confucius were ashamed to speak of them. Hence Mencius did not wish to speak about them. It better suited his principles, and his great intention to discuss the doctrines of the excellent monarchical government, exemplified by the celebrated Princes of ancient times.

‡ It was customary to sprinkle the sacrificial vessels with the blood of victims ‡‡

---

‡‡ This presents a striking coincidence, between some of the Chinese sacred rites, and those appointed by divine authority, and enjoined on the ancient Jews. See Exodus 29th chap.

Why (said the king), should we give it up? take a sheep in his place. I know not whether any such thing has taken place or not. (The king) said, there was such a thing. Then said (Mencius) this heart is capable of governing well. All the people consider that this act arose from a niggardly disposition, but your servant knows that it arose from your majesty's compassionate heart.

The king said you are perfectly right Sir: Yet truly the people do thus judge; but, although the Tse country is small, why should I thus hanker after one ox! The truth is, that I could not bear to see the innocent animal trembling on his way to the place of slaughter, and it was for that reason that I caused a sheep to be taken in his place. (Mencius) replied, it is not to be wondered at (or rather do not wonder) that the people considered your Majesty's having exchanged a large animal for a small as a proof of niggardliness. How could they know that your majesty secretly felt for the innocent animal, when on his way to the place of slaughter? for in this respect, what difference existed between the ox and the sheep (both being equally innocent)? The king smiling said, what in reality were my motives on this occasion! If I had not regretted the expence, why should I have exchanged the ox for a sheep? Is it not right that the people deem me parsimonious! *

12th 20th aud 35th verses and Leviticus chap. 1st. verses 15th and 19th and many other places of scripture, it is well known, that among the Hindoos there are a multitude of rites, which bear so strong a resemblance to those recorded in the sacred volume that it is self evident they must have come from the same divine original, although those who observe them, seem to have completely lost the knowledge of their original intention.

* Mencius was fully convinced that the king gave orders to exchange the ox for a sheep, because he could not bear to see the animal in such terror of death, and not because he regretted the expence, but in order to make him examine, find out and improve the compassionate dispositions of his nature, so as to extend his tender heartedness to the government of the people, he hinted that the people viewed his conduct, in this particular as indicating a parsimonious disposition. Finding that this expedient did not succeed he farther endeavored to urge him to self investigation by stating, that as both the sheep and ox were alike innocent, the act of exchanging the greater for the smaller looked more like parsimony than compassion. The king, however instead of being excited by this seeming difficulty and impeachment of his motives, to analyze his own dispositions, so as to lead to the happy result contemplated by the sage, found it beyond his power to extricate himself from the imputation of niggardliness, and tacitly acknowledged what in reality he was not guilty of. Thus were the benevolent attempts of the sage frustrated.

(Mencius) said, there is no harm in this (i. e. in what the people say). This is the nice hinge of benevolence, you saw the ox, but did not see the sheep. The superior man can look on animals when alive, but cannot bear to look on them when dying. If he hear their dying groans, he cannot bear to eat their flesh. Hence the superior man places his shambles at a distance. The king was delighted and said, the She King says, I guess other men's feelings by my own. You Sir have exactly expressed my feelings. I have been examining my motives and could not discover my genuine principle of action; but your words, Sir, have put my mind in motion. But pray what is there in this *Compassionate* disposition that fits me for governing well? *

Mencius said, suppose any one should say to your majesty, I am able to lift three thousand catties, but am not able to lift a feather; and that he could examine the point of an autumn hair, but could not see a waggon loaded with wood; would your majesty believe him? No indeed (said the king). Then consider, that at present your kindness is such as to extend even to the brutes, but your merit has not yet extended to the people, what is the cause of this? Truly a man's not lifting a feather is because he does not use his strength, and the reason why he does not see a cart loaded with wood, is because he does not employ his sight, and in like manner that the people are not protected, is because you do not put in practice your kind disposition. It is not for want of ability, that you do not rule well. †

* The King considered that the compassionate disposition which he manifested in reference to the ox, was a thing of the smallest importance, when compared with the vastness of governing a nation, hence he could not see how the possession of such a disposition could fit him for so great a trust: not knowing that to govern well, only required the proper cultivation of this tender heartedness, and the application of it to the government of men.

† Men are of the same species with ourselves, hence to love them is natural and easy; but brutes are of a different species, consequently to love them is neither so natural, nor so easy. Hence if we do the latter and not the former, it is self evident that want of will and not of ability is the cause.

What then said (the king), is the difference between want of will and want of ability? Mencius replied, suppose a man is required to take Tae Shan (a great mountain) under his arm, and leap over the north sea, if he say I am not able, this is real inability. But if a man be commanded by his superior to break a small branch of a tree, were he to say, I am not able, this is not inability, but want of will. Hence your majesty's not governing well is not such a thing, as that of taking Tae Shan under one's arm, and leaping over the the north sea, but is of a piece with not breaking the branch.

Let a man treat his own aged as they ought to be treated, and extend the same treatment to the aged of others. Let him act towards his own young relatives, as he ought, and then act in the same way towards the youth of other men: thus he may turn the Empire in the hollow of his hand.* The ode says have a rule for your own wife; extend this to your brothers, and to the government of a province: which means, extend this heart to all; nothing more is required.† Hence he that extends favor and kindness, may protect the four seas (China); he who does not extend favor, cannot protect his own family. That in which the ancients excelled other men, consisted merely in thus extending to all what they practiced. At present your majesty's favor extends to the brute animals, but its merit reaches not to your people: what is the cause of this?‡ Weigh things, and you

* The aged refer to one's father and elder brothers, the young to one's children and younger brothers.

† The Commentator says that the passage quoted from the She King, refers to the excellent manner in which the ancient and famous King Wan regulated his family, and governed his province, this being the case, the passage would be better rendered thus. "He ruled his own wife well, this he extended to his brothers, and to the government of his province."

‡ The ancient kings from first treating their own relative properly, went on to extend the same benevolent conduct to their people, and ultimately to animals. They commenced with what lies nearest and proceeded to what is most distant. From practising what is easy, they by regular order, went on to practise what is difficult. But at present (said Mencius) your majesty has reversed this order. This must have some cause; hence you should turn round on yourself, and investigate this matter.

know what is heavy and light. Measure things, and you know what is short and long. Tais must be done with all things; and of how much more importance is mind! I beg your majesty to measure it. *

But if your majesty raise troops, endanger your Officers, and form enmities with the other princes, will such things give joy to your mind! The king replied, no indeed!—Way should I delight in such things. I only use them to accomplish my great wish. May I ask what your majesty's great wish is? The king smiled and made no reply. Mencius added, has not your majesty a sufficiency of fat and sweet for the mouth, of light and warm clothes for the body, of beautiful colours for the eye to look on, of pleasant sounds for the ear to listen to; or of flatterers to serve in your presence? Your majesty's ministers are capable of administering all these. The king replied, why should these be the objects of my reigning wish? Then I know what your majesty's great wish is: you wish to extend your dominions—subdue Tsin, and Tsoo—rule China and support the foreigners who inhabit the four quarters of the globe. But if you seek to obtain your wish in this manner, you resemble a person who climbs a tree to take fish. †

How can my plan be so very foolish as this, said the king? It is much more so replied Mencius. Suppose one climb a tree

* Since the king's kindness was manifested towards animals, and not extended to the government of the people it shewed that his heart was heavy and long towards animals, but light and short towards men, hence the necessity of weighing and measuring it in order that a proper share of its attention might be given to different objects according to their proportionate value. * *

† The sage meant that to raise armies, attack the neighbouring Princes, and thus rouse the anger and provoke the wrath of men, in order to the gaining of the Imperial throne, which was then the great object aimed at by the contending powers, was equally futile, with that of climbing a tree in search of fish. His principles led him to advise the king to gain the hearts of the people, by a kind and liberal government, and to assure him that in thus gaining the affections of his own people, all the subjects of the surrounding Princes (or rather tyrants) would flock to his standard: thus he would ascend the Imperial seat, by the universal suffrage of the people, which is the only pledge of being appointed by heaven to reign over men. Such were the excellent politics instituted and carried into practice by the famous Monarchs of antiquity, and constantly taught and illustrated in the schools of the sages.

Many love their fellow creatures ardently, who are totally destitute of love to the great source of all excellence, and fountain whence flow all the good things which they enjoy. Is not the guilt of such men infinitely greater than that of King Leang!

in pursuit of fish, although he do not obtain any, yet no dangerous consequences insue; but if your majesty seek the accomplishment of your wish by such measures, after you have exhausted your heart and strength, you will bring misery on yourself. May I hear how this will insue, said the king. Suppose then, replied the sage, the people of Tsow and Tsoo were to engage in hostilities, which of the two think you would prove victorious? The people of Tsoo would be victorious, replied the king. Hence, rejoined the sage, a small country should not engage in hostilities with a great nation. Few people should not go to war with many; nor should the weak fight with the strong. Now the four seas contain about nine thousand Le, † and the whole of the Tse country forms about one ninth part of this extent: if then you attempt to subdue eight parts by one, where is the difference between this and that of Tsow fighting with Tsoo? Examine the root of the matter.

If your Majesty exhibit a benevolent government, all the learned under heaven, will covet to stand in your court. The husbandmen will all wish to till your lands. Both travelling and stationary merchants, will desire to store your majesty's markets. Travellers will delight to walk on your high ways, and all under heaven, who are oppressed by their own Princes, will come to your Majesty with their accusations. In such circumstances, what can prevent you from accomplishing your wish? The king replied, my intellect is dull, I am incapable of advancing to such things. I beg you, Sir, to assist my inclination, and enlighten me by your instructions; although I am not of quick perception, I desire to try thus to act * (or try whether you can teach me to govern in this manner).

* The king having heard what the sage said as to the duty and effects of exhibiting a benevolent government, wished to know more particularly in what benevolent government consisted and how it was to be exercised.

---

† It would appear from the ancient Chinese writers frequently using the phrase "Four seas" to denote the whole of the Chinese Empire, that they had no accurate conception of the extent and boundaries of their native country: if so what could they possibly know about other nations, whom they courteously style barbarians!

Mencius rejoined, it is only men of learning and superior virtue, who without constant supplies (or in times of scarcity) can preserve even and steady minds. As to the common people, unless they are provided with constant supplies, they will not be stable, but will give way to depravity and go to all lengths of wickedness. Now thus to plunge them into crime, and then punish them, is taking them in the net. How could a virtuous Prince thus ensnare his people! Hence an intelligent Prince will so regulate the supplies of his people, that when they look up, they will have enough to serve their parents, and when they look down, they will have what is requisite to feed their wives and children. Thus in years of plenty, they will have sufficient for all and in years of scarcity as much as may save them from death. Then he will lead on the people to the practice of virtue, and they will follow readily. *

At present the mode of regulating the supplies of the people is such, that when they look up, they have not sufficient to nourish their parents, and when they look down, they have not enough to feed their wives and children. In plentiful years, they all suffer distress, and in times of scarcity they have not the means of escaping death. In such circumstances they can only seek preservation from death, and are always afraid that they cannot avoid it. What leisure have they to cultivate the knowledge of propriety and righteousness! If your majesty wishes to govern well, why not revert to first principles?

* The holy kings of high antiquity, made it a rule that a certain quantity of grain should be stored up annually, during the period of plentiful crops, in order to afford supplies during the years of scarcity. For it was a self-evident principle with them that the virtue of the common people could not be preserved, not to say increased, unless government took such measures, as to prevent them from being starved by cold and hunger. And the Prince who neglected to pursue such measures was reckoned the murderer, instead of the father of his people. * *

---

* * Might not some of our wise legislators of the present day take a lesson on this point from those ancient politicians?

Around the dwelling places of five Mow, plant the mulberry tree, for the purpose of nourishing the silk worm, thus persons of fifty years of age, will have silks to wear. In the breeding of fowls and dogs * do not neglect the proper seasons, thus those of seventy years may eat flesh. Do not rob those who till farms of one hundred Mow of their time, and families of eight mouths will not suffer hunger. Pay great attention to the education of the schools, that you may extend the knowledge of filial piety and fraternal affection; and let not the grey headed bear burdens on the roads. It has never been the case that when a man could cause the aged to wear silks, and eat flesh, and the young did not suffer hunger or cold he did not become Emperor.

CHAP. II.

1. Chwang Paou having had an interview with Mung Tsze, said, I have seen the King (Leang Hwuy Wang) his majesty talked to me about his love of music, but I made no reply; what is your opinion about the love of music? Mencius replied if the king loved music aright, the kingdom of Tse would not be far from approaching to good government. On another occasion Mencius waited upon the king, and asked him whether he had not spoken to Chwang Paou about his fondness for music. His majesty's colour suddenly changing, he replied, I am incapable of delighting in the music of the ancients; I am only fond of the vulgar music of the day. † On which the sage said, if your ma-

* The Chinese are fond of dog's and swine's flesh.

† His majesty was self conscious, that his love of music was not of the right kind; hence his blushes when questioned by the penetrating sage.

jesty love music properly Tse is near prosperity. The music of the present day proceeds from that of ancient times. *

Let me hear your opinion (said the king). Mencius—Is it more delightful to rejoice in music alone, or to share one's delight in music with others? King—It is more delightful to share it with others. Mencius—whether is it more joyful, to share our delight in music with a few, or with all (or a multitude)? King—To share it with all is more delightful. Your servant begs leave to talk a little to your majesty on the subject of music. Suppose when the people hear the sound of your majesty's drums and bells, and the notes of your pipes, they all knit the brows of their aching heads, and say to each other how our king delights in music! but why does he bring us to this extremity? Father and son cannot see each other: wives and children are scattered.—Or if at present when your majesty goes to the chase, the people on hearing the sound of your majesty's chariots, and horses, and on seeing the splendor of your standards, wrinkle the brows of their oppressed heads, and say to each other, how our king delights in the sports of the field! but why does he bring us to this extremity! Father and son see not each other, brothers, wives and children are scattered abroad;—this arises from no other cause than that of your majesty not causing the people to participate in your joy. †

But if when the people hear the sound of your majesty's drums and the music of your pipes, they rejoice with joy beaming in their countenances, and say to each other, our king is,

* The sage perceiving that the king was put to the blush from a consciousness that he had not a genuine relish for true music, wished to dissipate this feeling, and lead him on to see the importance of relishing music, so as to induce him to make all his people happy in order that they might heartily rejoice with him, hence he intimated that it was not of such consequence to distinguish between the ancient and modern music, as it was to enter into the spirit of the thing.

† Both this and the following paragraph, are suppositions, and do not mean that the king of Tse, ruled either so badly, or quite so well as is here supposed.

we hope, in good health; for if he were sick, how could he have such music! or, if when your majesty goes to the hunt, the people, when they hear the sound of your majesty's chariots, and see your splendid banners, exult and with joyful countenances say to each other, our king is not far from being well, for were he sick, how could he thus engage in the sports of the field! This would arise from no other cause, but that of rejoicing with your people. If therefore your majesty would rejoice with your people, you might become sovereign of the empire. *

2. King Seuen of Tse asked whether it were true that Wăn Wang had a game park of seventy Le? Mencius replied, ancient records have it so. King—If it was so, was not this too large? Mencius—The people seemed to think it small. King—My game park is only forty Le, and yet the people appear to think it large; how is this? Mencius—Although Wăn Wang's game park was seventy Le in extent, the people being permitted to cut grass, gather fuel, and take game in it, the same as the king himself, was it not with reason that they considered it small! When your servant first arrived at your borders, I asked what were the great prohibitions of the country, then I presumed to enter. Your servant was informed, that within the out-skirts of the city, there was a game park of forty Le, and that he who killed a deer within this park was liable to the same punishment, as he

* During the time in which the various Provinces contended for Empire, the people were reduced and their property exhausted, hence if any one of the Princes had established a mild and wise system of goverment, the whole Empire must have reverted to him; so that he would have become Emperor. At that time the different petty Princes, only occupied the seat of government, and employed their music to gratify themselves; hence Mencius, intent on the salvation of the people, laid hold on the circumstance of the Prince of Tse being fond of music, and endeavoured to show him that the only way to come at the full enjoyment of its pleasures, was to rule his people in such a manner, as that they would cheerfully unite with him in participating the delights of his music. So that although the ancient and modern music were very different, he wished to shew the king that it was of much more importance, that his people should rejoice with him in the pleasures of music, than that the music which was used should be the same as that of ancient times, assuring him that if he could once bring his people to enter with spirit into his amusements, and thus share his pleasures with them, he would soon have the Empire under his hand.

who killed (or murdered) a man. Thus there is a pit of forty Le, in the middle of the country; is it not reasonable then that the people deem it large! *

3. Seuen, King of Tse, asked whether there were any principles upon which a friendly intercourse might be kept up between neigbouring nations? Mencius replied, yes there are.—It is only the virtuous (the word often seems to mean perfectly virtuous) who can so rule a great nation as to assist (or rather serve) a small country. † Hence Tang served Kŏ and Wan Wang served Kwan E. It is only the wise who, if they rule a small country, can serve a great nation, hence Tae Wang served Heun Yŭh and Kow Tsëen served Woo. He who with a great country serves a small one, pleases heaven, and he who with a small country serves a great nation, reverences heaven. He who pleases heaven will preserve the Empire, and he who reverences heaven will preserve his own country. The She King says, "Reverence the majesty of heaven and you preserve your country."

His majesty exclaimed, exalted words! I poor man have an infirmity, I love valour. Mencius replied, I intreat your majes- not to love low valour. If a man strike his sword and with a fierce countenance call out, who will oppose me (rather fight me)? this is the low valour of a common man.‡ I beseech your majesty to cultivate high valour. The She King says, "The king (Wăn) flashed rage,—his armies were drawn up,—he stopped the invading armies of Keu, made abundant the happiness of Chow and answered the expectations of the Empire. Such was the bravery of Wăn Wang. Wăn Wang once in ire and he gave tran quility to the whole Empire. ¶

* All the people of Wan Wang shared the advantages of his game park with their sovereign, how then could they deem it too large! On the other hand, the game park of Seuen Wang, although not so extensive as the other, yet being a sort of trap for the people, had they not solid reasons for considering it large!

† The truly virtuous do not consult about power but about reason and justice.—Hence they can bear with the rudeness of others and treat them with reason and compassion.

‡ Low valour is the valour of mere blood and breath, but high valour, is the bravery of justice and reason. The valour of mere blood and breath (animal passion), none ought to have. The bravery of justice and reason no man ought to be without.

¶ This refers to Wan Wang having prevented the invading army of Meih, or Keu, from making an attack on the people of Yuen.

The Shoo King says, "Heaven sent down this people, and appointed them rulers, and teachers, with the intention that they should assist the High Ruler * in extending favor to all quarters. To reward the innocent and punish the guilty depends on me alone. Who in the whole Empire would have dared to transgress his will!" If one man † in the Empire acted perversely (or raised rebellion) Woo Wang was ashamed of him. This was the valour of Woo Wang. Woo Wang being once angry (or with one frown) gave peace to the Empire. Can your majesty by being once angry, give peace to the Empire! The people only fear that the king does not love bravery.

4. Mencius having been received by king Seuen of Tse in his snow Palace, (pleasure House) the king said, have the virtuous (referring to Mencius) such enjoyments as this? Mencius replied, they have.

† One Commentator says, that the one man here spoken of refers to the tyrant Chow last Emperor of the house of Shang whom Woo Wang cut off.

---

* High Ruler, or as some render the original characters 上帝 Shang Te "Most High God," has been deemed, by some Chinese scholars, the best Chinese term which Christian writers and teachers can employ as the designation of the true God, and it is certain that the Chinese pay a considerable degree of reverence to the being, whatever he may be, which bears this name. But after weighing the matter with considerable care, we are inclined to think that 天 Teen ought to have the preference, as a purely Chinese designation of the Deity to any other which can be met with in their writings. It must be acknowledged, however, that in the passage under consideration, as well as in many others, the same supreme power, is ascribed to Shang Te which is uniformly attributed to Teen Yet the text speaks of Princes and teachers rather as the assistants of Shang Te than as his ministers, and one of the Commentators says, plainly, that they are appointed to supply the defects, or short comings of Shang Te in his government of men. It may admit of a query whether after all, this Shang Te be any thing but a personification of that principle which they call Le 理 and which is said to be Teen 天 Heaven, or rather heaven is said to be Le. † If this be the case 上帝 and 天 are but one and the same divinit .

† See page 19 Line 10 of the Shang Mung Ho Keang, where it is said 天 is 理 and nothing else. For the sense of the word Le 理 see Morrison's Dictionary under the word

If men do not obtain such pleasures, they blame their superiors (or rulers). But when they do not obtain them and therefore blame their superiors, they err. On the other hand, when rulers do not share their enjoyments with the people they are likewise in fault.* When the ruler rejoices in the joy of his people, they likewise rejoice in his joy, and when he sympathizes in the sorrows of his people, they also sympathize in his sorrows. It never has been the case, that he who rejoiced with the whole Empire, and grieved with the whole Empire could not act the true sovereign (i. e. secure the allegiance of the people).†

Formerly, King, Prince of Tse asked Gan Tsze, saying, I wish to take a view of the Chuen Foo and Chaou Woo hills and to return by the southern coast to Lang Yay. How shall I do, that I may imitate the tours of the ancient kings? Gan Tsze, in reply, exclaimed, excellent question! When the Emperor visited the tributary Princes it was called *Seun Show. Seun Show* means to inquire into their government. When the Princes went up to have an audience of the Emperor they termed it *Shŭh Chĭh. Shŭh Chĭh* means to give a statement of the manner in which they had discharged the duties of their office. None of these were without some useful end in view. Farther, the Emperor every year in the spring, examined the tilling of the fields and supplied those with seed who were short of it. In harvest he examined the reaping, and assisted those whose crops were deficient. In Hea they had a proverb which said, "If our King do not take a pleasure tour, how can we find rest. If our king is not cheerful, how shall we be assisted." Every tour and

* When inferiors do not patiently bear their lot, and superiors do not compassionate the people, both are in the wrong.

† When the Prince causes his people to share his enjoyments, and himself rejoices in their happiness and grieves when they suffer distress, then the joys and sorrows of the whole Empire become as it were one, and the people, at all times and in all circumstances, look up to their sovereign with reverence, confidence and affection. That they should not submit to his government under such circumstances is impossible.

every pleasure ramble was a pattern to the tributary Princes. *

At present the case is different, when sovereigns travel, they must have a large retinue which consumes great quantities of provisions; hence the people are hungry and have nothing to eat and for those who labour there is no rest. They look askance at each other and mutually calumniate. The people are dissatisfied and grumble. The royal will is opposed, the people oppressed; eating and drinking go on like the down flowing stream, which forgets to return By hunting and feasting, in this manner, the petty Princes and governors are vexed and oppressed. To follow the downward stream and forget to return is called *Lew* i. e. to descend. To ascend the stream and forget to return back is called *Lëën*. To pursue the chase without being satiated, is called *Hwuy*. To delight in wine and never feel that you have enough, is called *Wang*. The former kings never delighted in the *Lew* nor the *Leen*, nor practised the *Hwuy* and the *Wang*.† It depends on your majesty how you will act.

* In ancient times, the Emperor every twelve years went in person and visited the tributary Princes. On these occasions he made inquiries how they had exercised the powers entrusted to them. Every six years, the Princes went to court and gave an account of the manner in which they had discharged the duties of government. Besides this, the Emperor every spring went through the Imperial domain, "which was about one thousand Le in extent," and examined how the fields were tilled, at the same time causing supplies of seed to be given to those who had not sufficient of their own. In harvest he went round the same extent in order to see whose fields were unproductive, and to order that the deficiencies of such should be made up from the national granary. The tributary Princes followed his example, and in so doing shewed the closest attention to the happiness of the people. Hence, in the time of the Hoo Dynasty, the people within the Imperial domain had a common saying that unless the sovereign took his usual pleasure tours, they would lose the assistance which they reaped from the royal country. * *

† This gives a black picture of the licentious government of the Choo How (or subordinate Princes) of those days. In this manner they opposed the authority of the Emperor, oppressed the petty rulers, and tyrannised over the people. In every respect they acted directly opposite to those excellent rulers mentioned above.

---

* * This statement as well as many others to be met with in ancient records, shows that the Princes of high antiquity paid great attention to husbandry and also to the wants of the people. My teacher informs me, that the shadow of this ancient system of inspection and assisting the needy exists at the present day.

Prince King was highly pleased, and issued a proclamation informing those who dwelt in the country, that from that time he had begun to open his stores, for the supply of those who were in want, and called on the officer of music to play music expressive of the mutual joy of Prince and minister. For they played the Che Chaou and the Keŏ Chaou. The ode was that which says, "What crime is there in a minister restraining his Prince! He who restrains, loves his Prince." *

5. King Seuen of Tse, asked saying, all men wish me to pull down my Hall of audience, shall I pull it down or not? Mencius replied. The audience Hall is the Hall where they who rule well, hold audience: if your majesty wish to practise the government of a good king, do not pull it down. †

His majesty said, may I hear what kingly government is? Mencius replied, in former days when Wăn Wang governed Ke the husbandman paid one ninth (as a rent or tax)—the descendants of government officers had salaries — the ports (or entries to the country) and markets were inspected, but no duty was paid by traders—the use of the lakes and marshes was not prohibited—the culprit did not involve his relatives in his guilt. The aged who had no wife were called Kwan—the aged

* The king was delighted that he had foun[illegible] what is difficult to obtain, a faithful minister, who by his clear and upright statements, had prevented him from imitating the vicious example of the other Princes of the da[illegible], who wallowed in sensuality and oppressed their subjects. On the other hand, Gan Tsze was delighted that he had the happiness to serve a Prince who listened to and punctually followed his good counsel, hence it was highly proper that their mutual joy should be expressed by music suited to the happy occasion.

† The Hall of audience, here referred to, was a Hall below Tae Shan where in former times, the Emperors when they went east on their inspecting visits, assembled the petty Princes for the purpose of making inquiries into their government. Hence the advice of the sage, that if he wished to practice kingly government, he ought not to pull down such Halls, which were essential to that system.

who had no husband were called Kwa—the aged who had no children were called Tŭh and the young who had no father were called Koo. These four classes are the poor of the world, and have none to speak for them. Wăn Wang, in the exercise of benevolent government, attended first of all to these classes. The She King says, "The rich may get through, but have pity on the destitute."

The king exclaimed, O excellent words! *Mencius* replied, since your majesty praises them, why do you not reduce them to practice? The king said, I, poor man, have an infirmity, I love wealth. *Mencius* answered, saying, formerly Lew Kung loved wealth. The She King (speaking of Lew Kung) says, "He collected and stored up and put dried provisions in bottomless and bottomed bags: wishing to make his people happy and to shed glory on his country, he bent his bows got ready his spears, lances and battle axes and then commenced his march." Hence those who remained had provisions in store, and those who marched had dried food in their bundles; thus he was prepared to commence his march. If your majesty would thus cause your people to share the benefit of your love of wealth, what obstacle could it prove to your governing the empire! *

The king rejoined, I have another failing, I love women. *Mencius* replied, formerly Tae Wang loved women, he loved his wife. The She King says, "Koo Kung, Tan Foo (i. e. Tae Wang) next morning rode his horse by the western coast

* The king supposed that in consequence of his love of wealth he might be induced to exact from the people beyond just bounds and thus prove unable to exercise a kind and benevolent government. The sage instead of criminating his majesty on this score, advised him to imitate Lew Kung's love of wealth and then his fondness for money might be productive of beneficial results, and aid rather than injure the exercise of good government.

till he arrived below the mountain Ke with Lady Keang, where they chose a place to live together. At that time, within, there was no grumbling among the women, without, no emptiness (i. e. want of wives) among the men. If your majesty would share your love of women with your people (i. e. make them reap the benefit of it) what detriment would it be to your ruling the empire! *

6. Mencius, conversing with King Seuen of Tse, said, suppose one of your ministers wishing to take a journey to Tsoo, should commit his wife and children to the care of his friend, and on his return find that his friend had allowed his family to suffer from cold and hunger, what ought he to do to such a man? The king replied, he ought to cut him off from his friendship.

Mencius added, suppose the head jailor, or criminal judge of a district, could not manage properly the officers under his charge, what would your majesty do with him? The king replied I would put him out of office. If then, said Mencius, within the whole boundaries of a country, there were no good government, what would you do? His majesty looked to his left, and right, and began to talk about something else. †

* Tae Wang, grand-father of the celebrated Wan Wang, being harassed and his country having been invaded by the northern barbarians (or tartar tribes), he took his wife Lady Keang, mounted his horse, and rode off to the Ke Mountain, where he built a town, to which his former subjects flocked, and where all enjoyed happiness—all the ladies had husbands, and all the gentlemen wives, hence there was no cause for grumbling or complaint. Thus did Tae Wang share his love for the ladies with his people, if your majesty follow his example what obstacle will your favor for the fair sex throw in the way of good government. **

† Mencius all along had in view this question, hence he made the two former suppositions, in order to introduce the subject. When he came to this point, his majesty could no longer reply; for he was afraid to condemn himself, and ashamed to ask the advice of an inferior; hence may be seen that he was not fit for any thing.

** In all the above mentioned instances where the king objected that his love of pleasure, war, wealth, and women, prevented him from ruling well, the sage reasons with him on his own principles, or rather endeavors to shew him that the very dispositions which he himself considered detrimental to his being a good Prince, would, if properly regulated, conduce thereto. We think there can be but one opinion as to the excellence of this mode of leading human beings to the practise of virtue. Hence the frequent adoption of it by the ancient moralists of China show that they knew something of human nature.

7. Mencius having waited upon Seuen, King of Tse, said, a country is said to be ancient, not because of its lofty trees, but because it has had a long succession of hereditary ministers. There is no mutual esteem, or confidence between your majesty and your ministers. Those whom you promoted yesterday, are off to day and you know nothing of it. The king rejoined, how shall I be able to know before hand those who are destitute of talent that I may not employ them.* Mencius answered, a Prince ought to exercise the utmost caution in promoting men of virtue and talent. In promoting inferiors above superiors, and strangers above relatives, ought there not to be the greatest care manifested !†

When all your immediate attendants say he is a man of talent and virtue, do not credit them. When all the high officers say, he is a person of superior virtue and abilities, do not credit them. When the whole nation says, that he is a superior man, then make inquiry and if he be found to be so, employ him. When all those who are constantly about you say, that a man ought not to be employed, listen not. If all the great officers say, that he ought not to be employed, do not listen to them. When the whole nation says, that he ought not to be taken into office, then examine into the case, and if you find that he ought not to be employed, send him away. If all your attendants say, that a man ought to be put to death, do not listen to them. If all the great officers say, that he ought to be put to death, do not comply. If the whole nation say so, then examine the matter.

* The king meant to insinuate that the reason why some of his ministers went off so abruptly, was that they were destitute of talent, and that on this ground, he was justified in considering their departure as of no importance; at the same time, he asked by what means he might previously discover who were distitute of abilities, in order that he might be prevented from taking them into office, and thus avoid the evil of which the sage complained.

† It is a general rule of propriety, to honor superiors, and treat relatives with tender affection, but it is not a fixed and necessary thing, that people of superior rank, or relatives, should possess virtue and talents. Hence it often becomes an imperative duty to promote inferiors in preference to superiors, and strangers before relatives.

and if you see that he deserves death, then put him to death. If you act thus, you will be the father and mother of your people *

8. Seuen, King of Tse, asked Mencius saying, did not Tang banish Kee and Woo Wang cut off Chow? Mencius replied, it is so recorded in History. May a minister put his Prince to death then? *Mencius* replied, he who injures (or robs) virtue, is called a robber—he who injures (or murders) justice, is called a tyrant. A robber and a tyrant is called a common (or private) man. I have heard that the private man Chow was put to death, but have not heard that the Prince (Chow) was assassinated. †

9. Mencius having waited upon Seuen King of Tse, said, suppose your Majesty wished to erect a fine palace, you would employ a master carpenter to find large trees. If the master mechanic found large beams, your majesty would be pleased, and consider them fit for the purpose. But if the carpenters should hew down and make them too small, your majesty would be displeased and consider them unfit for the intended purpose. Now if a man from his youth studies right principles, and when he arrives at manhood wishes to reduce them to practice, your majesty says to him you must lay aside what you have learned,

* The speeches of constant attendants (or courtiers) are certainly unworthy of credit. The whole of the great officers ought to be credited, but still there is danger of their being blinded by prejudice. As to the whole nation, they will in general form a just opinion, but even in regard to their opinion, it is necessary to examine, because they have partialities, for or against those whose manners and taste agree, or disagree with their own.

† The murderer of virtue, and robber of justice, such as Kee and Chow were, being rebelled against by the people, disowned by relatives, and abandoned by heaven, are no longer the legitimate sovereigns of their country, but ought to be considered out-casts from society, and treated accordingly. On this principle the sage vindicated the conduct of Woo Wang, in cutting off the monster Chow. For, according to the principles of the sages, the act was looked upon as the infliction of merited punishment upon a robber and murderer, and not as the assassination of a Prince. The remark was intended to awaken the king of Tse to a deep sense of his own duty.

and act according to my principles, what is to be said (or done) in such a case? *

Suppose your majesty had an unpolished gem, although only 30 Taels weight, you would call a lapidary to cut and polish it. In reference to the government of a country, if the king say you must throw aside what you have learned, and follow my directions, how does this differ from teaching the jeweller how to cut and polish! †

10. The people of Tse attacked and conquered those of Yen. Seuen the king, in conversation with Mencius, said, some people advise me not to take possession *of Yen*, others advise me to take possession. Now, that one country of ten thousand chariots should in the space of fifty days conquer another of ten thousand chariots, is beyond human power. Hence, if I do not take possession, heaven will punish me. What do you think of taking possession? ‡

Mencius replied, if when you go to take possession the people of Yen are delighted, then take it. He who did so in ancient times, was Woo Wang; but if the people are not delighted at your taking it, then you ought not to take it. He who acted in this

* This comparison was drawn for the purpose of satirising Leang who was incapable of finding out and promoting men qualified for discharging the duties of government, intimating at the same time, that when his majesty did find such characters, by preventing them from putting in practice the divine principles which they had learned in the schools of the sages, and causing them to follow his own selfish and erroneous notions, he imitated the unskilful carpenter, who hews the fine large timber, so small as to render it unfit for the intended purpose.

† The Prince would not presume to polish the gem himself, but would give it to the lapidary. Thus he would shew his high sense of its value. Hence, when a Prince follows his own selfish views, in governing a nation, and does not confide in, and listen to men of virtue and talent, he shews that he puts a higher value on a gem than on his country. Fan She says, the ancients who possessed virtue and abilities were constantly grieved, that the kings would not act according to their principles, and on the other hand the common (or useless) Princes of the day, were constantly distressed that men of superior virtue and accomplishments, would not comply with that which they loved. Thus, from ancient times, it has been a difficult matter to find a Prince and minister who suited each other. This was the reason why Confucius and Mencius did not during their whole lives, meet with a Prince of their own mind.

‡ The king of Tse made a pretence that it could only have been by the special interposition of heaven, that a nation only equally strong with that of the enemy, could have conquered it in the short space of fifty days, and that this circumstance indicated that it was the will of heaven, that he should take possession of the conquered country; but this was a mere pretence, employed for the purpose of screening his selfish and avaricious designs.

manner of old, was Wăn Wang.* If when with a country of ten thousand chariots you attack a country of ten thousand chariots, the people come to welcome your troops with buckets of rice, and pots of Tseang (some thick fluid), is it on any other account, than that you are about to save them out of fire and water. But if you deepen the water, and increase the heat of the fire, they will turn away from you.†

11. The people of Tse having conquered Yen and seized it, the Princes consulted how they might deliver Yen. King Seuen said, the Princes have many consultations about subduing me, how ought I to treat them? Mencius replied, I have heard of a *Prince* of seventy Le becoming ruler of the whole Empire. Tang was the man; but I have not heard of a Prince of a country of one thousand Le, being afraid of men. The Shoo King says, "Tang commenced chastising at Kŏ. When he began, the whole empire confided in him. When he went east to subdue, the strangers of the west grumbled. When he turned south to subdue, the people of the north grumbled, saying why make us last? The people looked to him

* When the tyrant Chow reigned, two thirds of the empire wished Wan Wang to become their sovereign, but as the whole nation had not declared for him, he induced these two thirds to continue in subordination to the house of Yin (or Shang). In the thirteenth year of Woo Wang (son of Wan Wang) he conquered Chow and obtained the Imperial throne. In the time of Wan Wang, the measure of Chow's vices and tyranny was not filled up, hence the decree of heaven was not fulfilled, nor the hearts of the whole empire lost. Under these circumstances it would have been contrary to the will of heaven, and the unanimous wish of the people to rebel against Chow, but when Woo Wang took the field against him, the minds of all the people had reverted from Chow to Woo Wang, hence it became decisively evident that it was the determination of heaven to take the throne from the Yin family and give it to the house of Chow. For the unanimous voice of the people, is the same as the decree of heaven, "Vox populi vox Dei".**

† Meaning that if Tsĕ proved more tyrannical than Yen, the people of the latter country would turn round, and look for salvation from some one else. Chaou She says, that in going to conquer and punish a bad Prince, the conqueror (or punisher) ought to accord with the desires of the people. If the people are pleased the will of heaven is obtained.

** According to the Confucian philosophy when the reigning Prince loses the hearts of the people, he loses his right to the throne, and consequently to the allegiance of the nation. On the other hand, when the hearts of the people all turn towards any individual of eminent talents, and virtue, this is a certain mark that he is appointed by heaven to ascend the Imperial seat. On these grounds the famous Tang is highly eulogized for dethroning the tyrant Kee, last Emperor of the Hea Dynasty, and Woo Wang is praised to the clouds for having put to death the monster Chow, last Emperor of the Shang Dynasty. Both these heroes are said to have saved their country out of the midst of fire and water.

with longing expectation, as in a great drought we look with anxiety to the clouds and rainbow.* When he arrived, selling and buying were carried on in the markets without interruption, nor were the labors of the husbandman disturbed. He cut off their Princes and comforted the people. The people rejoiced, as when the timely showers fall The Shoo King says, "Wait till our Prince come and he will revive us."

The government of Yen has tyrannised over the people, when your majesty went to subdue them, the people, supposing that you were coming to save them out of the fire and water, came with tubs of food and buckets of Tseang to welcome your armies. If you kill their fathers and elder brothers,—bind their sons and younger brothers,—destroy their ancestorial Temples and carry off their precious vessels, how can you in this manner save them! The whole Empire is really jealous of the power of Tse, and now that you have doubled your territories, if you do not practise benevolent government, you will excite the military forces of the whole Empire against you.†

Let your majesty speedily issue an order that the old and young be returned, and that a stop may be put to the carrying away of valuable vessels. Consult with the people of Yen, and appoint them a king, then withdraw your troops; thus you may

* The people of the west and north, refer to those who lived at the west and north extremities of the Empire. The whole Empire looked up to Tang, as their Prince, and each Province was anxious that he should turn his victorious troops against its tyrannical rulers. Hence they looked with the same anxiety for his approach as people in the time of great drought look to the clouds and rainbow. When the rainbow appears, the rain stops, so that when people see it they are afraid that the rain will not reach them; thus were the people afraid that Tang would not reach them. When he did arrive, he only put to death the tyrannical rulers, while he made the people happy. He revived their drooping spirits, and as it were raised them from the dead.

† Mencius intimated to his majesty, that the other Princes had formerly been jealous of the power of Tse, but had not found an opportunity of quarelling with him, but as he had now doubled his dominions, by the conquest of Yen, if he did not practice benevolent government, and thus meet the expectations of the people of Yen, the jealousy of the other Princes would be increased, and they would certainly unite all the military forces of the Empire and attack Tse; nay, that the king himself would as it were beat up all the troops to attack himself.

put a stop to it (i. e. to the intended attack of the Princes). *

12. Tsow and Loo having been engaged in hostilities, Mŭh Kung (Prince of Tsow) asked Mencius, saying, thirty three of my officers have been killed, and not one of the people died in their defence; if I were to punish them with death, I could not put them all to death, and if I do not punish them with death, they will look with contempt on their officers, and will not defend them. In what manner ought I to act in such a case? Mung Tsze replied, in bad years and times of scarcity, the old and feeble of your majesty's subjects, are rolled into the ditches, while the young and strong, to the amount of several thousands, are scattered through the whole Empire (or have wandered to other countries); yet there is abundance of provisions in your majesty's granaries and plenty of money in the treasury, but your ministers do not report. Tsăng Tsze says. "Be cautious! take good heed! what goes out from you will return again." The people have now retorted. Is your majesty blameless? † If your majesty would practise benevolent government, the people would love their superiors, and die for their rulers.

13. Wăn, Prince of Tsang, said *to Mencius,* Tăng is a small country and lies between Tse and Tsoo, ought I to serve Tse or Tsoo? Mencius replied, I am not capable of advising you in this matter, but if I must say something, I have just one word;

* The advice of the sage to the Prince of Tse was to consult with the ministers and people of Yen to select a man of virtue and talent,—place him on the throne, and withdraw his army. By these means he said, you may put a stop to the confusion which has been excited in Yen, and prevent the surrounding Princes from making your seizure of Yen a pretence for attacking you. This is the plan by which you may save yourself from the threatened vengeance of the Choo How.

† Fan She observes, that the Shoo King (an ancient classic) says, "The people constitute the foundation of a country. If the foundation be firm, the country is stable. To keep public granaries and royal treasuries, is the way to govern the people. In plentiful years, store up. In years of scarcity, distribute. Pity the cold and hungry,—save the sick and miserable. Then the people will love their superiors, and in the time of danger will risk their lives for them, as sons and younger brothers would protect their fathers and elder brothers, or as the hand protects the head and eyes." Muh Kung could not turn round and examine himself, but put the blame on the people; how erroneous!

deepen these ditches, raise these walls, and along with your people hold fast the *city* till death, and the people will not leave it: in this manner you may succeed. *

14. Wăn Kung of Tăng said, the people of Tse have fortified Sëë. I am very much afraid. What ought I to do? Mencius replied, formerly Tae Wang, when he dwelt in Pin, was attacked by the northern barbarians (perhaps Tartars); he left and went below the the mountain Ke: not that he chose to do so, but because he could not avoid it.

If you practise virtue, your posterity will yet reign. The superior man creates an inheritance, and hands it down to his posterity, who ought to enjoy it. † If you act thus, heaven will assist you. What can Tse do to you! Exert your whole strength in the practice of virtue. Nothing more is wanted.

15. Wăn, Prince of Tăng, asked saying, Tăng is a small country; suppose we do our utmost to serve these extensive kingdoms (Tse and Tsoo), we shall not be able to avoid being invaded by them. In such circumstances, how ought we to act? Mencius replied, formerly, when Tae Wang dwelt in Pin, his country was invaded by the northern barbarians;—he gave them skins and silks, but could not get clear of them;—he gave them dogs and horses, but still was infested by them;—he gave them pearls and precious stones, but could not get rid of them. On which he called a council of the old men, and informed them, saying, "That which these barbarians want is our country. I

* The Prince of a country should die when the altars of the local deities are destroyed, hence he ought to hold fast his country till death, but, unless he has gained a strong hold of the people's affections, he cannot accomplish this object aright.

† Although Tae Wang was compelled by the repeated incursions of the northern barbarians, to leave his small territory, yet his descendants came to the Imperial throne, hence the sage informed King Wan of Tang that if he would imitate the virtue of Tae Wang, although he might lose his kingdom, heaven would reward his virtue in his posterity, by giving the throne to them.

have heard that the superior man does not injure men, by that which should nourish them. Why should you my people be grieved that you have no Prince. I will leave this country." He passed over the mountain Leang, and built a town below the mountain Ke, and there resided. The people of Pin said, "He is an excellent man, we cannot (or ought not to) lose him." They followed him as people flock to the market. Some say, "Hold fast: you have no right to give it up; hold it fast till death.*" Your majesty may choose between these two.

16. Ping, Prince of Loo, being about to go out, his special favorite Chwang Tsang said, at other times, when your majesty goes out, you give orders to your Officers, but to-day your carriage is ready, and your Officers know nothing of it. I presume to ask about this matter. The Prince replied, I am going to visit Mencius. How is that! How can your majesty disgrace yourself by paying the first visit to a common man! Do you consider him a man of virtue and talents? Now propriety and justice flow from virtue, but Mencius was more liberal in discharging the funeral rites of his *mother*, who died last, than in observing those of his *father*, who died first: your majesty should not visit him. You are right, said the Prince.

Lŏ Ching Tsze a disciple of Mencius, having waited on his majesty, said, why did not your majesty pay a visit to Mencius? The king replied, a certain person has informed me that Mencius had given his mother a more splendid funeral, than he formerly had given his father; on which account, I have not gone to visit him. On which Lŏ Ching said, what does the king call "more". Formerly he buried his father according to

* Some say the country that has for ages been governed by our ancestors, from whom we have received it, we have no right on our own authority to give up, and therefore are bound to die rather than desert it.

to the rites observed by a scholar (or inferior officer). Afterwards, *he buried his mother* according to the custom of the great officers.* Formerly, he used three tripods; afterwards, he used five.† The king rejoined, that is not what I refer to, I speak of the beauty of the shrouds, and of the outer and inner coffins. *Lŏ Ching* replied, how can these be said to have excelled! This *difference* arose merely from the inequality of poverty and riches.

Lŏ Ching Tsze, having waited upon Mencius, said, I have spoken to his Majesty. The king was about to pay you a visit, when his favorite Tsang Tsang prevented him. On this account he has not come. Mencius replied, when a man is to get into office, some one will be instrumental in putting him forward; when he is to be stopped, some one will be instrumental in preventing him from getting forward; yet being employed, or being kept back, does not depend on man. That I did not meet with the Prince of Loo, is to be ascribed to heaven. How could Tsang She's son prevent me from meeting with him!‡

CHAP. III.

1. Kung Sun Chow asked, saying, if you, Sir, had obtained an important office in Tse, might we have expected again to see the meritorious deeds of Kwan Chung and Yen Tsze?

* When Mencius's father died, he was only one of the literati, therefore, propriety required him to bury him and attend to his funeral and sacrificial ceremonies after the mode prescribed for men of his own rank: besides, he was poor and unable to purchase rich shrouds and coffin. But when his mother died, he was in a high Official situation and in affluent circumstances, hence, both his rank and his circumstances required that he should observe more splendour in her funeral and sacrificial rites.

† A tripod is a kind of vase with three feet, and was employed in the Temples, when sacrificing to the dead. The Emperor used nine—the petty Princes seven—the great Officers of state five, and the Literati three.

‡ Although human instrumentality is employed in causing good principles to spread, yet, that they should, or should not obtain their proper sway, is decreed by heaven, and lies beyond the power of human strength.

Mencius replied, Sir, you are a true Tse man, you know only Kwan Chung and Yen Tsze. Some one asked Tsăng Se saying, whether do you, Sir, or Tsze Loo possess the greater virtue and talents? Tsăng Tsze appeared uneasy and replied, my grandfather venerated him (Tsze Loo). Then said the other, whether is my master or Kwan Chung the more virtuous and talented? Tsang Tsze's countenance shewed displeasure and in anger he replied, why compare me to Kwan Chung! Kwan Chung gained the heart of his Prince and was wholly trusted by him. He governed the country for a long time. But his merit was low indeed! why compare me to him? *

Mencius said, since Tsăng Se would not imitate Kwan Chung, do you, Sir, expect that I should? Kwan Chung said, (the other) aided his Prince to force the submision of the Choo How. Yen Tsze made his Prince illustrious. Are Kwan Chung and Yen Tsze not worthy of imitation? Mencius replied, were I received into office, the Prince of Tse might with the utmost ease govern the Empire. Sun Chow replied, this still increases my doubts. If you look at the virtue of Wăn Wang who died at one hundred years of age, even it did not pervade the whole Empire. Woo Wang and Chow Kung, carried on what he had begun: thus the great work of renovation was accomplished. † But, if w at you say about the facility of governing well, be true, then Wăn Wang is not worthy of imitation.

* Kwan Chung assisted Kwan Kung to suppress the petty Princes, and for more than forty years assumed the whole power in the Tse country. But he was not acquainted with the true principles of monarchical government. and acted on the principles of force or violent government.

† Wan Wang, Prince of a small country, under the tyrant Chow, died at the age of ninety seven. Such were his talents and virtue, that two thirds of the Empire wished him to become their sovereign. His son Woo Wang (i. e. the heroic king) conquered the monster Chow the last of the Shang family, and ascended the Imperial seat. His brother Chow Kung assisted Ching Wang, the son and successor of Woo Wang. He adjusted the laws, rites, and music. This was a mighty renovation.

Mencius replied, with Wăn Wang who can compare! From Tang to Woo Ting, there were six or seven holy kings †, so that the whole empire had been long attached to the house of Yin. This length of time made it difficult to effect a change. Woo Ting had all the petty Princes at his levees, and governed with the same ease as he could turn his hand. Chow reigned not long after Woo Ting, the manners of whose ministers and people, and the spirit of whose excellent government were still in some measure preserved. Moreover, he (i. e. Chow) had We Tsze, We Chung, His Royal Highness Pe Kan, Ke Tsze, and Kaou Kĭh to assist him. Hence he held the throne long, and at last lost it. There was not a cubit of ground which he did not possess, nor one of the people who did not serve him, and Wăn Wang possessed but one hundred Le; hence his difficulty. *

The people of Tse have an adage, which says "Although you possess eminent wisdom and intelligence, these are not equal to power (or influence): although you have the instruments of husbandry, these are not of so much importance as it is to wait for the proper season." Now when the Hea, Yin and Chow Dynasties were in the height of their prosperity, the royal

* Tang was the founder of the Shang Dynasty; between him and Woo Ting there were eighteen Emperors. Six or seven of these were men of great talents and virtue, but before the reformer Woo Ting rose, the Emperors had degenerated. From Woo Ting to Chow, the last Emperor of the Shang Dynasty, there were seven Emperors, and the spirit of Woo Ting's excellent government as well as the effect produced on the manners of the people, was in some measure preserved, even to the time of Chow. Hence, the people being by the excellent laws and mild government of the former sovereigns of that house, so long and so deeply attached to the Yin family, wicked and tyrannical as the monster Chow was, it was no easy matter, even for a man of Wan Wang's talents and virtue, to change their regard for the reigning family, and by so doing effect a thorough renovation in the government. Thus it is evident, that Wan Wang's not obtaining the Imperial seat, is to be ascribed to the existing state of things, and not to any deficiency in his virtue or abilities.

---

† There had been several good Princes during that period, but none of them seem to be of great fame among the Chinese, when compared with such worthies as King Wan, and his heroic son King Woo.

domain did not exceed one thousand Le. Tse has this extent of territory. Throughout the whole country the cocks can hear each other crow, and the dogs can hear each other bark; thus, Tse likewise possesses the *sufficient* number of people. Without enlarging your territories, or increasing your population, if you only practise benevolent government, none will be able to prevent you from ruling the whole empire. Moreover, never before has there been so long a period without a good sovereign, nor have the people ever suffered more under tyrannical government. It is easy to feed the hungry and give drink to the thirsty.*

Confucius says, "Virtue runs swifter than the royal postillions carry dispatches." If at present a country of ten thousand chariots govern with benevolence, the people will delight in it, as those do who have been relieved from being suspended with their heads downward. Hence, if you do but one half of the work which the ancients did, your success (or merit) will be double theirs. It is only now that such things can be accomplished.

2. Kung Sun Chow asked Mencius, saying, suppose you, Sir, were made a high officer (or prime minister) of Tse, and succeeded in bringing your principles into practice, so as to establish either the government of force or of reason; there would be nothing wonderful in the circumstance, but were this the case, would your mind be agitated or not?

* From the time that Wan and Woo Wang aid the foundation of the Chow Dynasty to the time when Mencius gave this counoil to the Prince of Tse, more than seven hundred years had elapsed, and during that long period no great and good king had arisen. The people were at that time groaning under the most violent tyranny, hence, as those who are hungry are not particular as to what sort of food you give them, and as the thirsty are not difficult to please, as to the drink given them, so the people under such circumstances, would be easily pleased as to the kind of government placed over them, provided it diminished their sufferings.

Mencius replied, it would not. I am now forty years of age and cannot be agitated (or intimidated.) * If so, you, Sir, greatly surpass Mung Pun. To do so is not difficult. Kaou Tsze, tho' younger than I preserved his mind unmoved. Is there any fixed principle by which the mind may be preserved unmoved? Yes, Pĭh Kung Yew cherished valour so, that when wounded he would not contort his skin nor wink his eye to avert the blow when struck on the face. He viewed the slightest insult from a person as if he had been beaten in the market, or at court. He would not receive an insult, either from one with a large hair cloak (or from a beggar in rags,) nor from the Prince of ten thousand chariots. He looked upon the stabbing of a Prince of ten thousand chariots, as he did upon the stabbing of a poor man. He feared not the tributary Princes. A bad word addressed to him he always returned.

Mung She Shay cherished a valorous spirit so that he said, I look upon not having conquered as having conquered, (i. e. I, am as void of fear, when I lose as when I conquer). He who first calculates the strength of the enemy, and then advances; who first vexes his mind, or thinks much about victory and then meets the enemy, is afraid of a large army. Why should I seek to be certain of victory? To be perfectly void of fear is my principle. †

Mung She Shay resembled Tsăng Tsze—Pĭh Kung Yew resembled Tsze Hea. ‡ I do not know which of these two gentlemen

* Kung Sun Chow did not mean that the mind of Mencius would be moved or puffed up by the riches or dignity of his high station, but that the great responsibility of such a station, was enough to make him afraid of entering into it, or of making him fearful when in it, but Mencius told him that having arrived at forty years of age, "the period when the mind, and temper become firm and settled," he was perfectly void both of doubt and fear.

† Those who will not engage in battle until they are certain, that they are more than a match for the enemy, and are void of fear, only in such circumstances, possess not true valour; as for me, said Mung Shay, I wait not to calculate whether I am certain of victory or not. To be void o: fear is my motto and ruling principle: hence, although I am defeated, I am as destitute of fear to attack again the victorious enemy, as if I had formerly conquered him.

‡ Yew bent his attention to the obtaining of victory over others. Shay exerted his strength to govern himself. Tsze Hea firmly believed the sages. Tsang Tsze examined himself. Hence, these two heroes although not of the same class with Tsang Tsze and Tsze Hea, yet, if you speak of their dispositions, each of them resembled one of these worthies.

excelled in valour, but Mung She Shay maintained that which is most important (i. e. self-government.)

Formerly, Tsăng Tsze conversing with Tsze Seang, said, do you love valour, Sir? I have heard my master *Confucius* say, if when I turn round, and examine myself, I find that I am not upright, ought I not to be afraid of a poor man, in a coarse garb! But, if after self-examination, I find that I am upright, then, although he be sovereign of a thousand chariots, I will meet him. Thus the conduct of Mung She Shay, in preserving his feelings, did not equal that of Tsang Tsze, in preserving reason. *

May I presume to ask an explanation of the principles on which you and Kaou Tsze maintain a firm unagitated spirit? May I hear your explanation Sir, (Mencius replied) Kaou Tsze says, that if on hearing words you do not fully comprehend them, you ought not to seek for the sense in your mind: or if your mind comprehend not, do not call in the aid of the passions. Now, not to call in the aid of the passions is proper; but when you do not comprehend language, not to reflect and employ your mind to find out the sense, is improper. † The will is the leader

* Tsang Tsze carefully examined, and accorded with reason, not with his feelings or passions: the other attended more to his feelings than to reason.

† According to Kaou Tsze, when we hear words or doctrines, which we do not at first fully comprehend, we ought not to ponder them in our minds, until we find out their principles and signification, but to give over troubling our minds about them; and in like manner if in the hurry of business, our minds feel uneasy, we ought not to attempt to soothe them by the aid of the passions. These were his rules for maintaining a firm unmoved mind. The last of these rules Mencius approved, on the principle that it gave great attention to the root and little to the branches: the former he disapproved, because, if followed, we could never become acquainted with the philosophy of things.

or general of the passions. The passions constitute the fulness of the body, (or fill the body.) Now, when the will is cultivated in the highest degree, the passions follow (or come next) to it. Hence the saying, "Hold fast the will, and injure not the passions."*

Since you say that when the will is cultivated in the highest degree, the passions follow, what is meant by saying that we should hold fast the will and not do violence to the passions? When the whole attention is given to the will, it agitates the passions, and when the passions are entirely followed, they agitate the will, as in the case of a man stumbling and falling. This is the action of the passions and agitates the mind.

I presume farther to ask in what respect you excel him? I fully understand language (or doctrines) and nourish well my "Vast flowing vigour." I beg to ask what you call, "Vast flowing vigour"? Mencius replied, the explanation is difficult! This vigour is supremely great, and in the highest degree unbending; nourish it correctly and do it no injury, and it will fill up the vacancy between heaven and earth. This vigour accords with and assists justice and reason, and leaves no hunger (or deficiency). It is produced by an accumulation of righteous

* Mencius maintained that the will being lord and the passions servant, they ought both to be cherished so as that the one might lead and the other follow, without any mutual injury. * *

---

* * I am not quite satisfied that our word "passions" is a perfectly accurate rendering of the Chinese term "Ke." This word has a multitude of significations, the most common of which, when applied to man, are spirit, temper, feelings, habitual disposition, ardour, elevation vehemence, courage, vigour of mind &c. Upon the whole, it appears to me that the term, "passions" taken in its most comprehensive acceptation, as comprehending all the affections and feelings of the soul, answers pretty nearly to the Chinese word as used in this place.

deeds and not by a few accidental acts.* If our actions do not give pleasure to our hearts, they leave an aching void: hence, I said that Kaou Tsze understands not rectitude, but deems it something external.†

You must labor and not previously calculate the result. Let not your mind be taken off from duty. Do not help what is growing. Be not like the man of Sung. In Sung there was a man who feeling sorry that his grain did not grow, went and plucked it up a little, and returned in a foolish, hurried manner, saying to his family. Ah! to-day I am much fatigued I have been assisting the growth of the grain. On which his sons went off in haste to see the grain, and found it withered. Now there are few person in the world, who do not assist the growth of the grain. Those who consider it useless, give it up for lost and do not clean away the weeds from it. But those

* He who knows words, or doctrines has exhausted his mental powers in attaining an acquaintance with nature, and has fully examined every doctrine under heaven, so as to obtain a perfect knowledge of the reasons why any thing is true or false, right or wrong. The 'Ke' (passions or vigour) is originally vast and universally diffusive, and is that which fills the whole body, but, if not properly nourished it becomes famished. As to Mencius, he nourished it so as to bring it back to its original fulness and strength. He likewise perfectly understood the priuciples of every thing under heaven, and hence was equally free from doubt and fear: thus he was fully qualified for a place of great trust.

† Ching Tsze says, Heaven and man are one. We at our birth obtained the straight Ke of Heaven and earth, hence, if we cherish aright this *Ke* it will fill up the gap between heaven and earth. ††

---

†† When they speak, as above, of so cultivating the superior mental powers and the passions, or affections as that the former may lead, and the latter follow, we can form some notion of what they mean, but what idea can we attach to such phrases as this—"The Ke spirit, or temper, or feelings of heaven and earth, are the same as that of man, and if properly cherished by the latter, will fill up the vacancy between heaven and earth." I have never met with a learned native, who can give any rational interpretation of such expressions; they seem to have no idea of their signification. Nor is this matter of surprise, for it is abundantly evident that no rational idea can be attached to such language.

who wish to assist its growth pull up the blade a little. This is not merely of no advantage, but truly injurious.*

What is called knowing words? It is to know what is under the cover of insinuating talk,—the destructive tendency of loose conversation,—the departure from rectitude to which obscene language leads,—and the hard pressure which lies at the bottom of evasive expressions. These produced in a man's heart will injure his politics, injuring his politics and will prove injurious to all his actions. Were a sage to rise again he would confirm my words. Tsae Go and Tsze Kung were eloquent speakers. Yen Yuen both spoke and acted well. Confucius united all these good qualities in himself; yet he said I am not a skilful speaker. Are you not a sage then Sir? †

What language is that! Formerly, Tsze Kung asked Confucius, saying, are not you a sage Sir? Confucius replied, I am incompetent to act the sage. I only learn without satiety, and teach without being wearied. On which Tsze Kung said, to study without satiety, is wisdom, and to instruct without being wearied is perfect virtue. Possessed of perfect virtue united with wisdom,

* The scope of this passage is, that the mind should not cherish any previous determination, that after the performance of a certain number of meritorious actions the superior and inferior powers of the mind must be brought to a state of perfection, and thenceforth proceed in an irregular manner to the accomplishment of such deeds, in order that the end may be speedily attained after the manner of the foolish husbandman; but, that in opposition to this irregular procedure, we ought to go on steadily with calm unprepossessed minds, in the performance of every known duty, and in the constant practice of every virtue; in the same manner as the husbandman ought to clear away the weeds and give the fruits of the earth a fair opportunity of growing of themselves. As in the one case the grain will grow naturally, if proper culture be applied, so in the other perfect virtue will, by a patient and steady practice of righteousness, at last be secured, and that without the least violence or force.**

† Kung Sun Chow said, each of these disciples of Confucius, excelled in some one virtue, but their master united all their excellences in his own person, yet he himself said, that he was not skilled in speaking. But you Sir (speaking to Mencius), say you fully understand all sorts of language, and can nourish your temper well; thus you unite eloquence with perfect, practical virtue;—are you not therefore a sage!

** There is some truth in this view of the subject, but it is marked by the same fatal deficiency that is to be met with in every branch of the ethics of the school. It makes no reference to "the healthful spirit of divine grace" as the great source of all genuine virtue in man,

are you not a sage Sir? *Mencius* replied, since the holy Confucius did not take the appellation of sage. How can you thus speak!

Formerly (said Kung Sun Chow), I heard that Tsze Kung, Tsze Yew, and Tsze Chang, taken altogether, made one member of the sage, (or of a sage) and that Yen New, Min Tsze, and Yen Yuen, made his whole body in miniature. I presume to ask what place you would take among them? Let us put these aside, said Mencius. *

What then do you think of Pih E, and E Yin? Their principles differ from mine. Not to serve a Prince whom he did not approve, nor rule people who did not suit him;—to go into office when good government prevailed and to retire in times of anarchy and confusion, were the principles and practice of Pih E. † To serve a bad Prince, and rule worthless people; go into office, whether the country was well or ill governed, were the principles aad conduct of E Yin. ‡ To go into office, when proper; to give it up when proper; to remain long in office when proper and leave his place quickly when proper, were the principles of Confucius. All these were ancient sages, nor am I capable of acting equal to any of them; but he of whom I wish to learn is Confucius. ¶

* Mencius meant to say, that in aiming at excellence, we ought to place before our eyes the most eminent examples, and that although these disciples of the sage were men of talent and virtue, yet he did not wish to compare himself to them, nor to take them as his patterns. Confucius alone, he considered as the example he ought to imitate.

† Pih E was the eldest son of the Prince of Koo Chuh. He and his younger brother, successively resigned the throne of their father to each other and left their country. Upon hearing of the virtue of the famous Prince Wan, they returned and served him; but when Prince Woo, son of Wan,—cut off Chow, they disapproved of his conduct, it being contrary to their principles for a tributary Prince, or minister to rebel against his sovereign, even if a tyrant; so they retired to the mountains where they died of hunger.

‡ When E Yin was in Sin, he was sent for and employed by the famous Tang, who sent him five different times to admonish the tyrant Kee, last Emperor of the Hea Dynasty; but the latter continuing to lend a deaf ear to his expostulations, he at last assisted Tang to dethrone the monster, ascend his throne, and establish good government. From this may be seen, that his principles and conduct differed widely from that of Pih E.

¶ As to Confucius, he far excelled these sages, in as much as he at all times, and under every circumstance, acted exactly according to what was perfectly right in the nature of things. Hence he was selected by Mencius as his great pattern of imitation.

Were Pih E, E Yin and Confucius equals? No! From the time that people were created to the present day, none have been equal to Confucius! Were they in any respect equal? Yes, had they had the government of one hundred Le, they would have brought all the tributary Princes to their court and have united the whole Empire under their sway. Supposing that one unjust action, or the putting to death of one innocent person, would have gained them the whole Empire, they would not have done any such thing. In these respects they were the same. * I presume to ask in what respects they differed? Tsae Go, Yew To, and Tsze Kung possessed intelligence sufficient to render them capable of knowing the sage, nor would they from low unworthy motives have over praised their favorite. Now, Tsae Go said, in my view Confucius was far more virtuous than Yaou and Shun. † Tsze Kung said, look at their music, and you may know their virtue. I have compared the kings of the last hundred ages, and not one has escaped my observation; but from the birth of people downward, none have equalled Confucius. Yew To said, why only men? the Ke Lin, is of the same species as other birds. ‡ The Tae Shan (great mountains) are of the same kind as mole-hills, and the seas and rivers are of the same class as the small streams of water; so is the sage of the same species as other man, only he rises above men

* These constitute the radical principles of a sage, were he not capable of acting in this manner he could not be a sage. Hence, although Pih E and Yin E equalled Confucius in these, he still far excelled them in other respects.

† If you speak of their intelligence and holiness, then they did not differ: but if you speak of their practical merits, they did differ. When it is said that Confucius was more virtuous than Yaou and Shun, it is practical merit that is referred to. Yaou and Shun established good government and Confucius handed down their doctrines for the instruction of all ages. The merit of Yaou and Shun was confined to one age, but that of Confucius reaches to all succeeding generations. Had it not been for Confucius, following ages would have known nothing of the principles of Yaou and Shun. Thus it is evident that he was far more meritorious than they.

‡ The Ke Lin, is the chief of haired animals, and the Fung Hwang is the head of the feathered tribes.

of ordinary attainments. From the first man to the present hour, none have equalled the fulness of Confucius.

3. Mencius says, that he who subdues a man by force, is called Pa. A Pa must have an extensive country in order that he may be able to conquer his neighbours. He who subdues men by virtue is a king. A king waits not for a large country, in order to be able to subdue the whole Empire. Tang had only seventy Le, and Wăn Wang had but one hundred Le. Those who subdue by force do not subdue the heart. Force is not adquate to that. But those who subdue men by virtue, delight the hearts of the subdued, and their submission is sincere. Thus the seventy disciples submitted to Confucius. The She King speaking of Wăn Wang says, "From the west from the east, from the south and from the north there was not one thought not brought in subjection to him." This is what we call a genuine victory. *

4. Mencius says, the virtuous have glory, the vicious disgrace. To hate disgrace and yet practise vice is like hating dampness and yet dwelling in a low room.

If a Prince hate it (disgrace), then there is nothing he can do better than to honor virtue and respect the learned. When the virtuous occupy official situations, and men of talents are in office, then when the members of government have leisure they will illustrate the laws, so that even an extensive country will fear and respect them.

The She King says, "Now that heaven does not send down rain, I take the skins of the root of the mulberry tree and weave my nest, and who of the people below will dare to insult me!"

* The great object of Mencius was to convince the petty Princes of the day, that if any one of them, surrounded as they were by tyrannical governments, would but imitate the famous Tang, or Wan Wang, however small his territory might be he would assuredly gain the hearts of the whole Empire, and thus in spite of all opposition, be elevated to the Imperial seat, where he might diffuse peace and happiness through the nation.

Confucius says, he who wrote this Ode knows right principles; in governing a country who would dare to insult him? * At present when government have leisure they give themselves up to all kinds of pleasure and extravagance and call down misery on themselves. Men have neither misery nor happiness which is not sought by themselves. The She King says, "He who constantly thinks of according with the will of heaven brings much happiness on himself." Tae Keă says, "The calamities sent by heaven may be avoided, but men cannot live under the calamities brought by themselves."

5. Mencius says, honor the virtuous, employ men of talents, and promote men of eminent abilities to high official situations, then all the learned under heaven will delight to stand in your court. If you tax their shops and not their goods (or if the laws of selling and buying be attended to and no duty charged), then all the merchants under heaven will rejoice to store your markets. † Let inquiries be made at the out-ports and no duty exacted, and all the strangers under heaven will take delight in travelling your roads. Let the husbandmen assist in tilling the public field and not pay taxes, and all the farmers under heaven will delight to cultivate your waste lands.

He who can faithfully practise these five things, will find that the people of the neigbouring countries will look up to him as to their father and mother. Now, from the birth of men to this day, never have the children been led out to attack their father and

* This Ode was composed by Chow Kung brother of Woo Wang.

† When those who declined tilling the ground, which is the prime source of support, and sought a livelihood by buying and selling, were numerous their shops were taxed, in order to prevent such numbers from neglecting the root and attending to the branches. On the other hand, when few engaged in merchandize, no tax was laid on their shops, but a very light duty was exacted according to the quantity of goods sold. These were the regulations of their good kings.

mother. If you act thus, you will have no enemy under heaven. He who has no enemy under heaven is commissioned by heaven; nor has it ever been the case, that he who was appointed by heaven did not govern the empire.

6. Mencius said, all men have compassionate hearts (or hearts that cannot bear to do any thing cruel). The former kings had compassionate hearts, and exhibited them in their compassionate government. He who possesses a compassionate heart, and practises compassionate government, in ruling the empire may turn it in the palm of his hand. What is meant by saying that all men have compassionate hearts, may be thus illustrated, if one see a child about to fall into a well, the latent compassion of his heart is suddenly aroused. Nor is this because he wishes to gain the favor of the child's parents, or to gain a name in the neighbourhood, or because he is afraid of a bad name. *

Look at the subject in this light and you will see that he who has not a latent principle of compassion in his heart, is not a man, that he who is void of shame and hatred is not a man,—that he who has no humility and modesty is not a man, † and that he who knows not right and wrong is not a man. A latent principle of compassion in the heart is the spring of benevolence. Humility and modesty constitute the source of a correct and polite behaviour. Shame and hatred form the rising principle of justice. A sense of right and wrong, is the germ of wisdom.

* All men by nature have hearts which cannot bear to treat their fellow men with cruelty, or harshness; but the greater part of people allow their lusts to domineer, and thus destroy their naturally compassionate dispositions. Hence they become unable to manifest this virtuous disposition in their conduct.

† By shame is meant being ashamed of one's own vices and by hatred hating the vices of others.

Man has these four sources in himself, the same as he has four members.* To possess these four principles and yet to say that we are not able to act well, is to rob ourselves, and to say that our prince is not capable of acting aright, is to rob our Prince.

All who possess these four principles, if they know how to expand and fill them up, they will resemble the breaking out of fire, or the rising of water;—carry them to perfection, and you will be able to preserve the four seas (all China). If you do not fill them up, you cannot preserve your own father and mother. †

7. Mencius says, why should the maker of arrows be less benevolent than the maker of armour? The only difference is, that the maker of arrows is afraid that his arrows will not wound men, and the maker of armour is afraid that they will. The same is the case with the Priest (or magician) and the coffin-maker. ‡ Thus every one cannot but be attentive to his trade. Confucius says, the virtue of villagers is beautiful. How can the man who does not select virtuous neighbours be wise! Virtue is the nobility which heaven bestows, and man's quiet abode. None

* That is, these are as essential to a man, as are two hands and two feet. **

† To carry the principles of virtue to the utmost perfection, depends entirely on one's-self. He who does not act thus, throws himself away. ††

‡ The benevolence of each of these classes of men, is originally the same, and the only difference that exists between their intention lies in the difference of their respective employments. For although the arrow-maker wishes his arrows to wound or kill, and the armour-maker wishes his workmanship to save from wounds and death, yet it does not follow that the former possesses less benevolence than the latter.

** We allow that to a good man these are absolutely essential, but that they actually exist in all men, will be difficult to prove against such a mass of facts which indubitably establish the contrary position.

†† The advocates of human merit and moral ability, meet with warm supporters in the sages of the celestial empire; but nothing can be more evident to the attentive and accurate student of human nature and of divine revelation than that there is a gross fallacy at the foundation of the system.

can hinder him from dwelling in it. Hence the bad man is void of wisdom. He who is void of wisdom and virtue, is rude and unjust, and the servant of others. Now to be a servant of others and yet ashamed to serve them, is like being an arrow-maker and yet ashamed to make arrows, or a bow-maker, and yet ashamed to make bows.

If you know how to be ashamed, there is nothing like practicing virtue. The truly virtuous man resembles the archer. The archer first adjusts himself and then shoots. If he shoot, and miss the mark, he blames not him who gains the prize, but turns round and blames himself.

8. Mencius said, when any one told Tsze Loo of his errors he was glad. *

When Yu heard good words he made a bow. The famous Shun was still greater then these. He shared virtue with men,—gave up himself and followed others, rejoicing to make the virtues of others his own. During the whole period in which he was successively a husbandman, a potter, a fisher and an Emperor, he constantly imitated others. † He who imitates others in the practice of virtue, assists other in the practice of virtue. ‡ Hence there is nothing the superior man does greater, than that of assisting men to practise virtue (by imitating them.)

* Confucius says, that Tsze Loo in rejoicing when any one told him of his faults, may be called the Instructor of an hundred ages.

† Shun was first a farmer in Leih Shan, then a potter in Ho Ping, afterwards a fisher in Seaou Tsih, and at last ascended the Imperial throne. He not only imitated the virtues of others when in humble circumstances, but after he rose to the highest earthly dignity he followed the same course.

‡ When you imitate a man's virtue, you excite him to strive after greater eminence of moral excellence, and thus increase his virtue.

9. Mencius said, Pih E would not serve a Prince who did not suit his mind, nor make one his friend whom he did not esteem. He would not stand in a bad man's court, nor even speak with a bad man. To stand in a bad man's court, or speak with a bad man, he viewed in the same light as he would that of sitting in the mire with his court dress on. He carried his detestation of vice so far, that, if standing with a common man whose hat was not properly put on, he turned away and kept at a distance from him, lest he should be defiled. Hence, although any of the Princes sent a polite invitation, offering him an official situation, he would not accept of it. He would not accept it because he did not deem it pure (or right) to do so. *

Lew Hea Hwuy was not ashamed to serve a polluted Prince, nor did he despise an inferior situation. When promoted, he concealed not his virtue, but acted on correct principles. If put out of office, he grumbled not.—When pressed by poverty, he was not grieved. For, he always said, " You are you, and I am I." Although you make bare your arm, and expose your person at my side, how can you defile me!" Thus, he made himself at ease in his intercourse with others, and yet never lost his own integrity. If any one wished to detain him, he remained. He remained when thus detained, because he did not think that purity of principle admitted of his leaving.

Mencius says, Pih E was narrow minded, and Lew Hea Hwuy, was deficient in gravity; therefore, the superior man follows neither of them. †

* He reflected that, although the invitation was polite and according to propriety, yet it did not follow that it came from a man of genuine virtue. Therefore, when he considered that compliance would be a prostitution of his principles, he refused.

† Mencius having narrated the history of these two men thus far, at last passed judgment upon them, by observing that although the conduct of Pih E was lofty and pure, yet it was a sort of exclusive loftiness which cut off others; and that although Lew Hea Hwuy was liberal and agreeable, yet he rather trifled with the age. The former was too narrow minded, and the latter too liberal, so that the superior man wished not to make either of them his pattern.††

†† Yet the former is said to be one of the ancient sages :—see above.

CHAP. IV.

1. Mencius says, heaven's time is not equal to earth's advantages, nor are local advantages equal to men's union. When a town of three Le with suburbs of seven Le, is surrounded and attacked on all sides, without success, during the time in which it could have been surrounded, and attacked, there must have been a lucky day, but the want of success shews that lucky days, are not equal to local advantages.* When the walls are high, the ditches deep, the armour strong, the weapons sharp, and the provisions plenty, and yet the people flee, it shews that local advantages, are not equal to harmony among men. Hence, it is said, that a nation is not united by mere local boundaries, a country is not defended merely by the dangerous passes of Mountains and dens; nor is the Empire kept in awe by sharp swords only. Those who govern well, many will assist. Those who violate good government, few will assist.—Nay even their relations will rebel against them. When many assist, this will lead to the homage of the whole empire.†

* Before such a town could be surrounded and fairly besieged, some fortunate day must have occurred; consequently, the want of success affords sufficient proof that the selection of such days, is not of equal importance with such local advantages as strong ramparts and deep ditches afford.

† The good Prince governs, protects and awes his people, by more powerful weapons than swords and spears; namely by invincible and awful virtue.

Thus, there will be a whole submissive Empire to attack those who are opposed by their very relatives. Hence, the good Prince needs not to fight, but if he do fight, he must conquer. *

2. On one occasion when Mencius was just about to pay a visit to the Prince of Tse, a messenger came from the king, saying, that his majesty had caught a cold and could not face the wind to come and visit him (Mencius), adding that he did not know whether he should have the pleasure of seeing him at court. Mencius replied, unfortunately I am also sick, and cannot go to court. Next day Mencius went to condole with Tung Kwo She. Kung Sun Chow said, yesterday you refused to go to court, because sick; to-day you wish to go and condole.—Perhaps this is not proper. Mencius replied, yesterday I was sick, to-day I am well; why then should I not go and condole? †

His Majesty sent a man to inquire about his sickness, and likewise a medical man. When they arrived, Mung Chung Tsze said to them, yesterday he had an order from the king to go to court, but he had a slight attack of sickness and could not go to court; to-day he is somewhat better and has gone to court in haste. I do'nt know whether he may have reached it or not. On which he sent several persons to meet him on the way, beseeching him not to return, but to go to court. Mencius

* Intimating that at that time when the other Princes had by their tyrannical government made their own kinsmen their enemies, a Prince who could by his kind and benevolent measures, gain the hearts of the whole empire, would have no need for war: for the whole mass of the people would be his children, and secure him a bloodless triumph; or, if he found it necessary to take up arms, he must without doubt prove victorious.

† Mencius' refusal to go to court on the grounds of being sick, while he went to condole, was of the same nature as that of Confucius in refusing to see Joo Pei and then taking his harp and playing. † †

---

† † In both cases these sages told deliberate falsehoods. For, according to their own confession, neither of them was sick at the time. It is a foul blot in the history of men who set themselves up as the immaculate and infallible teachers of the world, that they could thus violate the sacred principles of truth. Nor will it avail their admirers any thing, to say that these falsehoods were told in order to reprove an unprincipled monarch, and a rude young man. For, we are not at liberty to do evil that good may follow, nor will any man of sound principle think of employing such means for the instruction of others.

was obliged to lodge that night in the house of king Chow She.* King Chow She (addressing him) said, within, are father and son, without, are Prince and Minister. These are the greatest of human relations. The reigning principle between father and son, is kindness, what is most important between Prince and Minister, is respect. I have observed that the king shews respect to you, but I have not seen you shew respect to him. On which *Mencius* exclaimed, what do you say, Sir! The people of Tso do not speak of benevolence and justice to their king. Is it possible that they do not esteem benevolence and justice excellent! In their hearts they really say, how is he worthy to be spoken to about benevolence and justice! Than this there cannot be greater disrespect. I dare not speak to (or before) the king, but according to the principles of Yaou and Shun. Hence, none of the men of Tse shew such respect to his majesty as I do.

King Tszc said, this is not what I mean. The Le Ke says, "When your father calls, you must not wait to say yes; when your Prince calls you, you must not wait for your carriage." You intended to go to court, but on receiving the king's commands, did not go. This seems at variance with the doctrine of the Le Ke. *Mencius*,--why put this construction on my conduct? Tsăng Tszc said, "The riches of Tsin and Tsoo cannot be equalled. They take their riches and I my virtue, they their nobility and I my justice; why should I be inferior to them!" Is not this just?

* This does not mean that he was so pressed by circumstances as to be obliged to lodge that night in King Chow's house, but that he did so in order that he might cause the Prince of Tse to come to the knowledge of his reasons for not answering his call. For he really was not sick, but refused to go, only because he considered it contrary to the principles on which kings and scholars should visit.**

** Thus he preferred the telling of a downright untruth, that is violating the law of God, to the committing of a breach of common etiquette. In the present day he has many imitators, even among professed Christians, who are so totally void of the fear of God, as to prefer trampling on his sacred law, to the giving of the least offence to a fellow mortal. What will the end of such things be!

Have not the words of Tsăng Tsze a moral? Under the heavens there are three kinds of dignity. Nobility (or office) is one. Age is one, and virtue is one. In the court, nothing equals nobility,—in the village there is nothing equal to age,—in supporting the age and ruling the people, there is nothing equal to virtue. Why should those who possess the one despise those who possess the two!

Therefore, a great Prince will have ministers whom he will not call at pleasure. When he wishes to consult them, he will go to them. If he do not thus honor virtue and rejoice in just principles, he is not fit for his office. Hence, Tang first learned of E Yin, and then made him his minister; consequently he governed well without effort. Hwan Kung first learned of Kwan Chung and then made him his minister, therefore, without exertion he forced the people (or rulers) to submission. At present, all the provinces are of one class, and their virtue equal. No one excels the others. This arises from no other cause, than that they love to teach their ministers, and like not to be taught by their ministers.

Neither Tang in his treatment of E Yin, nor Hwan Kung in his treatment of Kwan Chung, presumed to send for them. Now if Kwan Chung would not be called, how much less should he be ordered, who will not imitate Kwan Chung!

3. Chin Tsin said, formerly, the Prince of Tse offered you an hundred pieces of gold and you did not accept of them, but when in Sung, on being presented with seventy Yih you received them and when in Sëĕ you accepted fifty Yih. Now, if your refusal in the first instance was right, then your acceptance on the two latter occasions was wrong; or if your acceptance on the two latter occasions was right, then your refusal on the former

occasion was wrong. You must, Sir, take one of these alternatives. Mencius replied, on all these occasions I was right.

When in Sung, I had a long journey to undertake. The traveller must have travelling expenses. When presented with travelling expenses, why should I refuse them? When in Sëë I was apprehensive of danger, and when the money was presented it was said, "I have heard that you are afraid of danger, hence present this to pay a guard for you." Why then should I not have accepted it? When in Tse, I had no occasion for money. When one is not in need and yet is presented with gifts, it is making merchandise of him, but how can a superior man receive money to be thus bought!

4. When Mencius went to Ping Lŭh, in conversing with one of the high officers, he said, if your soldiers should three times in one day err in their motions, would you put them to death, or not? * On which he replied, why should I wait till they err three times. Then Sir, you have erred often: in years of famine your aged people are starved and turned into the ditches, and your young people are scattered to the four quarters of the world, to the number of several thousands. This is not Keu Sin's concern (or what I can remedy).

Mencius said, if you were to be made a man's shepherd and to receive in charge his flocks and herds, then you ought to seek for grass and pasturage for them. If you sought and could not find it, would you deliver them up again to the gentleman, or stand still and see them die? † This said Keu Sin, is my offence.

On another occasion (Mencius) waited on the Prince and said, I know five of your governors, but it is only Kung Keu

* The word used in the text, means simply to put away, but the Commentator explains it by a word which means to put to death.

† Mencius meant, that if an officer of government is so circumstanced as not to be allowed to act as he ought (or not to have the means of governing well) he ought to resign his situation.

Sin who knows his own errors. He then related the circumstance to the king; on which the latter said this is my fault.

5. Mencius, conversing with Che Wa said, your refusing the office of Ling Kew and begging the office of criminal judge, appeared right, because it gave you an opportunity of speaking; but now after having been in this office several months, could you not have spoken? Che Wa reproved his Prince and he did not reform; on which he gave up his office and departed. The people of Tse said, he (Mencius) has done very well for Che Wa, but we know not how he acts for himself. Kung Too Tsze told *his master* of this, Mencius replied, I have heard that when a man who holds an office is not allowed to do his duty, he resigns, and that he who reproves *his Prince* and his reproofs are not attended to, leaves his office (that is, it is the duty of a minister thus to act). But I am neither in office nor have I used reproofs; am I not therefore at perfect liberty to do as I please. *

6. When Mencius held the office of king in Tse he was sent to condole with the Prince of Tăng and Wang Ta Foo of Hĭh was sent as his assistant. When on their journey, Wang Kwan morning and evening waited upon Mencius, but when they had returned to Tse, he never once spoke with him on the business of their mission. Kung Sun Chow said, the office of king of Tse is not a mean situation, nor is the distance between Tse and Tăng small, why not speak with him during the whole of this journey on the business you went upon? Mencius replied, these affairs having been previously arranged by the proper authorities, why should I speak to him about them. †

* The people of Tse thought as Mencius had stimulated Che Wa to reprove his Prince, and had thus led him to act a proper part in resigning his office, on not being listened to, he ought himself to have acted on the same principle, and as his doctrines were not followed by the government, taken his leave of the country; but Mencius gave them to know, that as he held no official situation, his own principles laid him under no obligation to act as the other had done.

† Wang Kwan was a minion of the crown and as such was no favorite of the sage; therefore though in office and favor he kept him at his proper distance.

7. Mencius having gone from Tse to bury his mother in Loo, on his way back stopped at Ying. Chung Yu said to him, you did not know my stupidity; when you placed me over the workmen, your pressure of business was such, that I did not presume to ask. Now I wish to know whether the wood (of the coffin) was not too fine.

Mencius replied, in high antiquity, there was no fixed rule for the making of coffins. In the middle ages the inside coffin was made seven inches thick, and the outside one equal to it. This was the general rule from the Emperor down to the lowest of the people, and was observed not for show, but as a manifestation of filial piety. What is improper should not be delighted in, nor should what you have not the means of doing. When rank and wealth admitted the ancients acted thus, why should not I?

For instance, to prevent the earth from coming near the dead, is it not pleasant! I have heard that the superior man will not, for the sake of any thing under heaven, treat his parents in a shabby manner.

8. Shin Tung asked Mencius, privately, whether the Yen country ought to be subdued? Mencius replied, it ought. Tsze Kwae had no authority to give up Yen to another, and Tsze Che had no right to receive Yen from Tsze Kwae. Suppose, for instance, you should, without informing the king, give your office and salary to an officer whom you loved, and he without receiving the king's command should accept of them from you, how would this do? Yet what difference would there be between that case and this? *

The people of Tse conquered Yen and some one asked Mencius whether he advised them to it, he replied, that he did not.

* The country and people of Yen were received from the Emperor, from whom former Princes inherited them, hence, Tse Kwae in taking upon himself to give them to another, without informing the Emperor, acted a most irregular part, and Tse Che in accepting the throne without Imperial orders, violated every principle of order, and therefore deserved to be dethroned.

Ching Tung (said he) asked me whether Yen ought to be subdued, and I answered that it ought; on which he went and invaded it. Had he asked me who ought to subdue it, then I would have said, a divine messenger ought to invade it. Suppose any one should ask me whether a murderer ought to be put to death, I should answer that he ought. If he farther asked, who ought to put him to death; then I would reply, the sheriff ought to put him to death. In this case why should I have advised Yen to invade Yen! *

9. The people of Yen rebelled, and the king said, I am very much ashamed to see Mencius. Chin Kea said, let not your majesty be troubled; whether was Chow Kung or you the more virtuous, and which is the more wise? The king exclaimed, what do you say! Chow Kung said, the other, set Kwan Shŭh over Yin (i. e. the son of Chow) and Kwan Shŭh rebelled with Yin. Now, if he (Chow Kung) knew that this would be the case and yet appointed him, he was deficient in virtue. If he did not know, and yet sent him, he showed a want of wisdom. Hence, Chow Kung was not both completely virtuous and completely wise, how much less can your majesty be so! I beg leave to wait on him (Mencius) and explain this. He waited on Mencius, and said, what kind of man was Chow Kung? An ancient sage. Did he send Kwan Shŭh to oversee Yin, and did he unite with Yin in his rebellion? Yes. Did Chow Kung know, that he would rebel and yet send him? He did not know. Then the sage likewise errs. Chow Kung was younger brother, Kwan Shŭh was elder brother, was not the error of Chow Kung reasonable! †

* Intimating that the government of Tse, the invading country, was as bad as that of Yen the invaded nation, and hence had no authority whatever to attack it.

† When Woo Wang conquered the tyrant Chow, and ascended his throne, he set Woo Kang son of Chow over a small country, and Woo Kang brother of Kwan Shuh, was sent to look over him and watch his movements. When Woo Wang died and during the time that his brother Chow Kung assisted, or rather acted for Ching Wang, successor to Woo Wang, Kwan Shuh and Woo Kang rebelled against the Imperial House.

Moreover, the ancients of superior rank when they erred reformed, but those of the present day, when they err, follow up their errors. The errors of ancient superior men, resembled the eclipses of the sun and moon; all the people saw them, and all the people looked with expectation for their reformation, but why do those of modern times indulge their errors and attempt to excuse them!

10. Mencius resigned his office and returned home. The king waited on Mencius, and said, formerly I wished to see you, Sir, and could not obtain my wish. When I had you to sit by my side, the whole court was highly delighted, now that you leave me (or rather reject me) and return, I know not when I my again see you. Mencius replied, I dare not speak decisively, but I really wish to see you again. *

On another day, the king said to She Tsze, I wish to keep Mencius in the middle of the country, and to allow him ten thousand measures of rice to maintain his students, in order that all the great officers, and the people may have an example which they may reverence. Will you not speak to him for me? She Tsze employed Chin Tsze to inform Mencius. Chin Tsze conveyed the wishes of the king to Mencius in the words of She Tsze. Mencius replied, yes, indeed! Did not She Tsze know that I would not remain! If I had coveted riches, how should I have refused one hundred thousand, and now accept ten thousand!

Ke Sun exclaimed, Tsze Shŭh E was an extraordinary man, he first pushed himself into office, and when they would not employ him, he pushed his son into the office of king, (one of the highest). Who does not love riches, but he alone was the "Lung Kwan" among those who seek riches! †

* When Mencius was in Tse, although he had no fixed salary, he held an office, but finding that his principles were not adopted nor reduced to practice, he resigned his office.

† Lung Kwan, was a sort of mound raised in the market places, on which a fellow stood who monopolised all the profits of the market,

In ancient times, in the markets where they bartered their goods, there was an officer appointed to keep order. At last some mean fellow got up on an elevated spot that he might see all around him, and take in all the profits of the market. All men deemed him a mean fellow, and a tax was laid upon his gain. It was from the conduct of this scamp that the tax on merchandize took its rise. *

11. When Mencius left Tse, he lodged one night in Chow. Some one wishing to retain him on behalf of the king, sat down by his side and conversed with him, to whom he made no reply, but leaned on his chair and slept. The stranger was displeased and said, I prepared myself, waited one night and then presumed to speak to you, Sir, and lo you have slept and have not listened! I beg leave to see you no more. Mencius replied, sit down till I explain matters. Formerly, if Mŭh, Prince of Loo, had not sent a man to wait upon Tsze Sze, he could not have retained him. If Sëë Lew, and Shin Seang had no person of worth sitting by the side of Prince Mŭh he could not retain them.

You Sir, are vexed about a superior man (i. e. me) and yet you have not treated me as Sze Tsze. Have you cut off the superior man, or has he cut you off? †

12. When Mencius left Tse, Yin Sze said to some one, if he did not know that the king could not act like Tang and Woo, he is not very intelligent. If he did know this, and yet came here, it must have been from a wish to get into favor. He came one thousand Le, and tho' he found that he could not act

* In ancient times an officer was set over the markets to keep order, but no tax was levied on buying and selling, till this low spirited fellow began to monopolise the profits.

† Meaning that the Prince of Tse did not send this gentleman, but that he took upon himself to come in a private manner. Which mode of procedure was not like the manner in which Muh, Prince of Loo, detained Sze Tsze and was in fact treating Mencius with disrespect.

he remained three days, and then went out to Chow. Why such lingering! I do not like this.

Kaou Tse informed Mencius. He replied, how can Yin Sze know me! To come one thousand miles, and wait upon the king, was what I wished to do. Not to agree with him and depart, how could that be my wish! This was force.* That I should remain three nights and then go out to Chow, seems to me to be quick. Perhaps his majesty may change, then he will call me back (or the king might have reformed and have called me back). Now, having gone out to Chow, and the Prince not having called me back, I then became fully determined to return; but although this was the case, why should I abandon the king? His majesty is capable of acting well. Would he employ me, why should only the people of Tse be made happy? The whole Empire would obtain peace and happiness. Perhaps his majesty may reform. I daily hope he will.

Why should I imitate a little minded man, who when he reproves his Prince and he does not listen, breaks out into a violent passion and with all his strength runs a whole day and then stops. Yin Sze hearing of this, said, I am truly a little man.

13. When Mencius left Tse, while on the way, Chung Yu said to him, you appear uneasy, Sir. I have heard you say, that the superior man neither grumbles with heaven, nor blames men. To which he replied, that was one time, and this is another. In the course of each five hundred years, a famous sovereign should arise, and in that time there should be a man of renown.† Since the rise of the house of Chow, to the present day, more

* He waited on the king because he wished to put in practice his political principles and do his duty in the service of his country. But when he discovered that this object could not be effected at present, he had no other choice but that of leaving.

† Men of renown refer to men whose names must be handed down to future ages; and who by their talents and virtue have assisted in promoting good government in their country.

than seven hundred years have elapsed. Calculate and you will see it is past the time. Examine the state of the times and you will see that the thing may (or ought to) be. *

Heaven, it seems, does not wish to give tranquility and good order to the Empire. If it were to be done in this age, then seeing I am rejected who is there besides? Why should I not be uneasy!

14. When Mencius left Tse, Kung Sun Chow asked him whether it were the principles of the ancients to hold an office, without receiving salary? He replied, that it was not. When in Tsung (said he) I had an interview with the king, after I retired I felt disposed to depart. This determination I did not wish to change, and therefore did not accept of salary. At that time, there was war, so that I could not ask leave to depart. My long stay in Tse was not what I wished.

CHAP. V.

1. When Wăn of Tăng was SheTsze (i. e. heir to the throne) in going to Tsoo he passed through Sung and had an interview with Mencius. Mencius talking to him of man's nature being virtuous, could not but praise Yaou and Shun (or name them as

* Mencius, reflecting that the period was past, when according to the course of things, a Great Monarch and a renouned prime minister ought to have appeared, and that he was the only man then living capab'e of being such a prime minister, felt deeply grieved that none of the Princes would adopt and put in practice his principles and thus become Emperor. * *

From Yaou and Shun to Tang, and from Tang to Wan and Woo, there were severally five hundred years and odds, between the birth of these great sages.

* * The sage did not manifest that modesty in this case, which we naturally look for in a truly great man, especially in one who is held up to all succeeding ages as an example of perfect virtue.

proofs of his doctrine). When She Tsze returned, he again waited upon Mencius. Mencius said, do you doubt my words? Virtue is one only (or all men are, originally, equally virtuous).

Ching Keen conversing with King? Prince of Tse said, they (i. e. sages) are men and so am I; why should he afraid of them? Yen Yuen said, who was Shun and who am I! If I wish I may equal him.

Kung Ming E said. Wăn Wang is my teacher why should Chow Kung mock me! *

At present, if the country of Tăng had its length curtailed and its breadth augmented, it might be a virtuous country of 50 Le. The Shoo King says, "If medecine do not confuse one by its workings it will not cure."

2. When Ting, Prince of Tăng died, She Tsze (the heir) said to Jen Yew, I shall never forget what Mencius formerly said to me when in Sung. At present I am unfortunate. I have a great work to perform, I wish first to send you to inquire of Mencius and then I may perform this work. †

Jen Yew went to Tsow, and asked the opinion of Mencius. Mencius said, is not this good! In burying parents, we should do our utmost. Tsăng Tsze said, while living to serve them with propriety, when they die to bury them propriety, and afterwards to sacrifice to them with propriety, may be called filial piety. I have not learned the ceremonies observed by the Princes of states, but I have heard that to mourn for three years, to wear coarse garments, without hems and to eat coarse food, are what have been observed during three dynasties, by all classes from the Emperor down to the lowest of the people.

* Chow Kung was the son of Wan Wang and imbibed his principles, hence he was accustomed to say that Wan Wang was his teacher, but Kung Ming E considering that all men were by nature alike virtuous, and that they might be so by practice if they chose, used to recite the words of Chow Kung as equally applicable to himself.

† Prince Ting was the father of Prince Wan (here styled She Ssze). Jen Yew was She Tsze's Tutor. A great work, means a great burial and sacrificial ceremony.

Jen Yew returned and delivered his report, and three years mourning were fixed upon. The old ministers of the same family name with him, and all the officers objected, saying that, "The Princes of Loo, the country of our ancestors, did not thus act; nor has any of our own former Princes done so; nor should any change be made when you, Sir, have succeeded to the throne." For, Che in speaking of burial and sacrificial rites says, "We ought to imitate our ancestors; meaning that, we have received the rules for these from our fathers." * He said to Jen Yew, formerly, I did not study, but delighted in horsemanship and sword exercise; hence, the aged ministers and all the officers deem me unfit for my station (or for this work), I am afraid that we shall not be able to accomplish this great work aright. Will you, Sir, once more ask the opinion of Mencius? Jen Yew went again to Tsow and inquired of Mencius. Mencius replied, yes, he is right. He ought not to blame others. Confucius says, when the Sovereign died, business was transacted in the office of the Prime minister. The *Prince* drunk gruel and his face was deep black (with grief). When he came to the seat of mourning, he wept bitterly, so that not one of the officers, great or small, dared not to manifest grief. He led them. What superiors love, inferiors will most carefully attend to. The virtue of the superior man resembles the wind, that of the mean man, the grass. The grass must yield to the wind, it truly depends on She Tsze.

Jen Yew returned and gave his report. She Tsze said, true! It really depends on me. For five moons, he lived in a grass house and gave no commands: all the officers said he know-

* The royal families of Loo and Tang were both descended from Wan Wang; but they had lost the custom of mourning three years for the dead which was observed by Chow Kung, and other ancient worthies. Hence, their ignorant censure of this promising young Prince, who wished to put in practice the doctrines of the ancient sages on this point.

† This refers to what Confucius said concerning the ancient rites. In ancient times, the successor to his father's throne took no charge of government affairs for the space of three years but dwelt in retirement all that time,—wore mean clothes, and fed on coarse fare; while the court was held and business transacted in the office of the Prime Minister.

propriety. When the funeral took place, people from all quarters came to behold it. He wore the appearance of deep grief, and shed tears in abundance. Those who came to condole were highly pleased with him. *

3. Prince Wăn of Tăng asked about the right mode of ruling a nation. Mencius replied, impede not the proper business of the people. The She King says, "In the day time gather reeds, at night weave them; make haste and get your houses in good repair. The time comes, when you must sow your grain."

The way of the people is this,—if they have constant supplies, their minds are steady; but, if they have not constant supplies, their minds are unsteady. If their minds are unsettled, they will break out into the most licentious conduct, and go to all lengths. When they are thus plunged into crime, and then visited with punishment, it is taking them in the net. Can a benevolent Prince thus entrap his people!

Therefore a virtuous Prince will be grave, economical and polite to those below him, and observe a proper rule in taxing his subjects.

Yang Hoo said, he who seeks riches will not be benevolent, and he who is benevolent will not be rich.

In the Hea Dynasty, one man received fifty acres, and paid a tax. During the Yin Dynasty, each farmer had seventy acres and the *tsoo* was practised. The people during the

* It was a rule that when a Prince died he was buried five months after his decease. In the days of Mencius the country was in such a state of disorder and men had so far lost their originally virtuous dispositions, that the custom of mourning three years for parents was fallen into disuse. But to mourn three years for one's parents, and to feel pungent grief are perfectly natural to human beings and unless where the dispositions are depraved to the last degree, will be exemplified by all. Hence, when this young Prince heard the doctrines of the sage, about the perfection of human nature in its original state, he instantly began to manifest this disposition. * *

* * It is certain that a mind under the influence of virtuous principles, will feel deeply sorry for the loss of revered and beloved parents, but how is it possible for a truly virtuous mind to manifest it's veneration for deceased parents, by that kind of worship and adoration, which every truly enlightened man knows, belong, to the supreme being alone?

Chow Dynasty, had one hundred acres each and they used *Chih*. In reality all took one tenth. *Chih* means equal, *Tsoo* means to borrow.

Lung Tsze said, there is no better mode of regulating the lands than the *Tsoo* and none worse than the *Kung*. By the *Kung* system, the average of several years' produce is taken, and a tax fixed according to that average. Now, in years of abundance, although a large quantity be taken as a tax, there is no hardship in it. Hence the fixed rate is small (in such cases). But in bad years, when they cultivate the fields and the produce is deficient, by taking the full (or fixed) amount he who should be father and mother of the people, enrages them. They labor hard the whole year and cannot get enough to nourish their fathers and mothers, but are obliged to borrow on interest in order to make up their taxes, so that old and young are turned into the ditches. How could the father and mother of his people act thus! *

Now, Ting really observes the hereditary salary system. The She King says, "Let the rain descend first on our public and then on our private fields." But it is only when the *Tsoo* is pursued that there are public fields. From this we may learn that even in Chow the *Tsoo* system existed.

Institute the Seang, the Seu, the Heŏ and the Heaou, in order to instruct the people. The Seang was intended to nourish the aged,—the Heaou to instruct the young and the Seu to practise

* By the Kung plan an average of several years produce was taken, and the tenth part of that average was fixed as a permanent tax laid on husbandry. This system prevailed during the reign of the Hea family and is considered the worst plan of taxation. Tsoo means to assist. According to this system as observed during the Yin Dynasty six hundred and thirty mow (or acres) of land were divided into nine parcels. One of these was set apart for the use of government and the other eight were given to eight different husbandmen who united in tilling the public field as a tax or rent for their several farms. In some parts of the Empire this system was practised, with this difference that each farmer had one hundred acres and twenty acres were taken off the government field for the purpose of building houses upon for the accomodation of the farmers. This mode of taxation was considered superior to all the other systems. According to the Chih, which chiefly prevailed during the Chow Dynasty, eight farmers united in tilling a piece of land and in the end of harvest calculated the whole amount of produce, gave one tenth as a tax and divided the remainder equally amongst themselves.

them in archery. In the Hea Dynasty, they were called, Heaou in the Yin, Seu and in the Chow, Seang. The education of the three Dynasties were the same. The intention of all was to illustrate clearly the human relations. When the great relations of human life are clearly illustrated by superiors, then inferiors will live in harmony *

When a true sovereign arises he will take his pattern of goverment from you; thus you will be the tutor of a good king. †

The She King says, " Chow although long a Province has newly received the divine decree." ‡ This speaks of Wăn Wang. If you, Sir, act vigorously, you also will renovate your kingdom.

He (Prince of Tăng) sent Peih Chen to ask Mencius about dividing the land according to the Tsing plan. Mencius replied, your king is about to practise benevolent government and has chosen you, Sir, to send on this mission, you must exert yourself. Now, benevolent government must commence by a proper division of the lands. If the land marks are not correct, the ground will not be equal, nor will the salaries be fair. Hence, tyrannical Princes and avaricious ministers will neglect the proper division of the lands. When once the land marks are properly regulated, then you may sit down at your ease to divide the fields, and regulate the salaries.

Although the soft, loamy country of Tăng is of small extent, yet it still requires learned men and rustics. Were there no learned men, there would be none to govern the rustics, and were there no rustics, there would be none to support the learned.

* Mencius considered that the custom of affording salaries to the descendants of government officers and the Tsoo system were the root of good government and ought always to go together; hence, observed that the former was attended to by the government of Tang, but not the latter; wishing the king to unite the two, and thus revive the good old way.

† Intimating that the country of Tang being very small it could scarcely be expected, that the Prince of it could by his people raise himself to the throne of the Empire, but at the same time encouraging him with the hope that his excellent example might be copied by some other Prince of a more extensive country, who by doing so might rise to the Imperial seat, and give peace and happiness to the whole realm.

‡ That is the Prince of Chow was appointed by heaven to ascend the Imperial seat on account of his eminent virtue and talents.

In the outside of the city suburbs they observed the *Tsoo* plan, and took one ninth as a tax. Within the suburbs one tenth of the produce of one's own field was given as a tax. *

From the highest officer of state downwards, each had an entailed field of fifty acres. † A young man received a field of twenty five acres. ‡

In burying the dead, or removing one's dwelling place, they left not the district. The district fields were divided into Tsings, the people held friendly intercourse and mutually protected each other. Thus the inhabitants lived in harmony.

The fields thus regulated and divided into Tsings. Each Tsing contained nine hundred acres: the centre field was public property. Each of the eight families had a field of one hundred acres and all united in cultivating the public field. When the public work was finished, then they presumed to do their own work. Thus the country people were distinguished (from their betters).

These are the great outlines of the system; to soften and fit it to circumstances depends upon your Prince and you Sir. ¶

4. Heu Hing taking the words of Shin Nung ‖ came from Tsoo to Tăng and stepping up to the door of Prince Wăn said, I am a

* Near the city, the population being thick it was difficult, if not impossible to put in practice the Tsoo plan, hence they paid the tenth part of the produce of their private farms as a tax or rent.

† These fields were given to government officers with the intention that the produce should be offered in sacrifice to their ancestors, hence, as every man whatever be his rank, ought to serve his ancestors with equal respect, no difference was made in the bestowing of these fields between superior and inferior officers. These fields were given to servants of government, over and above their regular salaries, by way of liberal treatment of the learned.

‡ If a man had in his family, a younger brother above sixteen, who had not arrived at the years of manhood, twenty five acres were given to him, thus the rustics were treated liberally.

¶ Intimating that while circumstances might render it proper to deviate a little, from the letter of those regulations laid down by the holy kings of antiquity, their spirit and intention ought never to be departed from.

‖ An ancient Emperor, the first or second after Fuh He. He is said to have been the first, who taught the people the art of husbandry, and on that account is worshipped at the present day. He died 3114 before Christ.

man come from a distance, who hearing that your majesty excercises benevolent government wishes to have a shop from you and to become one of your subjects. Prince Wan granted his request. He had some twenty or thirty followers, all of whom wore coarse clothes, and made shoes and wove mats for a livelihood.

The disciple of Chin Leang, Chin Seang with his brother Sin, took their instruments of husbandry on their back and left Sung for Tang, saying "We have heard that your majesty (of Tang) practices the system of government taught by the sages, and are a sage. We wish to become the sage's subjects."

When Chin Seang saw Heu Hing he was greatly delighted and laid aside entirely what he had formerly learned and imitated him. Chin Seang having waited upon Mencius said to him, speaking the words of Heu Hing, the Prince of Tang really wishes to be a virtuous Prince, but he has not heard the doctrine of good government.* A truly virtuous Prince will plough along with his people and while he rules will cook his own food. Tang has its royal granaries and treasuries while the people are oppressed in order to make the ruler easy and comfortable. How can this be deemed virtue!

Mencius replied, does Heu Tsze sow the grain which he eats? Yes. Does Heu Tsze weave cloth and then wear it? No. Heu Tsze wears coarse hair cloth. Does Heu Tsze wear a cap? Yes. What sort of cap? A coarse cap. Does he make it himself? No He gives grain in exchange for it. Why does he not make it himself? It would be injurious to his farming. Does Heu Tsze use earthen ware in cooking his victuals, or iron utensils in tilling his farm? Yes. Does he make them himself? No. He gives grain in barter for them.

* Darkly insinuating that he was unacquainted with the principles of the divine husbandman "Shin Nung."

Exchanging grain for these tools does no injury to the potter, and how can the potter's exchanging these implements for grain bear hard upon the husbandman? Why does not Heu Tsze act the potter, and take every thing from his own shop which he wants to use? Why should he be in the confused bustle, exchanging articles with the mechanics? Is Heu Tsze afraid of the labor this would cause? The work of the mechanic and that of the husbandman ought not to be united, replied the other. O then (said Mencius) are the government of the Empire and the labor of the husbandman the only employments that may be united? There are the proper employments of men of superior rank, and the appropriate labors of those in inferior stations. Were every man to do all kinds of work, it would be necessary that he should first make his implements, and then use them; thus all men would constantly crowd the roads. Hence, it has been said (by the ancients) that some labor with their minds, and some with bodily strength. Those who labor with their strength, are ruled by men. Those who are governed by others, support (or feed) others. Those who govern others, are fed by others. This is a general rule under the whole heavens. *

In the time of Yaou before the world was regulated, when a mighty flood flowed on and deluged the whole earth,—when grass and trees grew most luxuriantly,—and birds and beasts were multitudinous,—when the five kinds of grain did not rise,—when birds and beasts harassed men, and their traces were in the middle country, Yaou alone was grieved at this state of things. He promoted Shun and diffused good order. Shun sent Yih to

* Were there none in inferior stations, there would be none to support those who possess education and rank, and were there none possessed of education and rank, then people in the lower walks of life, would live in utter confusion. The mutual benefit which these different classes derive from each other's labors, resembles the advantage which results to the husbandman and the mechanic from the exchange of those articles which they respectively produce. Hence may be seen, that it is beneficial to the whole community, that those who govern others should be exempt from manual labor.

regulate the fire. Yih burnt the mountains and marshes, and the animals fled into concealment. Yu opened nine channels—removed the obstacles which chocked the rivers Tse and Tă, so that they flowed into the sea, cleared the channels of Joo and Han,—gave free vent to Hwae and Sze and they flowed into Keang. Yu was eight years abroad (regulating the water) and in that time passed his own door three times, without entering. Suppose he had wished to till the fields, could he have done it? *

How Tseih taught the people to sow, plant and rear the five different kinds of grain. When the grain was brought to perfection the people were fed. Men have by nature the principles of rectitude in themselves, but, if they are fed, clothed, and kept at ease, without being taught, they differ little from the brutes. The holy man was grieved about this, and employed Keih as an instructor i. e. appointed him to the office of Sze Too, that he might teach them the duties of the human relations, viz that father and son should be affectionate, Prince and minister should be upright, that husband and wife should observe a proper distinction,—that old and young should keep a just gradation, and that friends should be faithful.

Fang Heun (i. e. Yaou) said, make them labor,—lead them,—comfort them,—make them upright,—aid them,—wing them, and

* In the age of the flood, many people suffered, holy man successively arose, and gradually regulated things, but even in the time of Yaou a proper regulation had not been effected. * *

---

* * The famous Yaou is said to have died 2230 years before Christ, or 220 Years before Noah's flood. Some have conjectured that the Chinese deluge, and that recorded by the sacred Historian refer to the same event. It does not appear, however, by the above account of the flood that they mean to say that it was occasioned by any sudden outbreaking of the great deep, or any extraordinary opening of the windows of heaven, but that from the creation of the world, down to the time of Yaou, the earth had been overflowed with water, to an extent which was highly detrimental to the fruits of the earth, and in other respects very injurious to the human species and that the water was put into proper channels by human efforts. We do not mean to say that these circumstances are sufficient to lead to the certain conclusion that the Mosaic flood must have been perfectly distinct from that of the Chinese, but we think they deserve the consideration of those who plead for the doctrine that Moses and the Chinese Historians refer to the same event.

cause them to obtain their original rectitude, when they follow, stimulate them to advance in virtue. Thus did the holy man feel anxiety about his people. Had he leisure for husbandry think you!

Yaou was grieved that he could not obtain a Shun, Shun was vexed that he could not obtain a Yu and a Yaou Taou.* He who is vexed about an hundred acres not being tilled, is a mere farmer. To assist men with money is called "Hwuy" (liberality). To instruct men in what is good, is called "Chung" (fidelity). To obtain men to govern the Empire is called "Jin" (benevolence, or perfect virtue). Hence, to give away the Empire to another is easy, but to obtain proper men to govern the Empire is difficult.

Confucius exclaimed, great was Yaou as a Prince! It is only heaven that is great and only Yaou could imitate (or equal) it. Vast and magnificent! The people could find no words sufficient to praise him. As a Prince he was lofty and he viewed the mere circumstance of having the throne of the Empire as nothing. Did not Yaou and Shun employ their whole minds in governing the Empire? yet they did not plough the fields.

I have heard of the people of Hea (China) renovating the barbarians, but I have not heard of the barbarians renovating the Chinese. Chin Leang was born in Tsoo and being delighted with the doctrines of Chow Kung and Confucius went north and in China studied the learning of the north, and excelled in it. He was what is called a man of great talents and worth. Your brothers followed him some ten or twenty years, but when their master died they turned their back upon him (or opposed his doctrines).

When Confucius died, after his disciples had mourned for him three years, they prepared to return home and on this occasion

* That is they felt great anxiety for the good of the Empire, until once they obtained these worthy men who afterwards proved such eminent and extensive blessings to the whole community.

went in and bowed to Tsze Kung, and wept till they all lost their voices, and then returned home. Tsze Kung erected a shed at the tomb and remained three years longer, and then returned home. Afterwards Tsze Hea, Tsze Yew, and Tsze Chang, considering that Yew Jŏ resembled the sage in appearance and manner, wished to conduct themselves towards him, in the same manner as they did towards Confucius, and tried to compel Tsăng Tsze to this. Tsăng Tsze said, this ought not to be done; that which is washed in the Keang Nan and bleeched in the autumn sun is truly white and cannot be made more clean, nor more white. *

At present, you, Sir, oppose the principles of your preceptor, and follow this southern barbarian chatterer, who knows not the principles of the former kings. This conduct differs from that of Tsăng Tsze.

I have heard of birds leaving the gloomy vale and removing to the lofty tree, but I have not heard that they descend from the lofty tree and enter the gloomy cavern.

The Loo Tsung says beat the Jung Teih (barbarians) and correct the people of King Shoo. † Now since Chow Kung would beat them, you, Sir, have not made a good change in learning of them.

If men would follow the principles of Heu Tsze, then there would not be two market prices, nor any deceit in the country, so that if you sent a boy five cubits high to the market, no one could impose upon him. Cloth of the same length would be the same price, and hemp and all kinds of silk of the same

* The sage referred to the circumstance of the disciples of Confucius thus mourning for him and thus respecting his very appearance and manner as presenting a constrast to the manner in which the ungrateful and deluded pupils of Chin Leang acted. The intention of Tsang Tsze's words was to shew his fellow disciples that Confucius could not be equalled, and that it was his superemiuent virtue, not his outward resemblance, that was the proper object of their reverence.

† King was the original name of Tsoo Shoo a country near to Tsoo.

weight would be the same price. The same quantity of all kinds of grain would be the same price, and shoes of the same size would be the same price. Mencius replied, things are naturally unequal in value. They differ one, five, ten, one thousand and ten thousand fold. If you, Sir, make them all alike, you will introduce confusion into the Empire. For instance, if the price of small shoes were the same as that of large shoes, who would make large shoes? To follow the levelling system of Heu Tsze would lead to deception. How could it lead to the regulation of the Empire!

5. E Che, of the sect of Mïh, employed Seu Pe to ask an interview with Mencius. Mencius replied, I really wish to see him, but at present I am unwell. Wait till I get better and I will pay him a visit; it is not necessary that he should come here. At another time, he again begged to see Mencius. Mencius said, I can now see him, but, if I do not deal uprightly with him, our doctrines will not be clearly exhibited. I will therefore correct him, (or tell him his errors plainly). I have heard that E Tsze is a disciple of Mïh. Now, the sect of Mïh, in conducting their funeral ceremonies, consider plainness and narrowness proper. If E Tsze thinks of changing the world, why should he consider his own principles wrong and not honor them? But E Tsze buried his parents in a handsome manner: hence, he served them in a manner which he considers mean (or disrespectful). *

Seu Tsze told this to E Tsze. E Tsze replied, this is also the doctrine of the Joo, (or learned) sect. The ancients said, "Preserve the people as you would your little child." What do these words mean? I consider that there should be no difference in our love of men, but that in order of time it should be first manifested to our parents. Jen Tsze told these words to Mencius.

* According to the principles of Mih a sumptuous funeral is disrespectful.

Mencius replied, does E Tsze believe that he ought to love the child of his neighbour the same as his brother's son. The passage which he has quoted merely signifies that a little child's falling into a well is not its fault. * Heaven produces things from one root, but according to E Tsze they have two roots.

In high antiquity they did not bury their relatives. When their relatives, or parents, died they threw them into the ditches, Afterwards, when passing by, they saw the wolves and worms preying upon the corpses. The perspiration came out on their foreheads,—they looked askance and could not bear to see them. They returned, brought baskets and spades, and covered the dead, Their covering of them was right. Thus there is a principle in nature which leads men (good and filial children) to bury their parents. †

Seu Tsze reported this to E Tsze, who instantly adopted the principle (or recognized it as just.

CHAP. VI.

1 Chin Tae said, not to wait on the Princes is right, but to do so seems but a small thing. If you would once wait upon them, the greatest advantage that might result from it, would be, that they would be led to rule according to the ancient royal laws, and the least consequence would be, that they would be induced to imitate those who have ruled by force. The book Che says, "Bend one cubit to straighten eight." Thus it

* E Tsze being at a loss how to extricate himself from the dilemma in which he was caught, endeavored to get off by referring to the words of the Kang Kaou. But the meaning of these words is, that when a little child tumbles into a well it is not its fault, nor is it the fault of ignorant people when they violate the laws ; and that on this ground they should both be treated with equal tenderness.

† From this the custom of burying took its rise. If, then, it be right in the very nature of things to cover our dead, it cannot be honoring them to do it in a shabby manner.

appears you might do it, (i. e. visit the Princes). Mencius replied, formerly, King, Prince of Tse, when going out to hunt, called the officers who had the charge of the game parks, by the Tsing flag; on which account they did not answer the call.* The king wished to put them to death. A determined scholar (said Confucius), forgets not that he may be cast into a ditch, and a hero forgets not that he may loose his head. Why did Confucius thus praise them? Was it not because they did not answer the wrong signal? Why then should I go uncalled? Besides, thus bending one cubit to straighten eight, is done from a gain seeking spirit; but once indulge this spirit, and it will seem right to bend eight cubits in order to make one straight.

In former days, Chaou Keen Tsze sent Wang Leang to drive the hunting chariot of his favorite servant He. They were out the whole day without killing any game. On his return, he said he is the worst charioteer under heaven. Some one having informed Wang Leang of this, he begged to go out again with him, and after much entreaty he prevailed upon him to go. In one morning they caught ten birds. When they returned, he reported that he (Wang Leang) was the best charioteer under heaven. Kēěn Tsze said, I will always send him with you to drive your chariot. This was told to Wang Leang. Wang Leang said, I will not do it. When I drove according to the proper rule, in one whole day, we did not kill any game; but when I violated that rule, in one morning we caught ten birds. The She King says, "Let the driver keep his course, let the archer hit the mark." I am not accustomed to ride with mean fellows. I therefore beg to be excused.

* The Tsing was the flag by which the Ta Foo officers were called out, but the Po Kwen (or leather cap) wss the signal by which the officers of the pleasure parks were summoned to the chase.

Now, if the charioteer was ashamed to bend to the will of the archer, although, by so doing, he might have taken hills of animals, why should I bend my principles to follow another? You are under a mistake, Sir, he who bends himself cannot straighten others.*

2. King Chun said, were not Kung Sun Këĕn and Chang E men of worth and valor? Once angry and all the Princes were afraid, when calm all under heaven was at rest. Mencius replied, how can they be considered great men? Have you not studied the Le Ke. It is the father who caps the young men, and the mother who manages the marriage of her daughters. On this occasion, she accompanies her to the door, and cautions her: "Saying married women ought to reverence their husbands, and be careful not to offend them and consider obedience to be the right path." These are the duties of wives and concubines. †

To dwell in the wide house of the world—to sit in the upright seat of the world—to walk in the great road of the world—if he get into office to practise his principles with the people—if not to practise them alone—not to become licentious by riches—not to be moved by poverty—nor bent by martial awe, such a person may be called a great man.

3. Chow Seaou asked whether superior men of ancient times wished to be in office? Mencius said, yes; ancient records say that when Confucius was three months out of office, he seemed vacant and at a loss. When he left a country he carried the proper introductory presents along with him. Kung Ming E says, that if the ancients were three months out of office they condoled with each other.

* The ancients would rather, that their principles should be adopted, than that they should go into or retire from office in an irregular manner. On this account neither Confucius, nor Mencius succeeded in bringing their principles into practice.

† Meaning that these two men by flattery and crutching stole their power and thus acted as wives or concubines ought to do.

4. Pang Kang asked, saying, is it not extravagant to be followed by some tens of carriages, and some hundreds of men, and to be supported by Princes of states? Mencius replied, unless it accord with justice a single bamboo or bucket of food ought not to be received from others; but since it accorded with justice I do not think it was extravagant in Shun to accept of the Empire from Yaou. Do you, Sir? No; I do not, said the other; but it seems improper that a scholar should have salary who is without merit.*

Mencius said, if, Sir, you do not interchange and barter, so as to supply those who are deficient, then the husbandman will have too much grain, and the women will have too much cloth. But, if you make an exchange of labor, then cutters of wood and cart wrights will have support from you.

Now, suppose there is a man here, who within exemplifies filial piety, and without brotherly affection:--observes the principles of the former kings and hands them down for the instruction of future ages, and yet does not obtain support from you. Why should you honor cutters of wood and carriage wrights and at the same time lightly esteem those who practise benevolence anu justice! †

But, the object of the mechanic, is to get a livelihood; is tha also the object of the superior man, in practising right principles? Why do you, Sir, ask about his object? If he do work for you, Sir, he ought to have support from you. Do you, Sir, reward him for his intention? Suppose then, that a man in ornamenting the walls of your house, should destroy them; his intention being to find support, would you give him wages or not? No. Then, Sir, you do not reward a man for his intentions, but for his merit.

* At that time Mencius, had succesively paid his respects to the different Princes, wishing to be employed and was followed by a great number of students and carriages. Pan Kang was doubtful whether such a retinue together with the support required from the Princes was not rather extravagant.

† Mencius meant to teach Pang Kang that the advantages resulting from having the literati in the country, being of a moral nature and tending to establish the people in the knowledge and practice of right principles as well as to prevent the spread of false doctrines, were far greater than mere mechanics could boast of.

5. Wan Chang, inquiring said, Sung is a small country, if at present it should put in practice the government of the ancient kings, Tse and Tsoo would hate and invade it. What should be done in this case? Mencius replied, when Tang dwelt in Pŏ he was neighbour to Kŏ, whose Prince acted irregularly and did not sacrifice to ancestors. Tang sent a messenger to inquire why he did not offer sacrifices. His reply was, that he had no victims. Tang sent him oxen and sheep. Kŏ Pih ate them and did not offer them in sacrifice. Tang sent a messenger to ask why he did not sacrifice. He replied, that he had no grain for that purpose. Tang sent his people to till the fields for them. The old and young carried food to the laborers. Kŏ Pih led out his people and seized the wine and food which they carried. Those who would not give up what they carried, they slew. They killed a little boy who was carrying rice and flesh, and seized these. This is what the Shoo King refers to when it says that "The people of Kŏ were enemies to those who carried food to them." *

He went on account of the murder of this boy and conquered, or punished them. All within the four seas said that he took revenge in behalf of common men and women, and did not wish to enrich himself by obtaining the Empire. Tang commenced his conquering, (or chastising) career in Kŏ and subdued eleven Provinces, and found not an enemy under heaven When he turned his face eastward, and conquered, the strangers of the west grumbled, and when he went southward to subdue, the nothern people complained, saying, why make us last? The people looked for him with the same anxiety, that we look for rain in the time of great drought. The people returned to the markets without any interval, ror did any change take place in the labors of the husbandman. He cut off the tyrannical Princes and comforted the people. His coming, like the fall of

* Wan Chang did not know, that where there is genuine virtue, the small may become great, and the weak strong, hence, Mencius referred to the conduct of Tang to prove that this might be the case.

seasonable rain, made them glad. The Shoo King says, "Wait till our Prince come; he will not be cruel."

There were some who did not submit to him (Woo Wang). He went eastward, subdued them and gave peace to the people. The people filled baskets with black and yellow silks, and went to meet him, saying "Welcome! our Chow sovereign; we shall now be happy." The officers put black and yellow silks in baskets, and went out to meet the officers of Woo Wang; and the common people put food in buckets, and drink in bottles, and went out to welcome his people. He saved the people out of the fire and water and cut off those who oppressed them.

The Ta She says, our Woo displayed his martial glory, entered the borders, and cut off the tyrants. His conquering glory was brighter than that of Tang. Sung does not practise kingly government. If he exemplified benevolent government all within the four seas would lift up their heads and long for his approach, wishing him to be their Prince. Were this the case, although, Tse and Tsoo be great, what occasion would there be to fear them? *

6. Mencius, conversing with Tsae Pŭh Shing, said, do you, Sir, wish your Prince to govern well? I will clearly explain this matter to you. Suppose a Ta Foo of Tsoo wished his son to learn the language of Tse, would he employ a Tse man to instruct him, or would he employ a Tsoo man? A Tse man said the other. But if you employ one Tse man to teach him, while they are all Tsoo men who daily converse with him, although you daily beat him, wishing him to learn the language of Tse, he will not succeed. If you place him in Chwang Yŭh for several years, although you daily beat him wishing him to learn the language of Tsoo you will not succeed. †

* Some of the officers of Chow assisted him to tyrannise over the people, and did not submit to his conquerer Woo Wang, hence the latter punished them and delivered the victims of their oppression. His glory in cutting off the monster Chow, and rescuing the Empire from the most cruel oppression, was truly splendid. The Prince of Sung did not in reality wish to practise benevolent government, and was totally ruined by Tse.

† Tsae Puh Shing was a government officer of the Sung country. Chwang Yuh is the name of a village in the Tse country.

An officer of government loosing his situation is like a Prince loosing his throne. The Le Ke says, "The Princes ploughed in order to prepare sacrificial grain. The Queen cultivated the silk worm, in order to make ready sacrificial robes."* If the victims were not prepared, nor the grain dressed, nor the clothes in trim, they presumed not to sacrifice. But if the scholar has no lands, he cannot sacrifice. If the victims, vessels and robes are not prepared, they presume not to offer sacrifice nor to have feasts. Was it not then with reason that they required to be condoled with?

But why did they carry introductory presents along with them, when they went out of office? The scholar's being in office resembles the husbandman's ploughing the fields. Why should the farmer on leaving a place leave his farming implements behind him? The Tsin country is a country where men of talent and worth are employed, but I have not heard, that they are so eager to get into office as this. Why have men of worth such difficulty in getting into office? Mencius replied, when a son is born his parents wish him married, when a daughter is born, they wish her wedded. This is the heart of father and mother, and all men have it. But, if without waiting the commands of father and mother, or the mediation of the go-between, the young pair should bore holes in the wall to peep at each other, both their parents and the whole nation would despise them. The ancients really wished to go into office, but they scorned to do so in a disorderly manner. To go into office not according to the proper mode, they viewed like boring holes through the wall.

* It has been and is still the custom in China for the Emperor and high officers of state to hold the plough on the first day of the new year, to show how much importance they attach to the cultivation of the ground. The Emperess in ancient times was accustomed to shew her female subjects an example of industry by rearing the silk worm with her own hand.

You, Sir, say that Sëë Keu Chow is a virtuous scholar. Were he placed in the Palace, and were all the others, whether old, or young, high or low, who live at court, Se Kew Chows, with whom could his majesty practise what is bad? On the other hand, were none of the courtiers, whether high, or low, old or young, Sëë Keu Chows, with whom could the king do what is good? What can one Sëë Keu Chow do for the king of Sung when left alone?

7. Kung Sun Chow asked Mencius, why he did not visit the tributary Princes? Mencius replied, the ancients, if they were not in office, did not visit. *

Kwan Yu Múh leaped over a wall to avoid it (seeing a Prince). Sëë Lew shut the door, and did not receive him, (the Prince). These carried the matter too far. When such earnestness as this is manifested, it is proper to see them. †

Yang Ho wished to see Confucius (i. e. to call him), but hated doing what was rude. When a Ta Foo sends a present to one of the literati, if the latter be not at home to receive it, he must go and pay his respects at the door of the giver. Yang Ho spied out when Confucius was from home, and sent him a fat pig, dressed. Confucius likewise found out when Yang Ho was from home, and went to pay his respects. In this case Yang Ho was first in observing etiquette; how could Confucius help going to visit him? ‡

Tsing Tsze says, those who shrug up their shoulders and force a flattering laugh, labor harder than the man who in summer

* The ancients who possessed learning and virtue, shewed the high value they put upon themselves, by not paying the first visit to a Prince, under whom they did not hold an office. If the Prince wanted their counsel it was his duty to wait on them in person.

† Kwan Yu Muh lived in the reign of Wan Prince of Wei, and See Lew in the time of Muh Prince of Loo. Wan and Muh wished to see these two gentlemen, but they not being in their service, were determined not to see them. But they were too stiff: because, these Princes proved the sincerity of their wishes to have an interview, by coming in person and ought to have been granted this favor.

‡ Although Yang Ho wished to send for the sage, yet he disliked the idea of doing what was contrary to etiquette; hence, used a scheme which at once accorded with propriety, and at the same time laid Confucius under an obligation of paying him a visit; but the sage, not wishing to have an interview with this gentlemen, took an opportunity of paying his respects and returning his thanks when the other was from home.

tills the fields Tsze Loo says, when speaking to a man with whom you are not intimate, (or do not accord), look how he blushes. I know not such people. Look at this and you will see the mind of these gentlemen.

8. Tae Ying said, I cannot just now put in practice the Tsing system, nor abolish the market duties, but I will lighten the dues a little, and next year abolish them. How will that do? Mencius replied, this resembles a man who daily steals his neighbour's fowls, and who upon any one saying to him, "this is not the conduct of a superior man," answers, I will take one less every month till next year and then I will stop. If you know that the thing is unjust. then give it over instantly, why wait till next year?

9. Kung Too Tsze said, outside people say that you, Sir, are fond of disputation. I presume to ask what is the cause of this? Mencius replied, how should I be fond of disputation? I cannot avoid it. The world has existed for a long time and there has been an alternate succession of order and confusion ever since the beginning. In the time of Yaou the waters flowed not in their proper courses, but inundated the middle country; which was inhabited by serpents and dragons, and the people had no where to rest. On the low grounds they dwelt in nests on the trees. Those who lived on the heights made caves for themselves. The Shoo King says, "The irregular water alarmed me." The irregular water, means the deluge of water. Yu was employed to cut channels for the water that it might flow into the sea; and to drive the serpents and dragons into the marshes. The water was put into the channels Keang Nang and Ho Hwae. Then the dangers were removed to a distance, the birds and beasts which injure man dispersed, and men lived on the even ground. *

* The Chinese account of a deluge bears more resemblance to the remains and effects of some tremendous flood than to the thing itself. Whether any of the posterity of Noah on wandering to that country found it in the state in which it is discribed in the above and some other passages of Chinese writings, or not, is difficult to say, but to us it seems, at least, highly probable.

After the death of Yaou and Shun, the principles of the sages gradually decayed, a succession of tyrannical kings arose, who pulled down the houses of the people, and turned them into fishing ponds. The people had no place of rest. Their fields were taken from them and converted into pleasure grounds, so that they had neither food nor clothes:—false principles and oppression prevailed: pleasure parks, fishing ponds and marshes were numerous, and birds and beasts came near. When Chow came to the throne the confusion of the Empire was still greater. Chow Kung assisted Woo Wang to cut off Chow and conquer Yen. For three years they punished the *cruel* Princes,—drove Fei Leen into an Island of the sea, and there slew him,—cut off fifteen Provinces, and drove the tigers, unicorns and elephants to a distance.* The empire rejoiced. The Shoo King says, "Great and illustrious were the deeds of Wăn Wang and gloriously did Woo Wang continue them. We their descendants are protected and enlightened by them and know not want."

The world degenerated again,—good principles dwindled away,—false tenets and wicked conduct prevailed,—ministers killed their Princes and sons their fathers.

Confucius got alarmed and composed the Chun Tsew, which treats of Imperial affairs. Hence, Confucius says, "They who would know me let them attend to the Chun Tsew, and let those who blame me also attend to it."

Holy kings did not arise and the Princes gave way to licentiousness. The doctrines of Yang Choo, and Mĭh Teih filled the empire. If the learning of the empire did not accord with Yang, it fell in with Mih. Yang taught that we should love ourselves only, hence we should have no Prince. According to Mih we should love all men alike: this is to have no father. They who have neither father nor Prince, are mere brutes. Kung Ming E says,

* All these governors and courtiers which Woo Wang thus punished, assisted the tyrant Chow in his cruel and oppressive measures.

when in the cook house there is plenty of fat meat,—in the stable abundance of fat horses, and people wear the aspect of hunger and the desarts are covered with those who have been starved to death; this is leading on the brutes to eat men. If the doctrines of Yang and Mih had not been stopt, the doctrines of Confucius could not have been exhibited, and false principles would have deceived the people, and choked the sources of benevolence and justice. The sources of benevolence and justice once filled up, the brutes would be led on to devour men.

On this account, I am afraid that the doctrines of the sage should be shut up, and wish to oppose the sects of Yang and Mih, and put away licentious expressions and false principles, that they may not prevail. If they rise in the mind, they injure the conduct, if they injure the conduct, they will hurt the government. When a sage rises again he will not alter my words.

In former times, when Yu repressed the flood, the empire enjoyed tranquility and peace. When Chow Kung united the western and northern barbarians (perhaps to China), then the people enjoyed rest. When Confucius wrote the Chun Tsew, rebellious, (or disorderly) ministers and their sons were afraid.

The She says, " Fight the foreigners and reform the people of Shay." Now I (Mencius) cannot but support the sages. Chow Kung would have beat those who are for neither father nor Prince. I also wish to rectify men's minds,—to stop depraved talk,—oppose artful conduct, and drive away licentious conversation, in order to second these three sages. Why do you say that I love disputation? I cannot avoid it. He who can reason down the sect of Yang and Mih is a disciple of the sages. *

* The three sages referred to, are Yu, Chow Kung, and Confucius. The doctrines of Yang and Mih, as they tended to lead men to act as if they had neither father nor Prince, were as injurious as the wild barbarians and savage beasts were dangerous, from this it followed that whoever was able by reasoning to confute them altho' he might not possess intelligence and virtue equal to the ancient sages, still he deserved to be considered their follower.

10. Kwang Chang exclaimed, was not Chin Chung Tsze a moderate a scholar! When in Ling he was three days without food, till his ear heard not, nor did his eye see. On the side of the well there was a Le (a sort of plum) which the Tsaou insect had more than half eaten; he crawled to it, attempted to eat it, and after three efforts, managed to swallow it, after which his ear heard, and his eye saw.

Mencius replied, I must consider Chung Tsze as chief among the scholars of Tsze, but, nevertheless, I cannot deem him moderate. Were he to act up to his own principles, he ought to become an earth worm; then he might be considered moderate. *

The worm above, eats dry earth, and below, drinks muddy water. † Was the house which Chung Tsze lived in built by Pih E (a sage) or by Taou Chih (a robber some say)? Was the grain which he eat sown by Pih E, or by Taou Chih. This he could not know. What injury can there be in that, said the other? He made shoes and his wife prepared hemp and gave these in exchange for food.

Mencius rejoined, Chung Tsze belonged to the ministerial family of Tse. His brother Tae had ten thousand Chung of salary. He deemed his brother's salary unjust and would not eat of it. He considered his brother's house unjust and would not live in it.

He avoided his brother, left his mother, and dwelt in Woo Ling. Having afterwards returned, it happened that some one presented a live goose to his brother, on seeing which he gathered

* Kwang Chang considered that moderation was the beauty of a scholar, and that as Chin Chung was born of a rich family, he manifested an extraordinary degree of moderation, by retiring to Ling, and living three days without asking of any one. But, Mencius, while he allowed him the highest place among the literati of Tse, still contended that as Chin Chung held, that we should not be at all dependant on others, he could not on his own principles, be considered moderate, unless he became an earth worm.

† Meaning that the worm depends not upon men, either for food or house room, but as Chung Tsze maintained that we should not use any thing which comes through the hands of bad men, and yet dwelt in houses built by men, and eat grain raised by men, he did not follow up his own principles.

up his brows, and said, why use that cackling thing? On some other day, his mother killed this same goose and gave it him to eat. His brother happening to come in, said you are eating the flesh of that cackling thing! on which he went out and spewed out what he had eaten. What his mother gave him, he would not eat; what his wife gave him, he eat. He would not dwell in his brother's house, but resided in Woo Ling. How did he follow up his own principles! Had he become an earth worm, then he would have acted up to his own tenets.*

* Of all that heaven produces, or earth nourishes, man is the greatest, and the most importent part of man's duty, is to maintain the human relations, but Chung Tsze violated these. How can he who does so be deemed moderate!

End of Vol. I.

CHAP. VII.

1. Mencius said, that even the quick sight of Le Low and the ingenuity of Kung Lun Tsze could not make things square and round without the compass and square, nor could the bright talent of the music master Kwang have formed the five notes, had he not used the six rules, neither can the principles of Yaou and Shun without the practice of benevolent government give peace and tranquility to the empire. Suppose a man have a benevolent heart and a benevolent character, if the people are not benefited by his favor, he cannot be an example to future ages, this is because he does rot put in practice the principles of the former kings. Hence, it is said, that empty, (or dormant) virtue is not sufficient for government, nor can dead laws reduce themselves to practice. The She says, " He who neither errs, nor forgets, is the man who accords with the ancient canons." It never has happened, that those who have followed the laws of the former kings have erred. When the sages had to the utmost exerted the strength of their eyes, they used the compass, the square, the measure and the line to make things square, round, even, and straight. These are inexhaustible in their use. When they had exerted to the utmost the strength of their ears they employed the six rules to render the five sounds correct. The use of there is inexhaustible. When they had ployed their minds to the utmost, they added compassionate government, and benevolence covered the empire. *

* The intention of this section is to shew, that all good government must be formed on the models laid down b the ancient kings, and to reprove those who merely know and praise the principles of those worthies, but do not reduce them to practice in governing the people.

Hence, it is said, that those who wish to make a thing high, ought to rear it on an eminence, and that those who wish to make a thing deep should begin in the channel or marsh. * How can those who in governing do not follow the first kings, be said to be wise! Hence, it is only the benevolent who ought to occupy a high situation. If a man who is destitute of benevolence holds a high situation, he disseminates his vices among the multitude. When superiors have no principles by which to regulate things, inferiors have no rules by which to regulate themselves. When the Prince does not pay sincere regard to the path of rectitude, his ministers will not respect the laws. When superiors violate justice, inferiors break the laws. It is mere good chance, if the nation be preserved in such circumstances. Hence, it is said; that the want of strong fortifications and numerous armies, are not the calamity of a city, nor is the want of extensive territory and great riches injurious to a nation, but when superiors know not propriety, and inferiors are untaught, then rebellion and rapine will rise among the people, and will be followed by speedy ruin. The She says, "Heaven is about to overthrow (the house of Chow) be not delatory in saving it." He who is unjust in the service of his Prince, destitute of propriety in his daily conduct, and who speaks not according to the principles of the former kings, is delatory and sluggish.

Hence, it is said, that he who exhorts his Prince to do what is difficult, reverences him; he who explains the principles of virtue and represses the licentiousness of his Prince, may be called respectful, but he who says, "my Prince is not able," is called a robber.

2. Mencius says, that the square and compass are the perfection of the square and round; so is the sage the highest example of the human relations. He who wishes to be a Prince,

* As men ought to avail themselves of local advantages in this manner, so those who would govern well, must avail themselves of the principles established by the royal sages of high antiquity. If they do so, they will easily accomplish great things.

ought to do the duties of a Prince, to the utmost, and he who wishes to be a minister, ought to do the duties of a minister to the utmost. He who does not serve his Prince as Shun served Yaou, does not respect his Prince, and he who does not rule his people as Yaou did, robs them. Confucius says, there are only two paths, virtue and vice. He who carries tyranny to the highest pitch will be slain, and his throne will be lost (to his posterity). He who does not go so far, will endanger his person and diminish his territories. If once one get the name of being dark and cruel, although he may have filial sons and grand-sons they will not be able, for one hundred ages, to wipe of the stain. The She says, "The beacon for Yin is not distant; it is only in the Hea Dynasty." This is what I mean.

3. Mencius says, three families gained the Empire by benevolence, and lost it again by the want of benevolence. * The Provinces of the tributary Princes decay, or flourish, are preserved, or lost by the same means. If the Emperor is not benevo lent, he cannot protect the four seas. If the tributary Princes are void of benevolence, they cannot protect the local deities. If the high officers of state are not benevolent, they cannot protect the Ancestorial Temples, and if the literati and common people are without benevolence, they cannot preserve their four members, (own persons).

The men of the present day hate death, and yet rejoice in vice; thus, they resemble those who hate drunkenness, and yet drink violently.

4. Mencius says, if you love others, and they do not shew affection to you, examine your benevolence. If you rule men and they prove disorderly, examine your wisdom. If you show res-

* These three families, or dynasties, were Hea, Shang and Chow. Yu, Tang, Wan and Woo gained the Empire by benevolence, and Kee, Chow, Yu and Le, lost it by the want of benevolence.

pect to others and they do not return it, examine your respect.* If you do not succeed according to your wishes, turn round upon yourself. If you be correct in your own conduct, all under heaven will follow you. The She says, " He whose mind always accords with divine reason, seeks abundant bliss."

5. Mencius said, men are all in the habit of speaking of the Empire and of the Provinces: Now, the foundation of the Empire lies in the provinces, the foundation of provinces in families, and the foundation of families in individuals.

6. Mencius says, to govern is not difficult:—offend not the ministerial families. What these high families desire, the whole Province desires, and what whole Provinces desire, the whole Empire desires:—when this is the case, your virtue and instruction may fill the four seas.†

7. Mencius says, when the Empire is virtuous, those of inferior virtue will serve those of superior, and those of inferior talents will obey those of superior abilities;—but when the Empire is not in the right path, the small must serve the great, and the weak must serve the strong. These two things are fixed by heaven. He who accords with the will of heaven, will be preserved, but he who disobeys it, must perish.

King, Prince of Tse said, to be neither able to command, nor willing to obey, is to be cut off from men, and weeping gave his daughter in marriage to Woo.

At present, a small country imitates a large country, and yet is ashamed to receive its mandates; this is just like the scholar

* If I love others, and they do not love me, I ought to examine myself lest my benevolence be not perfect. In the same manner I ought to act in reference to wisdom and respect.

† When the tributary Princes, under the Chow family, were at war, each struggling for the Imperial throne, the high officers of state had lost the path of virtue, and had assumed great authority to themselves. Moreover, the minds of the people had long depended on them, hence had their Princes attempted to subdue them by force they might have failed and brought misery on their own heads. Therefore, Mencius advised them to go to the root of the evil, and by virtuous personal conduct subdue the hearts of their ministers; assuring them that by so doing, they would obtain the hearts of the whole empire; after which they might with ease diffuse good education through the country, and thus bring all the people under their gentle sway,

who is ashamed to be commanded by his master. * If it (a small country) be thus ashamed, its best course is to learn of Wăn Wang. If Wăn Wang were imitated, a large country in the space of five years, and a small country in seven years would give laws to the Empire (i. e. its Prince would ascend the Imperial throne.)

The She King says, " The descendants of Shang were more than ten thousand. When Shang Te gave the decree, the descendants of the Shang family submitted to Chow, for the divine decree does not always rest in one. The able and talented men of Yin assisted at the sacrifices in the capital of Chow. Confucius says, great numbers cannot withstand the benevolent. Hence, if a Prince delight in benevolence, he will not have an enemy under heaven.

Now, if any one wishes to have no enemy under heaven, and does not practise benevolence, he resembles a man who on taking hold of something hot, does not cool his hand in water. The She says, " Who handles any thing hot without cooling his hand in water."

8. Mencius says, can the unbenevolent be advised? They sit at ease on the brink of ruin, esteem their calamities profitable, and rejoice in what proves their ruin. If the unbenevolent would be reasoned with, how could their countries be lost, and their families destroyed? Formerly, a boy sung, " When the streams of the Tsang Lang are clear, I will wash the strings of my cap in them, and when they are muddy I will wash my feet in them." Confucius said, listen to this my children, (disciples). When clear he washed his cap strings, when muddy his feet. This depended on the water itself. Now, if a man first lightly esteem himself, he will afterwards be lightly esteemed by others.

* The descendants of the royal House of Shang were numerous, but were all completely subdued by the eminent virtue of Wan and Woo, so that they cheerfully submitted to the house of Chow.

If a family first destroy itself, it will afterwards be destroyed by others; and if a nation first conquer itself, it will then be conquered by others. * The Tae Keä says, the calamities which heaven sends may be avoided, but the miseries which we bring on ourselves we cannot live under.

9. Mencius said, Kee and Chow lost the Empire by having lost the people, and they lost the people by loosing their affections. There is a proper mode of obtaining the Empire. He who obtains the people; will obtain the Empire. There is a way of obtaining the people, to obtain their affections is the way to obtain the people. There is a way by which you may get their affections, that is to give and take what is pleasing to them, and not to do that to them which they hate.

The return of the people to the benevolent, is like the downward flowing of water, or like the roaming of animals in the wide wilderness. Thus it is the Tà that drives the fish into the deep waters, and the Chen that drives the birds into the thick forest; and it was Këë and Chow, that drove the people to Tang, and Woo. † Were there at present, a Prince under heaven, who delighted in virtue, all the tributary Princes would drive the people to him, so that although he did not wish to become Emperor, he could not avoid doing so.

At present he who wishes to become Emperor must resemble the man who has a seven years sickness and who seeks a three

As it depended entirely on the water being clear or muddy, whether it should be employed to an honorable, or dishonorable purpose, so it depends on ourselves, whether we are respected or dishonored, whether we be happy or miserable. * *

† Ta is an animal resembling a small dog. It lives in the water and is said to eat fish. Chen is a bird of prey. As ravenous animals drive the fishes and birds to their proper element in like manner did the monsters Kee and Chow, drive the whole people of the empire to the benevolent Tang and Woo.

---

* * The Confucian school seemed to know nothing of those absurd ideas respecting the divine decrees, which attributes all evil, moral and natural, to the supreme being, or the gods, and which are so prevalent among eastern philosophers. On the contrary, they uniformly, and most unequivocally maintain, that man is the alone author of his own guilt and misery. At the same time they profess firm faith in the divine decrees, and in an overruling Providence.

years caustic. If he do not continue to take it, he will never get well. If his inclination be not bent towards benevolence, to the end of life he will have sorrow and disgrace and in the end ruin. *

The She says, "Who can practise virtue? They only assist each other on the way to ruin." This is what we mean.

10. Mencius said, you cannot reason with the self-tyrant nor act with the self-cast-away. He who slanders propriety and justice, is a self-tyrant, and he who cannot habituate himself to benevolence, nor walk in the paths of rectitude is a self-cast-away. Benevolence is man's quiet habitation, and justice his straight path. To have an empty, quiet house, and not to dwell in it, to abandon the straight path, and not to walk in it, how lamentable!

11. Mencius says, right principles are near and men seek them in something distant:—the practice of good principles is easy, and men seek it in what is difficult. Would men love their relatives, and honor their superiors, the world would have happiness and peace.

12. Mencius said, when those who occupy inferior situations have not the confidence of their superiors, they cannot rule the people. There is a right mode of getting the confidence of superiors:—those who are not believed by their friends, have not the confidence of their superiors. There is a way by which you may be trusted by your friends:—If in serving your parents you do not please them, you will not be trusted by your friends. There is a way of pleasing your parents:—If when you examine yourself, you find that you are not sincere, then you cannot please your parents. There is a way of obtaining personal sincerity:—If you do not clearly understand the principles of virtue, you cannot be sincere (or perfect). Hence, perfection (or sincerity) is the way of heaven, and to wish for perfection is the duty of

* Intimating that the people had been so long accustomed to vice and the disease was so deeply rooted in their frame, that he who wished to renovate them, must begin by a long course of accumulating personal virtue.

man. It has never been the case, that he who possessed genuine virtue, in the highest degree, could not influence others, nor has it ever been the case, that he who was not in the highest degree sincere could influence others. *

13. Mencius said, *Pih* E avoided Chow and dwelt on the shores of the northern sea, when he heard that Wăn Wang had arisen he exclaimed, " Why should I not return ? I hear that Se Pĭh (Wăn Wang) nourishes the old in an excellent manner." Tae Kung concealed himself from Chow, and dwelt on the shores of the eastern sea, when he heard of the rise of Wăn Wang he said " Why should I not return? I hear that Se Pĭh nourishes well the old." These two old men were the heads of all the aged persons in the Empire, and when they went over it was the going over of the fathers of the Empire. When the fathers went over, where could the children go? † Were there any of the tributary Princes who would govern as Wan Wang did, in the space of seven years he would rule the Empire.

14. Mencius said, Kew was first minister to Ke She, and was unable to bring him back to the path of virtue, but doubled his taxes. Confucius said, Kew is not a disciple of mine. My little children, (students) you may drum him, and thus expose his crimes. From this it may be seen, that when one's Prince, does not practise benevolent government, and yet he enriches him: Such a man would have been rejected by Confucius, and how much more those who violently fight for emolument. Those who wrangle and fight for territory, and fill the wastes with dead bodies, and who fight for cities, so as to fill the cities with dead bodies, may be said to lead on the earth to eat human flesh. Death is not a sufficient punishment for such crimes.

* That is he who possesses the highest degree of Sincerity * * will be confided in by his superiors, believed by his friends, and delighted in by his parents and relatives.

† These two were extraordinary old men. Both in age and virtue they were the fathers of the whole empire.

---

* * The word 誠 Ching which we have here rendered sincerity, genuine virtue, and perfection, is defined by Chinese moralists, to be reality, without any mixture of guile, or falsehood, or deceit. It is difficult to find any English term, which exactly corresponds to the Chinese word. Sincerity does not seem to express the meaning fully, and perfection seems to do more than express it.

Hence those who delight in war, deserve the highest punishment,—those who stir up the Princes deserve the next degree of punishment, and those who oppress the people cultivating the wastes, in order to increase their lands, the next.

15. Mencius says, nothing watches over the body equal to the pupil of the eye. The pupil of the eye cannot conceal a man's vices. When the breast is upright, the eye is bright, but when the breast is not upright, the eye is confused. Listen to his words, observe his eye; how can a man conceal himself?

16. Mencius says, the respectful will not insult a man:—the moderate will not plunder men. It is only the insulting, plundering Prince, who is afraid that men will not obey him. Have such respectfulness, and moderation. How can a sweet voice, and smiling countenance be esteemed respect and moderation?

17. Shun Yu Kwan asked whether it accorded with etiquette that men and women in giving and receiving should not hand any thing to each other? Mencius answered in the affirmative. Then said the other, if my sister-in-law were drowning ought I to rescue her with my hand or not. He, (said Mencius) who would not rescue a sister-in-law from drowning, is a wolf. That males and females should not hand a thing to each other, when giving and receiving is proper: to rescue a sister-in-law from drowning by the hand, is necessity caused by circumstances. Then said Shun the Empire is drowning, why do'nt you, Sir, save it. When the Empire is drowning, save it by right principles, when a sister-in-law is drowning, save her by the hand. Do you wish me to save the Empire by my hand? *

18. Sun Woo asked, why superior men do not instruct their own children? Mencius replied, it is not expedient. He who teaches must teach right principles. If he do so, and is not obeyed, then he must be angry. Anger breeds animosity, and thus alienates the affections. Then the son says, my father teaches me to be correct and he himself is not correct. Thus the affections of father and son are alienated which is very bad.

* Shun Yu Kwan thought that when the empire was sinking into ruin, a slight departure from the straight course might be justified in order to save it, but Mencius held no such opinion.

The ancients exchanged their children, and educated them.* Between father and son there should not be mutual reproof. Where there is mutual reproof, alienation takes place, than which nothing is more unfortunate.

19. Mencius said, whom is it of most importance to serve? To serve parents, is most important. What is of most importance to maintain? To keep ourselves is of most importance. I have heard of those who have governed themselves, being able to serve their parents. But I have not heard of any who neglected to govern themselves, and yet were able to serve their parents.

Whom should we not serve? But to serve parents is the root. What should we not keep? But to keep ourselves is the root.

Tsăng Tsze in nourishing his father Tsăng Seih always gave him wine and flesh. When he was about to draw the table he always asked to whom he would give what was left. When his father asked whether there were still any more (of what he had been eating), he always replied, that there was. When Tsang Seih died Tsang Yuen in waiting upon his father, Tsang Tsze always gave him wine and flesh. When about to draw the table he did not ask to whom he would give the fragments. When asked whether there was still more, he answered that there was not. He wished to present what was left to his father. This may be called feeding the mouth and body. But he who acts like Tsang Tsze may be said to nourish the mind, or inclination He who serves his parents, as Tsang Tsze did, may be said to be a filial child. †

* By this system the kind feelings between father and son were preserved complete, while the education of youth was not neglected.

† Tsang Tsze thinking that his father wished to give what was left to some one, would not hurt his feelings by saying that there was nothing left. Thus he nourished his fathers feelings. Tsang Yuen on the other hand wished his father himself to enjoy what was left of any thing good. Thus his object in saying that there was not any thing left, to nourish his fathers body. ††

†† We think it the duty of children to humour their parents, as far as their duty to God will permit, But as the plan pursued by Tsang Tsze, and Tsang Yuen, must have led them to tell downright falsehoods, at least on some occasions and as this is passed over by the sage, as a thing of no importance, we must warn the admirers of Mencius, against being encouraged by his authority, to violate the holy law of God, in order to please their parents, or any other human being.

20. Mencius said, it is not enough to reprove a Prince for employing improper men, or for bad government. It is only the great man that can expel vice from his sovereign's heart. If the Prince be benevolent, not one will be without benevolence. If the Prince be unjust, not one will not be upright. Once make the Prince upright and the Empire is settled.

21. Mencius says, it sometimes happens, that a man is praised when he does not expect it, and some are reviled who seek perfection (or who labor to avoid being reviled).

22. Mencius says, the reason why men speak lightly, is that they are not reproved.

23. Mencius says, the great disease of men, is, that they wish to be teachers of others.

24. When Lŏ Ching Tsze accompained Tsze Gaou to Tse, Lŏ Ching Tsze waited on Mencius. Mencius said, Ah! Sir, have you called on me? Why (said the other) does my teacher use these words! How many days is it since you arrived? I arrived yesterday. Are not my words reasonable then? I had not fixed on my lodgings before. Have you learned that one should first fix his lodgings and then wait on his teacher? I have done wrong. *

25. Mencius said to Lŏ Ching Tsze, you, Sir, accompained Tsze Gaou merely for the sake of food and drink. I did not think that having learned the principles of the ancients, you would have so esteemed a little food and drink.

26. Mencius said, there are three things which are unfilial, but to have no posterity is worst of all. The reason why Shun married without informing his parents, was, lest he should be without posterity. This, in the estimation of the superior man, was the same as if he had informed them. †

* Propriety requires, that when a student comes to a place, where his teacher lives, he ought immediately on his arrival to wait upon him. At that time, Lo Ching Tsze had comitted two faults. He had both associated with a mean man and at the same time neglected to call on his master directly on his arrival.

† Had Shun informed his parents that he intended to marry, they would not have given their consent, and the consequence would have been, that he would have had no posterity, and thus have been guilty of the greatest violation of filial piety. Hence, his filial piety was manifested by his not having informed them.

27. Mencius says, that to serve parents is the reality of benevolence, (or perfect virtue,) and to obey elder brothers, is the reality of justice. The reality of wisdom is to know these two things, and not to abandon them. The reality of propriety, is to ornament these. The reality of music is to rejoice in these:—rejoice in them, and they naturally grow. When they grow, they cannot stop. When they cannot stop, then you unconsciously shake your feet and move your hands to dance.

28. Mencius said, the whole Empire was greatly delighted and came over to himself (Shun.) It was only Shun that could look upon the whole Empire, joyfully submitting to him, as the grass under his feet. He considered that he who did not gain the affections of his parents, was not a man, and that he who did not obey his parents, was not a son. Shun exhausted the duties of filial piety. He brought round, and even delighted his father Koo Sow. Koo Sow once subdued and delighted, the whole Empire was renovated. Koo Sow when converted and pleased, the duties of father and son throughout the Empire were established. This is what we call great filial piety. *

CHAP. VIII.

1. Mencius said, Shun was born in Choo Fung, removed to Foo Hea, and died in Ming Tcaou. He was an eastern stranger. Wăn Wang was born in Ke Chow, and died in Peĭh Chin. He was an eastern foreigner. Their places of abode were distant more than one thousand miles, and the time between their births more than one thousand years. But when they got their wish and became rulers in the middle country, they resembled the

* While Shun was not loved by his parents, the Empire itself, and the love of all his people, were like the grass under his feet in his estimation. Hence, he persevered in acts of the greatest filial piety, till at last the obdurate heart of his father was overcome. The effects of such unexampled filial piety were felt through the whole of his dominions. Thus, his filial piety was unequalled.

two parts of a divided seal. The former and latter sages were formed after the same pattern.

2. When Tsze Chan was in office in the Chin country, he was in the habit of giving his carriage to people to carry them over the Tsin and Wei rivers. Mencius said, this showed kindness, but did not discover the knowledge of good government.

In the eleventh month, make foot bridges and in the twelfth make bridges for carriages and the people will have no difficulty in crossing the rivers.

When the Prince governs with equity, he may when travelling require the people to go aside. But how can he assist every one?

If he who governs wishes to please every one, time will prove too short.

3. Mencius told Seuen, King of Tse that when the Prince looks on his ministers as his hands and his feet, they consider him to be their bowels and heart; but when the Prince esteems his minister as his dogs and his horses, they view him as a common man; and when the Prince looks on his ministers as the grass of the earth, they view him as a thief and an enemy.

The King said, the Le Ke says you should wear mourning for a Prince whom you have formerly served. How do they act when their old ministers should wear mourning for them? Mencius replied, when the admonitions of a minister are followed, and his words listened to, so as to prove beneficial to the people, if he should have cause to leave and the Prince send an escort with him, till he leave the borders of the country, and send a recommendation to the place where he goes;—if he remain three years and do not return, his lands may be taken. This is called San Yew Le, or the three-fold politeness. The Prince who thus acts, will be mourned for by his former servants. The advice of ministers of the present day is not followed, nor their words listened to, so that they cannot benefit the people. When they have reason to leave their situations, and depart, they are seized, or pursued to the place whither they go. Their lands are taken on the day of their departure. These Princes are called robbers and enemies. How can men mourn for robbers and enemies!

4. Mencius says, when inferior officers are put to death, without being guilty, superior officers ought to resign, and when the innocent among the people, are put to death, inferior officers ought to give up their places.

5 Mencius said, if the Prince be benevolent, none will be wanting in benevolence, if the Prince be just, none will be unjust.

6. Mencius says, what is near propriety, but is not true propriety, what is near justice, but is not true justice, a great man will not practise.

7. Mencius says, when those who are in the middle path, bring on those who are not in the right way, and those who possess talents lead forward those of inferior abilities, then men will rejoice that they have able and virtuous fathers and elder brothers;—but when those in the right way, abandon those who are not, and those who have abilities give up those who have not, there is not an inch of difference in this case between the good and the bad.*

8. Mencius said, the man who will not do every thing, is the man who will act properly.

9. Mencius said, those who talk of men's vices, what future misery ought they to suffer!

10. Mencius said, Confucius carried the principle of not doing every thing to the highest pitch.

11. Mencius says, that a great man does not predetermine that his words are true, nor that his actions will accord with them, but is guided by what is just and right.

* If we are fathers or elder brothers, and do not instruct our children and younger brothers who are vicious, then we pass the medium. In this case where is the difference between us and them!

12. Mencius says, the great man never loses child-like simplicity.

13. Mencius says, those who merely nourish the living, are not worthy of being considered fit for great things:—It is only those who attend properly to the dead, that are competent for a great work.

14. Mencius says, the superior man lays the foundation deep in sound principles: wishing to possess them in himself. When once he becomes possessed of them, he enjoys them with composure,—enjoying them with composure, he relies upon their depth,—relying upon their depth, on the left and right he meets with their source. Hence, the superior man wishes to possess the thing himself.

15. Mencius says, learn extensively, and discuss clearly,—then you may turn round and draw the whole under one general principle.

16. Mencius says, those who attempt to subdue men by their own virtue, will never subdue them. But cherish men by your virtue, and you may subdue the Empire. If the Empire is not subdued in heart, there is no such thing as governing it.*

17. Mencius says, words that are not true, are inauspicious, but to conceal the virtuous is inauspicious in the highest degree.†

Lew Tsze said, Confucius praised the water, saying, "Water! Water!" Why did he thus extol the water? (or why take such delight in it).

Mencius said, a spring plays on, and stops not day nor night. It fills the channels, and proceeds till it reach the ocean. Thus it is with those who have the root (or reality) of virtue: hence he praised the water.

18. But, if water have no permanent source, then during the seventh and eighth months, when by the abundant rains, all the

* That is he who practises virtue merely that he may surpass others, will never gain their hearts, whereas the man who leads on others gently, by his example, kind offices and instructions, will win their affections.

† Choo Foo Tsze says, that the sense of this passage is doubtful. He suspects that the text is incomplete.

furrows and tanks overflow, you may stand by till they are dry again; hence, the superior man is ashamed of unmerited fame.

19. Mencius says, the difference between men and brutes is but small. The common herd lose this difference, but superior men preserve it. *

Shun was well versed in the principles of things, and examined the human relations. He acted from benevolence and justice, and did not labor to be benevolent and just.

20. Mencius said, Yu hated sweet wine, and loved good words Tang held the due medium and gave official appointments to men of worth, without respect of persons. Wăn Wang looked on the people as if he had injured them, and looked up to right principles, as if he had not yet seen them. Woo Wang did not slight those who were near, nor forget those who were distant. † Chow Kung wished to unite in himself these four excellencies of the three former dynasties. If in any thing he did not accord with them, he thought on it night and day, and when so fortunate as to find it out, he sat till morning, that he might put it in practice.

21. Mencius says, when the traces of kingly (or good) government were extinguished. The She (poems) were lost, when they were lost then the Chun Tsew was compiled. The Shing

* When men and brutes come into existence they equally receive the 理 Le or principle of heaven and earth as their nature, and also equally receive the 氣 Ke, breath, or subtile fluid of heaven and earth, as the form or substratum of their frame. The only difference is, that men receive the correctness of this breath, or subtile fluid, and have the power of carrying their nature to the highest perfection. Although, this is said to be a small difference, yet the distinction between men and the brutes really lies here. The common herd know not this, and put away the difference, hence, although they retain the name of men, they really do not differ from the brutes. * *

† Although Mung Tsze praised each of these worthies for one particular virtue, we are not from hence to suppose, that each of them was not capable of uniting all these virtues in himself. For their is nothing in which the sages are not complete.

* * If we comprehend this philosophy, it appears to us to convey the notion, that the difference between men and brutes, lies in something connected with the body rather than in the mental powers. Now, while we grant that a vicious man, is in some respect below the brutes, yet both reason and revelation teach us that with regard to mental powers, and moral responsibility, the difference between men and the brute creation is immense.

of Tsin the Taou Gih of Tsoo and the Chun Tsew are one. Records the transactions of Kwan of Tse, and of Wăn of Tsin. Its style is historical. Confucius says, I borrowed the ideas.

22. Mencius says, that in the course of five ages the influence of a superior man is lost, and in five ages the influence of a mean man is obliterated. I was not personally a disciple of Confucius, but I learned his principles from others.

23. Mencius says, there are cases in which you may receive and others in which you ought not to receive. There is a receiving which is injurious to moderation. There are cases when you may give, and others in which you ought not. There is a giving which hurts benevolence. There are cases in which you ought to die and others in which you ought not. There is a dying which is injurious to bravery.

24. Pung Mung learned archery of Yu. When he had made himself completely master of Yu's principles, he thought none under heaven surpassed himself, except Yu, and on that account killed him. Mencius said, Yu was also to blame. Kung Ming E said, he ought to be considered innocent. Mencius said his fault was light, but how could he be blameless!

The people of Chin sent Tsze Chŏ Joo, to make a secret attack upon Wei. Wei sent Yu Kung Che Sze, to pursue him. Tsze Cho Too said, to-day I have had an attack of sickness, and cannot hold my bow; I must die. He then asked his servant who it was that pursued him? The servant replied, it is Yu Kung Che Sze. O then said he I shall yet live. To which the servant rejoined Yu Kung Che Sze is the best archer of Wei; what does my master mean by saying that he shall yet live. Because, said he, Yu Kung Che Sze learned archery from Yin Kung To, and Yin Kung To learned archery of me. Now Yin Kung To, is an upright man and those whom he selects as his friends must likewise be upright. When Yu Kung Che Sze came up, he said, why do you not grasp your bow; Sir? The other replied, I have had an attack of sickness to-day and am unable to hold my bow. To which he rejoined, I learned archery of Yin Kung To and Yin Kung To learned the art of you, Sir, I cannot bear to employ your own skill to your injury. But although this is the case, still I am sent to-day on the king's business which I dare not neglect:—he then took out his arrows, struck off their steel points against the wheels of his chariot, shot four of them at him and returned.

25. Mencius said, even if Le Tse were dirty all men would cover their noses in passing her. *

Although a man be ugly, yet if he purify and wash himself, he may offer sacrifices to Shang Te.

26. Mencius says, in discussing nature, investigate its causes and no more. Causes take following nature to be the root. That which is hateful to men of wisdom, is boring out some by-road for oneself. They who act as wise men, imitate Yu in making courses for the water of the flood. Then they do nothing abhorrent to wise men. Yu in damming of the water, used no force. They who act the part of wise men, likewise act without effort. †

Although heaven be high, and the stars distant, yet if you investigate their laws, you may sit and calculate their revolutions for a thousand years.

27. When Kung King Tsze buried a son, Ke Yew Sze went to condole with him. On entering the door some people went and spoke with him and others went up to his seat and conversed

* Se Tsze although a beautiful lady yet if covered with filth, men would hate to come near her.

† There are many who from ignorance of nature, and from the want of a thorough investigation of the causes of things, act by force, and know not how to follow the plain, easy course of nature.

with him, but Mencius did not speak to him, at which he was displeased and said that all the gentlemen had spoken with him, except Mencius, who alone had not spoken to him, this said he is treating me with disrespect. Mencius hearing this, said, in the court etiquette requires that you should not pass the seat of another to speak with each other, nor should you pass the steps to bow to each other. I wished to observe etiquette, and Tsze Gaou deems me rude; is not this something wonderful!

28. Mencius says, that by which the superior man differs from other men, consists in keeping his heart. The superior man, keeps his heart by virtue and propriety. The virtuous (or benevolent) love others, and the polite respect others. Men constantly love those who love them, and he who treats others with respect, is always respected by others. If any one treat the superior man in an unreasonable manner, he will turn round on himself and say, I must be deficient in benevolence and etiquette, else why should I meet with such treatment. If after self examination, he find that he is both benevolent and polite, and that the other still treats him rudely, he will again turn round on himself, and say I must be unfaithful, or why should I be treated thus? *

If on turning round and examining himself, he find that he is faithful, and the other still treats him rudely, he says to himself, this wild fellow! in what respect does he differ from a brute? why should I trouble myself with a brute! Hence, the superior man has anxiety all his life, but not one morning's distress from wrangling with others. If he have anxiety, it is because he considers that Shun was but a man as well as he, but that Shun was an example to the world, which may be held up to future ages, and that he is but a common villager. This is cause of an-

* The superior man thus reasons with himself, viz that every thing which takes place, must have a cause, hence when he meets with rude treatment, he concludes, that it must have been occasioned by his own previous deficiency in virtue and politeness.

xiety; what then is he anxious about? merely that he may equal Shun. As to misery coming from external causes, the superior man is free from it. What is contrary to virtue he does not; what is rude he practises not. Although he may appear to have one morning's distress, yet in reality the superior man has no such misery. *

29. Yu and Tseih lived in an age of peace and order, and three times passed their own doors without entering. Confucius pronounced them virtuous. Yen Tsze lived in times of disorder and confusion, and lived on a bamboo of rice and a shellful of water. Other men could not bear such hardships, but they changed not the joys of Yen Tsze. Confucius pronounced him virtuous. Mencius says, that the principles of Yu, Tseih and Yen Huwy were the same. Yu thought that if any one under heaven was drowned it was he himself who drowned him, and Tseih thought that if any one under heaven suffered hunger, it was he himself who had caused it. † Hence, their extreme ardour. Had Yu, Tseih and Yen Huwy changed places they would all have acted the same part. If people in the same house with you are fighting, go and rid them, although your hair be dishevelled and your cap untied you may go.

If people of the same village with you are fighting and you run with your hair and cap in disorder to rid them, you manifest ignorance. You may shut your door.

20. Kung Too said through the whole country Kwang Chang is considered unfilial and yet you keep company with him, and treat him with respect. I presume to ask why you do so? Mencius replied, according to the common opinion, there are five things which are unfilial.—To indulge in sloth and pay no attention to the support of one's parents is unfilial—to gamble and drink without regarding the support of parents is unfilial,—to love wealth and selfishly bestow it on one's wife and children while

* The superior man on self-examination finds himself faithful, sincere and respectful, hence the wild abuse of those whom he accounts no better than the brutes, gives him not a single moment's trouble, because he expects no more of such men, than he does of a brute. The only anxiety which he feels arises from his not being equal to Shun in wisdom and virtue.

† This was because the former was appointed to drain the world after the deluge, and the latter to regulate the agriculture.

the support of parents is neglected, is unfilial—to follow the lusts of the ear and the eye, so as to bring disgrace upon one's father and mother, is unfilial—to be fond of wrangling and fighting so as to endanger our parents, is unfilial:—was Chang Tsze guilty of any one of these?

But there was reproof between Chang Tsze, and his father, hence they did not agree. Why should not Chang Tsze have wished to maintain the relations of husband and wife, and of mother and son? but because he had offended his father and could not come near him, he put away his wife and sent his children to a distance, and to the end of life, received no service from them, supposing that unless he acted thus, he would increase his fault: such is the case with Chang Tsze.

31. When Tsăng Tsze dwelt in Woo Ching, robbers came from Yu. Some one said to him, why should you not depart? the robbers have come. He said let no one occupy my house, lest he destroy the wood. When the robbers retired, he gave orders to have his house put in good repair, saying I am about to return. When the robbers retired he returned. His attendants said, the government has treated you faithfully and with respect, perhaps it was not right of you to go off first of all, when the robbers approached, and to return, when they have retired, thus shewing an example to the people. Chin Yew Hing said, you do not understand this matter. Formerly Chin Yew She was attacked by the grass carriers, our master had then with him seventy disciples and none of them met with any harm.* When Tsze Sze dwelt in Wei, robbers came from Tse. Some one said ought you not to leave! Tsze She said if I leave who is to protect the Prince?

Mencius said, the principles of Tsăng Tsze and Tsze Sze were the same. But Tsăng Tsze was a teacher, hence equal in rank to a father or elder brother. Tsze Sze was a minister and

* The disciples of Tsang Tsze thought that as the officers of government had treated him so respectfully, he ought to have remained when the robbers came and have assisted in opposing them rather than have set the people the example of fleeing from them. But they did not consider that as a teacher, who held no office under the crown, it was his duty to avoid danger, and not to risk his life in an encounter with banditti.

of low rank. Had Tsăng Tsze and Tsze Sze exchanged places, they would have acted the same part.

Choo Tsze said to Mencius, the king has sent a man to look at you, whether you really differ (in outward appearance) from other men or not. Mencius replied, why should I differ from other men, even Yaou and Shun were the same (in appearance) as other men.

32. There was a man in Tse who had a wife and concubine living in the same house. When their husband went out he always returned crammed with flesh and wine. When his wife asked with whom he eat and drank, *he said*, always with the rich and honorable. His wife informed his concubine saying, when our husband goes out he is sure to return full of flesh and wine, and when I ask with whom he eats and drinks, he says that they are all rich people.

But I have never seen them come here, I will spy out where our husband goes. She rose early in the morning and looked after her husband. In the town no one stood to speak with him. At last he went to the east suburbs of the town among those who were offering sacrifices at the tombs and begged what was left, which not satisfying him, he looked round for more. This was the way in which he crammed himself. His wife returned and informed his concubine how the man on whom they depended for life was acting and then united with his concubine in reprobating their husband. Both sat down in the hall and wept. The husband ignorant of all this, entered in a jovial manner and behaved in a pompous way. Mencius said, according to the views of a superior man there are few of the wives and concubines of those who seek riches, honor and profit, who have not occasion to be ashamed and weep.

CHAP. IX.

1. Wan Chang asked saying, when Shun went to the fields to till them, he called out and wept towards heaven? what was the cause of his lamentation and weeping! Mencius said, he was vexed and anxious. Wan Chang said, when your father and

mother love you, then rejoice and forget them not. If your parents hate you, labor hard and grumble not; did Shun grumble with his parents then? Mencius replied, Chang Seih asked Kung Ming Kaou saying I understand why Shun went to till the fields, but I know not, why he lamented and wept towards heaven respecting his parents.*

Kung Ming Kaou replied, you are not capable of knowing this. Now, Kung Ming Kaou considered that the heart of a filial son would not be free from care. He (Shun) would say to himself, to exert my whole strengh in cultivating the fields, is no more than my duty as a son. What is there still wrong in me, that my parents do not love me! The Emperor gave him his nine sons, and two daughters, all his officers, his oxen, and sheep and all his stores whilst he remained in the country. All the learned followed him. The Emperor took the whole Empire and gave it over to him; but because he could not gain the affections of his parents still he seemed a man possessed of nothing. To have all good men delight in him, is what every man wishes, but this could not dispel his grief. Beauty is what all men love, he married the Emperor's two daughters, but that was not sufficient to dispel his sorrow. Riches are what all men wish;—he possessed the Empire, but that could not dissipate his grief. Honors, are what all men are fond of;—he was Emperor, but that likewise was not enough to dispel his sorrow. Neither the affection of all men, nor the love of beauty, riches and honors, could assuage his grief. It was only the gaining of the hearts of his parents, that could dispel his grief.

When men are in infancy, they think ardently on their father and mother;—when they become susceptible of knowing beauty, they think with ardent desire on beautiful young females; when

* Although Shun's parents treated him with extreme harshness, and even attempted to take his life, yet he never grumbled at their treatment in the least, but was deeply grieved with himself, because of his being unable to gain their affections.

they are married their thoughts are occupied about their wives and children;—and when they get an official situation under the crown, their minds are taken up about their Prince. If they fail to secure his favor, they burn to the very soul. Men of great filial piety, think ardently on their parents during their whole life. I have seen from the conduct of the great Shun that there are those who at the age of fifty do so. *

2. Wan Chang asked saying, the She King says, " How ought a man to contract a marriage? He ought to inform his parents." True are these words. None knew propriety so well as Shun, why then did Shun mary without informing his father and mother? Mencius said, had he informed them, he could not have married. Now the matromonial bond, is the greatest of human relations. Had he informed them, he would have violated the greatest of human relations, and opposed his parents, hence he did not inform them.

Wan Chang said, I have heard why Shun married without informing his parents, but why did the Emperor (Yaou) give him his daughters in marriage without informing his (Shun's) parents? Mencius replied, the Emperor also knew that if he had announced it to them, he could not have married them to Shun.

Wan Chang said, Shun's father and mother sent him to repair the top of a granary and when he was up removed the ladder, and set fire to the house. They also sent him to clean out a well and when he was down they closed the mouth of it. Seang his brother came and said, the merit of covering up Too Keun (Shun) is all mine. Now his oxen and sheep shall be my father and mother's; his stores shall likewise be my father and mother's; but his arms and musical instruments shall be mine, and his wives shall make my bed. On saying this, Seang went in to the ap-

* It is the case with common men, that their hearts and affections are changed by circumstances; it is only the holy man that never loses his original heart.

partments of Shun, where he found him on this couch playing on his harp. Seang said, I have been vexed about you, but at the same time wore the aspect of shame. Shun said will you assist me in managing these servants? * Was Shun aware that Seang wished to kill him? Why should he not? But when Seang was sorrowful so was Shun, and when Seang rejoiced so did Shun.

Then Shun feigned joy, did he not? No. Formerly some one presented a living fish to Chin Tsze Tsan, Tsze Tsan ordered his pond keeper to nourish it. The pond keeper dressed it and eat it, and reported, saying that at first when I let it go, it moved with difficulty, but in a short time it went off in fine style. Tsze Tsan exclaimed it has got into its element, it got into its element! The pond keeper went out and said, who says that Tsze Tsan is an intelligent man? I dressed and eat the fish, and lo he exclaimed it has got into its element! it has got into its element! Therefore the superior man may be deceived by what appears reasonable, but you cannot trick him by what is opposed to sound reason. † He (Seang) came as an affectionate brother ought to do, hence, he truly believed him and rejoiced, why should he have feigned joy?

3. Wan Chang said, Seang made it his business to take Shun's life, when he became Emperor, why did he banish him? Mencius replied, he appointed him to a principality, and some one in a mistake said he banished him. ‡

Wan Chang said, Shun banished Kung Kung to Yew Chow, placed Hwan Tow in Tsung Shan, slew San Meaou in San Wei, and put to death Kwun in Yu Shan. When these four punish-

* Shun said will you assist me in overseeing these servants? I do not know, said Wan Chang whether Shun knew that Seang intended to kill him or not? Why should he not, said Mencius. When Seang was sorry so was Shun, and when Seang was cheerful so was Shun.

† The conduct of the pond keeper did not prove him to be a wise man, nor did his master by giving credit to his report, prove himself deficient in wisdom. What the pond keeper said exactly accorded with reason, hence Tsze Tsan believed him. The conduct of Seang on the occasion in question was what brotherly affection dictates, hence, Shun gave him credit and really felt joyful at the circumstance.

‡ Wan Chang thought that such had been the conduct of Seang towards his brother, that when the latter ascended the throne, he ought to have inflicted a severer punishment than banishment, even that of death, but Shun could not bear even to banish him, far less to inflict a heavier punishment

ments were inflicted the whole Empire submitted. He cut off the vicious. Seang was eminently vicious and yet he made him Prince of Yew Pe. Now what crimes were the people of Yew Pe guilty of, that they should have such a man for their ruler? Others he cut off, but his brother he made a Prince, will the truly virtuous man really act thus? Mencius replied, the truly virtuous man, in his conduct towards his brother, will not cherish wrath, nor harbour resentment, but will treat him only with affection. Feeling affection for him, he will wish him possessed of rank, loving him he will wish him rich. Now (Shun) in appointing him to the principality of Yew Pe, give him both rank and wealth. Had his brother been only a common man, while he himself was Emperor, how could it have been said, that he loved him! I presume to ask why some people said, that he was sent away (or banished)? Mencius replied, Seang had no power in the government. The Emperor sent an officer to govern the country and collect the taxes. Hence, it was said that he was sent off. How could he have power to oppress the people? still Shun constantly wished to see him, and he uninterruptedly went to see him. He did not wait till the time when the tribute was paid to give an account of the government of Yew Pe. This is what ancient books say.

4. Han Kew Mung said, report says that among men of finished virtue, a Prince cannot act the minister nor a father the son, but that Shun sat with his face to the south and Yaou led in all the Princes with their faces to the north to his court, and that Koo Sow also came into his court with his face to the north, * and that when Shun saw Koo Sow he appeared uneasy, and that Confucius said that at that time, the Empire was in danger and on the brink of ruin. I am at a loss to know whether this report be true or not. Mencius replied, it is not true. These are not the words of a superior man, but of some rustic from the eastern borders of Tse. When Yaou became old,

* The Emperor when seated on the throne, sat with his face to the south and his ministers entered the court with their faces to the north.

Shun acted for him. The records of Yaou say, that after Shun had acted for Yaou twenty eight years, Yaou died,* and that the people mourned for him three years, the same as for a father or mother; and all within the four seas refrained from music. Confucius says, that in the heavens there are not two suns, nor have the people two Lords; but if Shun had been Emperor (before the death of Yaou) and yet led all the Princes to mourn three years for them there must have been two Emperors at one time.

Han Kew Mung said, I have heard why Shun did not treat Yaou as his minister, but the ode says, "There was no land under heaven that did not belong to the Emperor, nor were there any of the people within the borders, who were not his servants." Since then Shun was Emperor, I presume to ask why Koo Sow was not his servant? *Mencius* replied, the ode does not mean this, but speaks of one who was so employed in the service of the king, that he had no leisure to nourish his parents; on which account he said, all ought to serve the king, why should I alone be esteemed able and thus severely worked. Therefore, in explaining the ode we must not interpret a phrase, so as to injure a sentence; nor on account of a single sentence injure the scope of the writer; but ought to meet the ideas of the author; thus, we may come at his meaning. If we follow single expressions, then, since the Yun Han ode says, that none of the people of Chow were left, it would follow, if these words are taken in their literal sense, that not one of the people of Chow was left.

There is no greater filial piety, than to honor one's parents. Parents cannot be more highly honored, than by taking the whole Empire and feeding them with it. There is no higher honor than to be the father of the Emperor. To nourish them with the whole Empire, is the highest degree of nourishment. The ode says, always speak of filial thoughts, (or he always

* The original says he ascended and descended, for when man dies one part ascends and the other descends, hence the ancients said when a person died that he had ascended and descended.

spoke of filial thoughts.) By his filial thoughts he was an example. This speaks of Shun.

The Shoo King says, with what reverence he waited upon Koo Sow! With what respect and awe did he stand before him. Koo Sow at last gave him credit (or yielded to him). This shews that the father did not act the Son.

5. Wan Chang said, did Yaou give the Empire to him? Mencius replied, no. The Emperor cannot give the Empire to another. But (said the other) Shun got the Empire; who gave it to him? Heaven gave it to him. When heaven gave it to him, did it command him in explicit terms?

No, heaven did not speak; it merely revealed its will by actions and events.* In what manner did it reveal its will by actions, and circumstances? The Emperor, said *Mencius,* may recommend a man to heaven, but he cannot cause heaven to give him the Empire. A tributary Prince may recommend a man to the Emperor, but he cannot cause the Emperor to make him a Prince. A high officer of state, may recommend a man to a Prince, but he cannot cause a Prince to make him a high officer. Formerly, Yaou recommended Shun to heaven, and heaven accepted him;—he exhibited him to the people, and they received him. Hence it is said, heaven did not speak, but merely made known its will by deeds and events.

I presume to ask in what manner he recommended him to heaven, and how it accepted him?—how he exhibited him to the people, and how they received him? He sent him to superintend the sacrifices, and all the gods were pleased, thus heaven approved of him. He sent him to direct the officers of state, and he succeeded, so that the people were happy under him, in this manner did they accept him. Heaven gave it to him, and the people gave it to him: hence it is said, that the Emperor cannot give the Empire to another. Shun was prime minister to Yaou for the space of twenty eight

* Actions and events refer to *Shun's* personal and official conduct

years, and when Yaou died and the three years of mourning for him were finished, then Shun gave place to Yaou's son, and retired to the south of Ho Nan. But all the Princes of the Empire waited upon him and not on Yaou's son. All who had law suits applied to Shun and not to Yaou's son. The songsters sang the praises of Shun and not of Yaou's son.

Hence, it is said that he was chosen of heaven. Afterwards he ascended the throne of China. Had he remained in Yaou's Palace and forced out Yaou's son, it would have been usurpation and not the gift of heaven. The Tae She says, "I know the views of heaven from the views of my people, and I know how heaven accords with me by the way in which my people listen to me. This explains the matter."

6. Wan Chang asking said, people say, that Yu's virtue was on the decay, because he did not leave the Empire to a man of worth, but to his son. Is this inference true? By no means, said Mencius.—When heaven gives it to the virtuous, it should be given to them, and when heaven gives it to the king's son, it should be given to him.

Formerly, Shun introduced Yu to heaven and seventeen years afterwards Shun died:—after the period of three years mourning for him was finished, Yu went out of the way of Shun's son, and lived in Yang Ching. The people of the Empire followed him, the same as when Yaou died, they did not follow Yaou's son, but followed Shun. Yu recommended Yih to heaven, and seven years afterwards, died. After the period of three years mourning for him was completed, Yih gave place to Yu's son and dwelt in a valley in Ke Shan. The Princes and those who had law-suits waited upon Ke and not on Yih, saying he is our Prince's (Yu's) son. The songsters did not celebrate the praises of Yih, but of Ke; for they said he is the son of our Prince.

Tan Choo (Yaou's son) was a degenerate young man, and Shun's son was likewise degenerate. Shun was prime minister to Yaou, and Yu was prime minister to Shun for a long succession of years. The people had long reaped the benefits of their administration. Ke was possessed of virtue and abilities, and was able reverently to continue the ways of his father. Yih had been prime minister to Yu, but for a short time. The people had only for a few years enjoyed the benefits which he diffused. There was a great difference between the length of time which Shun, Yu, and Yih were prime ministers. Their sons' being virtuous or degenerate, depended altogether on heaven, and was not in the power of man. When that which man cannot do, is done, it is heaven which accomplishes it, and when that which man brings not, comes, it is decreed. When a common man obtains the Imperial throne, he must have virtue equal to Shun, or Yu; and farther, there must be an Emperor (i. e. a good one) to recommend him (to Heaven). Hence, Confucius did not obtain the Empire. *

When the reigning family are the succesors of meritorious ancestors, before heaven cuts them off, they must be as bad as Këë or Chow. For this reason Yih, E Yin, and Chow Kung obtained not the Empire. †

E Yin assisted Tang to govern the Empire. When Tang died Tae Ting did not *live to* ascend the throne. Wae Ping reigned two years and Chung Jin four years. And then came Tae Keă who overturned the laws of Tang. But E Yin placed him three years in Tung (at the grave of Tang). He repented, abhorred himself and cultivated virtue. In Tung he practised benevolence and became just. When he had listened for three years to the admonitions of E Yin, he returned to Pŏ.

* Intimating that although the virtue of Confucius, was equal to that of Yaou or Shun, yet there was not an Emperor who could recommend him to heaven.

† If the reigning family be not extremely bad, heaven does not reject them; hence, although Ke, Tae Kea, and Ching Wang were not equal to Yih, E Yin, and Chow Kung, yet heaven did not take the throne from the former and give it to the latter.

The reason why Chow Kung did not get the Imperial throne was the same as that which prevented Yih in the Hea and E Yin in the Yin dynasties from being Emperors.

Confucius said, in Tang and Yu (the dynasty of Yaou and Shun) the Empire was presented to other men, but in the Hea, Yin, and Chow dynasties, the throne was obtained by hereditary succession. The intention of all was the same.

7. Wan Chang asked saying, men have said, that E Yin sought an introduction to Tang by becoming cook: was it so or not?

Mencius replied, no; by no means. E Yin tilled the fields in Yew Sin, and delighted in the principles of Yaou and Shun. He would not do what was unjust or contrary to reason:—suppose you had offered him the Empire to do it, he would not have regarded it. If you had offered him four thousand horses to do what was unjust, or unreasonable, he would not have looked at them. Nay he would not contrary to justice and reason either have given, or taken a single straw.

Tang sent presents, begging him to enter his service. He exclaimed, with perfect self possession, what are Tang's presents to me! To me what is equal to living in the fields and rejoicing in the ways of Yaou and Shun!

Tang sent three times entreating him. At last, he was moved and said, compared with my living in the fields and rejoicing in the principles of Yaou and Shun, is it not better to cause this Prince to become a Prince of the same stamp as Yaou and Shun? Is it not better for me to make this people, the people of Yaou and Shun? What is equal to seeing these things with my own eyes?

Heaven created this people, and sent those who are first informed to enlighten those who are last informed, I am one of heaven's people who are first aroused. I will take these principles and arouse this people. If I do not arouse them who will? *

He considered that if a single man or woman under heaven, did not reap the benefits of the principles of Yaou and Shun, it was as if he himself had pushed them into a ditch. Thus, did he take the heavy responsibility of caring for the Empire on himself. Hence, he went to Tang and exhorted him to conquer Hea and save the people.

I have not heard that a man who bends himself is able to straighten others, how much less can he who disgraces himself correct the Empire! The actions of the sages have not always been the same. Some went to a distance, some remained near, some went out of office, some did not; yet all agreed in keeping themselves pure.

I have heard that E Yin by the principles of Yaou and Shun sought to be employed by Tang, but have not heard that he sought this by becoming a cook.

E Yin says, "Heaven commenced at Mŭh Kung to cut off and attack, I began at Pŏ."

8. Wan Chang asked, saying, some one said, that Confucius lived with the ulcer doctor when he was in Wei, and that when in Tse he lived with the king's favorite, Tseih Hwan. Was this the case? Mencius replied, by no means. Some busy body has invented this. When he was in Wei he lived with Yen Chow Yew. Me Tsze's wife and Tsze Loo's wife were sisters. Me Tsze said to Tsze Loo, had Confucius lived in my house, he might have been one of the first officers of Wei; Tsze Loo told this to Confucius. Confucius replied, these things are decreed by heaven. Confucius went into office according to propriety, and retired according to justice. Whether he obtained

* They all possess good principles, but are asleep, and know not that they do possess them. I only can awake them to a sense of the worth of those principles which they originally possess.

office or not, he said it is the will of heaven. Had he lived with the ulcer doctor or with the royal favorite Tseĭh Hwan, it would have been unjust and not according to the divine will.

When Confucius was displeased in Loo and Wei, going to Sung, Tseih Hwan, who was Sze Ma, wished him to come, that he might kill him; but he changed his clothes and left Sung secretly. At that time when Confucius was in danger, he lived in the house of Ching Tsze, who held the office of Sze Ching and is now minister to Prince Chow of Chin.

I have heard that we should observe who are lodged by the ministers who reside at court, and with whom distant ministers lodge. If Confucius had lodged with the ulcer doctor, or with Tseih Hwan how could he have been Confucius!

9. Wan Chang asked, saying, some one said, that Pih Le He sold himself to a feeder of cattle in Tsin for the skins of five sheep, to feed cows, in order to obtain the favor of Prince Mŭh. Is this true? Mencius replied, by no means, some busy body has invented this story. Pih Le He, was a man of Yu; the people of Tsin sent gems of Chuy Keih, and four horses of Keŭh breed, begging of the Prince of Yu to grant him a passage through his country, that he might invade Uh. King Che Ke advised his Prince against this, but Pih Le He did not.

When he knew that the Prince of Yu would not be admonished and hence went to Tsin, he was 70 years of age. Had he not known that to feed cattle in order to get the favor of Prince Mŭh of Tsin, was a low, dirty thing, could he be considered wise? To know that one would not be advised, a nd not to advise him, could that be considered unwise? To know that the Prince of Yu was near ruin, and to go off before hand, cannot be called foolishness. When he was employed by Prince Mŭh of Tsin, to know that Prince Mŭh might be made to act well, and to assist him, can this be called want of wisdom! He assisted Prince Mŭh made him illustrious through the whole Empire, and handed down his fame to future ages, had he not been a man of eminent virtue and talents could he have done so? To sell himself in order to accomplish his Prince, is what a common villager who loves himself would not do, can it then be said that a man of virtue and education would!

CHAP. X.

Mencius said, Pih E's eye would not look upon a bad colour, nor would his ear listen to a bad sound. Unless a Prince were of his own stamp, he would not serve him, and unless people were of his own stamp, he would not employ (or rule) them. In times of good government he went into office and in times of confusion and bad government he retired. Where disorderly government prevailed, or where disorderly people lived he could not bear to dwell. He thought that to live with low men, was as bad as to sit in the mud with his court robes and cap. In the time of Chow he dwelt on the banks of the north sea, waiting till the Empire should be brought to peace and order. Hence, when the fame of Pih E is heard of, the stupid become intelligent, and the weak determined.

E Yin said, what of serving a Prince not of one's own stamp! what of ruling a people which are not to your mind! In times of good government he went into office, and so did he in times of disorder. He said heaven has given life to this people, and sent those who are first enlightened, to enlighten those who are last, and has sent those who are first aroused to arouse those who are last, I am one of heaven's people who am first aroused I will take these doctrines and arouse this people. He thought that if there was a single man or woman in the Empire, who was not benefited by the doctrines of *Yaou* and Shun, that he was guilty of pushing them into a ditch. He took the heavy responsibility of the Empire on himself.

Lew Hea Hwuy was not ashamed of serving a dirty Prince, nor did he refuse an inferior office. He did not conceal the virtuous and acted according to his principles. Although he lost his place he grumbled not. In poverty he repined not. He lived in harmony with men of little worth, and could not bear to abandon them. He said, you are you and I am I, although you sit by my side with your body naked, how can you defile me? Hence, when the fame of Lew Hea Hwuy is heard of, the mean man becomes liberal and the niggardly becomes generous.

When Confucius left Tse, he took his rice from the water, in which it was washed, and walked off, but when he left Loo, he said I will walk slowly. This is the way to leave a father and mother's country. When it was right to make haste, he made haste; when it was right to be dilatory, he was dilatory; when right to remain, he remained, when right to be in office he went into office: this was Confucius. Mencius said, Pih E was an example of purity among the sages. E Yin was the person among the sages who took responsibility upon him. Lew Hea Hwuy was an example of harmony among sages; and Confucius of acting seasonably.

Confucius may be said to have been a complete constellation of excellence. His being entirely complete may be conpared to that of the golden and diamond sounds. The golden note constitutes the commencement of music, and the diamond finishes it. To commence is the work of knowledge, to finish the work of holiness.

Knowledge may be compared to ingenuity, holiness resembles strength. If an archer shoots at the distance of an hundred paces, and reaches the mark, it is because of his strength, if he hit the mark, it is not on account of his strength.

2. Pih Kung asked concerning the degrees of rank and salary of the house of Chow? Mencius replied, you cannot hear them clearly explained. The tributary Princes, being afraid that they would injure themselves, took away all the records. But I have heard the general outlines of the thing. The Emperor was one rank, the Kung one, the How one, the Pih one and the Nan one.

In all there were five ranks. *In a Province* the Kuen was one rank, the Kung one, the Ta Foo one, the Shang Sze one, the Chung Sze one, and the Hea Ssze one. In all there were six ranks.

The Emperor had the immediate government of one thousand Le. The Kung and How had each a district of one hundred Le. The Pih had each seventy Le, and each of the Tsze Nan had fifty Le. In all there were four divisions. Those who could not get fifty Le, could not in person have access to the Emperor, but were attached to the Choo How, and were called Foo Yung. The Prime Minister of the Emperor, received territory equal to the How. The Ta Foo had land equal to the Pih. The Shang Sze had land equal lo the Tsze Nan. In a large country of 100 Le the Kuen had ten times as much as the King,—the King four times as much as the Ta Foo—the Ta Foo double that of the Shang Sze, the Shang Sze double that of the Kung Sze, the Chung Sze double that of the Hea Sze and the Hea Sze had the same salary as the common people, who served in government offices. Their salary was sufficient to supply the want of tilling of the fields.

In a small country of fifty Le, the Kuen had ten times as much as the King—the King had double that of the Ta Foo—the Ta Foo double that of the Shang Sze—the Shang Sze double that of the Chung Sze—the Chung Sze double that of the Hea Sze and the Hea Sze had the same as the common people who were in government offices. Their salary was sufficient to make up for their not tilling the ground.

Each of the husbandmen got a field of one hundred acres. Those who manured their fields best could support nine persons—the next class could support eight persons—the next seven—the next six and the next five. Those who had situations under government, had their salaries regulated in this manner.

3. Wan Chang asked saying, I presume to ask the mode of holding intercourse with friends? Do not value yourself for your age, high station, or brothers, in holding intercourse with a friend. When you choose a friend choose him for his virtue. Do not value yourself on any thing.

Mung Hëën Tszè had one hundred chariots and five friends. Two of them were Lŏ Ching Kew and Mŭh Ching, the other three I have forgotten. Mung Hëën Tsze in his treatment of these five friends appeared not to possess this high rank, nor did these five men act as if Hëën Tsze had such rank. If that had been considered they would not have been friends.

It is not only in countries of one hundred chariots, that this is the case. The same holds good with Princes of small countries, Prince Fei Huwy said, Tsze Sze can teach me, Yen Pawn can be my friend, as for Wang Shun and Chang Seih they may serve me.

It is not merely in a small country, that this is the case, but also in large countries. Ping, Prince of Tsin in his intercourse with Kae Tang, if asked to go in, he entered, if asked to sit down, he sat down, if asked to to eat he ate, although coarse herbs and gruel. He never was dissatisfied. For he would not presume not to be satisfied. But here the matter ended. He did not give him an official appointment—nor a salary—nor employ him. This was merely a scholar honoring the virtuous, and not a Prince honoring the virtuous.

When Shun was introduced to the Emperor, he made him his son in-law and gave him a dwelling near the palace. Thus the villager Shun was the guest of the Emperor. This was the Emperor making a friend of a common man. When an inferior honours a superior, it is called Kwei Kwei, and when a superiors honor an inferior, it is called Tsun Heen; the meaning of both is the same.

4. Wan Chang asked, concerning the spirit and manner of receiving presents. Mencius replied, it should be done with grave respect. But to refuse them, is not respectful. How ought one to act in this respect? If the giver be your superior, and you reflect whether he got the gift by justice, or not, and then receive it, you do not behave respectfully; hence you should not refuse. I beg to ask how it would do, not to refuse

in direct terms, but to refuse it in the mind, reflecting that it has been unjustly taken from the people, and making some other pretext for not accepting it? If he offer it in a proper manner, receive it with politeness. In this manner Confucius acted.

Wan Chang asked, saying, suppose a robber outside of the city meets with a man and behaves with reason and presents what he has taken by violence with propriety, ought he to receive it? He ought not. The Kang Kaou says, that he who kills a man and robs him of his property fears not death. All men should detest him. He ought to be put to death without waiting to teach him. The Yin dynasty received the laws of the Hea; and Chow those of Yin.

The Princes of the present day take from the people in the same mananer as the robber does. If they present it with propriety the king receives it. I beg to ask what can be said of this? Mencius replied, do you think Sir, that if a good sovereign were to rise, he would at once cut off the Choo How, or would he first instruct them, and afterwards, if they did not reform, cut them off? If you say that taking what you have no right to, is robbery, you press the point to the utmost extent of rigorous justice. When Confucius was in office in Loo, he shared the game with others, (or wrangled for his share.) If he would do so, how much more receive what is presented?

Then Confucius did not take office in order to practise good principles. Yes he did. Was going with them to the chase practising right principles? Confucius wrote a book to regulate the offerings and the sacrificial vessels, which did not require the productions of the four quarters to use in sacrifices. Why did he not leave? He first made a trial. If the example was worth practising and the Prince did not practise it, he then left. Hence he never was detained in a country for three years.

Confucius, if he saw that he could act, went into office. If received according to propriety he went into office. If the Prince supported him in a proper manner, he took office. He saw that he could act under Ke Hwan Tze and went into office. When in Wei he was received with propriety and went into office. And in Wei during the time of Heaou Kung because he supported him properly he went into office.

5. Mencius said, men should not go into office on account of poverty; but there are times when they may do it on account of poverty. Men should not marry for the sake of being taken care of, yet in some cases they may do so. When a man goes into office on account of poverty, he should refuse a high place, and take a low one. He ought to refuse a great salary, and choose a small one. Now, when a man on account of poverty, refuses a high place, and takes a low place one—refuses a great salary, and takes a small one, what place ought he to hold? * He may watch the gates and beat the Tŭh.

Confucius was once store keeper; at that time he used to say, let me keep my accounts correct, that is all my charge. When overseer of the grazing parks for the herds, he was accustomed to say, all my concern is, that the cattle be fat and thriving.

He who occupies a low station, and speaks high words, (or things belonging to a high station) is guilty, and he who stands in a man's court, and does not practise right principles, ought to be ashamed.

6. Wan Chang asked, why a learned man should not cast himself on a tributary Prince for support? (i. e. take his living without being in office). Mencius said, he dares not.

* A man should go into office to put in practice his principles, but if his principles be opposed to the times, and his family or parents be poor, he may on that account take a low situation where his responsibility is small, just as a man ought not to marry for the sake of being nourished, but in order to preserve the line of succession, yet if he be so feeble as to be unable to act for himself, he may marry for the sake of being taken care of.

When a Prince loses his country, it accords with propriety that he should receive support from another Prince. But it is contrary to propriety, for a scholar to accept of support from a Prince whom he does not serve.

Wan Chang asked, whether one ought to accept of grain presented as a gift. Mencius replied, that he ought to accept of it. Why is it right to accept of it? Because in such a case, the Prince treats him as one of his common people, and relieves his wants.

Since one ought to receive what is presented as a gift, why (when not in office) not receive what is offered as a salary? * He presumes not. I beg to ask, why he presumes not to receive it? Mencius replied, even the gate keeper and drummer have fixed duties and hence ought to receive wages from their superiors, but, when one who has no official duties receives a salary from superiors, he shews want of respect. †

If the Prince's gift be merely for the supply of your wants, you may receive it, but I do not know in the event of the Prince continuing for a length of time, thus to supply your wants, whether you ought to accept of it, or not. Mencius replied, Prince Mŭh thus treated Tsze Sze; he several times sent to ask for his welfare, and frequently sent him roast meat. At last Tsze Sze became displeased, and waved to the messenger to go to the outside of the large gate, where he bowed and refused to accept the gift; saying that from that time and ever after, I know that the Prince wishes to treat me as his dog or his horse. Hence, from that time, the messenger did not come again to present his gifts. To delight in the virtuous and yet not promote them, nay not even to nourish them, how can this be called delighting in the virtuous!

* Formerly, Mung Tsze for some time received his support from the Princes by way of gift, and would not accept of a fixed salary, hence arose these questions put by Wan Chang.

† To receive a constant salary without being in office is equivalent to casting one's self on the Prince for support and hence improper.

I presume to ask how a Prince should do, who wishes to support the virtuous? At first he should send his orders, with the gift, and the receiver should bow and receive it, then afterwards, the store keeper should have orders to continue the supply, without formally sending the Prince's orders. Tsze Sze considered that the roast meat was sent to vex him with bowing. This was not the way to nourish a superior man. *

Yaou in his treatment of Shun sent his nine sons to serve him, and gave him his two daughters in marriage, and gave him likewise a complete retinue of servants and a complete supply of oxen, sheep, and stores for his support, while in the country. Afterwards he promoted him to a high situation. Hence it was said, that his Majesty honored men of superior worth (or this may be said to be the way in which a Prince honors men of great worth).

7. Wan Chang said, I presume to ask wherein lies the propriety of not waiting on the tributary Princes? Mencius replied, in the town there are the servants of the market and of the well, and in the country the servants of the grass: all these are styled common men. Common men cannot take the customary presents (or sign of office) and wait on the Princes. Thus not to presume to visit the Princes is according to etiquette. † Wan Chang rejoined, when the common people are called to do work, they go and do it. When the Prince wishes to see them and calls them and they do not go what is the reason of this? To go and work is right, to go and visit is not right. ‡

* By sending his formal orders with the first gift a Prince honors the superior man, but if he continue to send his orders with every new supply, he only vexes him by the laborious ceremony of receiving it.

† Mencius said, that some of the literati lived in the town, and some of them in the country; they not being in office, were considered on the same footing as the common people, and consequently ought not to presume to visit the Princes.

‡ Wan Chang rejoined, since such of the literati as are not in office are considered on the same footing as the common people, why do they not visit the Princes when sent for, the same as the common people do work? Mencius said, to do work when called by government, is the duty of the common people, but when a Prince knows that a man is a scholar, and sends for him, in that character, he cannot go without violating his principles in order to please man.

Why do Princes wish to have interviews with such men? Either on account of their extensive learning, or of their superior virtue. If on account of their extensive learning, even the Emperor should not call a scholar; how much less should one of the tributary Princes? If on account of their superior virtue, then I have not heard of any, who wishing to see men of worth, sent for them. Prince Mŭh went often to see Tsze Sze and asked why ancient Princes of countries of one thousand chariots, wished to be the friends of the literati? At this question Tsze Ssze was displeased, and said there was a saying among the ancients, that they were their friends!

Now, does not the fact that Tsze Sze was displeased say that as to station, he is my Prince and I am his minister, how can I presume to treat him as my friend? But on the other hand as to virtue, he ought to learn of me, how can he treat me as his friend? If then a Prince of one thousand chariots sought and could not be granted the place of friend to a scholar how much less could he call such a one. *

When Prince King of Tse wishing to go to the chase, called the keepers of hunting parks, by the Tsing flag; they did not come. The king wished to slay them. The determined scholar fears not the being thrown into a ditch, nor does the brave soldier fear loosing his head. Why did Confucius praise these men? He praised their not answering to a flag which was not their own.

Wang Chang said, I beg to ask how the master of the hunting parks should be called? By a Pe Kwan, the common people by a Chen,—the literati by a Ke, and the great officers by a Tsing. If the masters of the hunting parks, are called by the flag of the great officers, they will rather die than dare to go.

* In regard to station, the difference between a Prince and a scholar, is too great to admit of the familiarity of friendship. On the other hand, the superiority of the great scholar, and man of eminent virtue, to the common class of Princes, on the score of knowledge and virtue, is so great, that the Prince ought not to presume to treat the scholar with the freedom which is allowable between mutual friends. How much less ought he to send for such men, as if they were to be treated as common workmen! Propriety requires, that when a Prince wishes to ask the counsel of a scholar, he should go in person and wait upon him, and he should listen to his instructions, with all the docility of a learner when receiving the lessons of a teacher. Thus did all the famous monarchs of antiquity.

If the common people are summoned by the signal of the literati, how would they dare to go! How much less should men of high worth be called by the signal of men of no worth!

Those who wish to see men of great worth, and do not treat them with propriety, act like those who wish to enter a house, but first shut the door. Now, in this case, justice is the road and propriety the door. It is only men of superior virtue, that can walk in this way, and go out and in by this door. The She King says: "The way of Chow is as even as a whet-stone and as straight as an arrow. Superior men tread in it, and inferior men view it as their pattern."

Wan Chang said, when Confucius was called by the commands of his Prince, he waited not for his carriage, but instantly walked off; did he not err? Mencius replied, Confucius held an official situation, and was called according to his rank. *

8. Mencius, in a conversation with Wan Chang, said, the most virtuous in a village may form friendships with the most virtuous of a village. The most virtuous in a province may unite in the bonds of friendship with the most virtuous of a province. The most virtuous in the Empire, may make the most virtuous in the Empire their friends. Such not deeming it sufficient to have all the virtuous under heaven as friends, will converse with the ancients. They recite their poetry and read their books. Can they be ignorant of the men? They therefore examine into their times, and choose friends among them also.

9. Seuen, King of Tse, asked how a prime minister should act! Mencius said, what sort of prime minister does your Majesty refer to? The King said, are there different kinds of prime ministers? There are, said the other. There are some prime

* Wan Chang, not distinguishing between those in office and those who are not, supposed that Confucius erred in answering the calls of his Prince with such prompitude.

ministers, who are relatives of the Prince, and some who are of a different family name. I beg then; said his Majesty, to ask how a prime minister, who is of the blood Royal should act? When the Prince is guilty of great errors, he should reprove him. If after doing so again and again, he does not listen, he ought to dethrone him, and put another in his place.* At this his majesty suddenly changed his countenance. Be not astonished, said Mencius, when your majesty asked me, I dared not do otherwise than give a correct reply. When the king's countenance became composed, he said, I beg to ask, what is the duty of a prime minister, who is of a different family name? If the Prince be guilty of errors, he should reprove him, and if after he has done so repeatedly, he is not listened to, he should leave his place.

CHAP. XI.

1. Kaou Tsze says, human nature resembles the willow, and justice is like a wand vessel; in forming human nature to justice and virtue we must do as we do when making a vessel of the willow.

Mencius said, can you Sir, follow the nature of the willow and make the Pei Keuen vessel? Must you not cut and split (or thwart and twist) it, before you make the Pei Keuen? Would you, as you thwart and twist the willow to make the Pei Keuen, in the same manner thwart and twist human nature in order to form it to justice and virtue? Your doctrines would lead all men to consider justice and virtue to be misery.

* When the country is in danger, a prime minister, who is of the blood royal, ought not to sacrifice justice to the feelings of kindness, which should be cherished among relatives, nor sit and quietly see the nation ruined, but ought to depose the unworthy Prince, and place a worthy relation in his stead.

2. Kaou Tsze said, human nature resembles the flowing of water. Cut a channel to the east, and it will run east: cut one to the west, and it will flow west. Man's nature, originally, is neither inclined to virtue nor vice, just as water is not inclined to run either east or west. *

Mencius said, true, water prefers neither east nor west, but does it neither incline to run up nor down? The virtue of man's nature resembles the downward flowing of water. Men are all naturally virtuous, the same as all water naturally flows downwards. If you strike water and leap in it, you may cause it to rise above your face. Dam its course, and you may raise it to the hills: but is this the natural inclination of water? It is impelled to do so. Human nature, in the same manner, may be made to practise vice.

3. Kaou Tsze said, life is called nature.† Mencius rejoined, do you mean, that life is nature, in the same sense as white is called white? I do. Then do you mean that the whiteness of a white feather, is the same as the whiteness of white snow? and that the whiteness of white snow, is the same as the whiteness of a white gem? Yes, I do. Is then the nature of a dog the same as the nature of an ox? and the nature of an ox, the same as the nature of a man? ‡

† By life is meant the power of knowing and moving, or acting, which men and brutes possess.

‡ Then said Mencius, if life be nature, it will follow, that as dogs and oxen can know and act their natures are the same as man's.

According to my opinion nature is the reason which man obtains from heaven, and life is the breath which man receives from heaven, or nature is heaven's reason, and life is heaven's breath. Nature is the superior principle, and life is the inferior. No man, nor animal when born, is without this nature, nor is any of them without this breath. If you speak of the breath (or life) then man and brutes, do not differ as to their knowing and acting, but, if you speak of reason (or nature) then how have brutes benevolence, justice, propriety, and wisdom in perfection? This shows how man is the soul of all things. Kaou Tsze knew not that reason was nature, hence, taught that breath or life, was nature.

* This seems to come near the idea of the celebrated President Edwards, who was of opinion that man is created with such powers, as constitute him a moral agent, without any bias either to virtue or vice, and that the inferior principles of human nature soon overcome the superior, in consequence of divine influence being withheld as a punishment for Adam's first sin, so that all men at an early period of their existence become inclined to evil and averse to good.

4. Kaou Tsze said, to relish food and love beauty, is nature. Benevolence is internal, not external. Justice or fitness is external, not internal. Mencius said, what do you mean by saying, that benevolence is internal, and justice * is external? A man, said the other, is old and hence I revere him: the age (or cause of reverence) is not in me. That thing is white and I esteem it such, because its whiteness is manifested externally. Therefore, I say that justice is external. Mencius said, the whiteness of a white horse does not differ from the whiteness of a white man; I know not whether there be any difference between the respect which you would shew to an old horse and that which you would shew to an old man; or whether justice be in the object reverenced, or in the agent who reverences.

Kaou Tsze said, I love my own brother, but I do not love the brother of a man of Tsin. The reason is, that the affection of love arises from my delight in him, hence it is said to be internal. I revere the age of an inhabitant of Tsoo, and I likewise revere the age of a relative. The reason is, that age produces the delight, or desire to revere; therefore, we say, that justice is external. † Mencius rejoined, a relish for food dressed by an inhabitant of Tsin, does not differ from a relish for food dressed by my own countryman. The things are the same, but is the relish for the manner in which they are dressed external?

5. Mung Ke Tsze asked Kung Too Tsze, saying, what is meant by saying, that justice is internal? We put in practice our respect, said the other, therefore, it is said to be internal. Should one pay more respect to his own elder brother, or to a neighbour who is one year older than his brother? One should pay most respect to his own elder brother. When drinking to,

* The word here rendered justice means what is just, proper and fit in the nature of things.

† That is, the affection of love reigns in me, and therefore is said to be internal, but respect rests on him, hence is said to be external.

which of them should one first give wine? To his neighbour. Then the cause of respect depends on that man, and the cause of precedence on this, and is in reality external, not internal.

Kung Too Tsze, unable to reply, informed Mencius. Mencius said, ask him whether he ought to pay most respect to his uncle, or to his younger brother, and he will say to his uncle. Then say, suppose your younger brother were the representative of the dead,* which would you show most respect to? and he will reply to my younger brother: then you may say, how then does the cause of respect rest in your uncle? and he will say, it depends on the place one occupies: then you may say, since it depends on the place one holds, I reply that in general, my highest respect is due to my elder brother, and is due to a neighbour only for a short time (i. e. while my guest).†

When Ke Tsze heard this, he said, when it is proper to show the highest reverence to my uncle, I do so, and when proper to give the highest honor to my younger brother, I give him the highest honor; but in reality this depends on external circumstances. Kung Too Tsze said, in winter we drink hot and in summer cold water; is then the sense which thus directs our eating and drinking external?

6. Kung Too Tsze said, Kaou Tsze says, that human nature is originally neither virtuous, nor vicious. Some say that nature may be led to virtue, or vice. Hence, when Wan and Woo reigned, the people loved virtue, but when Yew and Le reigned, the people took pleasure in cruelty. Some say that there are people whose natures are radically good, and others whose natures are radically bad. Hence, when Yaou reigned there was a

* Referring to to the custom of some persons being placed on the seat of a deceased parent, or ancestor, while sacrifices were presented to the manes of the person so represented. In this case, even a younger brother has the honors due to the person, whom he for the time personifies.

† The case of a younger brother being honored for a short time, on account of the seat, he occupies, was brought forward as a complete counter part to the case of a neighbour, or uncle proposed by Ke Tsze and to which Kung Too Tsze was unable to reply.

Seang (a wicked man). When Koo Sow was a father there was a Shun, and when Chow was an elder brother's son, and a sovereign, there were Wei Tsze Ke and Wang Tsze Pe Kan.* Now, since you say that nature is virtuous, these things could not have been. Mencius replied, if you observe the natural dispositions, you may see that they are virtuous: hence, I say, that nature is virtuous. If men practise vice, it is not the fault of their natural powers.

All men have compassionate hearts—all men have hearts which feel ashamed of vice—all men have hearts disposed to shew reverence and respect—and all men have hearts which discriminate between right and wrong. A compassionate heart is benevolence—a heart which is ashamed of vice is rectitude, a heart which respects and reveres, is propriety—and a heart which distinguishes right from wrong, is wisdom. Now, benevolence, rectitude, propriety and wisdom are not melted into us from something external: we certainly possess them of ourselves. But many think not of this. Hence, it is said "Seek and you shall obtain, let go and you shall lose." Some lose one fold, some ten, some beyond number. Thus, they do not improve their natural powers. † The She says, "Heaven created all men having their duties and the means, or rules, of performing them.

* Intimating that the holy Princes Yaou and Shun could not change the vicious nature of the wicked Seang, nor of the no less wicked Koo Sow, nor could the virtuous uncles of the brutal tyrant Chow, turn his feet into the path of virtue, and that consequently the nature of the one class, was radically good and that of the other radically bad. * *

† It is not that all man do not possess perfectly benevolent and upright hearts, nor that they have not hearts which are ashamed of vice and can distinguish clearly between right and wrong, but the evil lies in their not making a right use of their original virtue and talents, so as to bring them to consumate perfection. On the contrary, many thoughtlessly sink into vice and degrade themselves till they become no better than the brutes.

---

* * From the premises a conclusion some what different might be fairly drawn, namely, that the one class had so trained their minds to the contemplation of virtue, and had so far mortified the original depravity of their nature, that their conduct exhibited a happy contrast to that of the other. But, till it be fully proven, that their lives were perfectly free from the least deviation from perfect virtue, it cannot be shewn that their natures were orginally perfectly virtuous.

It appears that while the sages of antiquity, to a man, held the notion that human nature in its original state, i. e. as received from heaven is perfectly holy, there were others who maintained a very different doctrine. Let experience say whether the latter were not nearer the truth.

It is the natural and constant disposition of men to love beautiful virtue." Confucius says, that he who wrote this Ode knew right principles. Wherefore, since there are duties, there must be the means of performing them, which is the original nature of man. Therefore he loves beautiful virtue. *

7. Mencius said, in years of plenty, sons and younger brothers, (or young people) have abundance to depend on, but in bad years, they do much mischief. The difference does not arise from the talents, or natural powers, which heaven bestows, but from that which drowns their minds in vice. † If you sow and plant wheat in the same kind of land, and at the same time, it springs up, and ripens in season If the produce be unequal, that is to be ascribed to the fatness, or poverty of the land, to the abundance, or scantiness of the rains, or to the difference of labor bestowed on it. Wherefore, all of the same species resemble each other. Why should we doubt this rule in reference to man only? The sages are of the same species with us. Hence, Lung Tsze said, if a man without knowing the size of my foot, make shoes for me, I know, that he will not make baskets. Shoes resemble each other, because all the feet under heaven are of the same shape. ‡

This is the case too in reference to flavors. The relish of all mouths is similar. Yih Ya (a man well skilled in flavors) knew beforehand what my taste would relish. Since his taste was

* Human nature in its orginal state accords entirely with divine reason. In this respect there is no difference between Yaou, Shun and the man of the lowest situation. * *

† Intimating that in years of plenty, having abundance of food, they are disposed to learn and practise the principles of virtue, but on the other hand, when they are pressed by want their virtuous nature is forced by stern necessity to commit numerous acts of wickedness. † †

‡ These similies are meant to prove, that all men are by nature equally virtuous.

---

* * It seems a little strange how the sages did not perceive, that if human nature had been immaculately pure, and absolutely perfect as they uniformly represent it to be, man would have spontaneously walked in the path of perfect virtue, and could not without an absolute change of his nature, such as they never hint at, have deviated from the path of rectitude in the slightest degree.

† † Sound philosophy teaches us, that true virtue never shines so bright as in the time of severe adversity. Old experience teaches the same lesson. What are we then to think of that perfect virtue which is transformed into vice by adversity.

thus, if his nature had differed from other men as that of dogs and horses differ, how could all men follow the taste of Yih Ya? This proves that the tastes of all men are similar. The same holds good with regard to the ear. Sze Kwang knew beforehand what sounds would please the ears of all mankind. This proves that the ears of all men are similar. So it is with the eye. For instance, there was no one who did not esteem Tsze Too beautiful. Those who were insensible to the beauty of Tsze Too had no eyes.

Hence, it is said, that all men's mouths have a similar relish, and the ears of all have the same faculty of hearing, or are pleased with the same sounds, and their eyes love the same beauties. Why should their minds alone differ? In what do men's minds accord? It is said to be in reason and rectitude. The sages found out beforehand in what our minds are alike. Hence, reason and rectitude are delightful to our minds in the same manner as the mouth is delighted by eating herbs and flesh.

8. Mencius said, the wood on the New mountain was once beautiful, but being the out-skirts of a great city, it was cut down by the hatchet: how cannot it now be beautiful! Yet being nourished by the revolutions of day and night, and by the genial influences of rain and dew, the tender sprouts rise again, but are eaten up by the cattle and sheep. Hence, it appears a naked waste. When men see this naked waste, they suppose that, it was never covered by wood. But is this the original state, or nature of the mountain?

If man would preserve it, has he not a just and benevolent heart! But the means by which man loses his virtuous heart, resembles the cutting down of the wood by the axe. If you daily cut it down, how can it look well? The good feeling which he acquires in the night, leads him to unite nearly with all men in what they originally love and hate. But the business of the day checks and destroys it. When thus frequently checked and destroyed, at last the nightly feeling is not sufficient to keep his heart. When once his nightly feeling is not sufficient to keep him, he is not far from being a brute. When men see such brutes they suppose that they never possessed good abilities (or a virtuous nature), but is this human nature!

Hence, if it obtain its proper nourishment, there is nothing, that will not grow, but if that is lost, there is nothing that will not go to ruin.

Confucius says, hold fast and you will preserve it; let go and you lose it. It (the mind) goes and comes in no time. No one knows where it may go to. This can only be said of the mind.

9. Mencius said, I am not astonished that your majesty is defective in wisdom. Suppose you take a thing which of all others under heaven is most easily made to grow, yet if you give it one day's genial heat, and anon ten days chilling cold, it cannot grow. I am seldom with you, and when I retire those who cool you approach. How can my doctrines bud.

For instance, the talents required for chess are but small, yet if a man do not bend his whole mind and attention to it, he will not succeed. Yih Tsew is the best player in the country, suppose you employ Yih Tsew to teach two men to play at chess, and one of them bends his whole mind and attention to the thing, and only listens to the instructions of Yih Tsew; the other, although he listens, yet in his mind he sees a bird coming and thinks how he should handle his bow and arrow to shoot it. Hence, although he learn along with the other, he will not equal him. Is this because his knowledge is not equal to his companion? By no means. *

10. Mencius said, I love fish, so do I Heung Chang (a kind of wild boar's feet,) but if I cannot get both at once, I give up fish and take Heung Chang. I love life, and I love justice, but

* This section is intended to shew that it is in consequence of man coming in contact with external objects, the internal purity and rectitude of his mind are gradually corrupted.

if I cannot preserve both at once, I would give up life and hold fast justice. Although I love life, there is that which I love more than life, hence I will not act irregularly to obtain life. Although I hate death, yet there is that which I hate more than death, hence there are evils, or danger, which I will not avoid.

If it were the case that man desired nothing more than life, then why not use every means by which it may be preserved, and were it true that there were nothing which man hated more than death, then why not use every means by which danger may be avoided? *

From this virtuous nature a man will not do what is wrong to save life, nor what is unjust to avoid calamity. Hence, there is that which is desired more than life, and that which is hated more than death. Nor is it only men of superior virtue and talents who possess this heart, but all men originally possess it. The virtuous are able to preserve it. †

Suppose one in such a state that one bamboo of food, or one dish of soup would save his life, while the want of them would occasion his death, if you call rudely to him and give these to him, even a man on the high way will not receive them. If you strike the ground with your foot and offer them to a common beggar he will deem them unclean.

Now, if I without asking whether it is just or not, receive ten thousand Chung, of what consequence will these be to my person (compared with the bomboo of rice and dish of soup), but to beautify my mansions, afford me the attendance of wives and concubines, and the praises of the harum. ‡

* These remarks are intended to prove that man's nature is originally virtuous; so much so, that if followed, it leads a man to part with life rather than do what is unjust. * *

† This last clause is intended to shew to what length human nature will go, and what excuses it will make for an act of injustice, when once it loses its original rectitude.

‡ It is suspected that this conversation was held with the King of Tse, The intention of the sage was to shew his majesty, that his getting possession of, and holding fast that wisdom which his station required and depended on what sort of men he kept about him.

* * That there have been eminent examples of such conduct even among heathens cannot be denied, but the fact is by no means conclusive in support of the doctrine of the original rectitude of human nature. For a man may die a martyr to his own pride, or to public fame, as well as to his natural love of rectitude.

Formerly to save you from death, you would receive, but now you receive in order to beautify your mansions. Formerly you would not receive to save you from death, but now you receive to obtain the services of wives and concubines. Formerly you would not receive, to save your body from death, but now you receive to obtain the praises of the poor. Is it not time to stop?* This is what we call losing the original heart.

11. Mencius says, benevolence is man's heart, and justice is man's path. To lose the way, and no longer walk therein—to let one's heart go, and not know how to seek it, how lamentable! If a man lose his fowls, or his dogs, he knows how to seek them There are those who lose their hearts, and know not how to seek them.

The duty of the student is no other than to seek his lost heart.

12. Mencius says, suppose a man's nameless (4th.) finger, was bent so that he could not stretch it out, it would neither be painful, nor would it much impede his business. Yet were there any one who could straight it, he would not think the distance between Tsin and Tsoo too great to go for that purpose, just because his finger was not like other people's.

Now, if one knows how to feel ashamed that his fingers are not like other men's, and yet knows not how to be ashamed that his heart is not like that of other's, such a man may be said not to know the relative importance of things.

13. Mencius says, if a man wish to rear the Tung and Tsze trees, which may be grasped by one or both the hands, every one knows how to nourish them. If one knows not how to nourish himself, does he not love the Tung and Tsze tree,

* Formerly you would not receive a small morsel of food, even to save your life, because it was offered in a rude, insulting manner, but now in order to obtain splendid mansions, animal gratification, and human praise, you make no scruple to receive ten thousand Chung, although they come in an improper and unjust manner. What a striking proof, that you have lost your original virtue!

more than himself? This is the height of thoughtlessness.

14. Men in the treatment of their persons, love the whole body, and loving the whole body, they nourish the whole body. There is not a cubit nor an inch of skin, which they do not love, and hence there is not a cubit nor an inch of skin, which they do not take care of. Therefore, in examining whether one be virtuous or not, why should there be any other rule than what we find in ourselves.

In the body there are more honorable, and less honorable, less important and more important parts. We ought not on account of the less important to injure the more important, nor on account of the less honorable, to injure the more honorable. He who nourishes the less important, is a low man, but he who takes care of the more important, is a superior man. If a gardener were to neglect the Woo and Kea trees, and cultivate the Urh and Keih shrubs, he would prove himself a worthless gardener. The man who takes care of his little finger, and neglects his shoulder, without knowing, is a sick wolf man. * A man who merely eats and drinks, men despise, because he attends to what is of little moment, and neglects what is of great importance. If the man who gives himself to eating and drinking, did not neglect what is of great moment, then would not the mouth and belly be accounted among the cubits and inches of skin i. e. there would be no fault in taking care of them.

15. Kung Too asked, saying, all are equally men; what is the reason, † that some are great men, and some mean? Mencius replied, those who follow their superior faculties, are great men and those who follow their inferior faculties are low men.

* The wolf is expert at looking over its shoulder, but when sick it cannot to do so, hence it is employed as metaphorical of losing, or neglecting the back of the shoulder.

† Intimating, that if those who give themselves to eating and drinking, did not neglect more important concerns, they could not be blamed, but that this is never the case.

All are equally men, why do some follow their superior faculties, and some their inferior? The ear and eye cannot think, but are corrupted by external objects. When mere material things come in contact, they lead each other away. It is the mind that can think. When one thinks, he finds the right way; but if he do not think, he will not find it. * This is what heaven has bestowed on us. If we first establish our superior faculties, then our inferior faculties will not injure us. This only is the way to be great men, (or those who do so are great men).

16. Mencius says, there is a divine nobility, and a human nobility. Benevolence, justice, fidelity, and truth, and to delight in virtue without weariness, consitute divine nobility. To be a Prince, a prime minister, or a great officer of state, constitute human nobility. The ancients adorned divine nobility, and human nobility followed it.

The men of the present day, cultivate divine nobility, in order that they may obtain human nobility, and when they once get human nobility, they throw away divine nobility. This is the height of delusion, and must end in the loss of both.

17. Mencius says, all are equally desirous of honor, and all have honor in themselves; but they think not of it. The honor which men give is not genuine honor. Those whom Chaou Mung (the chief minister) raises to honorable stations, he can degrade or put down. †

The She King says, "Drunk with wine, and filled with virtue." Intimating, that those who are full of benevolence and justice, wish not for the fine flavored food which others would give them, nor do those whose praises are great and far known, wish for fine robes from others.

* It is only by the right employment of our our rational powers, that we come to the knowledge of those principles on which our conduct should be formed in all our intercourse with the world.

† The honor which man confers, he can give and take at pleasure, but the genuine honor which flows from the possession and practice of virtue, man can neither give nor take away.

18. Mencius says, virtue is superior to vice, as water is to fire. The moderns in the practice of virtue, resemble those who throw one glass of water on a cart load of burning wood, which not quenching it, they say, that water cannot overcome fire. Those who act thus, in the highest degree assist the practice of vice, and in the end lose their own virtue.

19. Mencius says, the Woo Kŭh when sown is beautiful, but if not ripened it is not equal to the Te Pae, and thus true virtue consists in maturity.

20. Mencius says, that Yu in teaching men to shoot taught them to bend their attention to filling the bow, and he who studies must bend his attention to filling up. When a master carpenter teaches, he must use the compass and square, the learner must also learn by rule.

CHAP. XII.

1. A man of the Jin country asked at Uh Loo Tsze whether eating or propriety was most important, and whether the love of women or propriety be most important? Propriety is most important said the other. If then one by eating only according to propriety should thereby die of hunger, but by eating contrary to propriety could obtain food, ought he in such a case to prefer propriety? If by meeting his bride he could not be married, but if by not meeting her in person he could obtain marriage, ought he in such a case to meet her. Uh Loo Tsze would not reply, but went next day to Tsow and informed Mencius. Mencius said, what difficulty is their in replying to this.

If you do not measure the root, and only wish to make the tops equal you may place an inch of wood higher than the top of a mountain. Gold is heavier than feathers, but how can you say that one clasp of gold is heavier than a cart load of feathers. If you compare what is most important in reference to eating, with what is least important in propriety, is not eating most important, and if you compare what is most important in the duty of marriage with what is least important in propriety, is not marriage the more important. * Go and answer him, saying, if by twisting your elder brothers arm and taking it from him by violence you could obtain food, but other wise could not, would you twist his arm, or not? If by leaping over the wall of the east house and dragging out a lady, you could obtain marriage, but if you did not so, could not obtain marriage, would you drag her or not?

2. Tsaou Keaou asked, saying, it is said, that all men may become Yaous and Shuns, is it so or not? Mencius answered, in the affirmative. Keaou said, I have heard, that Wan Wang was ten cubits and Tang was nine; at present, I am nine cubits and four inches high and can do nothing but eat rice. This being the case what must I do that I may succeed. †

Mencius said, why should this be the case, it is only necessary to act. Suppose a man who formerly could not overcome a chicken; then he was weak, but if he now can lift one hundred Keun, he is now strong. ‡ Thus he who can do what Woo Hwŏ did, is just Woo Hwŏ. § Why should men grieve themselves about want of ability? it is in want of exercise that the evil lies. He who walk slowly a little behind a superior, is said to act the part of a younger brother; but he who walks sharply and

* To hunger one's-self to death, or not to preserve the line of succession, are greater breaches of propriety, than to take a little food offered in a rude manner, when that is the only way of saving life; or breaking through the rules of obtaining in marriage, when that is the only way of obtaining it.

† How can I equal Yaou and Shun?

‡ The difference did not lie in his strength, but in the will to exert it or not.

§ Woo Hwo was a man of great muscular strength.

goes before his superior, is said to violate the duties of a younger brother. Now are not men able to to walk slowly behind? It is only that they will not do it. The way of Yaou and Shun. was filial piety and fraternal affection and nothing more. *

Now, Sir, if you wear such clothes as Yaou wore, recite Yaou's words, and perform Yaou's actions, you will be Yaou. But if you wear such clothes as Kēĕ wore, recite the words of Kēĕ, and do the actions of Kēĕ, then you will be Kēĕ.

Keaou said, when I obtain an audience of the Prince of Tsow I will ask him to lend me a house, that I may remain here and receive instructions in your school. Mencius replied, right principles resemble a great road, why should they be difficult to learn? The failing of men is, that they do not seek them. You may go home, Sir, and seek after them, and you will have abundance of teachers. †

3. Kun Lun Chow, inquiring, said. Kaou Tsze says, that the author of the Seaou Pwan is a mean man. ‡ Mencius said, why does he he say so? Because it complains. Mencius replied, how bigoted are Kaou Sow's criticisms on the poets! Suppose there was a man here, and a person of Yue were to draw his bow to shoot him, then I might dissuade him, and laugh, and for no other reason than that he was a relative of mine, but were my own brother to bend his bow to shoot him, then I would weep and dissuade him, and from no other cause, but that he was my brother. The complaint of the Seaou Pwan shews the affection of a relative. To feel affection for relatives is virtue. How narrow and bigoted Kaou Sow's remarks on the poets! But, said the other, why is there grumbling in the Kae Fung?

* Yaou and Shun carried the practice of the duties connected with the various relations of life, to the highest perfection; yet they only practised filial piety, and fraternal affection in perfection; why should not every man become a Yaou or a Shun!

† The proposal of Keaou, shewed that he considered the knowledge and practice of right principles very difficult to attain, but the sage wished him to know that so far from that being the case he might learn both theory and practice by paying proper attention to the every day circumstances of his situation.

‡ The Emperor Yew, having disinherited his oldest son, and sent away his mother, by the Seaou Pwan was composed to complain of such treatment.

Mencius replied, the Kae Fung points out the small faults of parents, and the Seaou Pwan points out the great faults of parents. When parents are guilty of great faults, not to complain is treating them with distance, when they are guilty of small faults and we complain, we shew want of forbearance. To treat them with indifference is unfilial, and want of forbearance is likewise unfilial.

Confucius says, Shun possessed filial piety in the highest degree. At fifty years of age, he felt ardent anxiety about his parents.

4. When Shun Kang was on his way to Tsoo, Mencius met him in Shĭh Mow and said, where are you bound Sir? To which he replied, I have heard that Tsin and Tsoo are raising armies. I am going to wait on the king of Tsoo, that I may persuade him to stop. Should the king of Tsoo not be pleased, I wish to wait on the king of Tsin and entreat him to stop. Perhaps I may succeed with one of these two Princes.

I do not, said Mencius, ask the particulars of your plan, but I wish to hear the general scope of it. In what manner will you persuade them? I will speak of the unprofitableness of the thing (i. e. war). Ah Sir, your intention is noble, but its name is improper. If you exhort the Princes of Tsin and Tsoo (not to go to war) from motives of gain, they will delight in gain and stop their armies; the armies will also joyfully stop and delight in profit. Ministers will serve their Princes from the love of gain. Sons will serve their parents from the love of gain. Younger brothers will serve their elder brothers from the love of gain. Thus, in the end Princes, ministers, fathers, sons, elder brothers, and younger brothers will abandon benevolence and justice, and perform their respective duties from mere mercenary motives. In such circumstances ruin is certain.

But, if you, Sir, exhort the Princes of Tsin and Tsoo to stop from a regard to benevolence, and justice, then the kings of Tsin and Tsoo will delight in benevolence and justice, and stop their armies; the armies will joyfully stop, and rejoice in benevolence and justice. Ministers will serve their Princes from the love of justice. Sons will serve their fathers from the love of benevolence and justice. Younger brothers will serve their elder brothers from the love of benevolence and justice. Thus, Princes, ministers, fathers, elder and younger brothers will all put away the love of gain, and perform their respective duties from the love of benevolence and justice. Were this the case one must govern the Empire. Why speak of gain?

5. When Mencius resided in Tsow, Ke Jin, then acting Governor of the place, sent presents to him, which he received without returning thanks. When he lived in Ping Leŭh, the prime minister Choo Tsze, sent presents to him, which he likewise received without returning thanks.

Some time after this, having gone from Tsow to Jin, he waited on Ke Tsze, but when he went from Ping Lŭh to Tse, he did not visit Choo Tsze. Uh Loo, greatly pleased at this, said, now I have obtained an opportunity (of asking). On which he asked, saying, Sir, when you went to Jin you visited Ke Tsze, but when you went to Tse you did not visit Choo Tsze; was this because he was only prime minister? Mencius said no. The Shoo King says, in presenting gifts let there be abundance of respect. If the respect do not equal the gift, it is said not to be presented, because the mind is not engaged in presenting it, hence the act is not completed. Loo was pleased, some one asking him about this affair, Uh Loo replied, Ke Tsze could not come to Tsow, but Choo Tsze could have come to Ping Lŭh.*

6. Shun Yu Kwan (speaking to Mencius) said, when a man esteems his name and merits of the first importance, he labors for the good of others. But, when he puts his name and merits in the back ground, he only acts for his own good. When you

* Ke Tsze was acting Prince of Jin, and could not go to another country to visit Mencius, hence, he in presenting his gifts, shewed sufficient respect. But Choo Tsze was only prime minister of Tse, and might have gone to the borders of Tse to see the sage, hence, although he sent presents, yet not having gone in person, he was deficient in respect, and consequently was not visited by Mencius.

Sir, held the office of middle King, your name and merits were of no use, either to superiors or inferiors, and you have left your place. Will the truly benevolent act thus.* Mencius replied, he who preferred holding a low situation, and would not employ his virtue and intelligence in the service of the vicious, was Pih E. He who went five times to serve Tang, and five times to serve Këë, was E Yin. He who was not ashamed of serving a vile Prince, and who did not refuse a low office, was Lew Hea Hwuy. These three gentlemen, did not act in the same way, but their aim was one. What was that? Benevolence. The superior man is truly benevolent, why should all act in the same way? †

In the time of Prince Mŭh of Loo, when Kung E Tsze was his Premier and Lew Tsze and Tsze Sze were ministers, Loo was greatly diminished, from which may be seen that these sages are of no advantage to the state.

Mencius replied, Yu would not listen to Pih Le He and consequently lost his country. Mŭh, Prince of Tsin, employed him and consequently subdued the Princes. If the advice of the man of virtue and talents is not followed, the country goes to ruin; how would it be possible to give part of it away.

The other replied, formerly, Wang Paou lived in Ke, and the people of Ho Le became good singers. Meen Ke lived in Kaou Tang, and the people of Tse Yew became good singers. The wives of Hwa Chow and Ke Leang wept well for their husbands, and the manners of the country were renovated. If it be within, it must appear without. For one to do his duty and not to influence by his merit, is what I have not yet seen, therefore at present there is no man of worth. If there were I must have seen them.

* Here Shun Yu Kwan saterises Mencius for having held a high office in Tse, without having done any thing meritorious for the good of the country.

† Intimating that a man's virtue, is not always determined by his going into, or his leaving office, and that truly good and great men, may pursue a different line of conduct, while all have the same end in view.

Mencius said, when Confucius was criminal judge in Loo, he was not listened to; when at a sacrifice no flesh was sent him, he waited not to put off his cap, but went off. The ignorant supposed that it was on account of the flesh that he left. The intelligent thought that rude treatment sent him away, but the truth is, that Confucius only waited for some little cause of leaving, and wished not to go away irregularly. The actions of the superior man are certainly not known by the multitude. *

7. Mencius said, the five Pa (Princes who ruled by force) offended against the laws of the three kings,—present tributary Princes are guilty of offences against the five Pa, and the present great officers of state are worse than the Princes. †

Formerly, when the Emperor went to see the Princes, it was called Seuen Show; and when the Princes attended at court, it was called Shuh Shih. In the spring season they examined the plowing of the fields, and supplied those with seed, who had not enough. In the autumn they enquired whose crops were deficient. When they entered a Province, if the lands were well cultivated, and the fields in good order—the aged nourished, superiors respected—and men of virtue and talents in official situations, they rewarded the Princes by a grant of land.

When they entered a Province, and found the land waste, and covered with weeds—the aged neglected, men of virtue and talents lost,—and avaricius men holding official situations, then they inflicted punishment. If a Prince was once absent from a levee, they diminished his salary,—if twice absent from a levee, they took part of his lands away—if thrice absent from a levee,

* Intimating that Shun Yu Kwan had not discernment to know who possessed eminent virtue and talents, which really was the case.

† The five Pa were Kwan Prince of Tse, Wan of Tsin, Muh of Tsin, Seang of Sung and Chwang of Sung all of whom departed in some measure from the politics of the former kings, and governed too much by force. The three kings were Yu of the Hea Dynasty, Tang of the Shang and Wan and Woo of the Chow. The two last being reckoned one only.

they sent an army to remove him. Hence, the Emperor inquired into crimes, but did not execute punishment, tributary Princes did not inquire into crimes, nor give orders to punish. But the five Pa dragged on the Princes to punish the Princes. Hence it is said, that the five Pa offended against the three kings.

Among the five Pa, Hwan Kung was most famous, he assembled the tributary Princes in Kwei Kew,—bound the victims, and brought the books, but shed no blood. The first clause of the oath declared, that the unfilial should be cut off,—that the legal heir should not be changed, and that concubines should not be made wives. The second declared, that men of virtue should be honored—talent should be cherished, and excellence made manifest. The third declared, that the old should be revered, the young treated with tenderness, and that strangers, (travelling merchants,) should not be disrespected. The fourth clause declared, that there should not be hereditary offices, that one man should not hold two offices, that proper men should be chosen to official situations, and that the Prince would not take upon himself to put to death high officers of state. The fifth clause declared, that the water courses should not be turned for private advantage, that no hinderance should be made to foreign trade,—that no one should be installed in the government of a country, without announcing it to the Emperor. It concluded by saying, let all of us who have unitedly sworn ever after attend to our oath, and live in harmony. But the Princes of the present day have violated all these five prohibitions, and hence, have offended against the five Pa.

He who connives at the faults of his Prince is guilty of a small crime, but he who leads on his Prince to commit the crimes to which he is secretly inclined, is guilty of a heavy crime. The present high officers of state all thus lead on their Princes to the commission of crimes to which they are secretly inclined. Hence it is said, that the present high officers of state, offend against, or are worse than, the Princes of the present time.

8. The Prince of Loo wished to give Chin Tsze a military command. Mencius said, to employ the people in war without teaching them, * is said to be ruining them; in the time of Yaou and Shun, those who would ruin the people would not have been endured. Suppose you were by one battle to be victorious over Tse, and thus get possession of Nan Yang, it would still be improper to go to war. Chin Tsze suddenly manifested displeasure, and said, thus I do not understand. Then said, Mencius I will clearly explain it to you; the Imperial domain, is one thousand miles, were it not one thousand miles, it would not be sufficient to treat the Princes aright. The country of a tributary Prince is one hundred miles, were it not one hundred miles, it would not be sufficient to produce victims and grain for the sacrifices in the ancestorial Temples.

When Chow Kung was made Prince of Loo it was one hundred Le of extent; not but that there was abundance of ground to give him, but he was restricted to one hundred Le. When Tae Kung was made Prince of Tse, it was likewise one hundred Le of extent; this was not for want of plenty of land, but he was restricted to one hundred Le. At present Loo is five hundred Le of extent. Do you suppose, Sir, that in the event of a good Emperor arising Loo would be increased, or diminished?† The truly virtuous, will not without cause take from that, and give to this; how much less will they take territory at the expence of men's lives!

* "Teaching the people" means teaching them propriety and justice, so that, within, they may obey their fathers and elder brothers, and without, serve their superiors.

† According to the principles of the famous Monarchs of antiquity the Emperor's Royal domain, was one thousand Le, and that of tributary Princes one hundred Le. This divison being founded by the sages, and according as it did with the nature of things, ought always to be attended to. Hence as Loo the country of a tributary Prince had so far violated this principle, of division as to have increased to the extent of five hundred, if an Emperor of the true ancient stamp should arise it would be diminished.

9. Mencius said, at present those who hold government offices, brag and say, we can for the benefit of our Prince cultivate the waste lands, and fill the stores and treasuries. Those who at present are called good ministers, in ancient times would have been called the robbers of the people. If the Prince's mind be not inclined to right principles, nor his inclination turned towards benevolence, then to enrich him is to enrich Këë.

They say we can for our Prince unite in alliance other countries, and if we fight, we must conquer. Those who are at present called good ministers, in ancient times would have been called the robbers of the people. When the Prince is not disposed to the right way, nor his inclination turned to virtue, and yet seek to profit him by violence and war, is to assist Këë. If (Princes) follow the principles of the present day, and do not change the present customs, although you give them the Empire they would not hold it one morning.

10. Pih Kwei said, I wish to take one twentieth as a tax, how will that do? Mencius replied, your principles Sir, are the principles of the Mih (northern barbarians.) Is one potter sufficient for a country of ten thousand houses? He is not enough, he could not make a sufficient number of vessels for use. In Mih the five grains do not grow, it produces millet only. They have no cities, no palaces, no ancestorial Temples, no sacrificial rites, no Princes, no presents of silks and food, no officers of government. Hence one twentieth is a sufficient tax.

How would it do for the inhabitants of China to abandon the duties of the human relations, and have no men of superior learning! If a country cannot be without a sufficient number of potters, how much less can it be without learned or superior men. Those who wish to make the taxes lighter than Yaou and Shun did, are great Mihs, and small Mihs, and those who wish to make them heavier than Yaou and Shun did, are great Kēēs and small Kēēs. *

11. Pih Kwei said, I have regulated the water better than Yu did. Mencius said, you are mistaken Sir. Yu regulated the water according to its own principles. Hence Yu made the four seas his reservoirs, while you, my dear Sir, have made the neighbouring states your reservoirs. When water runs not in its proper channels, it is called an inundation. An inundation, the benevolent man hates, you are under a mistake my friend. †

12. Mencius says, if the superior man is not fully grounded in the truth, how can he conduct affairs aright.

13. The Prince of Loo wished to employ Lŏ Ching Tsze in a government situation, or rather as Prime Minister. Mencius said, when I heard of it, I was so much delighted, that I could not sleep.

Kung Sun Chow said, is Lŏ Ching Tsze magnanimous, (perhaps valiant.) No. Is he a man of deep council? No. Is he possessed of extensive knowledge? No. How then were you so much delighted that you could not sleep? Because he is a man who loves virtue. Is the love of virtue enough? The love of virtue is more than sufficient to rule the Empire, how much more the Loo Province. For if a man love virtue, then all within the four seas will esteem it a light thing to come a thousand miles to instruct him. ‡

But, if they do not love virtue men will say they appear self-sufficient, and seem to say we know it. Their self-sufficient air,

* To levy one tenth as a tax was the principle on which Yaou and Shun acted. He who takes less, is a barbarian, and he who takes more is a Kēē, because less is not sufficient to defray the expences connected with the proper rites and ceremonies of a well governed country.

† Pih Kwei in carrying off the overplus of water from his own country, had sent it into the neighbouring states and thus produced a sort of deluge, which proved injurious to others, while Yu sent the overplus of water into the sea, where it could do no harm to any one.

‡ Men of superior abilities and great information will come from all quarters to assist him, so that he will be more them sufficient for the government of the Empire.

and manner will drive men one thousand miles distant from them. When good and learned men remain one thousand miles distant from them, then time-serving sycophants will come about them. When they dwell among sycophants, although they wished to govern well, how could they succeed.

14. Ching Tsze asked, what rules the ancients who were possessed of superior virtue, observed in accepting of an official appointment. Mencius replied, there were three things which induced them to go into office, and three which induced them to give up their offices. When they were met and received with respect and politeness, and it was said, that their instructions will be attended to, they went into office. But although they might be treated with undiminished respect, yet if their words were not attended to, they withdrew. In the second place, although their doctrines were not practised, if they were received with politeness and respect, they went into office. But when respect began to diminish they left.

In the last place, if morning and evening they had nothing to eat, and were so hungry, that they could not go out at the door, and if the Prince on hearing of it should have said my high officers cannot practise their principles nor follow their instructions, but I am ashamed, that they should be starved with hunger in my country; and, if he supplied their wants, then they accepted of his gifts merely to save them from death.

15. Mencius said, Shun was elevated from the tilling of the fields, Foo Yuë from being a house-builder, Kaou Kih from selling fish; Kwan E from prison, Shun Shŭh from the sea, and Pih Le He from the market. Hence, when heaven was about to place these men in important trusts, it first severely tried their minds, excercised their limbs, hungered their bodies, made them poor, and crossed them in their actions: thus it moved their hearts and taught them patience.

When a man has been accustomed to err, and is afterwards able to reform; when he has been distressed in his mind and crossed in his purposes, then he begins to act. It buds in his color, is sent forth in his voice, and then he understands.

If within, there be no minister who can rule the house, nor any minister that can assist the Prince, and without, no distress from a hostile country, then the nation will go to ruin. From this it will be seen, that life springs from sorrow, and affliction and death from ease and mirth.

16. Mencius says, there are many ways of teaching. To teach a man by deeming him impure (and cutting him off) is likewise to teach him.

17. Mencius says, he who employs his whole mind will know his nature. He who knows his nature knows heaven.

To keep the heart and cherish the nature, is the way to serve heaven.

To cultivate virtue with undeviating singleness of intention, without regard to a long or short life, is the way to fulfil the divine decree.

18. Mencius says, there is not any thing, but is decreed; accord with and keep to what is right. Hence, he who understands the decrees, will not stand under a falling wall. He who dies in performing his duty to the utmost of his power, accords with the decree of heaven. But he who dies for his crimes, accords not with the divine decree.

19. Mencius says, seek and you obtain it, be regardless of it, and you lose it. This kind of seeking is advantageous. To seek depends on us.

There is a proper rule by which we should seek, and whether we obtain what we seek or not, depends on the divine decree.

In this case seeking is of no advantage. To seek in this case depends on something external. *

20. Mencius says, all virtue (literally all things) is contained complete in ourselves. There is no greater joy than to turn round on ourselves and become perfect.

Let us vigorously exert ourselves to act towards others as we wish them to do to us. There is nothing easier than thus to seek virtue.

21. Mencius says, there are many who practise without a clear knowledge of principles, who become habituated to the thing without having examined it, and who to the end of life, do the thing without understanding its principle.

22. Mencius says, a man ought not to be shameless. Not to be ashamed of the want of shame is to be without shame indeed!

Mencius says, shame is of great moment to man. It is only the designing and artful that find no use for shame.

23. He who is not ashamed of being unlike others in one point, how can he be like them in any point? (Or he who is not) ashamed of being unlike others how can he become like them.

24. Mencius said, the virtuous Monarchs of antiquity loved virtue and forgot their power. Why should the ancient virtuous scholars alone be unlike them, i. e. the kings. They rejoiced in their principles and forgot the power of men. Hence, if the kings did not treat them with respect and politeness, they could not see them often. And, if they could not see them often, how much less make them their ministers.

25. Mencius speaking to Sung Kow Tsëen said, are you fond of travelling, Sir? I will give you a lesson on the subject. When men know and give credit to what you say, be perfectly

* It is the will of heaven that all should be virtuous and just, and it is within our own power to obtain these, and hence our duty to seek them. But whether we shall be rich or occupy high stations, depends on heaven's decree, hence it is not our duty to seek after these, nor is it certain that we shall obtain them, although we do seek them.

yourself and at ease, and when men do not know nor credit your words, be likewise at ease. How may I, (said the other) in such circumstances maintain self-composure? Honor virtue and rejoice in justice, then you may always be at ease, and maintain self-possession.

Hence the scholar in poverty, loses not rectitude, nor does he depart from the right path in the time of prosperity.

When he loses not rectitude in the midst of poverty he preserves himself. When he departs not from the right path in the time of prosperity, the people's hopes are not disappointed.

When the ancients got into office, they benefited the people. When they did not get into office, they cultivated personal virtue, and manifested it to the world. When poor (or out of office) they practised virtue alone, when in office, they united with the whole Empire in the practice of virtue.

26. Mencius says, he who would wait for a Wăn Wang, before he exert himself, is a mere common man. If one be a man of superior talents, and eminent virtue, he will put forth his strength and exert himself, although there be no Wăn Wang.

27. Mencius says, that he who, though you add to him the houses (or riches) of Han and Wei, still looks dissatisfied, far surpasses men in general.

28. Mencius says, employ the people on the principles of ease, and though you make them work hard they will not grumble. Put men to death by the principles, which have for their object the preservation of life, and though you kill them, they will not grumble.

29. Mencius says, the subjects of the Pa, (those who ruled by force) were joyful; thus, the people of the Wang, (those who ruled by reason,) were easy and self-possessed, thus.

They (the kings) put the people to death and they grumbled not, promoted their advantage and they praised not—so that they daily advanced in virtue without knowing the cause of it.

Wherever the superior man passes, renovation takes place. The divine spirit which he cherishes, above and below, flows on equal in extent and influence with heaven and earth. What is there with him of the making up of slight deficiencies!

30. Mencius says, good words do not enter so deeply into the heart of men, as does the fame of good actions, (or are not equal to the fame of good actions entering &c.) Good laws, are not equal to gaining the people by good instruction. Good laws the people fear. Good instruction the people love. Good laws obtain the people's money. Good instruction gains the people's hearts.

31. Mencius says, that which a man does without having learned, is from natural ability. What he knows without much thought is from natural knowledge. There is not a single child, who is carried in the arms, but loves its parents, and when they grow up there is none of them, but know how to reverence elder brothers. To feel affection for relatives, is benevolence—to reverence superiors, is justice. There is no difference in these under the whole heaven.

32. Mencius said, when Shun lived in the mountains, dwelt with stones and trees, and played with the stag and wild hog, he differed but little from the rustics of the mountains. When he heard a single good word, or saw a single good action, his zeal resembled the breaking out of a river, which nothing can stop.

33. Mencius says, do not what ought not to be done, wish not for what should not be wished for. To act thus is enough.

34. Mencius says, a man's having the wisdom of virtue, and the knowledge of managing affairs, depends on his having suffered trials. A minister kept at a distance, and a son treated with coldness, being grieved in their minds, and deeply vexed, become intelligent.

35. Mencius says, among those who serve Princes there are some who serve them for their pleasure, and some who give

tranquillity to the country, and who make tranquillizing the country their pleasure. There are some celestial people, who knowing perfectly what ought to be done in the Empire, go forth to do it, and there are some great men who being correct themselves. correct others.

36. Mencius says, the superior man has three causes of joy amongst which ruling the Empire has no place. When his father and mother are both alive and his brothers without trouble, this is his first source of joy. When he can look up to heaven without being ashamed, and down to men without blushing, this is a second source of joy. When he obtains men of the best talent under heaven, in order to teach and nourish them, this is a third source of joy. These are the superior man's three sources of joy, none of which consists in ruling the Empire.

37. Mencius says, to extend his territory and increase the number of his subjects, is what the superior man desires, but his joy consists not in these things.

To stand in the middle of the Empire, and give peace and tranquillity to all the people within the four seas, is what the superior man delights in, but his heaven-derived nature rests not in these. The nature of the superior man is such, that although in a high and prosperous situation it adds nothing to his virtue, and although in low and distressed circumstances it impairs it in nothing. The superior man's nature consists in this, that benevolence, justice, propriety, and wisdom have their root in his heart, and are exhibited in his countenance. They shine forth in his face, and go through to his back. They are manifested in his four members. The four members need not to be spoken to, in order to make them understand.

38. Mencius said, Pih E to avoid Chow dwelt on the borders of the north sea. When he heard that Wan Wang had arisen, he exclaimed, why should I not return ! I hear that Se Pih (Wan Wang) takes good care of the aged ? Tae Kung avoided Chow and lived on the coast of the eastern sea: when he

heard of Wăn Wang's government, he exclaimed, why not return! I hear that Se Pih nourishes the old well. Now, if there were any one under heaven that would take good care of the aged, the virtuous men would go over to him.

In a field of five Mow, they planted the mulberry tree round the walls. The women nourished the silk worm, and consequently the aged wore silks. They kept 5 breeding hens, and 2 breeding sows, and did not lose their season, so that the aged could obtain flesh to eat. A farm of one hundred Mow which one man tilled kept a family of eight, so that they did not suffer hunger. That which we mean by saying, that Se Pih nourished the old well, is this: he regulated their fields and small farms—taught them how to plant, and how to breed cattle—led on the women and children to cherish the aged. If people of fifty do not wear silks, they cannot be warm: if those of seventy do not eat flesh they cannot be satisfied. Those who are neither warm, nor satisfied, are called the cold and hungry. But none of Wan Wang's people were either cold or hungry.

39. Mencius says, manage well the cultivation of the fields, and lay on moderate taxes, and you will enrich the people.

Eat things in the proper season, and use them with propriety, and you will have more wealth than you can use.

Without fire and water, people cannot live. If you go at night and knock at a man's door, asking for fire or water, there is none who will not give you what is sufficient. The sages so govern the Empire, as to cause the grain to be as abundant as fire and water. When grain is as abundant as fire and water, will the people be vicious (or be void of benevolence)!

40. Mencius exclaimed, great was Confucius! Ascend the Tung mountain and Loo appears small—ascend the Tae mountain and the Empire seems small. Hence, look at the sea, and it is difficult to speak of water, and if you enter the sage's door, you will find it difficult to speak of virtue.

There is a way of observing water: notice its bubbling. The sun and moon, have brightness: suffer it and it will illuminate.

The flowing of water is a thing which if it fill not its circles in the fountain to the brim, it cannot flow out. The superior man's mind, although bent towards right principles, yet if he do not complete his education, he cannot communicate to others.

41. Mencius says, he who rises at cock-crowing, and applies with unremitting diligence to the practice of virtue, is a disciple of Shun, and he who rises at cock-crowing, and diligently pursues gain, is a disciple of Chih (a robber). If you wish to know the difference between Shun and Chih, it is no other than what lies between gain and virtue.

42. Mencius said, that Yang Tsze (the founder of a sect) acted only for self. If the plucking out of a single hair, could have benefited the Empire, he would not have done that much. Mih Tsze teaches to love all men alike; so that he might be of advantage to the Empire, he would have suffered being rubbed to powder from the crown of the head to the sole of the foot.

Tsze Cho held the medium between these two. To hold the medium is near the truth, but to hold the medium without weighing circumstances, is like sticking to one thing only. That which renders sticking to only one way, is that which injures right conduct, by taking care of one thing, and neglecting an hundred.

43. Mencius said, to the hungry any food is sweet, and to the thirsty any drink is pleasant, because they have lost the proper relish, being injured by hunger and thirst. But why is it merely the mouth and belly, that suffer injury by hunger and thirst! Men's minds also are injured by them. *

The man who can prevent the injury suffered from hunger and thirst, from hurting his mind, has no occasion to be distressed about not being equal to others. †

* Hunger and thirst injure the mouth and belly, and poverty injures the hearts.

† When man's heart is not moved by poverty he far surpasses others.

44. Mencius said, Hea Hwuy, would not, for the office of Sun Kung, (a high situation) have departed from his principles or changed his line of conduct.

45. Mencius says, some act like one who in digging a well, digs nine jin (about 72 Chinese cubits), but does not dig till he reaches the source, which is the same as the abandoning of the well altogether (i. e. the same as if he had not digged at all).

46. Mencius said, Yaou and Shun were perfect by nature, Tang and Woo by personal effort, and the Woo Pa in name only. When they continue for a long time to pretend to an attainment how can they know that they do not possess it?

47. Kung Sun Chow said, E Yin said, I would not constantly look on his bad behaviour. I placed Tae Keă in Tung. The people were highly pleased. When Tae Keă became virtuous, and returned the people greatly rejoiced. * Ought then a virtuous minister, when his Prince is not virtuous, to remove him to a distance? Mencius replied, he who has the views of E Yin may do so, but to do so without E Yin's views is usurpation.

48. Kung Sun Chow said, the She King says, eat not the bread of idleness. How is it then that learned men eat and yet do not till? Mencius replied, if a superior man dwell in a country, and is employed by the Prince, peace, riches, honor, and glory will be the result. The youth following him, will become filial, fraternal, and faithful. Where is there a greater instance of not eating the bread of idleness?

49. Tëen, son of the king (of Tse), asked what the business of the scholar consists in? Mencius replied, in elevating his mind and inclination? What do you mean by elevating the mind?

* Tae Kea was grand-son of the famous Tang, founder of the Shang Dynasty, He became heir to his grand-father's throne, and being put under the care of the renowned sage E Yin proved rather perverse, on which account his guardian sent him to live three years at the tomb of his worthy grand-father. This measure had the desired effect, for he on his return proved a good Prince.

It consists merely in being benevolent and just. To kill one innocent person is not benevolent. To take what one has no right to is unjust. Where is his (the scholar's) abode? In benevolence. Where is his road? Justice. To dwell in benevolence, and walk in justice, is the whole business of a great man.

50. Mencius said, suppose one had offered Chung Tsze the kingdom of Tse, contrary to justice, he would not have accepted it. Hence, all men confided in him, (or gave him credit); but this was only like the justice of giving up a bamboo of rice, or a pot of soup. A man cannot be guilty of a greater crime than that of obliterating the relations of kindred, of Prince, and minister, and of superior and inferior. Why should men on account of what is of small moment, give credit to what is of great importance? *

51. Taou Ying asked saying, when Shun was Emperor, and Kaou Yaou was minister of penal law, suppose Koo Sow (Shun's father) had killed a man, what ought to have been done (or what would Kaou Yaou have done).

Mencius replied, why he would have seized him to be sure. But would not Shun have prohibited him? How could Shun have prohibited him? He had received power from the laws. What would Shun have done in this case? He would have viewed relinquishing the Imperial throne, like casting away a pair of grass shoes, and would have stolen his father, put him on his back, fled to the sea coast, and lived there all the remainder of his days in joy, forgetting his Empire. †

52. Mencius on leaving Fan for Tse, saw the king of Tse's son, on which he exclaimed, one's dwelling alters his air (or spirits), his nourishment alters his person. How much depends on one's residence (or situation). Is he not merely a man's son?

* He left his mother and brother and would not receive a salary from the king.

† In case of Shun's father having violated the law, Kaou Yaou would only have known the law, and would not have known the Emperor's father. On the other hand, Shun would only have known his father, would not have known that he had the Empire. These are the principles on which a father and a minister should act.

Mencius said, the palaces, chariots, horses, and clothes, of the King's son much resemble other men's. Now, since his station makes him thus, what would be the effect, if he dwelt in the world's vast abode (universal benevolence).

The Prince of Loo having gone to Sung, when he called at the Teih Tseih gate, the porter said, this is not our Prince, how is it that his voice is so like our Prince's? This arose from no other cause than similarity of station.

53. Mencius says, to feed one, and not to love him, is to treat him like a pig. To love and not respect him, is using him as you would your dog.

The man (or Prince) who truly respects, and reveres you, does so before he presents his gifts. The superior man cannot be detained by a mere profession of respect, without the reality. *

54. Mencius says, the human figure and colour possess a divine nature: but it is only the sage who can fulfil what his figure promises (or that acts in character).

55. Seuen Prince of Tse wished to shorten the period of mourning for parents. Kung Sun Chow said, to mourn one year is better than to give it up altogether. Mencius said, this is like saying to one who should take a rude grasp of his elder brother's arm, you should take a slight hold. Teach him filial piety and fraternal affection, and all will be right. †

About that time the king of Tse's son's mother died, and his preceptor begged for him, that he might be permitted to wear mourning for several months. Kung Sun Chow asked, what was to be said respecting this case? Mencius replied, he wished to complete the period of mourning, and was not allowed; hence although he did it but for one day, it was better than not to do it at all. In the case I spoke of, no one prohibited, but the person was unwilling.

* This section speaks of the manner in which the Princes of those days treated the literati of merit.

† Intimating that were a man well acquainted with the principles of filial piety and fraternal affection, he would never think of either shortening the period of mourning for parents, nor of treating his elder brother rudely.

56. Mencius says, the superior man has five modes of communicating instruction.

1st. By administering instructions which affect like the timely shower. 2ndly. By perfecting men's virtues. 3rdly. By drawing forth their talents. 4thly. By answering enquiries. 5thly. By secretly influencing others. In these five ways, does the superior man impart knowledge.

57. Kung Sun Chow said, high and excellent are right principles! Learning them ought to be viewed as ascending to heaven, and as unattainable. Why not lower the study of them to suit the capacity of the learner, in order to encourage his daily exertion? Mencius replied, the Master carpenter does not change his lines for the sake of a dull apprentice, nor does the archer change his mode of handling the bow, for the convenience of a stupid learner. The superior man bends his bow, but shoots not; the arrow goes off of itself. He stands in the middle way, and those who can, follow him.

58. Mencius says, when the Empire possesses good principles, let good principles accompany your person to death, when the Empire is destitute of good principles, let your person accompany good principles to death. I have not learned that good principles are to bend to men.

59. Kung Too Tsze said, Tang Kang (younger brother of the king of Tang) is in your school, and asks according to propriety, why do you not answer him? Mencius replied, those who value themselves on their high station, their virtue, age, or merits in their enquiries, I do not answer.

60. Mencius says, he who stops where he ought not to stop will stop short in every thing, and he who treats rudely those whom he ought to treat handsomely, will treat every one shabbily. He who advances too fast will soon retreat.

61. Mencius says, the superior man, in his conduct towards animals, loves them but does not exercise benevolence towards them. He manifests benevolence to men, but does not

treat them with the affection which he shews to relatives. He treats relatives with tenderness, and shews benevolence to men; shews benevolence to men and loves animals.

62. Mencius says, the intelligent know all things, but pay the greatest attention to what ought to be diligently attended to. The benevolent love all, but love the virtuous with the greatest ardor. Even the knowledge of Yaou and Shun did not extend to every thing, but they applied ardently to what was of the utmost moment. The benevolence of Yaou and Shun did not extend to every man, but they ardently loved the virtuous.

He who disregards the custom of mourning three years, and attends to that of mourning three or five months, who in eating his food makes a rude slubbering noise, and yet asks others not to tear the meat with their teeth, does not know what is of the most importance. *

CHAP. XIII.

1. Mencius exclaimed, how destitute of benevolence was King Hwuy of Leang! The truly benevolent begin with those whom they ought to love most, and from them proceed to those whom they ought to love least. Those who are destitute of benevolence begin with those whom they ought to love least, and from them proceed to those whom they ought to love most. Kung Sun Chow said, what do you mean? Hwuy king of Leang destroyed his people in battle for the sake of territory. After great defeats he sent them again, and fearing that they would not prove victorious he sent his beloved son to die with them. This is what I mean by saying that some begin with what they ought to love least, and proceed to what they should love most.

* Such a man while he is anxious to attend to matters of lesser moment neglects what is of more importance.

2. Mencius says, that the Chun Tsew records no just wars, yet some were better than others. It is the duty of superiors to correct inferiors: hostile countries ought not to correct each other.

3. Mencius says, it were better to be without books, than to believe all that they record (or in their full literal sense). I credit only three or four slips of the Woo Ching. *

The truly benevolent man has no enemy under heaven. When the most benevolent conquer those who are the least so, why should the blood flow from the mortars? †

4. Mencius said, when man says I know well how to draw up an army, I am skilled in fighting, he is a great criminal.

If a Prince love virtue, he will have no enemy under heaven When he (Tang) went south to chastise Këé, the nothern people grumbled, and when he went east, the western strangers complained, saying, why make us last?

When Woo Wang conquered Yin, he had only three hundred leather chariots and three thousand brave men. The king said, be not afraid, I come to give you peace and security. I have no enmity to the people. They bowed their heads to the ground as houses fall. To conquer them was to rectify them, hence each wished him to correct them (or their own government). What use was there for fighting?

5. Mencius says, the master carpenter may teach his men by square and rule, but cannot give them ingenuity.

6. Mencius said, Shun when he eat dry bread, and vegetables, felt as if he could do so all his life, and when he was clothed in fine robes, attended by music, and had two ladies to wait on him, he was as if he had always had them. ‡

* A book which records the manner in which Woo Wang conquered the tyrant Chow.

† It had been said that when Woo Wang conquered Chow, the blood was flowing to the pestles which beat the rice, but this was on account of the people of Chow killing each other, and was not occasioned by the army of Woo Wang.

‡ Poverty could not make Shun covetous, nor could riches and honor make him proud. Through all the various conditions of life, in which he was placed, he continued the same.

7. Mencius said, from this time and ever after, I know the heavy consequences of killing a man's parents. If you kill a man's elder brother, he will kill your elder brother. Hence although you do not yourself kill them, you do nearly the same thing.

8. Mencius said, the ancients established custom houses to oppose tyranny, but the moderns employ them to assist oppression.

9. Mencius says, if a man himself does not walk in the right path, he cannot make his wife and children walk in it. If he employ men contrary to right principles, he cannot make his wife and children act aright.

10. Mencius said, the man who is sufficiently attentive to what is profitable, will not be injured by years of scarcity; nor will he who pays sufficient attention to virtue, be corrupted in an age of depravity.

11. Mencius says, a lover of fame, will resign (refuse to accept) a country of one thousand chariots, while a plate of rice or a dish of soup will shew his disposition. *

12. Mencius says, when men of virtue and talents are not confided in, the country is empty (of men). When there is no justice, nor propriety, superiors and inferiors are without proper distinctions. When there is no good government, there will not be sufficient treasure for use.

13. Mencius says, some who were destitute of virtue have the government of a province, but none who were destitute of virtue have obtained the Imperial throne. †

* In the former case, he forces himself for the sake of getting a name, but in the latter he unconsciously allows his true disposition to manifest itself.

† A bad man may, by pressing forward through his selfish views, steal the government of a country of one thousand chariots, but cannot so gain the hearts of the army and people, as to get raised to the throne of the Empire.

Tsoo She says, that from the time of Tsin downwards, some bad men have got the Imperial seat, but they have not kept it more than one or two generations, which is much the same as if they had never got it.

14. Mencius says, the people are of the first importance; the local deities and gods of grain next, and the Prince least of all. Wherefore he who gains the soldiers and people, becomes Emperor, he who gains the favor of the Emperor becomes a Prince, and he who gets the favor of a Prince is made a high officer.

When the Princes endanger the local gods, they must be deposed, and their places filled by others. When the victims are all prepared, and the grain dressed, and the sacrifices of the seasons offered, and still there are droughts and inundations, the local gods must be removed. *

15. Mencius says, a sage is the instructor of an hundred ages. Pih E and Lew Hea Hwuy were such. Hence, when the manners of Pih E are heard of, the stupid become intelligent, and the wavering determined. When the spirit of Lew Hea Hwuy is heard of, the careless become respectful, and the parsimonious liberal. They lived above one hundred ages, and one hundred ages below them. When they hear of them, not one but is roused. None but a sage could do so. How much more must they have influenced those who were about them.

16. Mencius said, to be benevolent is man. When man and benevolence are united, they are called Taou.

17. Mencius said, when Confucius left Loo, he did so very slowly. This was the proper way of leaving, the country of one's parents. But when he left Tse he took his rice in his hand, and walked off. This is the proper way of leaving a foreign country.

18. Mencius said, the reason why the superior man (Confucius) was in danger between Chin and Tsae was that he had no friendly intercourse with superiors and inferiors.

* These two circumstances shew, that the people are of more importance than either the Prince or local deities.

19. Mih Ke said, I am far from being praised by men's mouths. Mencius said, that is of no importance. The good man is the prey of many mouths. The She King says, "Sorry, sorry is my heart, I am hated by the low herd:" thus it was with Confucius. No effort could put a stop to their hatred, but they could not injure his fame: thus it was with Wăn Wang.

20. Mencius said, the virtuous employ their own light to illuminate others, but at present men employ their own darkness to enlighten others.

21. Mencius conversing with Kaou Tsze said, in the bye-paths of the hills the grass grows suddenly. If you constantly walk on them, the path will be formed, but, if there be any interval, the grass will suddenly rise and close it up. * Now at present your mind is closed up.

22. Kaou Tsze said, the music of Yu was superior to that of Wăn Wang. Mencius said, why do you say so? Because the joints of his instruments were eaten by insects. How does that prove the point? Is it the strength of two horses that cuts the tracks outside the city?

23. When the people of Tse were suffering from hunger, Chin Tso said, all the people of the country hope that you will again advise the king to open the public granaries, but I fear you will not again do it.

Mencius replied, this were to act like Fung Foo. In Tsin, there was one Fung Foo, who was famous at catching tigers with his hand. Afterwards he changed and became a good scholar and lived in the desert. On one occasion, when a multitude were in pursuit of a tiger, the tiger turned his back to the corner of a hill, and none dared to encounter him. Looking up they saw Fung Foo coming to meet them. Fung Foo

* The moral of this is, that if we cease for a moment to keep a guard over our hearts, vice will suddenly spring up and choke the growth of virtue.

bared his arm, descended from his carriage and seized him. The multitude were delighted, but the literati laughed at him. *

24. Mencius says, it is natural for the mouth to love a good flavor; the eye, beauty; the ear, sound; and the four members, ease. But there is a limit to these. The superior man does not call them nature.

Mencius says, benevolence is the duty of father and son; justice, of Prince and minister; politeness, of host and guest; wisdom, of the virtuous; and union with divine reason, of the sage. These are nature. The superior man does not say, that they are decreed.

25. Haou Sang Puh Hae asked, what kind of a man Lŏ Ching Tsze was. Mencius replied, he was a virtuous and faithful man. What do you call virtuous, and what do you call faithful? That which may be desired is called virtue. To have it (genuine virtue) in ones-self is called fidelity. To be full of sincerity is called beauty. To be so full of sincerity, that it shines forth in the external conduct is called greatness. When this greatness renovates others it is called sageship. Holiness (or sageship) which is above comprehension is called divine. † Lŏ Ching Tsze is between the two first, and below the four last.

26. Mencius says, if men run away from the Mih sect, they will go over to the Yang sect, and if they leave the sect of Yang, they will come over to the Joo sect (i. e. sages). When they come, let them be received.

At present those who reason with the followers of Yang and Mih, resemble those who pursue a stray sow. When they enter their sty, they forthwith bind them.

* They laughed at him, because he could not leave off his old habits. It is suspected that at that time, the king of Tse would not employ Mencius, hence he spoke thus; intimating that were he to obtrude his advice any farther, he would resemble the old tiger-catcher who knew not when to stop.

† What is called divine refers to the highest degree of the sage's wounderful excellence, which men cannot fathom, and does not mean that there is a class of divine men superior to the sages.

27. Mencius said, there is a tax on cloth, a tax on grain, and a tax on human labor. The good Prince takes one and spares two. If he take two, the people suffer hunger. If he take all the three, father and children are separated.

28. Mencius says, the Prince has three pearls, territory, men, and government. If he set his mind on jewels he will suffer misery.

29. Pan Ching Kwah went into office in Tse, Mencius exclaimed Pan Ching Kwah is a dead man! When Pan Ching Kwah was slain, the disciples (of Mencius) asked saying, how did you know Sir, that he would be put to death? Because said he, he was a man of small abilities, and never heard the great doctrines of the superior man: this was sufficient to lead to his death.

30. When Mencius went to Tang, he lodged in a public inn; and it happened that some people of the inn who made shoes, had laid the shoes in the window, and when they came to seek them could not find them.

Some one asked him saying, is this the way that your followers pilfer? Mencius says, do you suppose Sir, that they come here to steal? No I dont. You set up a school and those who go away from you, you follow not, those who come, you send not away. If their minds are well inclined, you receive them. *

31. Mencius said, all men have hearts which cannot bear to injure others. If we improve this disposition aright we are benevolent. All men have things which they will not do, if we apply this disposition to what we do we are just.

If a man perfect the disposition which does not wish to injure others, his benevolence will become inexhaustible:—and if a man can perfect the disposition which wishes not to commit

* The gentleman bethought himself, and finding that he was wrong, turned his tale in this manner.

burglary, his justice will become inexhaustible. If a man can perfect the reality of not wishing to be pointed at; wherever he goes he will practise justice.

The scholar who speaks when he ought not, in order to find out men's affairs, or who is silent when he ought to speak, in order to come at the knowledge of men's concerns, belongs to those who commit burglary.

32. Mencius says, he whose words are simple and easily understood, while they have an important and extensive meaning, speaks well. He who watches over himself with great strictness, and is liberal to others, acts well. The superior man's words go not below his girdle, but he maintains the right way.* The superior man watches over and adorns himself with virtue, and there is peace and tranquility all under heaven.

The failing of men is, that they neglect their own field and dress that of others. They require much of others, but little of themselves.

33. Mencius says, that Yaou and Shun were nature, Tang and Woo turned back to it.† When a man in every change of his circumstances hits true propriety, he possesses the highest degree of perfect virtue. Such a one does not weep for the dead on account of the living: he constantly practises virtue without any deviation, not that he may obtain the emoluments of office: his words will certainly be true, not with any view to making his conduct correct.

The superior man does what is right and waits the divine decree.

34. Mencius says, when you speak to men of high rank,

* That is his words although simple and easily comprehended are nevertheless important and have a deep and extensive signification.

† Yaou and Shun preserved entire the perfectly holy nature which they received from heaven. Tang and Woo although they in some measure lost their orginal perfection, yet by their own efforts regained it. The former were sages by nature, the latter by personal cultivation, so that in the end they were all one.**

** It is unnecessary to observe that these sentiments are at direct variance with the history of all ages, and of all countries, and with what passes before our eyes every day.

esteem them lightly, look not at their pomp and dignity. * Their palaces (i. e. present men of rank) are several jin high, with carved headed beams several cubits long. Could I get into office, I would not have such things. Their food is spread out on tables of a square Chang. They have several hundreds of concubines to wait upon them. Were I to get into office I would not act so. They indulge in mirth and drink wine, ride and hunt, followed by thousands of chariots; were I in office I would not thus act. I would not imitate them in any part of their conduct. In all my conduct I act according to the rules of the ancients, why should I fear them (i. e. the present grandees)! †

35. Mencius says, there is no better way of nourishing the heart than by diminishing our desires. If a man have few desires although he may slip in some things, it will be in few. But if a man have many desires, although he may in some measure preserve his virtuous nature, it will be but in a small degree.

36. Tsang Seih was very fond of dates and Tsang Tsze could not bear to eat them. Kung Sun Chow asked saying, whether broiled flesh cut small or dates were better? Mencius replied, broiled flesh. Then said Kung Sun Chow, why did Tsang Tsze eat broiled flesh, but did not eat dates? Because broiled flesh is what men generally eat, but he (i. e. Tsang Seih) was peculiar in his fondness for dates. Just as people avoid mentioning the name of the dead, but not their family name, because their family name is common to many, but their name is peculiar to themselves. ‡ Wan Chang asked saying, Confucius, when in Chin exclaimed, why not return; my scholars, or the scholars of my place, are bold and will advance, but cannot change their old

* Be not so overawed by the splendor of their station and the pomp by which they are attended as not to be able to speak your mind freely or to tell them all the truth.

† Yang She says, Mencius in this section compares his own good qualities with the short comings of others. This is a little failing in his disposition. No such thing was to be found in Confucius.

‡ It is customary among the Chinese, not to mention the name of their deceased parents and relatives. From the same motives of filial regard, Tsang Tsze refrained from eating dates because his father when alive was peculiarly fond of them.

ways. Why did Confucius when in Chin think of the forward scholars of Loo.

Mencius replied, since Confucius could not obtain men of the true medium, to whom he might commit his doctrines, he was obliged to take the high spirited and the firm. The high spirited would advance to the mark, and the firm would not do what was improper. Why should not Confucius wish to have men, who had attained the due medium! but since he could not find them, he thought on the next order of men, I presume to ask, who these high spirited men were? Those whom Confucius called high spirited, zealous men, were such as Kin Chang, Tsang Seih, and Muh Pe. Why did he call them high spirited? Their aim was high, and they talked big, constantly exclaiming, the ancients! the ancients! but when you examine their actions, they do not perfectly accord with their words.

When he could not obtain the zealous and high spirited, he sought those who would not disgrace themselves by doing any dirty action, and delivered his doctrines to them. These are the firm and steady and hold the next place.

Confucius said, of those who pass my door and do not enter my house, whom I am not displeased with there are only the Keang Yuen. The Keang Yuen are the thieves of virtue. Who are these Keang Yuen? They are those who (mocking the high spirited) say; how big and pompous their words, but when they speak, they think not how they are to act, nor do they regard what they have said, when they come to act. They are continually calling out the ancients! the ancients, and who (in derision of the steady) say why make ourselves singular. Let those who are born in this age, act as men of this age; this may be virtuous. Thus they secretly obtain the flattery of the age. This is the character of the Kean Yuen.

Wan Chang said, the inhabitants of the village all praise them Wherever they go they are attentive and generous; why did

Confucius consider them the thieves of virtue? If you wish to criminate them, there is nothing particular to take hold of—if you wish to reprove them, you find nothing in particular that you can reprove. They accord with the prevailing customs, and unite with a polluted age. They appear faithful and sincere, and act as if sober and pure. The multitude all delight in them. They consider themselves right and enter not the way of Yaou and Shun; hence they are called the thieves of virtue.

Confucius said, I hate appearance without reality, I hate the tares, and fear that they may injure the blade. I hate the loquacious, and fear that they will injure justice. I hate the sharp mouthed, and fear that they will confuse truth. I hate the music of Chin, lest it should spoil music. I hate a mixed colour lest it should spoil the true red. I hate the Keang Yuen, and fear that they will confuse virtue.

The superior man merely turns men back to correct, standard principles. This being done, the common people rise to the practice of virtue. When the people thus rise to virtue, there will neither be vice, nor wickedness.

38. Mencius says, from Yaou and Shun to Tang, there were 500 and more years. As to Yu and Haou Taou they themselves saw and hence knew them (Yaou and Shun). As to Tang he knew them from hearing. From Tang to Wan Wang, there were upwards of 500 years. As to E Yin, and Lae Choo, they knew him from personal sight. As to Wan Wang he knew him from hearing. From Wan Wang to Confucius, there were more than 500 years. As to Tae Kung Wang, and San E Sang, they knew him from personal sight; but Confucius knew him from having heard of him. From the time of Confucius to the present day, it is more than 100 years. From the time when the sage lived to the present day, is not long. Where I live is very near to his native place, but alas there are none who know him! None that know him indeed! *

* It is the general way of heaven, that once in 500 years, a sage should come forth, but sometimes the period is rather longer, and sometimes a little shorter.